Dear Karis,

Congratulations on this wonderful achievement. You're graduating from high school!

As God has helped, blessed, and led you thus far, He will surely be with you on your next adventure.

Always make Him first, best, and last. Keep your eyes on Jesus. He's coming back soon.

Your Louisville First Church Family

Amazing Testimonies of

Changed
Lives

Introduction

During the Second World War, a Dutch pastor and his family got into big trouble with the Nazis for hiding Jews. Late one night, they heard heavy boots outside their home and then a loud pounding on the front door. The entire family was arrested and loaded into a cattle car to be sent off to a death camp.

All night long, the family rode in the dark, jostling against one another and other prisoners jammed in the suffocating car. They were terrified of what was to come, wondering which extermination center they were being taken to. Auschwitz? Buchenwald? Dachau? So they earnestly prayed.

In the morning, the train stopped and the cattle car doors were swung open. Bright sunshine spilled into their confined quarters and onto faces filled with fear. The prisoners were marched outside and lined up beside the railroad tracks, expecting to be forever separated from their loved ones.

But in the midst of their gloom, they discovered astonishing news—good news beyond belief. They soon realized, as they viewed their surroundings, that they were not at a death camp. They were in the free country of Switzerland!

During the night, someone with great courage had tripped a railroad switch, diverting the route of the train to freedom. The soldiers meeting the train were not captors, but liberators! Instead of being marched through the gates of death, they were welcomed to a new life. Amid all this joy and relief, the Dutch pastor exclaimed, "What do you do with such a gift?"

That's the question we're asking you in *Amazing Testimonies of Changed Lives*. Throughout the following year, you'll be reading the conversion stories of hundreds of people just like you and me. You'll read familiar Bible accounts, like that of the apostle Paul, stories from great men and women in history, like Martin Luther and Fanny Crosby—plus testimonies from the Amazing Facts ministry, of people who turned from death to life when they accepted Christ.

May you be blessed as you read these amazing testimonies of transformed lives, and may it inspire you to share with others the story of your own turn to a new life of freedom in Christ.

Pastor Doug Batchelor
President, Amazing Facts International

Rosemarie

At Long Last, Part 1

"Hope deferred makes the heart sick, but when the desire comes, it is a tree of life" (Proverbs 13:12).

Rosemarie had never seen a Bible.

Even though she attended mass twice a week throughout her childhood and listened to the priest read Scripture passages, it wasn't until she was twelve that she actually saw a Bible.

One day, she was thrilled to find one by chance in her family's basement. Finally! Here was her opportunity to see what was inside a real Bible. Filled with great anticipation, she opened it and began reading. But her excitement quickly evaporated when she discovered strange words that didn't make sense. She soon gave up.

A couple of years later, she stopped attending church altogether. "As a Catholic, I was never shown, given, or instructed to read the Bible," she says. Yet she has always felt a strong interest for God's Word. The Lord was preparing the way to reveal Himself to Rosemarie.

Years passed, and Rosemarie went through some heart-wrenching times. She had a daughter out of wedlock. Then she lost her mother. Though they were not very close, she had longed for things to improve, but now that door was closed. She felt overwhelmed by the pain and confusion.

During these challenging years, she read a book that described a group of Christians who attended church together and then met for dinner afterward to read and discuss the Bible. The idea fascinated her. "Do people actually read and discuss the Bible like a textbook?" she wondered.

One day, Rosemarie sat eating lunch in a picnic-like area in front of the hospital where she worked. A woman she'd seen around the hospital asked to join her for lunch. As they ate, the woman introduced herself as Cynthia and shared how she'd found Christ at a community college in Sacramento.

At the end of their conversation, Cynthia gave Rosemarie her phone number and told her that she'd be happy to pick up Rosemarie and her young daughter any time they'd like to visit church with her. Before the week was over, Rosemarie called and accepted the offer—a decision that impacted the rest of her life.

Reflect: Do you have a strong and personal interest in the Bible? Amos 8:11 tells us that God will create a hunger for the Word in people's hearts.

Dig Deeper: Job 23:12; Acts 17:11; 1 Thessalonians 2:13

Rosemarie

At Long Last, Part 2

"Call to Me, and I will answer you, and show you great and mighty things, which you do not know" (Jeremiah 33:3).

Rosemarie had been hungering to learn more about the Bible and gladly accepted Cynthia's offer to attend church. She and her daughter thoroughly enjoyed the service, so Cynthia brought them again the following week. After that, Rosemarie and her daughter came on their own. Her daughter loved the Bible classes for children and even began memorizing Bible verses.

During this time, Cynthia and a woman named Freddie gave Rosemarie her first Bible study using the *Amazing Facts Bible Study Guides*. She was so excited to read the Scriptures for herself. "I remember discovering about heaven and ... that we were going to go and live there forever." It raised her hopes in seeing her mother again. "That lesson really stood out to me!"

Rosemarie marveled at how easy it was to understand the lessons. "I had never read the Bible and yet here I was reading and understanding about the Creation, how God created the world in six literal days and blessed the seventh day so I would always remember Him as Creator!"

Rosemarie treasured the studies she had with Freddie, because "that's how I met my best friend, Jesus!" After she completed the course, Rosemarie was baptized.

Soon Rosemarie became an active member of a Sabbath-keeping church, helping teach children in vacation Bible school, assisting with youth programs, and working as an outreach leader. Later, she began teaching a Bible class at church and worked as a Bible instructor. She also leads a Bible study group at her church using the very study guides that led her into the truth.

Years ago, Rosemarie longed to read a Bible. Today, she now goes door to door, offering Bible studies to others ... the very thing she longed for in life. She once cried out to God to give her the opportunity to learn more about the Scriptures, and the Lord now reminds her, "Before you call, I will answer." God's answer—at long last—was through loving Christians who opened the Bible to a longing heart!

Reflect: Think of one way you could share a Bible resource with someone today. Remember, you can be God's instrument to help lead someone to the Savior!

Dig Deeper: Job 13:22; Psalm 86:7; Isaiah 58:9

Peter, A Disciple
The Solid Rock, Part 1

> "One of the two who heard John speak, and followed Him, was Andrew, Simon Peter's brother. He first found his own brother Simon, and said to him, 'We have found the Messiah' (which is translated, the Christ). And he brought him to Jesus. Now when Jesus looked at him, He said, 'You are Simon the son of Jonah. You shall be called Cephas' (which is translated, A Stone)" (John 1:40–42).

Impulsive, unstable, boastful, vacillating, rash. Those are just a few adjectives used to describe the most famous (and outspoken) of Jesus' disciples. Peter was, in a sense, the first Christian convert. His brother, Andrew, learned of Christ and immediately brought Peter to meet Jesus.

The penetrating eye of the Savior looked upon this inconsistent, undependable, overconfident, and sometimes reckless fisherman and saw so much more. The Redeemer pictured what Peter could become through the power of the Holy Spirit—courageous, loyal, earnest, a leader, and a warmhearted disciple.

Jesus looked at Peter. Their eyes must have met as the Son of God spoke words of affirmation to a son of man He knew better than the impetuous Peter knew himself. Christ said, "'You are Simon the Son of Jonah. You shall be called Cephas' (which is translated, A Stone)" (John 1:42).

Peter was given a new name. It wasn't a nickname, a moniker, a pet name, or a byname. Jesus wasn't attempting to simply label this uneducated seeker who could run at a whim. The eye of faith saw how the moral weakling from Bethsaida would boldly preach to religious leaders who would murder him.

The conversion of Peter didn't take place in a moment. He still had many lessons to learn from the Master. But his first step forward began when Christ pushed aside the present being and held up for the wavering man a future reality.

Jesus will do the same for you when you turn to Him. He looks at you with tender, believing eyes and says, "My son, my daughter, you have been known by unflattering traits, you have been called cruel names, you have been handed a dismal future by others. But I see in you the precious and perfect man and woman you were meant to be."

Listen to the Savior. He promises to give you a new name and a changed life.

Reflect: Think of a character quality that you would like to be known for. God promises to turn your desire into a reality.

Dig Deeper: Isaiah 43:1; Jeremiah 1:5; Revelation 2:17

Peter, A Disciple

The Solid Rock, Part 2

> **"[Jesus] said to Simon, 'Launch out into the deep and let down your nets for a catch'" (Luke 5:4).**

A grade school test was created to help students learn to carefully follow instructions. It gives about 20 different steps to follow, but the very first step clearly states: "Write your name at the top of the page and turn your paper in to the teacher. Do not do any of the other steps."

Most students charge through the list, assuming they are to do all the steps, which include things like shouting out your first name and standing beside your desk and reciting the Pledge of Allegiance out loud. It's not hard to figure out who didn't carefully read and follow the instructions.

Jesus gave Peter a test, but while the fisherman agreed to follow His instruction, on the inside he obviously thought Christ knew nothing about fishing in broad daylight. He explained, "Master, we have toiled all night and caught nothing; nevertheless at Your word I will let down the net" (Luke 5:5).

When a miraculous catch came to the fishermen, so much so that the large haul nearly sank their boats, Peter became convicted that Jesus was no ordinary teacher. "When Simon Peter saw it, he fell down at Jesus' knees, saying, 'Depart from me, for I am a sinful man, O Lord!'" (v. 8).

The kindness of Jesus and the power of His miracle shed light on Peter's weak faith. Even though the doubting fisherman outwardly obeyed Christ's instruction, his heartfelt confession openly showed that his belief was small and weak.

The most amazing part of this step in Peter's conversion is that Christ worked with the reluctant man with feeble trust. Despite Peter's hesitating obedience, Jesus blessed his efforts. It gives hope to all who waver to believe in God's commands and promises. When we choose to faithfully follow the instructions of Scripture, even if our footsteps falter, God miraculously turns our tiny efforts into giant strides.

Reflect: Which Bible instruction do you struggle to obey? Don't forget that the Lord will bless your most feeble steps forward.

Dig Deeper: Matthew 17:20; Romans 1:17; 2 Corinthians 5:7

Peter, A Disciple

The Solid Rock, Part 3

"Having arrested [Jesus], they led Him and brought Him into the high priest's house. But Peter followed at a distance" (Luke 22:54).

It's called the two-second rule. This rule of thumb states that a car driver may keep a safe trailing distance at any speed if staying two seconds behind any vehicle that is directly in front of his or her vehicle. But it's a lousy rule when it comes to following Jesus.

When Christ was arrested and dragged to the house of Annas (a retired yet influential former high priest) and then to the judgment hall of Caiaphas, the current High Priest, "Peter followed at a distance" (Luke 22:54). The disciple apparently wanted to be close to Jesus, but not too close.

The Savior knew the heart of Peter. Before the agonizing night in Gethsemane, Jesus said, "Simon, Simon! Indeed, Satan has asked for you, that he may sift you as wheat. But I have prayed for you, that your faith should not fail; and when you have returned to Me, strengthen your brethren" (v. 31). Did Peter's faith fail? Yes, and no.

Peter told Jesus, "Lord, I am ready to go with You, both to prison and to death" (v. 33). He was confident and a bit boastful about his faith. But Christ predicted, "I tell you, Peter, the rooster shall not crow this day before you will deny three times that you know Me" (v. 34). And that's what happened in the courtyard of Caiaphas when the one who followed Jesus "at a distance" betrayed the Lord, three times.

When Peter denied Jesus the third time, the Bible says, "Immediately, while he was still speaking, the rooster crowed. And the Lord turned and looked at Peter. Then Peter remembered the word of the Lord ..." (v. 60, 61). How do we know Peter's faith did not completely fail? By looking at his response to the look of Christ after his failure. "So Peter went out and wept bitterly" (v. 62).

Though you may be converted and a disciple of Jesus, but are following "at a distance," you may know that genuine tears of repentance indicate your faith has not completely failed and that you are moving closer to the Master.

Reflect: Are you closely following Jesus or are you following at a distance? James 4:8 says, "Draw near to God and He will draw near to you."

Dig Deeper: Matthew 26:31–75; Mark 14:29–72; John 18:15–27

Corinne

Accepted by God, Part 1

"In my distress I called upon the , and cried out to my God; He heard my voice from His temple, and my cry came before Him, even to His ears" (Psalm 18:6).

Corrine grew up in a Mormon family but these ties dwindled when her parents divorced when she was 12 years old. "I always was a spiritual searcher and remember being afraid of hell. At the age of 14, I remember crying out to God to save me." She began attending a Pentecostal church which she stayed with until she was 28.

"At this point in my life I was doing a lot of soul searching. I felt I wasn't really living my life the way God intended." She explains, "I prayed that God would show me the truth and give me wisdom to discern what He wanted for me—and not what everyone else was telling me."

Corrine was working at a bank and occasionally had brief spiritual conversations with an elderly security guard. One day he loaned her a Christian DVD which contained a link to the Amazing Facts website (amazingfacts.org). During downtimes at work she began to peruse the whole site. She stumbled on the online Bible study lessons with worksheets and completed every single study and even received a certificate of completion.

The studies pressed on her heart, especially the Bible teaching about the observance of the Sabbath day. She says, "I remember questioning why we observed Sabbath on Sunday." The answers she had received, such as, "It was changed by early Christians to avoid persecution," were not biblical. She came to understand God had never changed the Sabbath.

Corrine also enjoyed studying about last-day events and was taught that Christians would be raptured before the seven-year tribulation period and the rise of the antichrist. But, once more, she could not find in the Bible any reference to a secret rapture before Christ's second coming. She also learned the antichrist was not a person but a false religion.

During this time Corrine admits, "My walk had taken a wrong turn. I had divorced my husband and was living with another man. I thought if I attended a Sabbath-keeping church I would not be accepted." So she continued to study on her own and the Holy Spirit kept calling to her heart.

Reflect: Have you ever cried out to God for help, but hesitated to fully surrender to Him? Remember, the only thing you really have to give up is a broken and sinful life.

Dig Deeper: 2 Samuel 22:7; Psalm 1:1, 2; Jeremiah 7:23

Corinne

Accepted by God, Part 2

"Depart from evil and do good; seek peace and pursue it" (Psalm 34:14).

Corinne cried out to God for help, but still hesitated to fully follow what she had learned from Scripture. One day she ordered some Bible books for her children. She says, "A book evangelist came to my home to deliver the books. He then shared about another series of books that I might find helpful. I bought the set, which included the book *The Great Controversy* which I delved into." Once more she felt a pull to attend church. But she hesitated to attend a Sabbath-keeping church, feeling that she would not be accepted.

Corrine was pregnant at the time. Through the encouragement of the book evangelist she married the father of her baby. She then began attending a non-denominational church but shares, "I still did not feel God's peace."

Sometime later she received an advertisement in the mail for an upcoming series of meetings in a tent pitched in the parking lot of a local high school. Evangelist Dave Steward from Amazing Facts would be speaking about last-day events and Corinne was very intrigued. "I wanted to refresh my knowledge on what I had learned a few years before through the *Amazing Facts Bible Study Guides*." Without realizing what church sponsored the meetings, she started attending and then learned they were Sabbath-keepers.

"And wouldn't you know," she shares, "all the fear I had of not being accepted vanished when I attended. I saw that the people were not only accepting of me, but also were genuine and kind. Their faith was not showy or loud. It was quiet and simple."

Corinne says, "I suddenly realized that at last I felt God's peace. I knew this was where my life's spiritual journey had been leading me all this time." She is now a member of that church.

"All I needed to do was surrender my fear and everything became easier. Even though God time and time again tried to prod me toward the church, it finally took me attending Dave Steward's prophecy seminar before I took that final step. God knows exactly how to gently lead His children when they call out to Him."

Reflect: Recall a time in your life when you experienced God's peace. Don't forget that Jesus can calm any storm you may be going through.

Dig Deeper: Psalm 119:165; Isaiah 40:11; John 14:27

Fanny Crosby

Blessed Assurance, Part 1

"Now faith is the substance of things hoped for, the evidence of things not seen" (Hebrews 11:1).

Life did not start well for Fanny Crosby. Born into a poor family, tragedy struck early. At just six weeks old, she developed a bad cold. When the family doctor was not available to provide help, a medical quack came and recommended a treatment that left her blind for the rest of her life. But she felt no resentment. At the age of eight, she composed the following poem:

Oh, what a happy soul I am!
    Although I cannot see,
I am resolved that in this world
    Contented I will be.
How many blessings I enjoy
    That other people don't!
To weep and sigh because I'm blind
    I cannot and I won't.

Fanny's father died when she was just a year old. Her mother and grandmother raised her in a Christian home that was centered on the Bible. She developed an incredible ability to memorize large passages of Scripture—including the entire books of Genesis, Exodus, and Leviticus.

At fourteen she was enrolled in the New York Institute for the Blind where she excelled as a student for eight years. Along with traditional subjects, she learned to sing and to play the piano and the guitar. She later taught at the school and became an ardent supporter for the blind, even speaking before Congress and with several presidents of the United States.

Fanny Crosby is best known as the most prolific hymn writer in history, creating over 8,000 hymns that were often published under a pseudonym because hymn publishers felt people would not purchase books that included too many songs from one author.

Some of her best-known hymns include "Pass Me Not, O Gentle Savior," "Blessed Assurance," and "To God Be the Glory." Fanny also composed over 1,000 poems, wrote two best-selling autobiographies, and was a public lecturer who was committed to Christian rescue missions.

Though raised from childhood as a Christian, she did not make a complete surrender to Jesus until she was an adult.

Reflect: When did you first think about making a full surrender of your life to Jesus? If you have not committed your heart to Christ, read 2 Corinthians 6:2.

Dig Deeper: Philippians 4:11; 1 Thessalonians 5:16–18; 2 Timothy 1:3–7

Fanny Crosby

Blessed Assurance, Part 2

"The work of righteousness will be peace, and the effect of righteousness, quietness and assurance forever" (Isaiah 32:17).

In 1839, when Fanny Crosby was about 19 years old, she began attending meetings at a Methodist church. She was timid and never spoke in public. In fact, she agreed to play music for the meetings on the condition that she would never be asked to speak.

A few years later, she developed a friendship with one of the teachers whom she would consult "concerning all matters in which I was undetermined how to act." Mr. Camp became a true friend and, according to Fanny, "I owe my conversion to that same friend, in so far as I owe it to any mortal."

When she was about 25, she dreamed that on a cloudy day someone invited her to visit Mr. Camp who was very ill. When she spoke with him, he asked, "Fanny, can you give up our friendship?" She replied, "No, I cannot. You have been my adviser and friend, and what could I do without your aid?"

Mr. Camp indicated that his time on earth was limited. He then asked Fanny, "Will you meet me in Heaven?" She said, "Yes, I will, God helping me." Then he responded, "Remember, you promise a dying man!"

When she awoke from her dream, the words resonated in her mind, "Will you meet me in Heaven?" Mr. Camp was in perfect health, but the dream left an impression on her and made her think deeply about salvation and whether she would meet her friend or anyone else in "the Better Land."

Just a few years after her dream, Fanny attended revival meetings at her church. She explains, "On two occasions I sought peace, but did not find the joy I craved, until one evening, November 20, 1850, it seemed to me that the light must indeed come then or never; and so I arose and went forward alone." As she earnestly petitioned the Savior, heavenly light flooded her heart as she realized for the first time "that I had been trying to hold the world in one hand and the Lord in the other."

At the age of 30, Fanny Crosby could now genuinely sing, "Blessed assurance, Jesus is mine!"

Reflect: Carefully read the lyrics to the hymn "Blessed Assurance," written by Fanny Crosby. Pray that God will help you sing these words from your heart.

Dig Deeper: Psalm 61:1; Acts 17:30, 31; Hebrews 10:22

Allyson

Messed Up, Part 1

**"For I know the thoughts that I think toward you, says
the , thoughts of peace and not of evil, to give
you a future and a hope" (Jeremiah 29:11).**

"I was a drug addict, involved in a destructive relationship with little desire for spiritual things," Allyson admits. "My sister and I were like light and dark, and I was the dark." Allyson's sister, Kathy, was a Christian music artist who blessed many people with her music. She once shared with Allyson, through a song she wrote based on Jeremiah 29:11, that God had a plan for her life. Allyson laughed it off. "God does *not* have a plan for me. My life is too messed up."

One day, Kathy gave Allyson, who was living in her home at the time, an ultimatum—clean your room, or else. Allyson refused. After Allyson returned from a weekend camping trip with a friend, Kathy told her, "You have to leave. I can't have this in my house anymore." That night, like Jacob, Allyson spent much of the night wrestling with God. She contemplated ending her life. In desperation, she cried out, "Okay God, I can't do this. I'm messed up and I don't know what to do."

The next morning, she visited a doctor to get help for her drug addiction. When she pleaded with her sister for a second chance, Kathy said, "You're my sister and I love you. I'll give you another chance to stay here, but you have to do two things"—she had to clean her room and attend a church camp meeting for ten days!

Allyson packed her clothes for camp meeting. In her suitcase, she secretly stashed drugs to help her "get through" the week. Strangely, she could never find them in her suitcase throughout the week she was at camp meeting even though they were in her possession the whole time. "So there I was, with no drugs, and it was already midweek at camp meeting. I was faced with detoxing there, and sleeping in a tent."

God was about to turn Allyson's life upside down.

Reflect: Have you ever come to a point in your life where you felt you could never straighten out a mess you created? That's not such a bad place to be.

Dig Deeper: Exodus 2:23; 2 Chronicles 14:11; Psalm 34:6

Allyson

Messed Up, Part 2

"Confess your trespasses to one another, and pray for one another, that you may be healed. The effective, fervent prayer of a righteous man avails much" (James 5:16).

Allyson, who struggled with a drug addiction and was involved in an abusive relationship, admitted to God, "I'm messed up and I don't know what to do." After her sister gave her the ultimatum to leave her home (where she was living) or attend a camp meeting for ten days, she chose the latter.

On Friday night, a new speaker came to camp meeting. Pastor Doug Batchelor gave his testimony. As he spoke of his growing up years and eventually shared about living in a cave and finding a Bible, Allyson was glued to her chair. Then Pastor Doug said, "God had a plan for my life, and he has a plan for your life too."

Allyson's heart was moved as she thought to herself, "Maybe God really does have a plan for my life. Maybe I'm not supposed to be addicted to drugs." Then and there she made a decision to give her heart to the Lord. "God took away my desire for drugs. It was immediate and it was permanent."

Allyson broke off her abusive relationship and began attending church. She took Bible studies from a kind elder named Duane, but continued to struggle with cigarettes. After attending a Christian retreat with a friend who also struggled with smoking, the two of them earnestly prayed together for victory and prevailed through God's power. With joy in her heart, Allyson was baptized and began a new life in Christ.

Sixteen years later, Allyson personally met Pastor Doug at another camp meeting where she shared her story. Hearing his caveman story, going through the *Amazing Facts Bible Study Guides*, gaining helpful information from the Amazing Facts website (amazingfacts.org) have all been helpful to maintaining her walk with God. She especially treasures her *Amazing Facts Prophecy Study Bible* with her name engraved on the cover—a special gift from a friend.

Allyson shares, "If God can change my life—a drug addicted, self-absorbed, miserable person—and give me a new life, He can do the same for you." In addition, she encourages others, "Don't ever stop praying. You never know what your prayers are going to do. I know I had people who never stopped praying for me. I believe it was those people's prayers that brought me to my Savior."

Reflect: What one person—someone who has not given their life to Christ—has God put on your heart to pray for on a daily basis? Don't give up praying earnestly for that person!

Dig Deeper: Job 42:10; Philippians 4:6; 1 Timothy 2:1

Isaiah

Beholding God, Part 1

> **"Woe is me, for I am undone! Because I am a
> man of unclean lips ..." (Isaiah 6:5).**

Isaiah was born during a time when the nation of Israel was in apostasy and rebellion against God. The northern kingdom was soon to be scattered and destroyed. The success and wealth of some had led to greed and the oppression of justice. There was no compassion toward widows, the poor, and the fatherless.

In the southern kingdom, Uzziah had been a very successful king, but his pride led him to presume he could enter the temple of God and offer incense. After the death of Uzziah, Isaiah went through a deep and transforming experience. While serving as a priest in the temple, he writes: "I saw the Lord sitting on a throne, high and lifted up, and the train of His robe filled the temple" (Isaiah 6:1). He saw angels who cried, "Holy, holy, holy is the of hosts; the whole earth is full of His glory" (v. 3).

It was as if the holy of holies had been thrown open before the humble priest and the glories of heaven were displayed before him. The glorious scene caused the whole temple to tremble. "The posts of the door were shaken by the voice of him who cried out, and the house was filled with smoke" (v. 4).

Isaiah was so moved by the revelation that he exclaimed, "Woe is me, for I am undone! Because I am a man of unclean lips, and I dwell in the midst of a people of unclean lips; for my eyes have seen the King, the of hosts" (v. 5). His admission revealed a knowledge of both the state of affairs in Israel and an understanding of his own heart.

But to this priest, bowed in humility of heart, came heaven's response. "Then one of the seraphim flew to me, having in his hand a live coal which he had taken with the tongs from the altar. And he touched my mouth with it, and said: 'Behold, this has touched your lips; your iniquity is taken away, and your sin purged'" (vv. 6, 7).

Isaiah's name means "the Lord has saved." All who, like Isaiah, respond to a true revelation of God by recognizing their own sinful condition, will experience a conversion of heart and a cleansing from sin.

Reflect: When have you last sensed the awesome presence of God? Take time today to prayerfully seek the Lord with a humble heart, just like Isaiah.

Dig Deeper: Exodus 24:10; Amos 9:1; Revelation 4:1–6

Isaiah

Beholding God, Part 2

"'Come now, and let us reason together,' says the , 'Though your sins are like scarlet, they shall be as white as snow; though they are red like crimson, they shall be as wool'" (Isaiah 1:18).

What are the hardest stains in the world to remove? One cleaning company lists five: hot cocoa, bodily waste, blood, permanent marker, and tomato juice. We could add stains made by grass, grape juice, and dirty car grease. Of course, there's always the question of whether you rinse something in hot water or cold water. Should you use mild detergent, citrus-based cleaners, hydrogen peroxide, enzyme cleaners, or bleach?

When God called Isaiah the prophet in the temple, the revelation of the Lord's glory humbled the priest and he immediately saw his own unworthiness. He recognized the stain of sin in his life, a mark so deep that it seemed impossible to remove. But the Lord did the impossible, and Isaiah was told, "Your iniquity is taken away, and your sin purged" (Isaiah 6:7).

One of the main barriers to conversion and coming to God is the belief that a person has committed sins so bad that the Lord could never forgive such iniquities. When Isaiah saw God's glory, the revelation was like that of Moses— he saw the merciful character of the Lord, traits that showed God's willingness to forgive and remove sin.

Isaiah was given the assurance that his sins were removed and, in turn, it motivated him to help his fellow Israelites receive the same peace. There is no need to worry over the impossible stain of sin, a blemish that, in our own power, can never be removed.

To God's people, he first pointed to their sin-stained lives: "Your hands are full of blood" (Isaiah 1:15). He pleaded, "Wash yourselves, make yourselves clean; put away the evil of your doings from before My eyes. Cease to do evil …" (v. 16). But how could this be accomplished? Only through the grace of God, revealed most perfectly by beholding Jesus who died on the cross for our sins.

The Lord said through Isaiah, "Though your sins are like scarlet, they shall be as white as snow; though they are red like crimson, they shall be as wool" (v. 18). When you humbly confess your sins, you may know that God—the true Stain Remover—can wash you clean.

Reflect: What's the worst clothing stain you've ever tried to remove? Did you ever successfully get it out? God can remove the deepest stain of sin from your heart.

Dig Deeper: Psalm 51:2; Ezekiel 36:25; 1 John 1:9

John and Mary

The Bargain, Part 1

"Call upon Me in the day of trouble; I will deliver you, and you shall glorify Me" (Psalm 50:15).

John and Mary were long-time, faithful members of a conservative Sunday-keeping church in Canada. For more than 30 years they served in many positions in their congregation, appreciated many of its teaching, and had many friendships. They were born into their church and never had intentions of leaving it.

Then tragedy struck. In 2011, Mary was diagnosed with cancer. At first the doctors were hopeful that she would recover after surgery and proper treatment. Their church family was very supportive and prayed that she would beat the 24 percent chance of survival given her.

John dropped Mary off at the hospital the day of her surgery and waited for a phone call to let him know when she'd be out. After the operation he rushed back to spend time with her and pray. They felt everything would turn out well. But the next morning three doctors met with them and stated that the surgery had not gone well. Her tumor was too big to be removed and if they tried to take it out she would have bled to death.

Then they told the worried couple that her chances for survival had dropped to just nine percent. "Never have I prayed for God's mercy like I prayed that day," John remembers. "I asked God to spare my wife's life." Then he told the Lord, "I will do whatever you want me to do."

After using some natural forms of therapy combined with chemotherapy, the tumor shrank in size and the doctors were able to successfully remove it. After more chemotherapy and radiation, Mary was on her way to recovery. John then explains, "God had answered our prayers, but now it was our turn to keep our end of the 'bargain.'"

Reflect: Do you personally know someone who experienced physical healing after they cried out to the Lord? What happened? Read about how Jesus healed people.

Dig Deeper: Psalm 28:1, 2; Isaiah 65:24; Jonah 2:2

John and Mary

The Bargain, Part 2

**"You will seek Me and find Me, when you search for
Me with all your heart" (Jeremiah 29:13).**

When John's wife, Mary, was diagnosed with cancer, he prayed, "I will do whatever you want me to do." After she recovered, the couple began searching the Scriptures for deeper truth. They shared their experiences with others as they continued seeking God's will for their lives. Some Bible passages raised questions in their minds about baptism, communion, and the Sabbath.

Then one day, in August 2014, they received a flier in the mail. It was an advertisement for a prophecy seminar conducted by Darrin Bartell from Amazing Facts. John recalls seeing the handbill lying on the counter for a few days. "I studied it some, but then went back to my other chores and didn't pay much attention to it. But in the back of my mind I wanted to know more."

John got busy with work. He and Mary also went to meetings at their Sunday church twice a week. But one day she said to her husband, "John, I'd like to talk to you about those upcoming meetings." At first he put her off, but finally she insisted, so they sat down and carefully studied the prophecy brochure. They finally agreed to check it out, though John was feeling a bit reluctant. "I assumed we were already attending the best church for us," he admits. "I have to thank my wife for being open to this new path we were about to embark on."

One Tuesday evening, they drove to the church for their first meeting. "I thought they would make a few interesting statements, pass the offering baskets to collect money and we'd go home," John says. "Then I'd show Mary where they were wrong. Wow! Was I wrong!"

John says they were "incredibly shocked" because they decided to double check everything the evangelist, Darrin Bartell, stated. "We were very skeptical. We looked everything up!" And they prayed earnestly to learn the truth. They kept attending the prophecy meetings and found themselves soaking up new light, including a clearer understanding about the Sabbath.

But this new pathway eventually led them to a crossroads.

Reflect: Have you ever prayed, "Lord, I will do whatever you want me to do"? Why not make a total submission of your life to God today?

Dig Deeper: Deuteronomy 4:29; Proverbs 8:17; Acts 17:11

John and Mary

The Bargain, Part 3

"When you pass through the waters, I will be with you;
and through the rivers, they shall not overflow you.
When you walk through the fire, you shall not be burned,
nor shall the flame scorch you" (Isaiah 43:2).

After John and Mary learned about the Sabbath in an Amazing Facts evangelistic meeting led by Darrin Bartell and then attended their first Sabbath service, Mary wasn't feeling good about going back to their Sunday-keeping church. "I wasn't quite ready to leave our old church," John admits. "I had a board meeting scheduled for the coming week and I was to be the chair. The pastor would attend with two other board members."

In the meantime, John called a district leader in his denomination and asked about the change of the Sabbath. "He told me in a few words that it had been moved to Sunday by the disciples," he remembers, "and that he didn't have a problem with it." Then John decided to call his local pastor to arrange a meeting so he could ask him some questions. The pastor insisted on knowing the topic and when John said he had some questions about the Sabbath his pastor agreed to talk with him.

Soon after this John attended the church board meeting. At the conclusion, the pastor announced before the other two members that he was ready to talk with John about the Sabbath. John was completely surprised and unprepared. He had carefully arranged his questions and made notes about specific Bible verses but left all of this at home. After his pastor repeated many of the first-day verses in the New Testament commonly used to try and support a change from Sabbath to Sunday, John did his best to share his new found understanding of the Sabbath. His comments were not received well and he was called a legalist.

Finally, John stood up and stated, "I don't like to call any man wrong, but I believe you are wrong." They politely shook hands and John left the church. The next week, John and Mary attended their Sunday-keeping church for the last time. A few months later, they were baptized into God's end-time church. The pathway to truth led John and Mary through some difficult times, but God was with them every step of the way. They were determined to keep their end of the bargain with God.

Reflect: Do you believe God will be with you through any trial you experience? David could say that even when "I walk through the valley of the shadow of death, I will fear no evil; for You are with me" (Psalm 23:4).

Dig Deeper: Exodus 15:2; Leviticus 26:3–10; John 14:27

"For whoever desires to save his life will lose it, but whoever loses his life for My sake will find it" (Matthew 16:25).

As he raised his slingshot and aimed at a bird, young Albert suddenly heard the church bells of his village in Alsace, what was then part of Germany, start ringing. He dropped his weapon and, to the surprise of his friend, ran toward the birds, waving his arms and scaring them away.

Even at an early age, Albert Schweitzer developed a reverence for life, a philosophy he carried with him for the rest of his life. Born into a wealthy family, Albert enjoyed privileges that others only dreamed about. His father, a Lutheran pastor, taught him to play music. He studied organ and later obtained a degree in theology at the University of Strasbourg in 1899.

Albert became principal of a theological college and enjoyed a career of teaching and writing. He was happy in his work and continued to pursue his love of music. But something tugged at his heart. A Bible verse summarized a pull he felt when he compared his happy life with the "care and suffering" he observed around him. "For everyone to whom much is given, from him much will be required ..." (Luke 12:48).

"Even at school [as a child] I had felt stirred whenever I got a glimpse of the miserable home surroundings of some of my schoolfellows and compared them with the absolutely ideal conditions in which we children of the parsonage at Günsbach lived," he once wrote.

Schweitzer wrestled with the life and teachings of Jesus. Liberal theologians of his time dismissed Christ as simply a moral teacher with humanitarian ideals. He wrote his own controversial views about Jesus while concluding that the only way to know Christ was to respond to His invitation, "Follow me ..." (Matthew 4:19).

During this time, Albert was following his love for music and pursued a career as a musicologist with dreams of becoming an expert on J.S. Bach. He studied the organ in Paris and even wrote a definitive edition on Bach's chorales and cantatas.

And then, one day, after reading an article from a missionary magazine about the giant medical needs in Africa, the gifted professor dropped a bombshell on friends and family that left them thinking he had lost his bearings.

Reflect: Can you think of a time in your life when you sensed God tugging at your heart? How did you respond? Remember that Jesus wants to lead you "in the paths of righteousness" (Psalm 23:3).

Dig Deeper: Luke 14:26, 27; Ephesians 5:1, 2; Philippians 2:5–9

Albert Schweitzer

Reverence for Life, Part 2

"I was hungry and you gave Me food; I was thirsty and you gave Me drink; I was a stranger and you took Me in; I was naked and you clothed Me; I was sick and you visited Me ..." (Matthew 25:35, 36).

Albert Schweitzer shocked his friends and family when, in 1905, he announced his decision to study medicine and then become a missionary doctor in equatorial Africa. A few years earlier, he wrote that after awakening one morning, "There came to me the thought ... that I must not accept this happiness as a matter of course, but must give something in return for it."

He had tried to settle the matter of Jesus' saying, "For whoever desires to save his life will lose it, but whoever loses his life for My sake will find it" (Matthew 16:25). So "with calm deliberation" he thought through the issue before getting out of bed. He concluded, "I would consider myself justified in living till I was thirty for science and art, in order to devote myself from that time forward to the direct service of humanity."

His first thought was to work in Europe, perhaps in orphanages helping unfortunate children. But those doors never opened up. That's when he stumbled upon an article from the Paris Missionary Society that outlined the need for medical work in the Congo. After setting down the magazine, "I quietly began my work. My search was over."

Schweitzer's friends and relatives thought he was making a foolish decision. They told him he was burying his talents. They pointed out that his best gifts were in the fields of science and art. One friend said he was like a general who wanted to stand at the front of the firing line. Another said he could do more good lecturing about the needs of medical work for the people in Africa than by actually serving the people on this large continent.

It was a far greater battle to follow his convictions than he realized—especially with so many well-meaning people who urged him not to go forward. But even though many "regarded me as a precocious young man, not quite right in his head," Albert stepped forward into the unknown, taking the words of Christ seriously. For years he had "talked about the love of Christ," but now he would "put it into practice."

Reflect: What one thing could you do this week to move beyond merely "talking" about the love of Christ to "doing" the love of Christ? The Lord once told Moses at the Red Sea, "Tell the children of Israel to go forward" (Exodus 14:15).

Dig Deeper: Psalm 140:12; Proverbs 31:8, 9; 1 John 3:17

Albert Schweitzer

Reverence for Life, Part 3

> "Then great multitudes came to Him, having with them the lame, blind, mute, maimed, and many others; and they laid them down at Jesus' feet, and He healed them" (Matthew 15:30).

"I wanted to be a doctor that I might be able to work without having to talk." So said Albert Schweitzer as he left his career as a teacher and musician to attend medical school and then travel to Africa where he would bring healing to the sick and diseased.

In 1911, he completed his medical training and offered to work, at his own expense, at a mission at Lambaréné on the Ogooué River, in what is now Gabon, in Africa (then a French colony). Schweitzer raised money by conducting concerts and was soon ready to equip a small hospital. In 1912, he married Helene Bresslau, and in 1913 they set off together to establish a hospital about 200 miles (14 days by raft) upstream from Port Gentil (Cape Lopez).

During their first nine months, Albert and his wife saw around 2,000 patients. Many had traveled over long distances for days to reach him. Besides injuries, he treated heart disease, eating sores, dysentery, malaria, sleeping sickness, leprosy, fevers, hernias, and tumors. At the same time, he had to deal with intentional poisoning, fetishism, and the fear of cannibalism by certain tribes.

They began their surgical work in a white-washed chicken coop where his wife assisted him as an anesthetist. Eventually, they constructed a two-room hospital. When World War I broke out in 1914, they were put under supervision by the French military (since Schweitzer was born a German citizen). By 1917, the couple were physically exhausted from their work and returned to Europe to recover.

When Schweitzer's health improved, he once more raised money for the mission hospital through giving lectures and organ recitals, and in 1924, returned to Lambaréné. He worked to rebuild the hospital, added new staff, and was able to use new advances in medicine to treat tropical illnesses.

In 1952, Albert Schweitzer was awarded the Nobel Peace Prize, and from that time until his death worked against the creation of nuclear tests and nuclear weapons. In one of his last great speeches before his death (in 1965), called "Declaration of Conscience," he concluded, "The end of further experiments with atom bombs would be like the early sunrays of hope which suffering humanity is longing for."

On September 4, 1965, Schweitzer died at his beloved hospital in Lambaréné. His grave, on the banks of the Ogooué River, is marked by a cross he made himself.

Reflect: What type of outreach do you feel God has called you to perform? What type of hurting people do you feel compassion toward most?

Dig Deeper: Matthew 21:14; Mark 6:56; Luke 4:40

Peggy

Mad at God, Part 1

> "My God, My God, why have You forsaken Me? Why are You
> so far from helping Me, and from the words of My groaning?
> O My God, I cry in the daytime, but You do not hear; and
> in the night season, and am not silent. But You are holy,
> enthroned in the praises of Israel" (Psalm 22:1–3).

Peggy was mad at God. She confesses, "I felt that He let me down when we moved [from Texas] to Detroit." She and her husband had two daughters and she prayed that the Lord would protect them from dangerous influences that would destroy their lives. Unfortunately, they got involved in destructive activities.

So she turned her back on God and started looking into the New Age movement. Even though she had been baptized into the Southern Baptist Church, she began reading books on reincarnation, witchcraft, and out-of-body experiences. "I never really got into it," she recalls. Eventually, her family moved back to Texas.

Then Peggy's husband began having serious health problems. Within a six-month period, he suffered from three strokes that disabled him. He needed help walking, his speech was slurred, and he couldn't use his right hand. He even had trouble swallowing without choking. On top of that, he suffered from diabetes and high blood pressure.

"My husband and I really began to battle depression. Life seemed to have come to a dead end," she remembers. Peggy felt like she was barely hanging on, trying to make it on her husband's Social Security check. She began to think a lot about death. "What is going to happen when my husband dies or my parents pass away?" Her daughters lived far away from home. "I felt so alone."

Peggy's husband felt pretty hopeless too. He once lived a full and productive life, including his hobby of working as a mechanic and racing cars. Now, he was stuck sitting in a chair most of the day with nothing to do but watch TV. "That was Satan's plan, to keep him in despair. But God had a better plan." They both felt they needed God back in their lives and started searching for a church to attend.

During this time, they began listening to different preachers on TV. And during all this channel surfing, God was about to reveal Himself to Peggy and her husband in a powerful way.

Reflect: Have you ever felt you were facing a hopeless situation? What happened? Paul the apostle once said, "My God shall supply all your need according to His riches in glory by Christ Jesus" (Philippians 4:19).

Dig Deeper: Job 3:23–26; Psalm 35:17, 18; Matthew 6:33

Peggy

Mad at God, Part 2

"Remember the Sabbath day, to keep it holy" (Exodus 20:8).

After going through several difficult circumstances and being mad at God, Peggy and her husband decided to turn back to the Lord. They began looking for a church to attend and at the same time started watching different preachers on TV.

Early one morning, when Peggy's husband couldn't sleep, he started flipping through TV channels and came across Amazing Facts with Pastor Doug Batchelor. He liked what he heard, and he began recording programs so his wife could listen as well. "We both really liked listening to Pastor Doug preach," she explains. They didn't know what denomination he represented and didn't think too much about it.

One day, while reading her Bible, Peggy was looking over the Ten Commandments. For some reason the fourth commandment kept standing out in her mind. She thought to herself, "God, what are You trying to show me?" She read the commandment over again, several times, and began to think she was not truly keeping the Sabbath. After attending church on most Sundays, Peggy would go shopping and do other things. Now she felt convicted that she should dedicate the whole day to God. "I decided I would start keeping the Sabbath right."

Just a couple of days later, when she sat down to watch another presentation by Pastor Doug, she was taken aback when he preached about the Sabbath! Because she had just been reading about the Sabbath, her interest was piqued. "After hearing Pastor Batchelor's message, I realized I truly had been keeping the Sabbath wrong, in more ways than I had realized."

Peggy and her husband suddenly became interested in knowing which church Pastor Doug was from. After doing a little research on the Internet, they discovered he was the pastor of a Sabbath-keeping church. They didn't know much about this church, but liked what they were hearing. Peggy looked in the phone book to see if there was a Sabbath-keeping church nearby. Sure enough there was. They decided to attend the next Sabbath, but when Saturday rolled around, they got cold feet.

But God was still calling to Peggy and her husband ...

Reflect: Do you recall a time when the Holy Spirit convicted you to do something? What was it? Read what the Bible says about pressing forward in Philippians 3:13, 14.

Dig Deeper: Isaiah 58:13, 14; John 16:13; Acts 2:37

Peggy

Mad at God, Part 3

> **"Your ears shall hear a word behind you, saying, 'This is the way, walk in it,' whenever you turn to the right hand or whenever you turn to the left" (Isaiah 30:21).**

Peggy became convicted to keep the seventh-day Sabbath, but when she and her husband decided to attend a local Sabbath-keeping church, they backed out at the last minute. Yet the Lord continued reaching out to Peggy and her husband.

Not long after getting cold feet over attending a local Sabbath-keeping church, Peggy was reading the book of Revelation through and was completely confused. She prayed for God to help her understand this book. A couple of days later, a flier came in the mail with what she called "crazy-looking beasts on it." There was a lion with wings and a four-headed leopard. But most eye catching was a line at the top that indicated it was sponsored by Amazing Facts!

My husband said, "Let's go!" They thought they would hear Pastor Doug, but were soon just as excited to listen to evangelist Jason Morgan, who was also a fascinating speaker. Peggy says, "I was so completely excited by the things I was learning from Jason that I didn't miss one single night. In fact, we came early for every meeting!"

As she sat through the seminar Peggy knew in her heart that God led her to this denomination. "So many of my questions were being answered," she shares. "I wondered about the Second Coming and Pastor Morgan made things so clear, right from the Bible."

On a beautiful spring day in March, Peggy was re-baptized. She explains, "This time it meant so much more to me. Now I truly understood what it meant to be buried in death with Jesus and raised to new life." Since this time, Peggy has shared her faith with her mother and niece who saw the Sabbath truth and also joined the church.

Though at one time Peggy was mad at God, she is now so grateful for the way the Lord did not forsake her. "When I look back over how God led me, I am amazed."

Reflect: What Bible truth did you discover that most changed your life? Pray about sharing that truth with someone else this week.

Dig Deeper: Deuteronomy 31:8; John 14:26; Ephesians 1:18

Andrew, Disciple of Jesus, Part 1

Saving Your Brother First

"Now the names of the twelve apostles are these: first, Simon, who is called Peter, and Andrew his brother ..." (Matthew 10:2).

"Where's my brother?" ten-year-old Jacob wondered as he looked around his bedroom. He had been playing with his toys when he noticed two-year-old Dylan had wandered out of the room. Jacob walked out to the backyard and saw his brother's shoe floating in their swimming pool. Jacob had just watched a movie about a hero saving a girl from drowning and the scene popped into his head. It motivated him on what to do.

Jacob jumped into the water, pulled his brother onto the deck and started doing compressions. In about 30 seconds, Dylan coughed up water and started breathing. After saving his brother's life, Jacob was hailed as a hero by his family and local law enforcement. But the fifth grader wasn't so sure about all the fanfare. After being asked if he felt like a hero, he replied, "kind of."

Andrew was a hero. After being a devoted follower of John the Baptist, he heard the wilderness preacher say, "There He is!" Then, pointing at Jesus, he exclaimed, "Behold the Lamb of God!" (John 1:36). At first, Andrew wasn't sure what John meant. But something deep inside motivated him and a friend to follow Jesus. They wanted to meet this Man. Could this be the Messiah?

When Christ sensed the two were following Him, He turned and said, "What do you seek?" (v. 38). They replied, "Rabbi ... where are You staying?" Jesus said to them, "Come and see" (v. 39). So the two spent personal time sitting at the feet of Jesus, drinking in His words.

At some point, Andrew must have looked around and thought to himself, "Where's my brother? I've got to introduce my brother to this Man!" Andrew's first action after meeting the Master was to think of his own sibling. "He [Andrew] *first* found his own brother Simon [Peter], and said to him, 'We have found the Messiah.' ... And he brought him to Jesus" (vv. 41, 42, emphasis added).

When we first meet Christ and experience His life-changing touch in our lives, we will naturally want to spring into action and think of those we love, just like Andrew who saved his brother's life by bringing him to Jesus.

Reflect: Have you ever met someone who saved a person's life? You can become an Andrew and bring others to Jesus, including your own family members.

Dig Deeper: Mark 16:15; Luke 19:10; 1 Peter 4:10

Andrew, Disciple of Jesus, Part 2

Faith to Feed the Hungry

> "Andrew, Simon Peter's brother, said to Him, 'There is a
> lad here who has five barley loaves and two small fish,
> but what are they among so many?'" (John 6:8, 9).

Maria, a high school teen, wanted to feed the hungry. Millions of Americans, she learned, don't regularly have enough good food to eat and yet a lot of food—up to 40 percent—is simply thrown out. So she teamed up with fellow students to develop a free online platform putting businesses that have extra food in touch with charities that feed hungry people. Her organization is run mostly by high school and college students and has redistributed more than 1.8 million pounds of food in the last five years.

After He had taught all day in a remote place, Jesus' disciples came and said to Him, "This is a deserted place, and the hour is already late. Send the multitudes away, that they may go into the villages and buy themselves food" (Matthew 14:15). A crowd of five thousand had gathered to hear Christ and now the disciples urged Jesus to let them go home or to a nearby village for food.

"But Jesus said to them, 'They do not need to go away. You give them something to eat'" (v. 16). Philip said, "Two hundred denarii (200 days' wages) worth of bread is not sufficient for them, that every one of them may have a little" (John 6:7). Then Andrew, who grew up in this region, said, "There is a lad here who has five barley loaves and two small fish, *but what are they among so many?*" (v. 9, emphasis added). You could hear doubt in his voice.

Jesus not only wanted to feed the hungry, but to also teach His disciples to trust Him to care for all their needs. Christ said, "Bring them here to Me" (Matthew 14:18). Jesus then invited the multitudes to sit down on the grass. "And He took the five loaves and the two fish, and looking up to heaven, He blessed and broke and gave the loaves to the disciples; and the disciples gave to the multitudes. So they all ate and were filled, and they took up twelve baskets full of the fragments that remained" (vv. 19–21).

Sometimes God allows us to go through testing experiences in order to strengthen our faith. Even though the situations we face seem like an impossibility, we may know that "with God all things are possible" (Matthew 19:26).

Reflect: Can you think of a time in your life when your faith was tested? Picture yourself standing next to Andrew while watching Jesus feed the multitude. Let this story strengthen your faith!

Dig Deeper: Matthew 14:13–21; Luke 9:10–17; John 6:1–14

Andrew, Disciple of Jesus, Part 3

Happy to Be Number Two

> "For I say, through the grace given to me, to everyone who is among you, not to think of himself more highly than he ought to think, but to think soberly, as God has dealt to each one a measure of faith" (Romans 12:3).

A fifth wheel camper is one of the largest types of towable RVs on the road. It's pulled by a large pick-up truck with a special "fifth wheel hitch" located in the bed of the truck. They can be quite spacious thanks to their extended length and slide outs. Plus, a fifth wheel can be parked and detached from the vehicle to allow for daily travel.

But the term "fifth wheel" is also an idiom for an extra and unnecessary person or thing. If you've ever been the third person on a date with just two other people, you may have felt like a "fifth wheel" or a "spare tool"—nonessential, redundant, and unneeded. Perhaps Andrew felt that way at times.

While Andrew was one of Jesus' first disciples, he was not part of the inner circle of three—Peter, James, and John. At the feeding of the five thousand, Jesus first approached Philip, though Andrew chimed in his thoughts. And in another story near the end of Jesus' time on earth, Andrew once more appears to be in second place.

After the triumphal entry of Christ into Jerusalem, an incident took place at the temple. "Now there were certain Greeks among those who came up to worship at the feast. Then they came to Philip, who was from Bethsaida of Galilee, and asked him, saying, 'Sir, we wish to see Jesus'" (John 12:20, 21). Philip seems to be the initial focus of this encounter, yet notice what happens next. "Philip came and told Andrew, and in turn Andrew and Philip told Jesus" (v. 22).

In all the references to Andrew in the gospels, he never seemed to mind being like a fifth wheel. It never appeared to bother him to be a team player, someone who didn't need to be captain or president. Like Philip, he was more focused on bringing people—even foreign "Gentiles"—to Jesus and uplifting the Savior. After all, when you are serving Jesus and others, you're never an unnecessary part of the team.

Reflect: Have you ever felt like a fifth wheel? Read 1 Corinthians 12:22 and never forget that every person is essential in the body of Christ.

Dig Deeper: Numbers 12:3; John 1:27; James 4:10

Carlos

From Partying to Preaching, Part 1

"Not many days after, the younger son gathered all together, journeyed to a far country, and there wasted his possessions with prodigal living" (Luke 15:13).

Carlos was born in Brooklyn, New York, but at age 10 he moved with his family to Puerto Rico, making him fluent in both English and Spanish. He grew up in a hardworking, loving, middle-class family who raised him up in the Catholic Church, yet even though he went through the sacraments, he never felt connected with these beliefs.

When Carlos was taught that if he turned from God he would be punished in hell for all eternity, he rejected God. "That's not fair," he thought to himself. "If God is just and I choose not to follow His way, then He should just take away what He originally gave to me—life." As soon as he wasn't required to attend church, he quit going and never looked back. "I didn't want anything to do with God."

Carlos enjoyed his high school years, where he played in sports and was popular. But when he entered university, things took a turn for the worst. "I partied and drank some before college, but when I started working in the restaurant business, I was exposed to a whole new environment." Carlos says, "I began partying every day of the week." He used alcohol and drugs on a heavy basis. "I partied like there was no tomorrow. I was doing all the wrong things in all the wrong places."

But his life was empty. "I thought I was having a great time, but I was looking for a purpose in life that I couldn't grasp," he shares. Carlos got depressed, which only pushed him deeper into drugs and alcohol. He finally hit rock bottom, even contemplating suicide.

During this time, Carlos was taking a psychology course that studied the human brain. "I was blown away by the powerful way our mind works," he shares, "and it led me to believe there must be some type of Supreme Being out there." But how would he discover this Creator? He definitely wasn't going to start with Christianity. "I believed the Christian's God must be sadistic to torture those who disobeyed Him." So he turned to non-Christian religions in search of truth.

Reflect: Was there ever a time in your life when you felt that God was not fair? The Lord is patient and will reveal His love for us if we open our hearts to Him.

Dig Deeper: Luke 15:11–24; Ephesians 5:11; 1 John 2:15–17

Carlos

From Partying to Preaching, Part 2

"Choose for yourselves this day whom you will serve ... But as for me and my house, we will serve the " (Joshua 24:15)

In his search for truth, Carlos read about the lives of Buddha, Socrates, and Mohammed. Then he decided to read a book about Jesus. "I knew Him as a cool hippie who healed the poor, but not much more." The book said that the Sermon on the Mount was the greatest speech ever given in history. "Since I loved history and politics," Carlos recalls, "I decided, for the first time in my life, to open a Bible. I read Matthew, chapters five through seven. I've never been the same since."

When Carlos finished reading these chapters, an unexplainable peace came over him. "It was something I had never before felt and had been searching to find for years." Though he couldn't understand what was happening, he realized it came from reading the Bible and listening to the words of Jesus. "So I decided to give Christ a chance." And the more Carlos read the Bible, the more attracted he became to the life of Jesus.

Now Carlos faced a new dilemma: Which church was the true church? There were so many denominations! "I had to study them all because I wanted to find the one closest to the truth," he shares. So he began to visit all sorts of churches, often going a couple times a week. People criticized him and told him he was confused. But Carlos wondered what if they were in the wrong church and didn't know it?—so he just kept searching.

One day, while flying from Tampa, Florida, to Puerto Rico, Carlos struck up a conversation with his seatmate. Near the end of their flight, the gentleman suggested he study the Sabbath truth in Scripture more carefully.

Memories from high school slowly came back to him. He recalled a classmate who didn't participate in Saturday activities and a friend who wouldn't work on Friday nights. He called this friend and asked about visiting his Sabbath-keeping church. His friend put him off, but God wouldn't let this opportunity pass by. One day, his friend's father stopped by Carlos' family business and invited him to visit their church. Carlos chose to go.

Reflect: What's the hardest decision you ever had to make in your life? Sometimes we need to be willing to give up one thing in order to have something much better.

Dig Deeper: Proverbs 19:20; 1 Corinthians 15:33; 2 Peter 3:9

Carlos

From Partying to Preaching, Part 3

"Jesus said to His disciples, 'If anyone desires to come after Me, let him deny himself, and take up his cross, and follow Me'" (Matthew 16:24).

When Carlos asked his Sabbath-keeping friend about his church, his friend put him off. But his friend's father, Jose, who was an elder in the church, invited Carlos to a Wednesday evening meeting.

Carlos' first experience at church was challenging for someone who had lived a worldly life. The music he heard felt to him like he was attending a funeral service. Carlos was used to partying music. "But I wasn't there to be entertained or looking for friends, I was seeking truth!" Carlos kept attending this church even though he continued visiting others. "I was still searching."

One day, Jose asked Carlos if he wanted to study the Bible at his house. Carlos agreed. They met twice a week. "We got deeper and deeper into the Bible. It came to life for me!" They went from Genesis to Revelation. When they hit the Sabbath topic, he was blown away by the abundant evidence on the seventh-day Sabbath.

"I started asking my friends," he remembers, "why they went to church on Sunday instead of Saturday." None of the answers he received made sense nor could they be backed up from Scripture. This experience caused him to look at his friend's Sabbath-keeping church in a new light.

A big turning point in his study came when they looked at the state of the dead and hellfire. "I realized that I had been presented a perverted image of a sadistic god, not the loving and merciful God of the Bible," he recalls. He learned there would be a judgment and the wicked would burn, but not forever. They would be consumed and then cease to exist. "I can serve a just and fair God like that," he concluded.

After many years of searching for truth about God, Carlos found a church that answered all his questions and practiced the teachings of the Bible. Soon, Carlos was baptized into God's remnant church.

Something else happened to Carlos while taking Bible studies. He began to feel a call to preach the gospel.

Reflect: Have you ever given someone a simple Bible study? If you feel hesitant, but interested in learning how to do so, why not simply accompany someone else in your church and watch.

Dig Deeper: John 10:27; 1 Corinthians 11:1, 2; 1 Peter 2:21

Carlos

From Partying to Preaching, Part 4

**"[Jesus] said to them, 'Go into all the world and preach
the gospel to every creature'" (Mark 16:15).**

While taking Bible studies, Carlos began to feel a call to preach the gospel. One day he watched a DVD titled *The Final Events of Bible Prophecy*. He shares, "I was captivated! I discovered the Amazing Facts ministry and went online and found many resources that I enjoyed." He especially liked a series by Pastor Doug Batchelor called *The Prophecy Code*. He also felt an even deeper call to study theology and become a pastor. "I wanted to do what Pastor Doug was doing."

But his partying days had left him in so much debt that he could hardly pay for school. So he moved from Puerto Rico back to New York to find a higher paying job. He began working as an elementary dual-language teacher and finished his master's degree. At the same time, he began attending a Spanish Sabbath-keeping church in Manhattan where he soon became an elder.

"I continued to have a strong desire to dedicate my life to full-time ministry," Carlos remembers. "I loved teaching, but wanted to work completely for God." One day he saw an ad for the Amazing Facts Center of Evangelism (AFCOE) training program and decided to attend. After paying off his debts, Carlos quit his teaching career and headed for Sacramento.

Carlos loved AFCOE. "I learned so much and was having a great time," he shares. One day, Pastor Jëan Ross, the director for AFCOE, asked Carlos about his future plans. "He told me he wanted me on their team and offered me a position as one of their full-time evangelists."

It was a dream come true. Carlos realized that the call he felt to preach four years earlier was more than a passing thought. It was the Holy Spirit revealing His plans for his life. Carlos accepted the invitation. "It's been the greatest journey in my life. I have the best job in the world!" He is now the director of the AFCOE program.

From partying to preaching, Carlos was a young man with a distorted view of God who longed to discover truth. Now, as a bilingual Amazing Facts evangelist, he leads others to find a God who truly cares.

Reflect: Have you ever preached a sermon? Maybe God is calling you to stand up and share the gospel before a group. Pray about it and talk with your pastor.

Dig Deeper: 1 Corinthians 1:21; 1 Timothy 4:13; James 3:1

John Calvin

Timid, Mild, and Cowardly, Part 1

"We have the prophetic word confirmed, which you do well to heed as a light that shines in a dark place, until the day dawns and the morning star rises in your hearts" (2 Peter 1:19).

Most do not think of the giant reformer from Geneva—John Calvin—as, to use his own words, "timid, mild, and cowardly." But God could read the devoted heart of this thoughtful youth who led a blameless life. It was apparent at an early age that this sharp student would be a force for good, if only he submitted his thinking to the Word of God and not church tradition.

Calvin grew up in the church and was destined—his father's wish—for the priesthood. Born in 1509, in France, he was the first of four sons to survive infancy. His mother died while he was a child. Early on, his intellectual skills were obvious and at the age of just 12, he was hired as a clerk by a local bishop. In college he learned Latin, studied philosophy, and then entered law school.

While in Paris, Calvin heard of the teachings of the Reformation and, loyal to the church, believed these Protestant heretics deserved to die at the stake. But God broke through the thinking of this honest student through Calvin's own cousin, Olivetan, a Protestant. Once, when the two met for one of their regular discussions about Christianity and the church, Olivetan told Calvin, "There are but two religions in the world. The one class of religions are those which men have invented, in all of which man saves himself by ceremonies and good works; the other is that one religion which is revealed in the Bible, and which teaches man to look for salvation solely from the free grace of God."

Calvin looked at his cousin and firmly stated, "I will have none of your new doctrines! Do you think I have lived in error all my days?"

But a seed was planted in the mind of this brilliant student, a thought that would not go away. A small ray of light broke through the thick walls of his thinking, walls of false teachings and intellectualism that kept God at a distance. But now, the Lord came near.

Reflect: Can you think of a time when you spoke against something and then the Lord later convicted you to reconsider? Don't forget, "The lifts up the humble ..." (Psalm 147:6).

Dig Deeper: 1 Samuel 16:7; Ecclesiastes 5:2; Mark 4:26–29

John Calvin

Timid, Mild, and Cowardly, Part 2

"O wretched man that I am! Who will deliver me from this body of death?" (Romans 7:24).

John Calvin's conversation with his Protestant cousin, Olivetan, wouldn't leave his mind. He became convicted of his own sins and sensed that he stood alone before the Judge of the universe. All of his good works, including the ceremonies of the church, did nothing to remove sin from his life and left him utterly hopeless. Though he earnestly increased his efforts at penance, he did not feel at peace with God.

During this time, while still a student in college, he passed by the public square and witnessed a heretic being burned at the stake. Calvin studied the face of the martyr and saw peace on his countenance. How could this heretic, who rebelled against the church's teachings, exhibit calmness of spirit while he [Calvin] perfectly sought to obey the church yet lived in despair?

John Calvin knew the Protestants rested their faith alone on the Word of God, so he was driven to study and find what gave them courage in the face of death. In the Holy Scriptures he discovered Jesus. The gospel message so gripped him that he knew he could never become a priest. Though he attempted to continue his studies in law, he finally abandoned this course and devoted himself to spreading the gospel.

But Calvin was, to use his own words, "timid, mild, and cowardly." He was naturally a quiet person who enjoyed retreating to his studies. He was not drawn to stand before people and speak. But through the influence of Christian friends, John began to teach in small villages and in the homes of simple people the truths that set him free.

During the turbulent years of the Reformation, Calvin found himself in difficult circumstances that led him to flee for his life. He eventually left Paris and on his way to Strasbourg made a stop in Geneva where William Farel, a fellow French reformer, convinced him to stay and work for a time. He was forced to flee for a period but eventually returned to carry on his work for nearly 30 years until he died at the age of 54.

Reflect: Do you know of any timid yet powerful Christians? Solomon described the righteous as "bold as a lion" (Proverbs 28:1).

Dig Deeper: Joshua 1:7; Proverbs 28:1; 2 Timothy 1:7

Barbara

When Your World Falls to Pieces

> "I will instruct you and teach you in the way you should
> go; I will guide you with My eye" (Psalm 32:8).

Barbara threw the Amazing Facts evangelistic brochure in the garbage. She was at the lowest point in her life. Over the last three years her mother had passed away, her husband died of cancer, and her father died from a stroke. As she tried to cope with family challenges, financial stresses, and deep grief, she thought she was going to go crazy.

Just the night before the brochure arrived, she had cried out to God for help. She felt like she was at the end of her rope. The Lord gave her calmness to make it through the night. The next day when the mail came she immediately saw the invitation to a prophecy seminar being conducted by Darrin Bartell. Something called to her heart to pull the big colorful mailer back out of the garbage. She was drawn to the pictures. Barbara later called a friend and they both attended the meetings.

Barbara shares, "When I heard Pastor Bartell preach, I knew God put him on earth to speak to me! I can still see him holding up a Bible and saying, 'Don't believe everything you are told. Go to the Bible for answers.'" When the meetings were transferred to a Sabbath-keeping church, she hesitated to attend. She had always been taught that these Sabbath-keepers were a cult.

"So I asked my friend, 'Should I go?' She said, 'Are you learning more about the Bible? Are you growing in Christ? If so, then go!'" The first time she entered this church, she says, "I felt like I was coming home. My best friends in the world are in that church. I have true friends there."

Barbara gratefully says, in light of her poor health, that if she had not found God's last-day church when she did, "I would probably not be alive right now. My health was so bad. I was under so much pressure. I hardly knew how to pray. I am so glad I pulled that brochure out of the garbage. My local church and Amazing Facts have been such a blessing to me because they have helped me to grow in Christ."

Reflect: Can you recall one time you sensed the Holy Spirit speaking to your heart? Did you follow the promptings of the Spirit? It will bring you joy!

Dig Deeper: John 14:26; Romans 8:26; 1 Peter 5:7

Mike

Getting Straight Answers, Part 1

"You will seek Me and find Me, when you search for Me with all your heart" (Jeremiah 29:13).

Mike was hungry for Bible answers.

In his early years, Mike was reared in a devout Catholic home in New York State where he was involved in many church activities. "I was an altar boy when I was young," he shares, "and did volunteer work in the church." One area of service was the Eucharistic ministry where Mike was ordained to carry out such services as taking communion to shut-in members, visiting the sick, and praying with those who could not attend church.

But as he became an adult, he found himself overwhelmed with worldly responsibilities and attractions that began to pull him away from spiritual things. "Like so many other people," Mike shares, "I became too concerned with my job. I was working with a local food bank. It occupied a lot of my time and required travel. When I wasn't working, I just wanted to go out and have fun. The last thing I was concerned about was waking up early to attend church. So the church was pushed aside."

As Mike's job responsibilities escalated, so did the demand for his time. He enjoyed the things that money could buy, but found little time to enjoy them. "I was lonely and depressed," Mike recalls, "and turned to drugs and alcohol." He found that he was not only disconnected from friends due to his busy workload, but he was also disconnected from his former spiritual self.

At a low point, things began to turn around. "I started to feel guilty about not being involved in church anymore. It was always gnawing at me, and I wanted to please the Lord and get into my Bible. But in the Catholic Church, we didn't do much of that."

Mike was hungry for Bible truth, so he started reading the Bible on his own. He began to discover many things in the Bible that did not correspond with what he had been taught growing up. This opened a door of searching and learning. He couldn't get enough of the Bible and read everything he could get his hands on. He studied church history, the Reformation, and carefully compared the teachings of different denominations with Scripture. And God rewarded his searching.

Reflect: Did you ever lose a precious possession? Do you recall searching earnestly for that item? Did you ever find it?

Dig Deeper: Deuteronomy 4:29; Proverbs 8:17; Luke 11:9

Mike

Getting Straight Answers, Part 2

> "No one can serve two masters; for either he will hate the one and love the other, or else he will be loyal to the one and despise the other ..." (Matthew 6:24).

Mike was excited about the truths that he was discovering in the Bible, but he was uncomfortable with how they clashed with the teachings of the Catholic Church. "Growing up as I did," he says, "you just didn't question the church. I was scared to death. I remember talking to my parents and my priest. I took out my Bible and asked about specific verses, but I couldn't get straight answers."

That's when Mike stumbled across Amazing Facts on television. What caught his attention was how Pastor Doug gave answers to the very questions Mike had been asking for years. "Amazing Facts always offered pamphlets at the end of the show," Mike adds. "After Pastor Doug talked on a certain topic he'd offer a pamphlet. I just couldn't wait to order it. I also ordered the *Amazing Facts Bible Study Guides*. I was learning all kinds of stuff and getting the answers I needed!"

One thing Mike appreciated about Amazing Facts is the way Pastor Doug always provided Scripture with his teachings. It was a welcome contrast to the hesitations he had received from other people he had asked for answers. "It made a huge difference in my life," said Mike, "to be able to have actual Bible references that I could go to and read plain as day."

Mike made a decision to leave the Catholic Church. "I felt totally lost," he recalls. "I was always taught that the Protestant denominations were evil, and if you joined a Protestant church, you were doomed to hell. So I didn't know what to do." Mike decided that he would join the Lutheran Church since it was most closely related to the Catholic Church. But conflicts with Bible teachings kept coming up. So his search continued.

Mike kept studying his Bible with the help of Amazing Facts and eventually found God's true church. Today he has a strong, personal relationship with Jesus. He no longer lives his old lifestyle of drugs and alcohol and partying. "You can't be married to your wife and then go out and cheat on her," he explains. "That's the way I feel about Jesus. I can't have a relationship with Him, my Lord and Master, and then go out and cheat on Him."

Reflect: Do you have a relationship with Jesus and serve Him because you love Him? Remember, obedience is an act of love!

Dig Deeper: Luke 10:27; John 14:15; 1 John 4:19

Lydia

Royal Hospitality

> "A certain woman named Lydia heard us. She was a seller of purple from the city of Thyatira, who worshiped God. The Lord opened her heart to heed the things spoken by Paul" (Acts 16:14).

The oldest military award still being given by the United States is a decoration called the Purple Heart. It is presented in the name of the President to soldiers wounded or killed in battle. It is the successor to the earlier Badge of Military Merit, first given by General George Washington who designed the badge in the form of a purple heart.

During his second missionary journey, the apostle Paul received a vision of a man pleading, "Come over to Macedonia and help us" (Acts 16:9). Without delay, the apostle, along with Silas, Timothy, and Luke, turned west to preach the gospel beyond Asia Minor. Arriving in Philippi, they went outside the city on the Sabbath "where prayer was customarily made; and we sat down and spoke to the women who met there" (v. 13).

Luke explains, "Now a certain woman named Lydia heard us. She was a seller of purple from the city of Thyatira, who worshiped God" (v. 14). Lydia, whose name in Greek means "beautiful one" or "noble one," was apparently a businesswoman, possibly a widow, who sold purple cloth. Thyatira was famous during the Roman era for its dyeing facilities and manufacturing of purple cloth. This cloth was difficult to make because of the tedious process, so it was sold for a high price. This is partly why purple is often associated with royalty.

The Bible says, "The Lord opened her heart to heed the things spoken by Paul" (v. 14). Lydia became Paul's first convert in Philippi and thus the first convert to Christianity in Europe. "And when she and her household were baptized, she begged us, saying, 'If you have judged me to be faithful to the Lord, come to my house and stay.' So she persuaded us" (v. 15). Lydia had an open heart and an open home, providing royal hospitality to these missionaries.

Paul and Silas—soldiers of Christ—could have received heaven's Purple Heart for the beatings they were about to unfairly receive in Philippi, but in another sense, so could Lydia for, like all Christians, she died to self in order to receive Christ (Galatians 2:20).

Lydia showed the royal colors of Jesus, for after Paul and Silas were released from jail, they went back to her home to recover and then continue their brave work for Christ.

Reflect: Do you personally know someone who has received an award for bravery?

Dig Deeper: Acts 16:11–15, 40; Romans 12:13; 1 Peter 4:9

Rachael and Mike

"Don't Join His Cult!", Part 1

**"A man's heart plans his way, but the
directs his steps" (Proverbs 16:9).**

"When it comes to religion," Rachael shares, "I was raised 'nothing.'" Her mother occasionally mentioned the importance of prayer before going to bed and there were the short prayers at the dinner table before eating. She had two older brothers and a younger brother. Her parents divorced when she was only two.

Her father remarried more than once and eventually became a Catholic. "I was really confused, especially when he had his first two marriages annulled. It felt like he was pretending he didn't have these two other families." There were few normal relationships in Rachael's life—lots of divorces, stepfamilies, kids born out of wedlock, and remarriages.

In high school, Rachael made friends who played sports together. Peers pressured her into having her first alcoholic beverage. "For the next seven years I was a pretty heavy drinker. But I didn't think it was a big deal since I was behaving like everyone around me," she remembers. "Even though I was one of the 'party girls' I was strongly against premarital sex and drug use. My friends would laugh at me when I would wear a shirt that said, 'Don't buy the lie—save sex for marriage.'"

Before graduating, Rachael began working with a juvenile court supervising teens that were court ordered to complete community service hours. After four months of working there she noticed a co-worker named Mike who was a case manager. "I didn't feel as a fellow worker that it was appropriate to show any interest, but my mother, who worked in the same building thought it was a great idea to set us up on a date," she recalls. "My mom had tried to set me up with men for years and knew I didn't date and was a virgin. She thought something might be wrong with me."

One thing she remembers her mother saying about Mike, "You should date him, but whatever you do, don't join his cult!" She laughed at her mom's comment and said, "I'm not an idiot." But inside she wondered, "Is this guy into the KKK or some extreme group?" Of course, the supposed cult she spoke of was his Sabbath-keeping church. Was Mike part of some weird organization? She would soon find out.

Reflect: Has anyone ever told you that you belonged to a strange church? Remember, we are called to be a "peculiar people" (1 Peter 2:9, KJV).

Dig Deeper: Psalm 32:8; Isaiah 30:21; James 1:5

Rachael and Mike

"Don't Join His Cult!", Part 2

"Train up a child in the way he should go, and when he is old he will not depart from it" (Proverbs 22:6).

Mike grew up in a Sabbath-keeping home and his family moved around quite a bit. "I've been home schooled, attended public school, and even a Christian boarding school." By the time Mike reached the 8th grade, he had rebelled against his parents and Christianity in general. He began drinking and using street drugs. His grades dropped and he quit coming home at night. "It was during this period that I professed, at least to myself, that I was an atheist. I believed that God and heaven were made up because people were scared of dying."

One night, when Mike returned from a party, instead of sneaking back into the house, he decided to lie down on the grass and look up at the stars. He remembers, "It was then that I realized there has to be a God. Our planet and everything in it couldn't have come from nothing."

When Mike turned 21, he started settling down and thinking about a career. Eventually he enrolled in a police academy. During this time, he had a child out of wedlock. He finished his schooling and was hired as a police officer for a couple years.

Mike's life as a new father was challenging, especially between himself and his daughter's mother. They parted ways and he later ended up taking a job as a case manager for juveniles and adults on probation/parole for drugs. He shares, "It was here that I met Rachael. She worked across the street at the courthouse." He decided to ask her out.

On their first date, during an awkward moment, Mike asked Rachael, "Do you believe everything in the Bible is true and accurate?" She thought that was an easy question to answer. "Yes," she said. But she thought, "That's a weird question. Of course if it's in the Bible it's true. But what I didn't realize is how much of the Bible I didn't even understand. I later understood he was thinking about the Sabbath. If he had brought that up right away, I would have known for sure he was crazy. What's funny is that this conversation took place on a Friday night at a football game!"

That weird question eventually led both Mike and Rachael to a turning point.

Reflect: Have you (or someone you know) ever been asked a "weird" question about religion? What was the question? The Bible says to always be ready to give an answer for your faith (1 Peter 3:15).

Dig Deeper: John 3:4; Acts 16:30; Hebrews 2:3

Rachael and Mike

"Don't Join His Cult!", Part 3

"You will show me the path of life; in Your presence is fullness of joy; at Your right hand are pleasures forevermore" (Psalm 16:11).

Mike's question to Rachael about the Bible at the Friday night football game didn't come out of the blue. He grew up knowing about the Bible. He also knew about Pastor Doug Batchelor and Amazing Facts. So as he began to think about the church of his childhood, he did a quick search on the Internet and in no time at all found amazingfacts.org. He read *The Richest Caveman* which launched him more deeply into studying the Bible. "I could really relate to Pastor Batchelor's story," he shares.

While dating, Mike and Rachael started attending a Sabbath-keeping church and began regularly watching Doug Batchelor videos. Mike also started listening to many of Pastor Batchelor's sermons on podcast. During downtime at work, he would fill his mind with more truth from these messages.

Mike and Rachael began attending church on a regular basis. As Bible truth convicted their hearts, their lives began to slowly change. After they were married, Rachael began asking Mike, "Why aren't we practicing more of the things we are learning?" So they began to return tithe, stopped eating unclean meats, drinking caffeine and alcohol, and threw out over a hundred DVDs. They soon became convicted to keep the Sabbath every week and the very weekend of their baptism, God miraculously opened up a new job for Rachael so that she could keep the Sabbath.

Today, Rachael loves sharing her faith at work. "One of the books I've handed out is Pastor Doug's *At Jesus' Feet.*" Since they drive an hour each way to church, they enjoy reading Amazing Facts materials while driving. At Christmas, they often wrap up truth-filled materials and give them to friends and family.

Mike reflects, "No matter how much society changes, Amazing Facts stays true to Bible truth. I thank God for Amazing Facts which has been used by the Lord to turn me in the right direction."

Rachael laughs as she looks back. "My mom warned me not to join Mike's cult. But instead, Amazing Facts led me to God's true church."

Reflect: Has God been convicting you to change certain behaviors in your life? What most needs to change right now for you to be at peace with the Lord? Step out in faith and watch the waters part.

Dig Deeper: Proverbs 12:28; Colossians 4:5, 6; 1 Peter 3:15

John Newton

Amazing Grace, Part 1

> **"For the grace of God that brings salvation has appeared to all men"** (Titus 2:11).

John Newton, an Englishman, was born on July 24, 1725, to a shipmaster. His mother—a godly woman who taught him the Bible and how to pray—died of tuberculosis when John was almost seven years old. He was sent to boarding school for a couple years and then rejoined his family after his father remarried. His mother's influence began to fade as he developed friendships with a bad crowd.

At age 11, Newton went to sea with his father who intended him to work on a sugarcane plantation in Jamaica. But John changed his plans and signed on with a merchant ship that was sailing to the Mediterranean Sea. He admits that he became weary of his religious efforts, and "instead of prayer, I learned to curse and blaspheme, and was exceedingly wicked when from under my parents' view. All this was before I was twelve years old."

When he was 18, John was pressed into naval service by the Royal Navy. When he tried to desert, he was stripped to the waist, tied to the grating, and flogged. He was so incredibly angered by the humiliation that he intended to murder the captain and then commit suicide by throwing himself overboard.

Newton eventually transferred to a slave ship bound for West Africa. He didn't get along with the crew and the captain finally left him with a slave dealer who made him a slave to an African princess. A few years later, thanks to a friend of his father, he was rescued by a sea captain and returned to England.

On this return voyage, the ship encountered a severe storm off the coast of Ireland and almost sank. It sobered Newton and he began reading his Bible and quit drinking, gambling, and swearing. Even though he still worked in the slave trade, he felt that March 10, 1748 was a turning point in his life. "I cannot consider myself to have been a believer in the full sense of the word, until a considerable time afterwards."

God was not finished working in the life of this soon-to-be captain of slave-trading ships.

Reflect: Do you think the influence of John Newton's mother had a lasting impact on his life? You can impact another's life when you lead by example.

Dig Deeper: Luke 19:10; 2 Timothy 1:5; 2 Peter 3:9

John Newton

Amazing Grace, Part 2

"By the grace of God I am what I am, and His grace toward me was not in vain; but I labored more abundantly than they all, yet not I, but the grace of God which was with me" (1 Corinthians 15:10).

John Newton experienced a heart-changing event in 1748, while returning on a ship to England. When the vessel nearly sank, he cried out to God for mercy. It was a turning point in his life. But he was still involved in the slave trade and eventually captained slave ships. During this time, he married his childhood sweetheart, Mary Catlett, in 1750. The couple adopted two orphaned nieces.

In 1754, John suffered a major stroke and had to give up his seafaring and slave-trading activities, though he still invested in slaving operations. God continued to work on Newton's heart and he eventually became a clergyman.

Eventually, John Newton not only became involved in the Committee for the Abolition of the Slave Trade, but wrote a pamphlet titled *Thoughts Upon the African Slave Trade*. He described the horrific conditions on slave ships and then apologized for participating in the trade. "It will always be a subject of humiliating reflection to me, that I was once an active instrument in a business at which my heart now shudders."

People struggling with faith would often seek his advice—including the young William Wilberforce, a Member of Parliament. Wilberforce's recent conversion led him to contemplate leaving politics, but Newton encouraged him to stay in Parliament and "serve God where he was." As an ally with Wilberforce, he worked against slavery and lived to see the passage of the Slave Trade Act 1807.

John Newton later made this confession of faith: "It is certain that I am not what I ought to be. But, blessed be God, I am not what I once was. God has mercifully brought me up out of the deep miry clay and set my feet upon the Rock, Christ Jesus."

In 1767, the poet William Cowper began attending Newton's church. Cowper and Newton worked together to create great hymns for the church, including "Glorious Things of Thee Are Spoken." But the greatest contribution Newton gave to the church was a hymn that captured his own conversion story. It reads,

"Amazing grace! How sweet the sound, that saved a wretch like me!
I once was lost, but now am found, was blind, but now I see."

Reflect: Find and read (or sing) the lyrics to the hymn, "Amazing Grace." As you go through the words, remember, Jesus died personally for you!

Dig Deeper: 1 Chronicles 17:16, 17; Ephesians 2:8, 9; 1 Timothy 1:15

Diana

A Leap of Faith, Part 1

"For we walk by faith, not by sight" (2 Corinthians 5:7).

Long-distance truck drivers will tell you that they have seen just about anything and everything out on the road. It's difficult to surprise a trucker, but that's what happened to Diana. She was standing on a four-lane bridge in Ohio, helping a stranded motorist when she looked up to see a semi-truck barreling straight toward her. Diana had seconds to respond. She could stay where she was and get hit, or she could jump off the 25-foot high bridge and pray she wouldn't land in traffic below.

Diana took a leap of faith and jumped. She felt herself falling through the air and, in answer to her quick prayer, landed on a median. When she awoke, she had to crawl over to her cell phone to call for an ambulance. At the hospital, Diana was told she had fractured her pelvis, broke ribs, fractured her neck, had a collapsed lung, and had internal bleeding. But God brought miraculous healing to Diana.

Life hasn't always been easy for her, especially as she sought for love in all the wrong places. Diana first ran away from home at the age of eleven. Her dad drank, and her parents fought constantly. She rode her bicycle five miles to her grandparent's where she found short-term peace in their home.

At age eighteen, Diana looked for happiness by joining the armed services. However, she found only alcohol and bad relationships there. A few years later she got married and, though she ended up with two beautiful daughters, her marriage went south. Sadly, Diana kept trying to fill a hole in her heart left by her father who had gone through multiple marriages. She was looking for love, but she ended up abused.

Later in life, Diana was working as a security officer and often read her Bible during breaks. One day, a fellow worker stopped by and asked if she believed in Christ. She replied, "I'm a sinner, saved by grace. I still have much to learn."

Diana's co-worker then said, "I have something for you to read." He handed her an *Amazing Facts Bible Study Guide*. She had been praying for more light and shared, "My spirit rejoiced, and I knew that this was an answer to my prayer!"

Reflect: When is the last time you had a close call? Do you believe angels were watching over you?

Dig Deeper: Psalm 91:11, 12; Matthew 21:22; Romans 10:17

Diana

A Leap of Faith, Part 2

"Blessed be the my Rock, who trains my hands for war, and my fingers for battle" (Psalm 144:1).

Diana's thirst for Bible knowledge grew as she studied the *Amazing Facts Bible Study Guide* given to her by a co-worker. When she learned of the Sabbath truth, she said, "It lit a fire in me that couldn't be contained. I came alive and was very hungry for the Word and to know my Jesus."

Soon she was listening to Amazing Facts programs on the web. Eventually, she began attending a Sabbath-keeping church where she was baptized. Diana, once a fighter in the armed forces, now refers to herself as a soldier for Jesus. "I am praying that my Father will transform me into a warrior for Christ."

"My step has a spring to it, I smile with confidence," she says. "I have been set free from my relationship addiction. Prayer and the Bible have become my sword, and faith has become my shield. It is a new day, and I am blessed."

Today, Diana is back on the road, driving and witnessing for Christ. "Amazing Facts has been my rock on this journey because I can listen to important truths as I travel down the road," she says. "I only return home once a month, so listening is very important to my getting fed by the Word."

She looks for opportunities every day to share her faith. One day, she offered a ride to a 21-year-old who was living on the road. The young adult, named Tyler, was struggling with depression and had recently lost three friends. Diana felt that he needed to hear Pastor Doug's testimony. So she played it for him while they started on a 550-mile stretch. She ended up playing one sermon right after another.

When she arrived at her destination, she gave him a Bible, covered one night's lodging in a motel, and bought him a bus ticket home. "I believe in my heart that he went away knowing Jesus a little better," she recalls. "I thanked my Father for the opportunity to show His love and prayed that Tyler would someday be fully committed to Him."

Diana understands what it's like to find your way home. It's been a long journey through pain, but by God's grace she has made the leap of faith into her Father's arms.

Reflect: Have you ever had to take a leap of faith in your Christian journey? What happened?

Dig Deeper: Galatians 2:20; Philippians 4:13; Hebrews 11:1

Crispus

"The Chief Ruler of the Synagogue"

"Then Crispus, the ruler of the synagogue, believed on the Lord with all his household. And many of the Corinthians, hearing, believed and were baptized" (Acts 18:8).

In terms of actual facts, we know less about Crispus than we do about many people in the Bible. In fact, we only know that he was "the ruler of the synagogue" in Corinth, and that Paul himself had baptized Crispus (1 Corinthians 1:14). We also know that Crispus had a "household," but we don't know what that household comprised, just that they were baptized along with Crispus, though presumably not by Paul himself.

But there's a great deal we can glean from the 25 words found in this verse. He was, first of all, "the ruler of the synagogue" in Corinth. This major city in the Roman world was a melting pot of ideas, cultures, and resources. It was a cosmopolitan environment, with a diverse and changing population, ideal for spreading new teachings and customs. Essentially, the city's religious life was eclectically pagan.

Among the Jews, then, a synagogue was an important center not only of worship, but also of learning, culture, and community. Having been commanded by God to be separate from the paganized influences around them, the Jews of Corinth would look to the "ruler" of their congregation for spiritual leadership and protection.

So to learn that Crispus "believed on the Lord," i.e., on Jesus, would be major news in that community. Think of what would happen in your town if a major religious leader from another faith showed up at your church and joined!

Second, we can deduce that Paul's teachings had an immediate effect on Crispus' family: "all his household" believed.

Third, we can see that Crispus was, himself, an evangelist: "And many of the Corinthians, hearing, believed and were baptized." What did they hear? Paul's words, yes, but also Crispus' testimony. It's one thing for a traveling evangelist to come and declare something, and it's good that they do. But when you hear from your friends and neighbors, and when you see a leader in your community respond, that's even more impressive.

We don't have a record of what Crispus said, or how he acted so as to influence "all his household" and many of his neighbors. But we have the record that it happened—and that's inspiration enough!

Reflect: Have you shared your faith with your family and neighbors? Who do you know that would benefit from your testimony? Sharing your testimony will help you be an overcomer!

Dig Deeper: Joshua 24:15; Mark 5:22; Revelation 12:11

Priscilla

No Cable? No Problem!

"Being confident of this very thing, that He who has begun a good work in you will complete it until the day of Jesus Christ" (Philippians 1:6).

Most people would be quite frustrated if their cable was disconnected, but Priscilla saw God's hand working in her life. When she couldn't afford to pay her cable bill, she hooked her computer up to her television and began watching programs through the Internet. Soon she discovered the Amazing Facts website and many sermons that she could watch for free!

Priscilla identified with Pastor Doug's personal testimony. She grew up in an orphanage and as an adult plunged into a life of drugs, shame, and time in prison. But the greatest pain she's ever known happened two years ago when her only child, her 21-year-old son, was killed in a car accident. "He had his whole life ahead of him. I attempted suicide in the days following his death. I felt my life was over and not worth living without my son."

Listening to Bible-based sermons gave her hope. She heard promises of a better tomorrow and sensed God leading her to learn more about the Bible. When she heard about Saturday being the Lord's true Sabbath day, it caused her to dust off her Bible and read for herself about the seventh day.

She was so hungry to learn about Bible truth that she set aside contact with the regular news in her community and in the world in order to discover the hidden treasures of God's Word. "I am so interested in Bible prophecy that I sometimes think I bore my friends because it is all I talk about!"

Priscilla has hesitated to join a church because she has never found one that truly teaches the Bible. She has been to services where there was lots of shouting during the sermon, but they never helped her really know more about God. She felt alone and rejected when others spoke in tongues and she did not.

Hearing God's Word preached through Amazing Facts is changing her mind about church. She shares, "Now I want to be baptized. I'm ready to make a public commitment to serve Jesus Christ. Please pray for me as I make a first step to find a church home. I want to become a member once and for all, and stay there!"*

Reflect: Do you know someone like Priscilla who is searching and about to make a decision for Jesus?

Dig Deeper: Ephesians 4:13–16; Colossians 1:9, 10; 2 Peter 3:18

*Amazing Facts helps connect people like Priscilla with a local Sabbath-keeping church.

David Livingstone

He Changed Africa for the Better

"For by grace you have been saved through faith, and that not of yourselves; it is the gift of God, not of works, lest anyone should boast" (Ephesians 2:8, 9).

Hardscrabble—which the dictionary defines as "marked by poverty"—certainly describes the childhood and youth of David Livingstone. Born in 1813, he went to work in a factory at age 10 and used his hard-earned wages to help his mother.

Such child labor is outlawed now in Britain, but a ten-year-old boy grows up quickly when thrust into the adult world of work. Young David learned self-reliance in a hurry—a trait which extended to his spiritual life. By the age of 20, when his working years equaled his childhood ones, he began to think about his standing with God.

"Great pains," he says, "had been taken by my parents to instill the doctrines of Christianity into my mind, and I had no difficulty in understanding the theory of a free salvation by the atonement of our Savior; but it was only about this time that I began to feel the necessity and value of a personal application of the provisions of that atonement to my own case."

But knowing that he needed to be saved and accessing that salvation are two different things. Even more challenging was Livingstone's impression that a young man could not receive salvation until the Holy Spirit had moved upon him. Thus, Livingstone waited a long time.

Eventually, the Lord spoke to his heart and revealed to him his error. He finally renounced all hope in himself and, as a bankrupt sinner, trusted in the power of Christ to save.

During his factory years, Livingstone managed to acquire an education, eventually studying theology and graduating from medical school. Thus armed, he set off for the heart of Africa, in what today is Zambia, and brought the gospel message to natives who'd never heard the Bible story before.

Livingstone was also a noted explorer who mapped much of Africa and who also searched for the source of the Nile River. He became the first European to see the Mosi-o-Tunya waterfall along the Zambezi, today known as Victoria Falls, the name he gave them.

Because David Livingstone trusted Christ for salvation, the young man from Scotland was able to change the lives of untold millions in Africa. When he died, he was kneeling beside his bed, begging God for souls.

Reflect: Do you have a total assurance of God's salvation? Is the Lord calling you to reach a certain people group?

Dig Deeper: John 1:12; Romans 10:9, 10; John 6:44

Taron

From Tonsillectomy to Testimony

"I beseech you therefore, brethren, by the mercies of God, that you present your bodies a living sacrifice, holy, acceptable to God, which is your reasonable service" (Romans 12:1).

When he was just six years old, Taron had an experience that confirmed the reality of God. He suffered from repeated bouts of tonsillitis and high fevers that kept bringing him back to the hospital.

"One evening," Taron recalls, "I was really sick and asked my grandmother if God would ever heal me. She said He would."

The following afternoon, Taron was in his bed when suddenly the entire room lit up. He remembers, "I saw Jesus descending from heaven into my room. He asked what was wrong and I told Him about my illness." Taron says Jesus placed His fingers in his mouth, removed his tonsils, and told him he would get well.

Actually, a kind surgeon removed Taron's infected tonsils, but nonetheless his vision of being healed "was a catalyst for my strong belief in God at a young age."

Later, as a teen, Taron began listening to Amazing Facts on Sunday mornings on TV. The messages led to his conversion while he was a high school sophomore. "I began to do the *Amazing Facts Bible Study Guides*. It was a critical point in my conversion," he shares, and it led to his baptism. His thorough study impacted his lifestyle. "While reading Amazing Facts materials, I saw parts of my life that needed to change—my diet, the music I listened to, the movies I watched, my whole life needed to go in a different direction."

Taron stopped hanging out with his friends on Friday nights and began keeping the Sabbath. "I stopped attending art class on Saturdays. That was hard to let go since I enjoyed painting so much. But when conviction comes, decisions have to be made," he explains. He had no regrets about his choice.

"I began to attend church and become active in ministry," he reveals. After attending a training program on soul winning, Taron now shares his faith with just about everyone he meets. Ultimately, Taron wants to enter full-time ministry. "I want to be a pastor and serve [others] for Christ," he says. He is currently working as an insurance agent. "I provide life and health policies to clients, but my primary job is to help others secure *eternal* life insurance!"

Reflect: Have you ever given up something for Jesus—without any regrets?

Dig Deeper: Matthew 19:21; Luke 14:33; Romans 12:2

Moses

Drawn Out by God, Part 1

> "The child grew, and she [Jochebed] brought him to Pharaoh's daughter, and he became her son. So she called his name Moses, saying, 'Because I drew him out of the water'" (Exodus 2:10).

Moses wasn't his first name. Well, it was the name given to the baby that was taken out of the Nile by Pharaoh's daughter. When the ruler of Egypt saw the Hebrews multiplying in his country, he commanded that all baby boys be thrown into the river. Amram and Jochebed feared God and decided to hide their beautiful new son. But after three months, something needed to change.

So Jochebed obeyed the Pharaoh's command—sort of. She wove a basket boat out of reeds and placed her boy in the Nile, a river that was worshiped as a god. When the Pharaoh's daughter found the baby, her heart was moved and she decided to keep the child. Miriam, the baby's older sister quickly offered to find a nurse (her mother) to help care for the baby.

The Bible then explains that when the baby grew to a certain age, he was brought back to the Pharaoah's daughter and "he became her son." Then it says "she called his name Moses, saying, 'Because I drew him out of the water'" (Exodus 2:10). Moses, which means "drawn out," was the name given by the Egyptian princess, not by the boy's mother.

Actually, many royal names in Egypt contained the root name of Moses, but had the added name of a god, such as Ahmose ("Ah" was a moon god) or Ramose or Ramses ("Ra" was a sun god). It's possible that Moses' full name was "Hapimose" in honor of "Hapi," another name for the Nile from which he was drawn.

It is evident that Moses' early upbringing left an indelible mark on his life. Though he was trained in all the highest schools of Egypt and learned all the secrets of warfare and religion, in his heart he was still a Hebrew.

After all, as a young man, when he saw an Egyptian whipping one of "his" people, he slew the Egyptian (vv. 11–13) then fled for his life. This adopted son of Pharaoh's daughter thought he would rescue God's people in his own way. But Moses first needed to learn that he was not drawn out by an Egyptian princess, but by a heavenly Prince for a great work.

Reflect: What does your name mean? Did you ever wish you had a different name? God will give each one of His followers a new name in heaven.

Dig Deeper: Exodus 2:1–15; Hebrews 11:23–27; Revelation 2:17

Moses

Drawn Out by God, Part 2

**"Humble yourselves in the sight of the Lord,
and He will lift you up" (James 4:10).**

You can buy a burning bush. It's also known as winged spindle, a beautiful flowering bush native to China, Japan, and Korea. *Euonymus alatus* is a popular ornamental plant in gardens and parks because of its brilliant orange and red foliage in the fall.

The bush seen by Moses in the Midian wilderness, after he had fled Egypt to avoid the wrath of the Pharaoh, wasn't just a pretty desert plant you could purchase at a local nursery. This bush was flaming with fire because "the Angel of the Lord appeared to him in a flame of fire from the midst of a bush" (Exodus 3:2).

The sight was so unusual because, though the bush was burning with fire, it did not burn up. When Moses approached the burning bush, God called to him and then said, "Do not draw near this place. Take your sandals off your feet, for the place where you stand is holy ground" (v. 5).

The Lord told Moses that He had heard the cries of His people enslaved in a foreign land and wanted Moses to bring "My people, the children of Israel, out of Egypt" (v. 10).

But the reluctant shepherd resisted. Though he had originally sensed his calling while in Egypt to use his inborn talents and education to free the Hebrews, he now shrank from this dramatic call by God. For forty years he had been raised in Egypt to the heights of power, but then fled in the face of a Pharaoh who wanted him dead. Now, after forty years of living in Midian, marrying the daughter of Jethro, and tending sheep, his heart had changed. Moses now had no confidence in himself.

Sometimes when God's people feel most prepared to answer His summons to service, when they feel most ready to take action, they are least in a place to lead. Like Paul, who spent three years in Arabia before he was in a position to conduct great missionary endeavors, Moses needed time away from Egypt to unlearn all he had gained in that culture in order that he might be more filled with the Spirit.

It's a necessary step in conversion for all God's people—distrusting self and trusting only in God.

Reflect: Can you think of a time you felt ready to tackle something big and didn't realize just how "not ready" you were? Go to God first before you go into battle!

Dig Deeper: Proverbs 11:2; Philippians 2:3–11; James 4:6

Kim

Hip-Deep in Hypocrisy, Part 1

"Do not rejoice over me, my enemy; when I fall, I will arise; when I sit in darkness, the will be a light to me" (Micah 7:8).

Kim's father fell quickly to cancer and died at age 64. It turned her world upside down.

"He was my everything. We were close. His death horrified me," she explained. "I comforted him through countless eight-hour chemo sessions, but the fear in his eyes ... it still bothers me today."

He didn't know where he was going when he died. Kim didn't either.

He called himself a Christian, but deep inside he was scared and confused because he was living a life of biblical disobedience, even though he considered himself to be a "good person." After all, he was a dedicated police officer who daily put his life on the line for others. Kim couldn't figure out how he rationalized his lifestyle to fit his professed beliefs, and she feared for his salvation.

Kim's father didn't believe in church, and dismissed attending by saying "it's just a club"—an offhanded comment that confused Kim while she was growing up. He taught Kim that obedience to biblical principles was unnecessary, fanatical, and downright weird. "Temperance in all things" seemed to be his motto, but Kim thought that just didn't make sense. How is living in sin temperate? Is it possible to sin just a little?

Hip-deep in hypocrisy, without solid biblical knowledge or a good church background, Kim got quite mad at God. She didn't understand why God would make such a good man suffer. She really felt he was being cheated of his life.

At the same time, Kim says, her life was a mess. At a young age she married a non-believer and pursued worldly lusts for more than 20 years. She had a big house, new cars, money ... whatever she wanted; but with babies at home, and a husband at the bar every night who ordered her not to call him, she drifted into despondency.

Swirling deeper into darkness, Kim divorced her husband. Shortly thereafter, her father died, and she remained very distant from God for a long time. Interestingly enough, she always sensed God was with her. Yes, the Lord was with Kim and had a special plan for her life.

Reflect: Have you ever felt the future was dark and it seemed God had left you? Remember Hebrews 13:5.

Dig Deeper: Deuteronomy 31:6; Psalm 119:105; John 8:12

Kim

Hip-Deep in Hypocrisy, Part 2

"If you love Me, keep My commandments" (John 14:15).

After Kim's marriage failed and she lost her father to cancer, she felt that Satan was keeping her in a prison of guilt. For a long time, she cried and drank wine daily. During this time, Kim also learned she had cancer.

Distraught, she went looking for answers.

And God responded.

Kim somehow began to feel His compassion and sensed a calling upon her heart. To her, it was inconceivable. She considered herself "a messed up, heartbroken, out of control, disobedient, worthless, fornicating, bad sinner;" yet here was God, tapping her on the shoulder telling her He loved her.

God was guiding Kim, drawing her step-by-careful-step through a spiritual process resulting in a new and deeper understanding. He sent Daniel, a new Christian, into Kim's life. Together, they began their search for a church. She and Daniel repented and were baptized, married, and eagerly started their new, Christ-centered lives.

Their new pastor encouraged the congregation to read the Scriptures to make sure he was on track. Kim and Daniel did just that—and discovered that he was teaching confusing doctrine contrary to the Scriptures.

In fact, the next eight churches they attended of varying denominations, and some of no denomination at all, were all doing the same thing. Pastors made allowance for those living in unrepentant sin to continue; and they all worshipped on Sunday, a point with which Kim was beginning to take issue. All they could see was hypocrisy and disobedience—and the music was so loud they couldn't hear the congregation singing.

When Kim questioned these pastors, they gave many excuses why obedience is necessary in some, but not all, biblical teaching. She didn't understand how her father, and now these pastors and church members, could pick and choose what they wanted to obey. She knew Jesus said to obey all, not some, of His commandments. And she knew there were logical, consistent, biblical teachings they could believe in.

Kim was determined to find a church that believed in keeping all of God's commandments.

Reflect: Have you ever struggled to get a clear answer to some Bible question? What did you do? Did you ever find a solid answer that lines up with God's Word?

Dig Deeper: Psalm 119:45; John 15:10; Galatians 5:1

Kim

Hip-Deep in Hypocrisy, Part 3

"Here is the patience of the saints; here are those who keep the commandments of God and the faith of Jesus" (Revelation 14:12).

Kim and Daniel were searching for a church that believed in all of God's commandments. Surrounded by hypocrisy and inconsistency, they felt that most Christians they knew were using "grace" as a "get-out-of-hell-free" card. With all her history, and all the confusing responses from pastors of different churches, they nearly gave up.

She desperately wanted to obey God's commandments—all of them—because she loved God and was thankful for what Jesus accomplished for her on the cross. She cherished the forgiveness He extended and wanted to fellowship with others who desired to obey Him too. God's Holy Spirit was unrelentingly tugging at her heart, and she knew that Christ's true church had to be somewhere, and she was going to find it.

One day, while searching online for sermons, a presentation by Pastor Doug Batchelor popped up on YouTube. She watched it. Then, she watched another. And another. Kim says Pastor Doug was "right on" with the truth of God's Word! Every issue dear to her, he explained biblically and sensibly. Finally, she began to understand.

Then, she watched a message on the seventh-day Sabbath. Everything that she had suspected was false or hypocritical was proving to be so. The veil was lifted. She knew she had found not only God's true church, but His remnant people of Revelation.

She sought out the local Sabbath-keeping church, and is happy to report that she and Daniel are now very joyfully attending a church that teaches and believes in all the Scriptures. Their previous conflict and confusion over Bible truth is completely gone, and they have so much peace and joy in their hearts.

Today, Kim credits God's grace for a successful cancer surgery and for keeping her cancer free. She and Daniel have been re-baptized in their new church where they have found true happiness in Christ.

Reflect: Have you determined, by the Lord's grace and power, to obey all of God's law? "With God all things are possible" (Matthew 19:26). "Without Me you can do nothing" (John 15:5).

Dig Deeper: Psalm 111:7, 8; Proverbs 3:1, 2; Ecclesiastes 12:13

Billy Graham

Just As He Was, Part 1

"Jesus said to him, 'I am the way, the truth, and the life. No one comes to the Father except through Me'" (John 14:6).

Just a few days shy of his 16th birthday, Billy Frank, as his friends knew him, was focused on baseball, not the Bible. Though barely making it onto his high school baseball team at Sharon High School in Charlotte, North Carolina, the lad still had dreams of playing professional baseball.

But William Franklin Graham, Jr., was destined for other things in life. The change began in 1934, at a "tabernacle" with an evangelist who had a strange name: Mordecai Ham. He was a fiery Baptist preacher who was described as a "fighter" when young Billy Frank resisted invitations to Ham's crusades.

As Graham would later recall, "'Is he a fighter?' I asked. That put a little different slant on things. I like a fighter.'"

Ham's direct preaching—including what Graham perceived as a finger pointing directly at him—made its mark: "I have no recollection of what he preached about, but I was spellbound. In some indefinable way, he was getting through to me. I was hearing another voice ... the voice of the Holy Spirit."

No longer reluctant to hear the evangelist Ham, Graham returned nightly. But to avoid the pointing finger, Billy Frank and a friend sat in the choir behind the preacher—even though neither could sing.

Finally, after hearing a sermon about God's love for us while we were still in our sins (see Romans 5:8), Graham responded to the preacher's persistent invitations to come forward and accept Christ.

As he later wrote, "No bells went off inside me. No signs flashed across the tabernacle ceiling. I simply felt at peace ... happy and peaceful."

Accepting Christ as Savior changed the direction of Billy Frank's young life. Gone were the dreams of pro baseball. Instead, he would finish high school and go to Bible school, first at a Bible college in Florida, and finally at Wheaton College near Chicago. There he met Ruth Bell, the daughter of missionaries, to whom he was married for 64 years until her death.

Graham ended up presenting the gospel message in person to more people than anyone else in history: 210 million people in more than 185 countries and territories. But first a personal crisis would test the commitment a young Billy Frank made in 1934.

Reflect: Have you made a commitment to follow Christ? How did you feel if and when you first made that commitment? Make it a habit to recommit yourself to Jesus every day.

Dig Deeper: Acts 4:12; John 17:2, 3; Revelation 22:17

Billy Graham

Just As He Was, Part 2

"Sanctify them by Your truth. Your word is truth" (John 17:17).

No longer dreaming of a baseball career, young Billy Graham's life as a preacher and evangelist began to take shape. He became involved in a local church and eventually was called, at age 28, to be president of Northwestern Bible College in Minneapolis.

He also was active in Youth for Christ, an evangelical organization aimed at reaching young adults in a world recovering from the Great Depression and the Second World War. Another brilliant young evangelist, Charles Templeton from Toronto, Canada, teamed with Graham and the two became fast friends.

But when Templeton told Billy of plans to go to Princeton Theological Seminary in New Jersey and how he wrestled with doubts about Scripture, a break loomed on the horizon. Graham's friend rejected the Bible's account of creation, while Graham affirmed it.

Templeton's divergence—he eventually called himself an agnostic—shook Graham. Did Billy also have to pursue an advanced degree to prove his faith? Did God want him to remain in evangelism, even when a 1949 campaign in Altoona, Pennsylvania, was what the young preacher called a "flop"?

During this time, Billy was invited to preach at a Presbyterian retreat center in California. Despite his Baptist connections, Graham went, walking the grounds reading his Bible. One phrase, "Thus saith the Lord," popped up again and again in his Bible readings.

Finally, on an evening stroll, Graham found a tree stump, placed that Bible on it, and prayed: "O God! There are many things in this book I do not understand. There are many seeming contradictions. There are some areas in it that do not seem to correlate with modern science. I can't answer some of the philosophical and psychological questions Chuck [Templeton] and others are raising."

Moved by the Holy Spirit, Graham then knelt down, and prayed, "Father, I am going to accept this as Thy Word—by faith! I'm going to allow faith to go beyond my intellectual questions and doubts, and I will believe this to be Your inspired Word!"

The next night, 400 people responded to Graham's invitation to receive Christ or recommit their lives. Within weeks, his Los Angeles tent crusade brought national attention and launched his global evangelism career.

When Billy Graham decided to unreservedly take God at His word, God blessed Billy's work and life beyond measure.

Reflect: Have you or a friend faced a crisis of faith? How did you resolve the conflict? Remember to always "trust in the with all your heart, and lean not on your own understanding" (Proverbs 3:5).

Dig Deeper: Psalm 12:6; Psalm 119:11, 160; 1 Peter 1:22, 23

Nancy

Breaking the Cycle, Part 1

"For I, the your God, will hold your right hand, saying to you, 'Fear not, I will help you'" (Isaiah 41:13)

With a shaking hand, Nancy slid the key into the brass lock and swung open the door to her new home. It was dark. There was no furniture anywhere. It was as barren as her battered heart. Alone and exhausted, Nancy fell to her knees with a gut-wrenching moan. "Lord, I'm a mess."

When Nancy was a child, it seemed that when it came to God, all she learned at home, church, and school was about His wrath, anger, and eternal damnation. Her little heart trembled as her teachers at school seemed to confirm this fierce picture, as the nuns were often cruel even toward the smallest children.

"It was horrible," says Nancy. The guilt and fear of seemingly unavoidable hellfire played into years of rebellion long after she left the Catholic Church. "All I heard was that you cannot do this or that or you will go to hell. That kind of perfection seemed impossible, so I felt like I wasn't worth anything." She rebelled against it all, and this tragic misunderstanding of her value in the eyes of God would torment her for years to come as she struggled to fill the spiritual void left in her heart.

While Nancy was baptized as a born-again Christian in her twenties, along with her husband, that nagging picture of God left big room for doubt. Her new church hinted at God's grace, but the place was more of a center for social events rather than a place to find a life-changing belief system. All the same, Nancy and her husband took their children with them to church every Sunday. They were happy—that is, until Satan crept in and brought a wave of destruction into their marriage.

Riddled with guilt and heartache over the demise of her relationship, Nancy slid further downhill, hitting one devastating pothole after another. She began drinking and partying, moving in and out of relationships.

This cycle of heartbreak continued in a desperate search for love and acceptance, but it amounted to little. To make matters worse, she was even diagnosed with cancer. "Why I didn't turn back to God at that point, I really don't know," says Nancy. But that was about to change.

Reflect: Have you ever struggled with making the same mistakes over and over again? God has great patience and goes to great lengths to reach out to you.

Dig Deeper: Deuteronomy 32:36; Psalm 86:15; Micah 7:19

Nancy

Breaking the Cycle, Part 2

"Hear the voice of my supplications when I cry to You, when I lift up my hands toward Your holy sanctuary" (Psalm 28:2).

Nancy's life was in shambles, and she knew it. After her last divorce, she got the keys to her new home, but there was no excitement, only the heartbreak of loneliness. She realized that she had looked into every dirty corner of her world to find the answer to her soul's cry for love, but only had failure and pain to show for it.

In those moments, she knew where she needed to turn. She prayed, "Lord, You promised to lift us out of despair. I need You. I need You to start guiding my life." Nancy asked God to be her husband—her captain and leader. It was then that her life began to really change.

Nancy soon returned to a church she had once attended only sporadically. There she met Gary, a spiritual man who invited her to attend Bible studies and services at a variety of churches. They became friends and eventually a couple. It was through Gary that Nancy met a group of Sabbath-keepers in a walking club. They joined the group, meeting several times a week. Nancy bonded with her group. "They are the most genuine people I have ever come across," she explains.

The pastor, Jeff, joined the group almost every day, and Nancy loved hearing his perspective on the Bible. She and Gary loved learning more about God, so when Pastor Jeff told them about an upcoming prophecy seminar, they were excited. "I didn't trust just anyone to teach prophecy," says Nancy, "but I felt like this was the right place to go for answers."

Amazing Facts evangelist Darrin Bartell did not disappoint. "He is really led by the Lord," Nancy shares. "And he is an amazing teacher. He talked in a way that I could understand and relate to."

Nancy attended every meeting, drinking in the many new teachings. "It seemed like Darrin was talking directly to me even when we were in a group setting," she says. "Amazing Facts really opened up the Bible to me. For the first time in my life, I felt comfortable learning the Bible. I was absorbing it like a sponge."

Reflect: Have you ever been so low that the only place you could look was up? That's not always a bad place to be for it can lead us to find that our only hope is in the God of heaven.

Dig Deeper: 2 Samuel 22:7; Psalm 119:147; Lamentations 3:56

Nancy

Breaking the Cycle, Part 3

> "Therefore, if anyone is in Christ, he is a new creation;
> old things have passed away; behold, all things
> have become new" (2 Corinthians 5:17).

Nancy was impressed by all the scriptural evidence for everything Darrin Bartell, an Amazing Facts evangelist, taught her. "I would always get something new, something that I hadn't heard in the past," says Nancy. "I finally knew the reality about God's love and His forgiveness. He wants to have fellowship with us—that's why He created us! And I understood that by being obedient to His Word, it brings harmony to our lives. I'm finally fulfilled. I don't have that empty void. God fills it!"

What she learned about God and the Bible filled Nancy's heart with lasting joy. She couldn't believe the amazing love of Jesus, and the prophecies provided an even clearer picture of God's loving character and His battle to save her from sin. "I had always known about the judgment," she reflects. "But learning about His love and character makes a huge difference in how you perceive His judgment. If you have a relationship with Him, you are not going to be judged that way."

Darrin spent a lot of time talking with Nancy and answering her Bible questions. When he spoke to her about recommitting to God through baptism, Nancy nearly shouted, "Yes!"

A few weeks later, she was baptized by Pastor Jeff on a Sabbath. "It meant so much that Darrin was there," says Nancy. "He taught me that this is the truth, and this is what I want for my life."

She is finally at peace knowing that God gave everything to save her and, through a daily relationship with Him, provides guidance for living in obedience.

Today, Nancy looks back on her life of turmoil, incredulous that she didn't turn back to God in the midst of difficult times. But for her, coming to God was about finding compassion. "It took the truth about His love, not a catastrophic event, to bring me into God's fold," she says. "When the time was right, it was the love of God's people that opened my eyes, and the honesty of the Word that brought me back to the Lord. And I couldn't be happier about it!"

Reflect: Can you think of a time God called you back from going the wrong direction? Who or what got your attention? The Lord has a thousand ways to reach us.

Dig Deeper: Psalm 98:1; Isaiah 42:9; Matthew 13:52

Jacob

The Unlikely Choice, Part 1

> **"And the said to her: 'Two nations are in your
> womb, two peoples shall be separated from your body;
> one people shall be stronger than the other, and the
> older shall serve the younger'" (Genesis 25:23).**

Imagine that you're a newlywed ready to begin a family. That's how Rebekah, beloved wife of Isaac, saw herself. She committed to marrying the son of Abraham without even seeing her future mate. God had impressed her heart that this was the one she should wed.

The wedding was joyous, to be sure. Abraham was wealthy, and God had promised great blessings to Isaac and his descendants (Genesis 12:3). Yet here was Rebekah, waiting for the greatest blessing of all—a child. Twenty years would pass before Isaac's prayers for his seemingly barren wife were answered.

Then, blessed news! Rebekah wasn't going to have one child, but two! The pregnancy wasn't easy: "But the children struggled together within her" (Genesis 25:22). Actually, the Hebrew translation is too mild. It should read, "the children *crushed* one another within her." Talk about prenatal sibling rivalry!

When Rebekah asked God, "If all is well, why am I like this?" (v. 22), God's response must have stunned her: "Two nations are in your womb, two peoples shall be separated from your body; one people shall be stronger than the other, and the older shall serve the younger" (v. 23). It was unheard of in Hebrew culture for the younger to rule over the older. The eldest always had greater rights.

The conflict between the two lives developing in Rebekah's womb was even revealed at the time of birth. As the babies emerged, the younger grasped onto the heel of the older. It presaged a lifelong battle between Jacob (which means "heel grabber" or "supplanter") and Esau (which means "hairy"). Hosea records, "He took his brother by the heel in the womb, *and in his strength he struggled with God*" (Hosea 12:3, emphasis supplied).

Though Jacob, the younger, was at odds with his older brother, the Lord was at work through this imperfect family with less than perfect children. As we will discover, Jacob, the unlikely choice to become a father of the Hebrew nation, most certainly struggled with God. It's a spiritual journey most everyone takes who becomes a follower of Christ.

Reflect: How long would you be willing to pray for something you desired from God? Be persistent in prayer. Don't give up too quickly!

Dig Deeper: Genesis 27:29; Malachi 1:2–5; Romans 9:10–13

Jacob

The Unlikely Choice, Part 2

"So he swore to him, and sold his birthright to Jacob. And Jacob gave Esau bread and stew of lentils; then he ate and drank, arose, and went his way. Thus Esau despised his birthright" (Genesis 25:33, 34).

Esau was sitting well. As the eldest son of Isaac, his future was bright and secure. His birthright assured him of great wealth that would come to him from a man—his father—who was the son of the wealthiest man in that country, Abraham. Plus, his rugged good looks were complemented by his skill as a superb hunter. He was an outdoor "man's man" and Isaac was proud of his oldest boy.

Jacob, on the other hand, liked to stay close to home. Some might go so far as to say he was "Momma's boy." Whereas Esau was forthright, bold, and reactive, Jacob was more reserved and thoughtful ... and cunning. With Esau, what you saw is what you got. But Jacob could be a quiet schemer. Surely, his mother told him of God's promise that the older would serve the younger.

When Esau came home from an unsuccessful hunt one day, Jacob saw an opportunity to help God out. His older brother was often focused on instant gratification and a quick reward. So in his famished state, he asked his younger brother for some stew. "But Jacob said, 'Sell me your birthright as of this day'" (Genesis 25:31). The timing couldn't have been more perfect, so thought Jacob.

"And Esau said, 'Look, I am about to die; so what is this birthright to me?' Then Jacob said, 'Swear to me as of this day.' So he swore to him, and sold his birthright to Jacob" (vv. 32, 33).

Jacob won that day, but his conscience would not rest easy. After his mother cooked up a plan to deceive her husband into blessing Jacob, Esau discovered his brother's deception and planned to later kill him. So the younger son ran for his life. Not until a momentous encounter with the Lord in a dream did the deceiver begin to learn that "God demonstrates His own love toward us, in that while we were still sinners, Christ died for us" (Romans 5:8).

Reflect: Can you think of a way God blessed
you, even when you were sinning?

Dig Deeper: Psalm 106:24; Philippians 3:18, 19; Hebrews 12:16, 17

> "'I am the God of Abraham your father and the God of Isaac;
> the land on which you lie I will give to you and your descendants. ...
> Behold, I am with you and will keep you wherever you go, and
> will bring you back to this land; for I will not leave you until I
> have done what I have spoken to you'" (Genesis 28:13, 15).

Esau made a vow to kill Jacob for stealing his birthright. He didn't take personal responsibility for his foolish choice, but blamed his younger brother. Of course, Jacob's scheming to personally receive his father's blessing with his mother's assistance wasn't much better. So the deceiver ran for his life, never to see his mother again.

On his run to Padan Aram (where his mother's family lived) Jacob stopped at Bethel to rest for the night. Lying down on the ground to sleep, he rested his head on a stone. During the night he had a vision of a ladder (or staircase, the Hebrew is unclear) that stretched from earth to heaven upon which angels ascended and descended. Then he heard God say to him, "I will not leave you until I have done what I have spoken to you" (Genesis 28:15).

We should be as surprised as Jacob in hearing this promise made to the one who grasped at his brother's heel—the one who convinced short-sighted Esau to part with the firstborn's birthright, the one who deceived his own father, and the one who fled from his enraged older brother.

Jacob, the unlikely choice, was promised great things by God. "Also your descendants shall be as the dust of the earth; you shall spread abroad to the west and the east, to the north and the south; and in you and in your seed all the families of the earth shall be blessed" (v. 14).

It was at Bethel that Jacob had his conversion experience: "'Surely the is in this place, and I did not know it.' And he was afraid and said, 'How awesome is this place! This is none other than the house of God, and this is the gate of heaven!'" (vv. 16, 17).

The next morning, Jacob set up an altar, vowing to return to this spot and make the anointed stone "God's house" (v. 22). Now, with a stronger faith and a divine blessing, God's chosen one continued his journey.

Reflect: Have you ever sensed God speaking directly to your heart? Did you experience His love and blessing flowing over you?

Dig Deeper: Exodus 3:15, 16; Ezekiel 37:24, 25; Matthew 22:32

Andy and Naomi

Conviction Won, Part 1

"He who loves father or mother more than Me is not worthy of Me. And he who loves son or daughter more than Me is not worthy of Me" (Matthew 10:37).

Andy and his wife, Naomi, live in the heart of Amish country with their seven children where he works as a carpenter, handyman, and furniture builder. Naomi and the older children work in a large vegetable garden on their farm. At first glance, one would assume the family fit perfectly in the Amish world.

But while they still maintain the Amish lifestyle they were happily brought up in, they have been shunned from the church and from their families as a result of becoming Sabbath-keeping believers. Taking a stand for their faith has come at a great price, but they claim without hesitation that it is worth it. "No one can deny our joy," says Andy.

How did Andy, an Amish man living in the heart of Amish country, become a Sabbath-keeper? It all began when a Sabbath-keeping neighbor gave Andy's brother a copy of an Amazing Facts magazine on Daniel and Revelation. When Andy and his brother compared the contents of the magazine to the Bible, they could see that the teachings were true.

Later, the neighbor shared a copy of a Christian book that caused Andy to spend long periods of time pondering new truths that were both wonderful and challenging. Then he received *The Great Controversy* and was familiar with stories of the martyrs. "But the second half was new! When I read that book, there was no question in my mind that it was inspired."

Andy and his wife, Naomi, had been taught the Ten Commandments since their childhood. But Andy had always wrestled with the question of why the Amish did not keep the fourth commandment. He also had suffered much inner conflict over the question of why a God of love would cause people to suffer in hell for eternity. "I would stay awake at night and think about these things," Andy recalls. "When I read the Amazing Facts magazine, I came to understand the truth."

Andy shares that it was a joy and relief to discover answers to questions he had struggled with for so long. But it was also a challenge to think about what would happen if he took a stand. Finally, though, conviction won. "I realized I was living a lie, and I could not do that."

Naomi also had challenges to work through.

Reflect: Have you ever wrestled with a decision to obey God when it might upset family or friends? The Lord promises to honor those who honor Him.

Dig Deeper: Matthew 10:33; Mark 8:34; Acts 5:29

Andy and Naomi

Conviction Won, Part 2

**"For you will be His witness to all men of what
you have seen and heard" (Acts 22:15).**

Naomi, who was studying with her Amish husband, also saw the truth in the Amazing Facts resources given out by a Sabbath-keeping neighbor. However, she had questions regarding what she felt was a conflict between two of the commandments: the fourth and the fifth. "I had understood the fifth commandment to mean that honoring our parents means to obey them," she explains. "I couldn't see how I could go forward in keeping the fourth commandment when it would mean disobeying my parents."

Naomi's mother was living with their family at the time, and Naomi worried what would happen with her mom if they went forward in their new understanding of Bible truth. "Then Andy explained to me that to honor our parents means to respect them. That helped me understand that I could obey God and still respect my mom. Then I was able to make my decision to go forward with Andy. It was a struggle, but it was worth it. We see more blessings as we continue in His light."

Andy explains that they do not think badly of the Amish for shunning them. "The reason we are shunned," he clarifies, "is because they truly believe we have been deceived, and they are trying to force us back into the fold. They are trying to save us." Andy further explains that it is the strong moral principles that he and Naomi were taught in the Amish religion that actually ended up giving them the strength to leave it.

Determined to help the Amish learn the Bible messages that they have gained such joy from, Andy and Naomi have started a ministry. They are supported by other Sabbath-keeping Christians who are determined to minister to the Amish community. In turn, the supporters are gaining wonderful blessings from being exposed to a wholesome and simpler lifestyle.

"I love Amazing Facts!" says Andy. "Amazing Facts is a huge part of how we came to understand the Sabbath, the truth about hellfire, and about prophecies like the Mark of the Beast. I have studied the magazine that was given to me so much, it is wrinkled. And I carry copies of the magazine with me now to share with other people." Andy's hope and prayer is that the same joy that came to him and his family will come to others as well.

Reflect: Have you ever shared a piece of Christian literature with someone? How was it received? The Bible promises, "Cast your bread upon the waters, for you will find it after many days" (Ecclesiastes 11:1).

Dig Deeper: Jeremiah 1:7, 8; Matthew 5:14–16; 1 Peter 3:15

Aleksandr Solzhenitsyn

Men Have Forgotten God

"The fool has said in his heart, 'There is no God'" (Psalm 14:1).

Aleksandr was a Marxist and a believer in the communist ideology of the Soviet Union in the early 1940s. Twice, during World War II, he was decorated for his service in the Red Army. But he began to have doubts about the moral foundations of the Soviet regime.

He later wrote, "There is nothing that so assists the awakening of omniscience within us as insistent thoughts about one's own transgressions, errors, mistakes. After the difficult cycles of such ponderings over many years, whenever I mentioned the heartlessness of our highest-ranking bureaucrats, the cruelty of our executioners, I remember myself in my Captain's shoulder boards and the forward march of my battery through East Prussia, enshrouded in fire, and I say: 'So were we any better?'"

In February 1945, Solzhenitsyn was arrested for writing negative comments in private letters to a friend about how Joseph Stalin conducted the war. He was accused of anti-Soviet propaganda and sentenced to an eight-year term in a Gulag (labor camp).

Late in his imprisonment, Aleksandr experienced a conversion from Marxism to Christianity. He wrote of it in his massive *The Gulag Archipelago*, a three-volume work that gives an inside look, in numbing detail, of the Soviet prison system. He concluded, "Nowhere on the planet, nowhere in history, was there a regime more vicious, more bloodthirsty, and at the same time more cunning and ingenious than the Bolshevik, the self-styled Soviet regime ..."

Looking back on his life and studies of this history, Solzhenitsyn concluded: "Over a half century ago, while I was still a child, I recall hearing a number of old people offer the following explanation for the great disasters that had befallen Russia: 'Men have forgotten God; that's why all this has happened.' Since then I have spent well-nigh 50 years working on the history of our revolution; in the process I have read hundreds of books, collected hundreds of personal testimonies, and have already contributed eight volumes of my own toward the effort of clearing away the rubble left by that upheaval. But if I were asked today to formulate as concisely as possible the main cause of the ruinous revolution that swallowed up some 60 million of our people, I could not put it more accurately than to repeat: 'Men have forgotten God; that's why all this has happened.'"

Reflect: Do you know of someone who has "forgotten God"? Stop and pray for them right now. The Bible repeatedly warns us not to forget God and encourages us to remember the Lord's kindness toward us.

Dig Deeper: Psalm 53:1; Ephesians 4:18; Jude 22

Dale

From Terror to Trust, Part 1

"He awakens Me morning by morning, He awakens My ear to hear as the learned" (Isaiah 50:4).

Late one Saturday night, Dale prayed for something worthwhile to come into his life. He had too much time on his hands and that meant too much temptation. The very next morning, God answered his prayer.

Dale had been raised in a Protestant church and made a profession of faith in his teens after hearing an extremely terrifying sermon on the eternal fires of hell. The teaching of the wicked being thrust into never-ending torment led to what he calls a "fire escape salvation."

Over the years, Dale always wondered how God could create something so horrifying in order to scare people into worshiping Him. "I questioned how a loving God could be so unfair and vindictive," he recalls. "I had no confidence in my salvation."

He asked many people—preachers, family members, religious co-workers, and friends—"Why would God want to force me into being saved?" Dale wanted to desire heaven the way a man lovingly desires to marry a woman. "It's not much of a marriage if her relatives point a gun at you and insist you get married." The most common answer people gave him was, "We're not supposed to question God."

Since he was a teen, Dale had also been fascinated by the book of Revelation and the prophecies about the end of time. An avid news follower, he knew the world was moving toward greater chaos and that Bible prophecies were being fulfilled. He was taught the secret rapture and the seven-year-tribulation theory and certainly didn't want to be left behind.

That's when Dale earnestly prayed one Saturday night for God to lead him to freedom from sin. The next morning, while scanning every religious channel on DirecTV for something to watch, he settled on the only speaker who was wearing a tie. "Seriously!" he recalls. "I wanted to see someone who appeared respectful in God's house."

The man in the tie ended up being Pastor Doug Batchelor and what Dale heard completely turned his life in a new direction.

Reflect: Have you ever prayed and asked God to speak to you? What happened? You can always turn to the Bible and hear God speak to your heart.

Dig Deeper: Jeremiah 33:3; John 10:27, 28; Romans 10:17

Dale

From Terror to Trust, Part 2

**"You shall know the truth, and the truth
shall make you free" (John 8:32).**

When Dale prayed one Saturday night and asked God to send him something worthwhile to watch, he found a speaker the next morning on TV ... the only one wearing a tie! "I wanted to see someone who appeared respectful in God's house," he recalls.

The program was from Amazing Facts and Pastor Doug Batchelor was speaking on "What is Truth?" Dale enjoyed Pastor Doug's style and manner of teaching so much that he went to AmazingFacts.org and found more presentations. The first two sermons he watched were titled "The Good News about Hell, Parts 1 and 2." Then he watched "Why is there Evil?"

These three presentations changed everything for Dale. "Pastor Doug answered the questions that I had wrestled with all my life," he remembers. "I'd never heard such truths." What really impressed Dale was how the teaching came straight from the Bible. "Ultimately, what persuades me is when someone shows me answers from the Scriptures."

For the first time in his life, Dale heard a preacher present a loving God who doesn't want anyone to perish. His heart was especially moved by the question, "If Jesus could save a demon-possessed man, why would you think you're so lost that He couldn't save you?" These sermons led Dale to a "real" understanding of God, true repentance, and a genuine experience of salvation. "After 40 years of doubt and disbelief I am finally getting used to blessed assurance in Christ!"

Dale makes Amazing Facts part of his daily walk with God and he is now keeping the Sabbath. "I have no doubt that God answered my prayer when I stumbled upon Amazing Facts on TV." He's enjoying the wealth of resources on the Amazing Facts website and especially likes to listen to *Bible Answers Live* and Joe Crews' sermons.

"Amazing Facts has helped change a man," he shares. "I thank God for His patience with me. Instead of asking people for answers, all I really needed to do was ask God."

Reflect: What have you found to be most helpful to your daily walk with God? The key practices include Bible study, prayer, worship, and witnessing.

Dig Deeper: Psalm 145:18; Matthew 6:6; John 16:13

The Philippian Jailer

How the Prisoners Freed Their Captor

"Sirs, what must I do to be saved?" (Acts 16:30).

We don't know his name. He's merely identified as "the keeper of the prison." But his urgent question, asked moments after he'd contemplated suicide, reverberates through the centuries to our time: "What must I do to be saved?" Before answering that question, let's look at some background to this story.

In vision, Paul had received a plea to share the gospel in Macedonia and support the nascent group of believers there. "Come over to Macedonia and help us" (Acts 16:9). While in the Macedonian city of Philippi, Paul and Silas met and baptized Lydia, a woman who accepted the message. But they also encountered a demon-possessed slave girl whose work made money for her owners.

The girl's latest message, however, was displeasing to many. Following Paul, she cried out, "These men are the servants of the Most High God, who proclaim to us the way of salvation" (v. 17). After "many days" of this, Paul rebuked the spirit that possessed the young woman and she was set free (v. 18).

Recognizing the loss of income they now faced, the girl's "masters" dragged the two evangelists before the magistrates, who beat them with rods and commanded them to be jailed. Now we meet the "keeper of the prison," who places the feet of the emissaries in stocks in the innermost part of the jail (vv. 20– 24).

God had far different plans for Paul, Silas, and the jailer. As the two Christians sang hymns and praised God, an earthquake shook the jail with such force that every prisoner's bonds were loosed, every jail cell opened.

Catastrophic would be too mild a word to describe the jailer's outlook. He was supposed to keep everyone in place, and now they were gone—or so he thought. Such an inexplicable circumstance could only lead to a grisly execution by his governors, so suicide seemed the only way out.

In the jailer's darkest hour, Paul's voice brought light: "Do yourself no harm, for we are all here" (v. 28). God's power kept the prisoners in their place. Then came the jailer's plaintive question: "What must I do to be saved?"

The answer was simple, yet complete: "Believe on the Lord Jesus Christ, and you will be saved, you and your household" (v. 31).

That promise is just as true today: Believe and you will be saved. What glorious good news!

Reflect: Who do you know that could benefit from being told the good news of salvation? Don't overlook the most unlikely people around you. God's power to move hearts is beyond our comprehension.

Dig Deeper: Isaiah 58:9; Acts 2:37; Job 25:4

Sandy

Lying Down in Peace, Part 1

"I will never leave you nor forsake you" (Hebrews 13:5).

Sandy grew up in a very turbulent home. Her father was a violent alcoholic who beat her so severely that eight times she landed in the hospital for broken bones from his rages. Her mother was cold and indifferent. She constantly criticized family members for the slightest things. Sandy knew about the Lord but had no interest in ever getting to know Him. "If my parents don't love me," she felt, "why would God?"

Many times Sandy ran away from home. Many nights she slept on train tracks praying for a train to come and put her out of her misery. She tried taking her life for the first time at nine, then 11, and then at 13 years old. "My last try," she recalls, "consisted of a sure-fire plan. I gathered all sorts of pills I found in my home and hid them in my bedroom closet. One night I mixed up a pitcher of strawberry Kool-Aid and consumed them all. Then I fell asleep."

A couple of hours later she awoke in severe pain. Her heart was racing uncontrollably; she was dripping in sweat and felt pins and needles pricking her all over. Though she was panting and shaking, her mind was still clear. In this state she tearfully cried out to God, "Why haven't You saved me from all this abuse? Why haven't You protected me? What is the point of being here just to be tortured? What good am I?"

A voice suddenly spoke to her heart. "How do you know God hasn't protected you? Most children your size would not have lived through all your beatings. God loves you more deeply than you'll ever know. He has plans for your life to prosper you and lift you up. He will never leave you!" After this she fell back to sleep.

In the morning Sandy felt perfectly well. At first she thought she had only dreamed of what she tried to do. But the evidence of the pitcher and empty pill packets lying around convinced her that an angel from heaven had spoken to her and saved her life. "I could even still taste the bitterness of the medicine in my mouth," she remembers. This dramatic encounter started her on a journey to discover God in the Bible.

Reflect: Have you ever felt so discouraged that you wanted to end it all? Never forget that Jesus will never leave you or forsake you.

Dig Deeper: 1 Kings 19:1–8; Psalm 18:16; Romans 8:37–39

Sandy

Lying Down in Peace, Part 2

> **"The is my shepherd; I shall not want. He makes me
> to lie down in green pastures ..." (Psalm 23:1, 2).**

Sandy had tried to end her life by lying down on railroad tracks as a teenager. But God's hand was watching over this broken and abused young woman. Several years later, while attending a homeschool convention with her two small children, she met Lisa.

"We began to share until my little ones needed to eat and take a nap," Sandy explains. "So Lisa sat down on the floor next to me and we continued talking. At one point she offered to hold one of my kids. I was a little uneasy about that. It's hard for me to trust anyone. But I finally let her rock one of my kids to sleep."

Lisa and Sandy talked for a couple of hours about children and education. Then Lisa shared a Christian book with Sandy and said, "God placed you in charge of your children. You are responsible for them. It's right that you carefully study and pray about how to bring them up properly." Sandy was deeply touched by Lisa's words.

After opening her heart more to Lisa about her painful past, including a traumatic incident that led to the birth of one of her children and her husband leaving her, Lisa prayed right there, on the spot, for Sandy, not worrying about who might be watching. Then she took the book and on the inside of the back wrote: www.amazingfacts.org and handed it to Sandy.

"I listened to my first Doug Batchelor sermon online soon afterwards. His sermon was uplifting to me and easy to understand." Sandy continued watching more talks. As she listened, she knew without a doubt that she was hearing truth from God's Word.

Eventually Sandy began calling the toll-free number on the screen and requesting free booklets. Later, she signed up for the free *Amazing Facts Bible Study Guides* and found a Sabbath-keeping church. She attended every week and began to absorb as much truth as she could. Eventually, she was baptized and continued attending every week with her two growing children.

Amazing Facts has helped Sandy to "begin to trust ... something and Someone," she explains. "Now I can say with full conviction, 'I am a new creation!' I lie down at night and sleep worry free because I know my heavenly Father is faithful and will protect me."

Reflect: Do you ever find it difficult to fall asleep at night because of fear? Claim God's promise that His angels will watch over you.

Dig Deeper: Psalm 4:8; Proverbs 3:24; 2 Corinthians 5:17

Millard Fuller

The Gift of Service, Part 1

*"May the God of all grace, who called us to His eternal glory
by Christ Jesus, after you have suffered a while, perfect,
establish, strengthen, and settle you" (1 Peter 5:10).*

Millard Fuller could sell just about anything. When he was six, his father gave him a pig which he fattened and sold for a good price. Soon he was selling more pigs, rabbits, chickens, and even worms to fishermen.

He eventually went to law school and, with a friend, formed a partnership to sell things to raise capital to buy rental real estate. Some items didn't sell very well (mistletoe) and some did (rubber doormats). When the two graduated in 1960, they discovered they were better at selling than at litigating. They started successfully selling everything from tractor cushions to cookbooks.

Millard married Linda Caldwell and they soon were living in an elegant home with a barn and pasture for saddle horses and a swimming pool. By the time Millard was 29 years old, he was a millionaire. But it all came at a price. He quit attending church, his values slid, and his marriage suffered.

One day, Linda left town to think about the future of their marriage. Millard was left home with their two children. He admits, "The rumbling thunderstorm inside me began to roil." He realized, "Never before or since have I suffered as I did during those days. Everything else—business, sales, profits, prestige, everything which had seemed so important—paled into total meaninglessness."

A week later, Fuller happened to hear a phrase on TV that caught his attention. "A planned life can only be *endured*." He thought to himself, "That's what I'm living. And I'm enduring it and suffering." His plan in life was to get richer and richer and make his company bigger and to acquire more things. And when he died, he would be buried among the rich in the local cemetery.

With the words still ringing in his ears—"A planned life can only be endured"—he phoned Linda and convinced her to meet and talk about their marriage. Perhaps God could save their marriage. Perhaps God could help change the direction of their lives.

Reflect: Sometimes it takes a crisis to jolt us into assessing the direction of our lives. Have you had a difficult experience that turned out to be a blessing?

Dig Deeper: Isaiah 41:10; Ephesians 5:20; James 1:2

Millard Fuller

The Gift of Service, Part 2

"But whoever has this world's goods, and sees his brother in need, and shuts up his heart from him, how does the love of God abide in him?" (1 John 3:17).

Millard Fuller was quite wealthy, but his marriage was in shambles. He could sell toothbrushes, but his family life was full of holes. When his wife left him, he realized that unless he changed directions, he would lose her. She agreed to meet and talk. While sipping orange juice in a café, she suddenly broke down and began crying and couldn't stop.

They stumbled outside and went for a long walk, eventually sitting down on the steps in front of a church. "There it happened," he remembers. "Linda faced me and bared her soul. She confessed the ways in which she had betrayed our relationship. I poured out my own agony and regret for ways I had betrayed her. The wall was broken down, and love rushed in like a mighty flood." They stayed up all night talking, singing, and praying.

When they returned home, they were determined to make God the center of their lives. They would give up their pursuit of wealth and refocus their lives on Christian service. The Lord convicted them to provide affordable housing for low-income families. They would use community volunteers for labor and donations, and only ask people to cover the cost of materials. They didn't charge interest and they made no profit.

Their dream began in Georgia, then took them to Africa, and then to Texas, and soon their ministry—Partnership Housing—reached clear around the world. By 1981, the program grew into Habitat for Humanity. By 2003, Habitat affiliates around the world had constructed over 150,000 houses and were active in 92 nations. In 1984, Fuller drew in Habitat's most famous volunteer—President Jimmy Carter. Eventually, Millard began a new program called the Fuller Center for Housing, and it's going strong today.

Millard Fuller could sell just about anything, but he discovered that the gift of unselfish service—and the joy that comes from living for others—cannot be bought or sold.

Reflect: Have you ever participated as a volunteer in serving others? There is no greater joy than to give to bring happiness to people around you.

Dig Deeper: Luke 12:33; John 3:16; 2 Corinthians 9:7

Roy

From Reggae to Jesus, Part 1

"For what will it profit a man if he gains the whole world, and loses his own soul?" (Mark 8:36).

When Roy was discharged from the military, he was told, "You have an attitude problem and won't conform to the rules." Growing up in New York City (NYC), Roy was a mischievous kid who was always getting into trouble. Even though his parents made him attend church, he never really connected with God. Yet he felt in his heart that there was a reason for his existence.

High school for Roy was filled with fighting, alcohol and "weed." After being arrested for trespassing and robbery, his lawyer recommended he enlist in the Air Force, which gave him six months' probation and some time to straighten out his life. "In basic training I got into a fight my first week. I was still a 'rainbow' and hadn't even received my uniform," Roy remembers. "Luckily, one of the drill instructors liked me and got me off the hook." His next six years in the service didn't change things. Now the drugs and alcohol simply happened in the different places he was stationed—Colorado, Florida, and Germany.

After his time in the service, Roy lived in Florida and then moved back to NYC. He had given up drinking and drugs, but still struggled with fighting. Old friends got him involved in smuggling drugs. One day his mother said, "That's enough! You need to get a job." So he did. "My family is Honduran and Jamaican, so I grew up in this culture and loved reggae music," Roy explains. "I had been deejaying for years, so when my partner at work mentioned he was also a disc jockey, I joined his team."

Roy loved this new side job of being a DJ in NYC. He served at several big night clubs and mingled with popular hip-hop artists and knew just about every Reggae musician at the time. He also was employed by the largest Black radio station in NYC on the Reggae show.

His regular day job paid well, but something was missing. "On my bucket list I intended to someday find a church to attend. The few I visited I didn't like. Besides, I was too busy partying and having a good time. Deep down inside, though, I knew something was missing in my life."

Reflect: Has there ever been a time in your life when you felt like something was missing? Jesus promises to fill the deepest voids in our hearts.

Dig Deeper: Psalm 81:10; Romans 15:13; Colossians 2:9, 10

Roy

From Reggae to Jesus, Part 2

"He who finds his life will lose it, and he who loses his life for My sake will find it" (Matthew 10:39).

One Friday night (actually it was early Saturday morning), Roy, a successful Reggae DJ, left the club where he was working and went home to watch music videos on TV. It was something he did to unwind on many Saturday mornings. "I turned on BET (Black Entertainment Television) only to find an older white gentleman speaking. I almost changed the channel, but the things he said were so captivating that I found myself glued to the TV for the next 30 minutes."

The speaker he listened to was a man named Joe Crews. Roy watched him for several months and eventually mailed in to receive free Bible studies. "I began learning so much about the Bible. I even tried to keep the Sabbath, but not very successfully."

"Sometime later," Roy continues, "this new white guy comes on one Saturday morning. He explained that Joe Crews passed away and that he was the new speaker for Amazing Facts. I was devastated," he admits. "Who could possibly know the Bible like Joe Crews?"

Roy confesses, "I grew to like Pastor Doug Batchelor." He invited people to attend an evangelistic series called 'Net '97.' "I intended to go only one night to see this Doug live. I had no intention of becoming part of a church." He soon discovered he would not personally hear Pastor Doug since this was a satellite program, but Batchelor's "preaching was so captivating that I came every single night."

On July 25, 1998, Roy was baptized into God's remnant church in Queens. He quit his job in the music business and never looked back. Roy became very active in church and was soon serving as a Personal Ministries leader, sharing his faith with others. Roy eventually became an elder in his church and also a director of youth for a church conference.

Having been involved in the music entertainment field, Roy has a heart for youth interested in contemporary music. "There's a lot of alluring and captivating music that sounds good," he warns, "but the pictures they paint are not as beautiful as they might look on the surface." He encourages youth to go to the source of truth—the Bible.

Roy shares, "I can't thank God enough for Amazing Facts. It literally saved my life."

Reflect: Have you ever struggled to give up something in order to have Jesus? Is there anything more important than eternal life?

Dig Deeper: Matthew 4:19; Luke 14:33; John 8:12

Samson

Remember Me, Lord!

> **"Then Samson called to the , saying, 'O Lord , remember me, I pray!'" (Judges 16:28).**

Samson's parents prayed for a child, and promised to dedicate his life to God's service. They agreed Samson's hair would never be cut, and the boy would never drink wine. In return, Samson had superhuman strength that allowed him to wreak havoc on Israel's enemies, the Philistines.

But while Samson kept his vows when it came to hair and drink, he allowed himself to be tempted by the idolatrous pagans around him. Samson insisted on marrying one of the Philistine women, even though she would quickly betray him on several levels.

Instead of learning from that experience, Samson found a prostitute named Delilah, who enticed him, and pleaded, and begged, until Samson revealed the secret of his power—his long hair. While he slept, Delilah shaved his head, and the Philistines attacked. Samson couldn't overcome them, at which point he learned "the had departed from him" (Judges 16:20).

They bound him, put his eyes out, and sentenced him to hard labor in Gaza. He had been a judge of Israel, but now he was an object of ridicule and scorn. Yet his devastation would lead to deliverance. It was while he was bound as a blind servant that his eyes were opened and his heart was broken. In weakness, he rediscovered his strength in God.

That bit of news was kept from his Philistine captors, who decided to make Samson the centerpiece of a festival celebrating their fish-god, Dagon. Thousands of worshippers thronged the temple, and ultimately Samson was brought out for show and to be scorned by the pagan crowd. This is when Samson uttered the prayer in Judges 16:28: "Strengthen me, I pray, just this once ... that I may with one blow take vengeance on the Philistines!"

God answered this request and he "took hold of the two middle pillars which supported the temple, and he braced himself against them, one on his right and the other on his left. ... And he pushed with all his might, and the temple fell on the lords and all the people who were in it. So the dead that he killed at his death were more than he had killed in his life" (Judges 16:29, 30).

Reflect: Can you recall any modern stories of a prodigal whose repentance brought a surprising result? God can do wonders with humble hearts when we admit we are blind.

Dig Deeper: Psalm 50:15; Jonah 2:1, 2; Revelation 6:10

"The fruit of the righteous is a tree of life, and he who wins souls is wise" (Proverbs 11:30).

Prea wanted to learn how to share her faith with others and was excited to attend an AFCOE to Go evangelistic training seminar held by Amazing Facts. "When I finished the course," Prea says, "the first thing I did was tell my church about the experience because they sponsored me. From there, I held a class at church on how to give Bible studies. It wasn't that scary since I used the tools that I had received at AFCOE to Go. I just passed on that same information."

Prea was anxious to use her training to win souls. In September, a visitor came to her home church. The guest had been watching a Christian satellite program and had discovered the Sabbath truth. She wanted to know more, so she decided to visit the Sabbath-keeping church that Prea attended. "I started talking with her," says Prea, "and at the end of the day I asked her if she would like to do Bible studies. She said yes, and we met once a week." Prea and Moucille completed the 26-lesson *Amazing Facts Bible Study Guides*, which include various Bible topics of interest.

"Moucille was so interested in knowing more and more Bible truth," Prea explains. "She was always on time to our studies, and she was very happy to be learning and she eagerly responded to every appeal at the end of each lesson." Moucille was so willing to follow truth, in fact, that when Prea shared the study guide on the topic of returning the tithe, Moucille thought she would not have the money to do that. But when she truly understood the lesson, she told Prea, "I didn't know that. I'm just going to do it."

Moucille, 75, was struggling with knee problems, but she faithfully came to every study even when she could barely move. She also shared recipes with Prea that she was using since becoming a vegetarian. "When we finished the Amazing Facts study guides, I invited Moucille to attend the live streaming presentations with Doug Batchelor called *Landmarks of Prophecy* that were being held at our church. She came to those meetings, too." Moucille was baptized, and she and Prea enjoy a close friendship.

Reflect: Have you ever given someone a Bible study? It's a deeply rewarding experience to open the Word and share God's truth with another person. Contact your pastor if you'd like to learn how to conduct a Bible study.

Dig Deeper: Jeremiah 1:7, 8; Matthew 5:16; 1 Peter 3:15

Prea

Unafraid to Witness, Part 2

> **"You shall receive power when the Holy Spirit has come upon you; and you shall be witnesses to Me in Jerusalem, and in all Judea and Samaria, and to the end of the earth" (Acts 1:8).**

After Prea attended an AFCOE to Go evangelistic training seminar with Amazing Facts, she was open to share her faith as God led. Another experience took place at a street fair where her church had a booth. "We hand out literature at the fair booth, and sometimes it just seems like nothing happens," says Prea.

A couple walked by her booth and were interested in what they were sharing. They were obviously open to learn more, so "we invited them to church, and they came!" Prea learned that Laura's husband was already a believer, so she didn't know if Laura would be interested in studying. "AFCOE to Go taught us to tell people who are already students of the Bible that we need to practice giving Bible studies," she says, "so that's what I told Laura. She agreed to study with me and ended up being very studious."

Laura, who was Jewish, took the studies very seriously and noticed points in the lessons that even Prea had not caught. Prea adds that she timed the studies to be completed just before the *Landmarks of Prophecy* series began. After attending those meetings, Laura was baptized and is now an active part of the church.

Prea shares an especially touching insight to the experience. "Laura has stage IV breast cancer. It touched me so deeply to see someone break down crying as she talked about Jesus and His love. Such love at a difficult time in her life really affected her, and it came out. It affected me, too."

The first advice Prea has for those who are thinking about giving Bible studies is, "Don't be afraid." She encourages people to not be worried about difficult questions that come. "If people are hungry, they are not interested in if you are a real teacher or if you have all the answers. If they ask you a question you can't answer, you can always say, 'We'll get to that in a later lesson,' or you can say, 'I don't know, but I'll find out.'"

Prea discovered, "There's always someone out there, and the Lord will help you if you have a willing heart. I pray for God to be my voice, and I don't have to be afraid."

Reflect: What is your greatest fear about witnessing? Remember, your role is to be faithful and leave the results in God's hands.

Dig Deeper: Mark 16:15; Romans 10:17; Colossians 4:2–6

Charles G. Finney

Wrestling with God in the Woods

"Seek the and His strength; seek His face evermore!" (1 Chronicles 16:11).

Charles was feeling distressed. Though he was a successful lawyer at the young age of 29, something troubled him. The New Yorker was expecting a new client to show up in his office the next day, October 11, 1821.

As a respected attorney, Charles had won admission to the bar the old-fashioned way—apprenticing with another lawyer. Now he used his gifts to help others navigate the legal system of that time. But first, he had some personal business to care for.

Charles Grandison Finney was worried about his own salvation. So he decided to head for the woods near his home in Adams, New York. "I will give my heart to God, or I never will come down from there," he declared to himself.

For hours, Finney wrestled with the Lord in prayer before returning to his office. He then played hymns on his cello, a favorite pastime. Then something happened. "The Holy Spirit descended upon me in a manner that seemed to go through me, body and soul," he would write more than half a century later. "I could feel the impression, like a wave of electricity, going through and through me. Indeed it seemed to come in waves of liquid love, for I could not express it in any other way."

When Finney's new client showed up the next morning, the visitor was likely unprepared for what Charles had to say. "I have a retainer from the Lord Jesus Christ to plead his cause," he declared, "and cannot plead yours."

Three years later, Finney was ordained a Presbyterian minister, but he shunned the strict Calvinism of that denomination. Instead, he placed an emphasis on personal conversion and public acceptance of Christ. His revivalism swept the nation and is credited with inspiring the later evangelism of Dwight L. Moody, Billy Sunday, and Billy Graham, among others.

Finney went on to help lead the fight for the abolition of slavery, serve as president of Oberlin College in Ohio, and author a "Systematic Theology" reference book still in use today. He passed to his rest in 1875 at the age of 85, though his legacy remains.

Reflect: Can you recall when you sought God and He responded in a powerful, life-changing manner? The Lord works in many different ways to touch hearts.

Dig Deeper: Psalm 27:8, 9; Amos 5:6; Hebrews 11:6

Connie

Awakened to the Sabbath

"It is high time to awake out of sleep; for now our salvation is nearer than when we first believed" (Romans 13:11).

After a routine mammogram came back abnormal, Connie became frightened and longed for a more spiritual connection. To deal with her fear, she would sing Christian songs, look up at the sky, and talk to God. When further testing proved that she was fine, she rejoiced and felt that God had allowed this experience to wake her up.

During this time, while faithfully attending church every Sunday, Connie recorded a couple sermons each week from a Sabbath-keeping network. When she heard the pastors on these programs saying "Happy Sabbath," she was puzzled because she thought Sabbath-keeping was a Jewish tradition.

When she watched an Amazing Facts program, an advertisement came up that encouraged viewers to visit sabbathtruth.com. Since she was curious about the Sabbath, she visited the site and her eyes were opened to what the Bible teaches about the seventh day.

Connie says, "It's amazing that it was all there in the Bible, but I never saw it before. When I started honoring the Sabbath, I shared it with my mother, and she wanted to as well." Both Connie and her mom had been keeping Sunday while learning about the Sabbath. She made a point of doing her shopping and other business on Saturday in order to keep Sunday holy. But when Connie learned about Sabbath being on the seventh day, she and her mother were convicted to keep Saturday as the Sabbath.

Connie continued watching Amazing Facts and began sharing what she learned with others. "I minister to inmates through the mail, using Amazing Facts study guides," says Connie. "The inmates love it! One wrote and asked me where I was getting this stuff. I tell them all about Pastor Doug, Amazing Facts, and sabbathtruth.com."

Connie's life is far different today from the life she lived before discovering Jesus. "I was chasing after the things of this world but still felt empty. I would drink so much that I couldn't even walk or talk," she says. "Now I feel complete. I honestly believe that if I had not listened to God's call to watch Pastor Doug, I would be dead today. I am so thankful that God used Pastor Doug to wake me up. I was asleep and didn't even know it."

Reflect: Have you ever fallen asleep (or nearly so) while driving? How much more dangerous is it to fall asleep to the sobering times in which we live.

Dig Deeper: Isaiah 50:4; Titus 3:5; Revelation 3:14–22

Dionysius and Damaris

A Joyful Failure

"So Paul departed from among them" (Acts 17:33).

Paul was a very successful evangelist and missionary. When he traveled throughout Asia Minor, crowds flocked to hear him, many were healed by God through him, and the huge number of churches raised up are attested to in his New Testament letters.

But one time, his work was a dismal failure. Or was it? The faithful apostle of Christ was passing through the famous pagan city of Athens in Greece, when he noticed many idols, hundreds of statues to all sorts of gods. Seeing all the false forms of worship, "his spirit was provoked within him" (Acts 17:16) and led him to witness to the Jews and some Gentile worshipers in the local synagogue.

Paul ventured into the marketplace to witness to others, including "certain Epicurean and Stoic philosophers" (v. 18). They decided to hear out the strange teacher and invited Paul to speak at the Areopagus, also known as Mars' Hill, which was the city council of Athens. He grabbed at this interesting opportunity to reach more people for Christ.

After affirming the religious devotion of his listeners, he explains that he would like to speak about "THE UNKNOWN GOD," words he saw on some altar in Athens. Paul then tells about the Creator who made all things and the impossibility of humans being able to make gods to worship. After quoting some of their own Greek poets, he ended with an appeal to prepare for God's appointed day of judgment through Christ who was raised from the dead.

Abruptly, interest in Paul's eloquent evangelistic sermon ended for the Athenians. "When they heard of the resurrection of the dead, some mocked, while others said, 'We will hear you again on this matter'" (v. 32). Before Luke concluded the story of Paul's departure from Athens, he added, "However, some men joined him and believed, among them Dionysius the Areopagite, a woman named Damaris, and others with them" (v. 34).

Admittedly, preaching to a crowd of philosophers was a tough assignment. Yet we must remember that Jesus' favorite audience was just one person, such as the woman at the well. By the baptismal numbers, this probably wasn't a report we'd rush to print in church papers. But the conversion of this handful of believers in Athens gives us hope that God isn't interested in numbers alone, but in even just one person, like you.

Reflect: Have you ever attended an evangelistic campaign where very few were baptized? Let's remember that heaven rejoices over just one convert!

Dig Deeper: Matthew 10:29; Luke 15:1–31; Acts 17:16–34

Scott

Getting Answers, Part 1

"I love those who love me, and those who seek me diligently will find me" (Proverbs 8:17).

"I should have died," Scott recalls. He was 27 years old and working on a race car when it exploded. The eruption was so violent that he lost his arm. Looking back, he gratefully acknowledges, "God was watching over me that day."

Scott learned about the Lord early on in his life. Each week, a school bus dropped by his home to take him to Sunday school. It was a good babysitting source for his parents and kept him busy and out of trouble. "I learned about Jesus but didn't really have a conversion experience," he explains. "I've always known Him, but I haven't always been a very good servant of Jesus."

After Scott's brush with death, he began attending a Charismatic church and helped with the music ministry. He played drums and was an important part of the church band for ten years. "But there was always something missing," he admits. "I wasn't growing spiritually."

During the last five years that he attended this church, people began "muttering nonsense" and speaking in tongues. "Several members told me that because I didn't speak in tongues, I must not have received the Holy Spirit," he shares. All the same, Scott felt that something wasn't right with this church.

When a new building was erected, many members left, including several friends from the church band. Then the main pastor had a stroke. As several other troubles occurred, Scott soon found himself starting to question the teachings of the church.

"What about the Sabbath?" The Holy Spirit kept impressing his mind with that question, over and over, like a ringing in his ears—"What about the Sabbath?" So he decided to ask his pastor, "What about the Sabbath?" The pastor explained that Jesus was the Sabbath now and that we didn't need to keep the seventh day since the Lord gave us the first day of the week. These answers didn't satisfy Scott.

Concerned about what was being taught from the pulpit, Scott met with the pastor to talk about what he was learning. He even explained how Constantine changed the Sabbath worship day to Sunday to please the pagans in his empire. Still, after an hour of discussion, Scott wasn't getting answers that made sense.

Reflect: Think of a time you were traveling and came to a dead end. What did you do? God will help you when you hit spiritual dead ends.

Dig Deeper: 2 Chronicles 7:14; Isaiah 48:17; Matthew 7:8

Getting Answers, Part 2

"You will seek Me and find Me, when you search for Me with all your heart" (Jeremiah 29:13).

Scott went to his pastor looking for clear Bible texts to his questions, but didn't get straight answers. The following Sunday the pastor stood before the congregation and resigned. Then, during the next week, the pastor died. It shocked everyone, including Scott.

At the wake for the pastor, one of the speakers got up and said, "It's okay. He's in heaven now." Scott suddenly knew something was terribly wrong with the teachings of this church and that he needed to make a change. "After studying about the Sabbath, I was determined to keep Saturday as God's day of worship." After trying once more to share his beliefs with other members, and being labeled a legalist, he decided to leave.

"I didn't know where to go," he says. One church in town had a Saturday-evening service and he was prepared to visit when the Holy Spirit led him to a different church. He knew nothing about this church except that some of the "talk on the street" claimed it was a cult. But Scott felt the Holy Spirit leading him to this church.

One of the first things Scott heard when he attended this Sabbath-keeping church is that they believed in the Bible and only the Bible. He attended the one-hour Bible study followed by a one-hour worship service. After his first Sabbath with this congregation, he says, "I knew that I had found a new church home."

Something more convinced Scott that God was leading him into the truth. One night, he was watching a Christian network when, "just before I fell asleep, Amazing Facts came on. Pastor Doug was preaching and he had such a nice, calm demeanor. He just explained things and didn't try to beat it down my throat."

Scott was so convicted that he downloaded the Amazing Facts app to his smartphone and began watching more programs. The things he heard matched much of what he had been reading in his own personal study. When he saw a link on a talk about God's true church, Scott watched the program and was excited to discover that the Sabbath-keeping church he was attending was the same church Pastor Doug spoke about.

Scott nearly died from a tragic accident years ago, but the Lord had a different plan in mind for this seeker of truth.

Reflect: What are three important qualities you look for in a local church home? What does the Bible say are the characteristics of God's true church?

Dig Deeper: 1 John 5:2; Revelation 12:17; 14:12

Jonathan Edwards

Finally Convicted—and Converted

"Now to the King eternal, immortal, invisible, to God who alone is wise, be honor and glory forever and ever. Amen" (1 Timothy 1:17).

Jonathan Edwards, a precocious young man from East Windsor, Connecticut, was already working on a master's degree at Yale University when just 17. He was later to become best known as the preacher of the first Great Awakening in the young colonies: "The God that holds you over the pit of hell, much as one holds a spider, or some loathsome insect over the fire, abhors you, and is dreadfully provoked: his wrath towards you burns like fire," he declared in his most famous message, "Sinners in the Hands of an Angry God."

But before the young man could become the preaching wonder of his day, Edwards knew he had to become a Christian. He studied, he prayed, but there was still doubt. During his time at Yale, a bout of pleurisy—inflammation of the lungs—triggered an intense search for salvation. He later recalled, "It pleased God, to seize me with a pleurisy; in which he brought me nigh to the grave, and shook me over the pit of hell."

Jonathan recovered, but was not yet thoroughly converted. It would only be when Edwards read the verse in 1 Timothy 1:17, that God was indeed the "King eternal," that the light began to dawn.

About 18 months later, as a student-preacher visiting western New York State, Edwards received the confirmation he sought: "I felt a burning desire to be in everything a complete Christian; and conformed to the blessed image of Christ; and that I might live, in all things, according to the pure, sweet and blessed rules of the gospel."

Edwards went on to apprentice as a pastor, then to take charge of a congregation on his own, and to preach sermons which spread throughout the nation during that revival in colonial America. He had 11 children, who, along with their 1,400 descendants, had an amazing impact on the United States: one U.S. Vice President, one law school and one medical school dean, three U.S. Senators, three governors, three mayors, 13 college presidents, 30 judges, 60 doctors, 65 professors, 75 military officers, 80 public office holders, 100 lawyers, 100 clergymen, and 285 college graduates.

Jonathan Edwards lived for only 55 years, but he packed those years full of spirituality and accomplishment. And it all started with a deep self-examination and a quest for God.

Reflect: Have you, or someone you know, ever been so convicted of sin that you searched for God and His answers? Jesus said, "Whoever exalts himself will be humbled, and he who humbles himself will be exalted" (Matthew 23:12).

Dig Deeper: 1 Chronicles 29:11; Psalm 90:2; Romans 11:36

Dan

Spiritual Surgery, Part 1

"The God formed man of the dust of the ground, and breathed into his nostrils the breath of life; and man became a living being" (Genesis 2:7).

Dan could barely breathe. He was taking in big gulps of air, but it felt as though he were trying to fill up a colander with water. Lightheaded and off-balance, he also felt an incredible tightness in his chest. Then, all of a sudden, it was like someone was squeezing his heart, like a wet rag being wrung out. It didn't stop. It was being wrung tighter and tighter ...

Later, Dan recalled staring at bright lights overhead while on his back in the doctor's office. It was Labor Day, and he had just survived a massive heart attack. The doctors had told him it was nearly a "widow maker." He closed his eyes and prayed, asking for more time with his family—if it was God's will. Four stents, prostate cancer, and a stroke later, Dan was still alive and kicking. God had a plan for his life.

Dan and his wife, Denise, were Christians. He came from a family who were actively involved in the church. His grandfather was a pastor and so was his only son. Family was also important to Dan and Denise and they believed in honoring their fathers and mothers, and following God's commandments.

So when Denise's parents began to need assisted care, the two picked up and moved to the next state to be there for them. When Denise's mother passed away, they moved again, this time more than fifty miles away from their work—a business they owned together. Because of the long drive to and from their store, they began to conduct some business out of their home. They signed up for Internet service, which also came with free cable television. They hadn't owned a television in years.

One evening, as Dan was channel surfing, he stumbled upon a Christian network. On the screen was a pastor named Doug Batchelor, who was recounting his testimony. Dan kept watching and felt something was different about this pastor who once lived in a cave and stole televisions! Fascinated, Dan watched the rest of the program, then started watching an Amazing Facts outreach series. He continued to tune in to Pastor Doug week after week.

By the end of the series, Dan was changed.

Reflect: Can you recall a time when you were flat on your back because of an accident or illness? Did you call out to God for help? He is only a prayer away.

Dig Deeper: Psalm 147:3; 1 Corinthians 6:19, 20; 3 John 2

Dan

Spiritual Surgery, Part 2

"Therefore, whether you eat or drink, or whatever you do, do all to the glory of God" (1 Corinthians 10:31).

After suffering a near-fatal heart attack and other serious health issues, Dan stumbled across Amazing Facts on cable television. He was inspired to watch an entire evangelistic series because he especially wanted to know what the Bible says about health.

Hungry to learn more, he sent away for the free *Amazing Facts Bible Study Guides* as he continued watching broadcasts. He searched AmazingFacts.org for more resources, discovered a documentary on the Sabbath called *The Seventh Day* on a website called SabbathTruth.com, and was shocked to discover the truth about the Sabbath even though he had read the Bible through several times.

After accepting the Sabbath, Dan faithfully studied and accepted many other biblical doctrines he had never before known—the truth about the afterlife, hell, prophecy, and more. He soon completed all of the *Study Guides*.

"Amazing Facts was very instrumental in teaching me how to let the Bible be its own interpreter and the importance of studying the Bible versus just reading the Bible," Dan says. "The thing that impressed me most was the instruction to not take one verse out of context, but to study [the Bible] in its entirety."

And he continued to learn about the Bible's laws of health. When he learned that "taking good care of our bodies is an act of worship," he began to change how he lived, what he ate and drank. And when he suffered a stroke from a blocked artery shortly after surgery for prostate cancer, he rehabilitated from a wheelchair to a cane in a matter of weeks. His physical therapists were shocked. But Dan attributes his miraculous recovery to God—to prayer and a biblical diet and lifestyle he first discovered through Amazing Facts.

A mere two-and-a-half years after finding the ministry, Dan was baptized into a Sabbath-keeping church. Now he serves as a deacon and has been cancer-free for over a year. "I can say without a doubt, I am definitely a life that was changed," he cheers. "It is my hope [that] I can bring help and encouragement to someone who may be struggling with the same issues or searching for answers as I was. And yes, I still faithfully watch Amazing Facts each week!"

Reflect: If you were to choose one area of your life where you need to make a lifestyle adjustment, what would it be? God will give you strength to grow in that area.

Dig Deeper: Genesis 1:29; Proverbs 3:7, 8; Romans 12:1, 2

Philip

Calculating Faith

"Philip answered [Jesus], 'Two hundred denarii worth of bread is not sufficient for them, that every one of them may have a little'" (John 6:7).

Scott Flansburg can calculate numbers fast. He is so quick with computing in his head that he has been dubbed "The Human Calculator." Even at an early age he could add up numbers with lightning speed. As a child, he would keep a running tally of his family's groceries so that his dad could write an exact check before the cashier rung up the total. Using the motor skills part of his brain, Flansburg can add, subtract, multiply, divide, and find square and cube roots almost instantly ... and with the accuracy of a calculator.

Philip, an early disciple of Jesus, was good with numbers. He was converted through the ministry of John the Baptist, and responded to Jesus' call, "Follow Me" (John 1:43). Like Andrew, Philip brought people to Jesus (Nathanael was his first convert).

But this calculating disciple needed to learn to stretch his faith beyond figuring things out on his own. "Now the Passover, a feast of the Jews, was near. Then Jesus lifted up His eyes, and seeing a great multitude coming toward Him, He said to Philip, 'Where shall we buy bread, that these may eat?' But this He said to test him, for He Himself knew what He would do" (John 6:4–6).

Philip, a native of Bethsaida in Galilee and familiar with the economy in that region, quickly calculated what it would cost to feed such a crowd. "Two hundred denarii (200 days' wages) worth of bread is not sufficient for them, that every one of them may have a little" (v. 7). In this case, Philip flunked this heavenly math test.

What happened next—Christ miraculously fed more than 5,000 people with just five barley loaves and two "small" fish—must have forever impressed the calculating mind of this genuine follower of Jesus. Philip learned that when doing the work of God, heaven's math is beyond human computation, for "with God all things are possible" (Matthew 19:26).

Later, when some Greeks came to the Passover in Jerusalem and wanted to meet Christ, they approached Philip. After he spoke with Andrew, the two disciples knew what to do—go tell Jesus! When you are faced with a problem, the correct answer is always to go to Jesus. He can solve any problem, no matter how complex.

Reflect: Have you ever faced a difficult problem and didn't know what to do? Jesus said, "I am the way, the truth, and the life" (John 14:6).

Dig Deeper: Psalm 90:12; Matthew 10:30; 2 Peter 3:8

Ryan

Not the End

"For this is good and acceptable in the sight of God our Savior, who desires all men to be saved and to come to the knowledge of the truth" (1 Timothy 2:3, 4).

One night, when Ryan was 23, he took a large amount of acid and thought, "This is it." Thankfully, it was not the end because during his recovery time he found the beginning of a new life through Amazing Facts.

Ryan had always been fascinated by different world religions. As a teen and young adult, he was part of several different churches. When just 15, he knew he wanted to be a minister, but was confused by the teachings he heard in his Catholic school and what he read in the Bible.

When tragedy struck his family and his younger brother died, he admits, "I was destroyed. My world suddenly went from a normal teenage world ... to a very dark and lonely place." The loss led him even deeper into his search for truth.

At 18, he joined the army and considered becoming a military chaplain officer. But after a back and knee injury during training, those plans came to a screeching halt, and he found himself lost and feeling very lonely. He couldn't understand what God's plan was for him anymore. Disappointment and confusion drove him to try other avenues besides studying—drugs, alcohol, and promiscuity. This lifestyle continued for many years until he almost died of a drug overdose.

One day, while he was recovering, he flipped on the television and discovered Amazing Facts. The more he watched, the more he became convicted by what he heard. His search for truth led him to amazingfacts.org and the *Bible Answers Live* radio program. He explains, "Concepts that confused me as a young Bible student began to make sense. I felt as if a dark veil that had been over me was starting to be lifted."

Today, Ryan's life has turned in a completely new direction. His former lifestyle is long gone and he now attends a Sabbath-keeping church. He also enjoys sharing with friends what he found—showing them Amazing Facts programs like *Final Events* and *Cosmic Conflict*.

Ryan is thankful to God for leading him to truth. "I truly believe that if I had not turned on the TV and found this ministry, I probably would not be here today."

Reflect: Have you ever been confused over the meaning of a Bible verse? Remember, you can always turn to the Author of Scripture for divine help in understanding truth.

Dig Deeper: Psalm 143:8; 1 Corinthians 14:33; James 1:2–5

John Bunyan

A Pilgrim's Progress

**"The blood of Jesus Christ His Son cleanses
us from all sin" (1 John 1:7).**

Life in seventeenth century Britain was no picnic. Many homes consisted of one or two rooms crowded with large families. Women often gave birth to eight to ten children; however, half of them often died in infancy. If you could regularly afford meat or fish, you were considered well-to-do; but if you were poor, then it was just bread, cheese, and onions—supplemented by pottage, or boiled grain—as your daily fare.

This was the world into which John Bunyan was born in 1628, and while his father was a tinker—a traveling mender of metal household utensils—the family was not affluent. Neither was young John, who learned the tinker's trade from his father. As a youth, John was rowdy and his language shocked even other reprobates in his hometown.

An early marriage to a Christian girl gave Bunyan a framework for "piety" of a sort: He would read the prayers and attend church twice daily, but it was all a formality, not an effort of the heart. Bunyan would try to "be good" and fail, try and fail, and occasionally give up for a round of sinful living.

Finally, he came across a copy of Martin Luther's commentary on the book of Galatians. The great reformer's words spoke to Bunyan's heart. One biographer said Bunyan's "happiness was now as intense as his misery had been."

Despite continuing struggles, Bunyan persevered, until the words of 1 John 1:7 gripped his heart. He would later recall, "I saw, moreover, that it was not my good frame of heart that made my righteousness better, nor my bad frame that made my righteousness worse, for my righteousness was Jesus Christ Himself, 'the same yesterday, and to-day, and forever.'"

Bunyan's conversion was final; he embarked on a career of preaching as a "non-conformist" minister, leading to a 12-year imprisonment at a time when religious tolerance was almost nonexistent. During that time, he wrote *Grace Abounding to the Chief of Sinners* and *The Pilgrim's Progress*, both of which remain in print today.

John Bunyan suffered much as a sinner and even more as a pilgrim on his Christian journey. But perseverance and prayer fortified his life, enabling him to leave a legacy that spans the centuries.

Reflect: Do you know anyone who has had the struggle John Bunyan did in finding peace with God? What would you say to them to encourage their journey?

Dig Deeper: Psalm 56:13; Zechariah 13:1; Hebrews 9:14

Glenda Sue

From Tragedy to Triumph, Part 1

"We know that all things work together for good to those who love God, to those who are the called according to His purpose" (Romans 8:28).

Kirk and Glenda Sue were shattered when their only son Jesse was tragically killed. Glenda Sue has no question that the Lord arranged for them to spend one last Thanksgiving with Jesse at his home. They had no idea this would be their last visit with their son. "Jesse enjoyed cooking Thanksgiving dinner for all of us. It was such a happy time together."

Unfortunately, she ignored a heavenly impression to contact Jesse the day before his death. She thought to call him but decided that she was too busy and would contact him the next day. But at eight a.m. the next morning her eldest daughter called to tell her that Jesse was gone. "I was completely devastated," she laments, "and realized I had missed the opportunity to talk to my son one last time."

Falling deep into grief, it took Glenda Sue a few months to realize that the impression she had received was from God. "Once I finally understood," she says, "I knew how much the Lord really cared for me." She started listening more carefully for the Lord to speak to her after this heart-wrenching experience. "I did not blame God for my son's death. I know our lives here are temporary."

A year later, Kirk's father passed away. It was during that time they received some *Amazing Facts Bible Study Guides* in a most unusual way. Two men began mistakenly dropping the studies off at their house for a few weeks instead of the next block down. After Glenda Sue read all the studies they left, she looked for more. "The materials re-ignited my interest in the Bible's facts about the Sabbath, something that had stirred me since I was a child."

When Glenda Sue was an inquisitive eight-year-old, she recalls reading about the Sabbath commandment in the Ten Commandments. She innocently asked her Sunday school teacher why they didn't go to church on Saturday. "She sent me to my parents," Glenda Sue recalls, "and my question was squashed like a nasty little bug. It was never biblically answered. For years I continued to wonder about the fourth commandment and if there was anyone who kept the Sabbath day."

Through the mistakenly-dropped-off study guides she was beginning to get the answer to this lifelong question.

Reflect: Can you think of a time when you witnessed God bringing good out of tragedy? Remember, the Lord does not cause tragedies. Satan is the instigator of all evil.

Dig Deeper: Isaiah 30:21; Luke 1:79; John 16:13

Glenda Sue

From Tragedy to Triumph, Part 2

"Ask, and it will be given to you; seek, and you will find; knock, and it will be opened to you" (Matthew 7:7).

When two men accidentally dropped off *Amazing Facts Bible Study Guides* at Glenda Sue's home, she eagerly read them and wanted to learn more. She eventually discovered AmazingFacts.org where she gladly found all the lessons online. She and her husband, Kirk, completed the web studies and then searched for a Sabbath-keeping church to visit.

Glenda Sue discovered both positive and negative statements about Sabbath-keepers on the web, but knew the Bible studies she completed spoke powerfully to her heart. She found two churches close by and when a friend mentioned that a post office worker attended one of them, that's where they decided to attend.

The pastor and church members warmly welcomed Kirk and Glenda Sue. The pastor went through all the Amazing Facts lessons once more to make sure they understood everything and then baptized them together into their newfound faith. "We love our new church! It's like a little bit of heaven just being there."

The Sabbath truth so deeply impacted Glenda Sue's heart that she felt impressed to go across the street from their home to witness to a retired Baptist pastor. After sharing literature with him, she prayed for him and then he prayed for her. Obviously he felt she needed her eyes opened. She felt discouraged when she went back home, so she just rested in the arms of Jesus. Then a song came to her heart. "Trust and obey, for there's no other way, to be happy in Jesus, but to trust and obey." Glenda Sue smiled, "Thank you, Jesus, for being by my side. I turn this situation over to you."

Kirk and Glenda Sue later found the two men who initially dropped off those first few Amazing Facts lessons. "Our story is one they love to tell others," she shares. "You never know who may be receptive. I did not even know that I needed them or how much they would impact my life. We have gone from tragedy to triumph because of these lessons."

Even when God's servants mistakenly leave Bible study guides at the wrong house, God can turn it into the right house for His glory!

Reflect: Did you ever witness God using a "mistake" or "accident" and making it an opportunity? Maybe some of these blunders were not errors after all!

Dig Deeper: Psalm 25:4, 5; Proverbs 16:9; John 14:26

Ethiopian Treasurer

Sent by an Angel

"Now an angel of the Lord spoke to Philip, saying, 'Arise and go toward the south along the road which goes down from Jerusalem to Gaza'" (Acts 8:26).

On the road to Gaza, Philip would find an Ethiopian official, the treasurer in the court of Queen Candace. He was also a eunuch—a class normally excluded from Jewish temple worship—so for Philip to find this treasurer returning from Jerusalem and reading a scroll of Isaiah was doubly surprising.

Don't forget, either, that Philip, a deacon in the church at Jerusalem, was not accustomed to roaming far and wide for converts. He had to be sent by the angel of God on this journey.

But the Ethiopian, too, had an angel prompting, did he not? Reading Scripture is one thing—millions have read the Bible, or parts of it, but without apparent spiritual impact. For instance, the noted atheist Richard Dawkins praises the poetic language of the 1611 Authorized (King James) Version of the Bible, but clearly the words haven't yet reached Dawkins's heart.

Yet this foreign visitor to Jerusalem, perhaps a follower of the Jewish faith, was eager to understand what he read in Isaiah 53. Who was this suffering Servant? Why did He have to suffer? And what does it mean? Those questions crowded this official's mind.

In Acts 8:30, 31, we read: "So Philip ran to him, and heard him reading the prophet Isaiah, and said, 'Do you understand what you are reading?' And he said, 'How can I, unless someone guides me?'"

The Ethiopian official, hearing Philip's exposition of these Bible verses in Isaiah, immediately asked to be baptized. It's most likely that the eunuch himself went home and spread the word of Jesus to others for, through the centuries, Ethiopia has had a strong Christian tradition despite numerous societal and governmental challenges.

Philip's response to this angelic call to reach out to the Ethiopian official is a challenge for each of us. We too should be willing to travel beyond our regular pathways to share the truth of Christ's love with hungry hearts. Let's not leave the work of outreach up to pastors, but, as people who have received Jesus into our hearts, become disciples, willing to go wherever God leads.

Have you heard the call? There just might be a traveler sitting next to you, wishing to learn more about the Suffering Servant.

Reflect: Immigration is bringing the world to our doorstep. Are there new people groups in your community you can try to reach? God wants you to step out of your comfort zone.

Dig Deeper: Psalm 25:8, 9; Mark 10:15; 1 Peter 2:1, 2

Kevin

Dumping a Heavy Load

**"Come to Me, all you who labor and are heavy laden,
and I will give you rest" (Matthew 11:28).**

Most dump truck drivers that work for paving companies unload sand, gravel, and dirt as part of their daily work, but Kevin had more he needed to unload. As his life spiraled out of control and his marriage headed for divorce, he stumbled across the Amazing Facts radio broadcast on a local Christian station.

Both Kevin and his wife Jody traveled down difficult roads in their early years. Though each had a moderate connection with church, both of their parents divorced when they were young. Kevin lived with his father and learned from an older sibling about some roads not to travel. Jody struggled with depression and suicidal thoughts through much of her teen years.

After getting married, Kevin was deployed for 18 months. When he returned home, Kevin shares, "Our lives were a mess. Divorce was on the horizon. Depression was taking over my wife. We were arguing frequently."

Kevin had plenty of time to listen to the radio while driving a dump truck for a paving company. One day he came across a program that caught his attention—*Bible Answers Live!* He tuned in to the program often and found some of the topics so intriguing that he wrote Bible verses on his hand while at work. Then he would call Jody to cross-check those Scripture references.

Jody was not easily convinced of the truths Kevin was learning until they ordered the *Amazing Facts Bible Study Guides* and began to carefully go through each lesson. She grew up with great fear about hell and was tormented about what could happen to her or her loved ones. The lessons on hell and death brought new light and deep peace to her heart.

Slowly Kevin and Jody began unloading things out of their lives that were weighing them down—collections of worldly music tapes, cigarettes, and caffeinated beverages. Kevin shares, "As we grew and the Lord led us along, we changed how we lived. Our marriage became stronger and it really impressed our oldest daughter who witnessed the improvements made in our lives."

Today Kevin still unloads materials from his dump truck, but he is now distributing more than sand and gravel. As the Lord opens doors for him, he shares his faith in the One who brought him rest from carrying heavy loads. "Trials still come, but God sustains us as we trust Him. We just keep moving forward in faith."

Reflect: Have you felt weighed down by a heavy burden in your life? Read the verse for today and claim Christ's promise for rest.

Dig Deeper: Psalm 55:22; Matthew 11:28–30; 1 Peter 5:6, 7

John Wesley

"I Felt My Heart Strangely Warmed"

> **"By which have been given to us exceedingly great and precious promises, that through these you may be partakers of the divine nature" (2 Peter 1:4).**

In 1703, John Wesley was born into the "family business." Rev. Samuel Wesley was the rector (administrator) of the Anglican church in Epworth, England. John and his younger brother Charles were raised to go into the ministry just as their father had.

For John, that career path almost didn't happen. In 1709, when John was still five years old, the rectory where his family lived caught fire and the lad was trapped in an upper bedroom. A parishioner, standing on another man's shoulders, rescued John from the fire. Later, Wesley would refer to himself as "a brand plucked out of the fire," quoting Zechariah 3:2.

In 1720, Wesley became a student at Christ Church college in Oxford, graduating in 1724. He was ordained the following year and eventually served as a parish priest in London. He went to America in 1735, along with Charles, to serve the new settlement in what is today's state of Georgia, returning two years later. Throughout this period, Wesley often just went through the motions of his religion. He saw the Moravians, German pietists, during his voyage to America and marveled at their faith and dedication. He could preach and see people come to faith in Christ, but he lacked assurance of his own salvation.

On the evening of May 24, 1738, John Wesley's life was to change forever. That morning, he'd read the words in 2 Peter 1:4 and noticed similar phrases elsewhere in Scripture. That evening, Wesley attended a meeting in the Aldersgate. At about 8:45 p.m., as the speaker read from Luther's treatise on the book of Romans, God's love broke through: "While he was describing the change which God works in the heart through faith in Christ, I felt my heart strangely warmed. I felt I did trust in Christ, Christ alone for salvation; and an assurance was given me that He had taken away my sins, even mine, and saved me from the law of sin and death."

Wesley's pastoral career took a different direction after Aldersgate. He preached personal holiness, brought forward the Arminian teaching that a saved person could be lost, and attracted followers who in turn preached the Wesleyan message throughout England and beyond. The lad literally "plucked out of the fire" lived a life that God used to change the world.

Reflect: How has the desire for holiness affected your life and approach to faith? Find a "great and precious promise" from the Bible and memorize it today.

Dig Deeper: Ezekiel 36:25–27; 2 Corinthians 6:17–7:1; 1 John 3:2

Jennifer

Rooted in Love, Anchored in Hope, Part 1

> **"In my distress I called upon the , and cried out
> to my God; He heard my voice from His temple, and
> my cry entered His ears" (2 Samuel 22:7).**

Pulling her car over to the side of the road, Jennifer buried her face in the steering wheel and began sobbing. She hated her life and her work as an exotic dancer. Jennifer cried out to God to be delivered, and He answered her prayer.

Jennifer grew up in a broken home ravaged by alcoholism. She spent years enduring abuse and shame as she moved in and out of foster care. "I grew up with so much hostility in me," she says today. "I didn't understand why I had so much pain inside, why I had to go through what I did. I grew up without an identity. I tried hard to find my purpose in life, but I just couldn't ever make sense of the world."

Her mom regained custody when Jennifer was seven years old, and they eventually began attending a Sabbath-keeping church. But Jennifer never developed a personal relationship with Jesus. Inside she felt rebellious, selfish, depressed, and damaged.

At age 18, Jennifer had her first child. To support herself and her son, she began working as an exotic dancer. She hoped it would be a temporary job, but it stretched into years. "My life was filled with one bad decision after another," she says.

Seeking to fill the painful void in her heart, Jennifer also explored New Age spirituality and occult practices. "I hated life," Jennifer admits. "I would do anything to try to attain happiness." And she did just about anything. But all the happiness she found was short lived and left her feeling worse than before.

Meanwhile, Jennifer's mother continually interceded in prayer for her. She also sent Jennifer videos and articles from Amazing Facts. Jennifer decided to give them a try because she was bored and found this as a way to pass time. But she didn't expect what happened next.

It was the first time ever that Jennifer actually felt hope in her heart for a better life. Even though she was still working as an exotic dancer, she felt God gently convicting her heart through the Bible truths.

Reflect: Have you ever felt utterly broken inside? If you, or someone you know, feel desperately in need of help, God promises to hear and answer every sincere prayer.

Dig Deeper: Exodus 2:23; Psalm 30:2; 1 John 5:14

Jennifer

Rooted in Love, Anchored in Hope, Part 2

"Peace I leave with you, My peace I give to you; not as the world gives do I give to you ..." (John 14:27).

When Jennifer cried out to God to be saved from her broken life of sin, the Lord reached her heart through Amazing Facts. As she watched ministry programs, she began to believe that she could trust her heavenly Father, who would never let her down.

During this time, Jennifer still went to work but began feeling an increasing presence of evil in the club where she worked as an exotic dancer. She hated being there. "I was filled with so much disgust that one day on my way to work, I pulled over to the side of the road and started sobbing—pouring my heart out to God. I surrendered to Him at that very moment." She went home, fell to her knees, and once more cried out to God, "Please deliver me out of this lifestyle."

Jennifer then made a promise to God that she would be His disciple and that He could mold and use her for His kingdom and glory—that she would serve Him for the rest of her life.

"I immediately felt His presence. He overwhelmed me with so much joy and peace. I felt truly loved and understood for the first time in my life. Here I was—living so sinfully, but He still loved me. He still pursued me, before I ever pursued Him. He gave my life a purpose. He had a hope and future for me just as He does for all His children."

Jennifer never went back to work at the club. Instead, she studied deeper into the myriad resources available from Amazing Facts. She soon found relief from the pain that had dominated her life for so long. She began to understand God's grace.

As her walk with God grew stronger, Jennifer was called by the Lord to participate in the Amazing Facts Center of Evangelism (AFCOE) training. "The very ministry that God used to get hold of me is the very ministry He used to educate and equip me in evangelism."

Today, Jennifer's life overflows with peace, security, and hope. "I am content and genuinely happy! Two days after my thirtieth birthday, I was baptized by Wyatt Allen of Amazing Facts and by the pastor of my church."

Reflect: When have you last sensed God's joy and peace in your life? Is there something standing in the way of receiving these gifts? Why not completely surrender that one thing to the Lord and have faith in His power to help you?

Dig Deeper: Isaiah 55:12; Luke 14:33; Romans 15:13

Gaius

A Footnote in History?

> "So the whole city was filled with confusion, and rushed into the theater with one accord, having seized Gaius and Aristarchus, Macedonians, Paul's travel companions" (Acts 19:29).

A footnote is a note of reference that is usually placed at the bottom of a printed page. But it can also describe a person or event that is considered of minor importance.

At best, the Gaius of whom we read in Acts 19 is a footnote in history. Much can be assumed about him, but little can be determined—especially since there are three others in the Bible with the name of Gaius.

But let's start with what we do know: This Gaius was with Paul in Ephesus, a town where the apostle ministered for three years. Indeed, Ephesus was more than just a "town"—it was one of the seven cities in Asia Minor where the nascent religion of Christianity had taken root, so much so that converts and their influence were having an impact on the local idolatry business.

In Ephesus, many were losing interest in praying to the goddess Diana; Paul's preaching turned people away from idol-worship, even as influential as the cult of Diana was in that place and that time. Being an associate of Paul on that trip, Gaius certainly shared his testimony and spoke with people who likely abandoned their pagan ways in favor of worshipping the true God.

And this Gaius was a Macedonian, from a prosperous area on the plains of Thessalonica in Greece, a land noted for timber and precious metals. Though the Christians of Macedonia were at times in distress, Gaius did hail from a prosperous and, one imagines, cultured region. It is probable that he was converted under the teaching of Paul. Imagine having the great apostle give you Bible studies!

Now Gaius is in Ephesus, dealing with a dangerous situation. Cooler heads prevailed and Aristarchus and Gaius were freed from captivity, unharmed. Paul, having avoided the mob, left Ephesus for Macedonia.

We learn no more of this Mr. Gaius, but what is known should encourage believers today. He found faith, placed his life alongside Paul's, and ventured forth to share the good news with others, not counting the cost of such a move.

There are still people, today, who need to hear the gospel. Would you be willing to be a footnote in the history of gospel evangelism?

Reflect: Have you ever shared the gospel in a setting where it was unpopular? Paul reminded Timothy, "All who desire to live godly in Christ Jesus will suffer persecution" (2 Timothy 3:12).

Dig Deeper: Acts 17:8; 1 Corinthians 4:9; 2 Corinthians 8:19

Jeremy

God Stopped Me, Part 1

"You shall not murder" (Exodus 20:13).

Jeremy's marriage was on the rocks ...

Even though he grew up in a Christian home that enjoyed outdoor activities such as fishing, hiking, and camping, these family outings often included alcohol, which frequently led to other substance abuse and family strife.

Unsurprisingly, Jeremy soon began experimenting with cigarettes, chewing tobacco, beer, and even marijuana. When his high school sweetheart caught him smoking pot at school, she gave him a look he'd never forget. She turned her back and walked away. He ran after her, and she gave him an ultimatum. "It's me or the drugs."

Jeremy says, "I chose her." At the young age of twenty, they got married. They eventually had three beautiful kids, but Jeremy could only wish they lived "happily ever after." Long work hours and a cross-country move led to serious and constant fighting. Even worse, as their relationship deteriorated, he began to wonder if she was cheating on him.

Friends contacted Jeremy, hinting that something was going on with his wife, but he lived in denial. "I tried to stay together with her, mostly for the kids. I started drinking alcohol, but numbing the pain just didn't work."

Jeremy eventually discovered that, indeed, his wife was having an affair. "I also knew of God, but I didn't have a relationship with Him," he admits. "I didn't know what to do at this point. I got down on my knees and prayed, asking God to show me what to do."

Two weeks later, Jeremy arrived home to find a strange man in his living room, watching TV with his wife, while their daughter was playing nearby. Jeremy's anger and rage welled up inside him as he went to their bedroom, found his rifle, and loaded a shell. He contemplated loading one for himself.

As he left the bedroom with the intent of ending the life of the stranger, he stopped in front of a picture of his children, hanging just outside the bedroom door. He loved the photo of his beautiful kids all dressed up in western-style clothes. He suddenly heard a voice in his head say, "Don't do this."

Jeremy fell to his knees, still holding the gun, as he began to sob. He knew his marriage was over. He prayed and asked God to forgive him for what he almost did—attempt to take another man's life. "God stopped me from ruining my kids' lives."

Reflect: Have you ever taken an action that you later regretted? Stay close to Jesus each day and ask the Holy Spirit to guide your thoughts and behaviors.

Dig Deeper: Psalm 37:8; Proverbs 14:29; James 1:20

"Peter said to them, 'Repent, and let every one of you be baptized in the name of Jesus Christ for the remission of sins; and you shall receive the gift of the Holy Spirit'" (Acts 2:38).

Jeremy's marriage was on the rocks and when he found his wife with a strange man, he almost ended that man's life. Jeremy and his wife soon divorced, going through a long and painful custody battle. He eventually moved back home near his parents, found work, and began drinking heavily, all the while missing his kids.

During this difficult time, Jeremy found encouragement in his relationship with his uncle—a Sabbath-keeping Christian. He had witnessed how the gospel had transformed his uncle's life. One day, his uncle invited Jeremy's parents to an Amazing Facts seminar, presented by Tyler Long.

"My folks invited me to go, but I refused." Jeremy was angry with God for his broken family and for his failure as a father. "I'll stay here and drink," he told his parents. He also prayed, "God, how could you allow all this happen to me and my family?"

The Lord was working on his heart, however, and Jeremy felt an impression to go to the meetings. "So I went," he remembers, "And God spoke to me at the presentation." One verse he heard Tyler share pierced his heart: "He who finds his life will lose it, and he who loses his life for My sake will find it" (Matthew 10:39). These compelling words convicted him to surrender his life completely to God. Immediately, peace flooded his mind; he then began a new journey as a disciple of Christ.

Jeremy spent hours studying the Bible as he searched for answers and sought to understand the life-changing truths taught in Scripture. He watched many Amazing Facts presentations and was especially impressed by Pastor Doug's suggestion: "If you choose to follow Christ, you need to stop dating the devil." As Jeremy put this advice into practice, he found his life was transformed in amazing ways.

Today, Jeremy enthusiastically shares his faith with those in his community and even with his own children when he sees them. His life since finding Christ has not been easy, but he continues to find peace, comfort, and hope in the Word of God.

Reflect: How do you respond to the nudging of the Holy Spirit? Jesus sends the Spirit to not only convict us of sin, but to teach us, guide us, and comfort us.

Dig Deeper: John 14:26; Romans 8:26; Galatians 5:22, 23

Martin Luther

Trembling Monk Finds Faith

"For in it the righteousness of God is revealed from faith to faith; as it is written, 'The just shall live by faith'" (Romans 1:17).

After being spared a lightning strike at the age of 21, Martin Luther, already possessing baccalaureate and master's degrees in law, fulfilled his vow. During the storm, he prayed to St. Anne and promised to become a Catholic monk if he survived.

A man of his word, Luther entered the monastery shortly thereafter. He endured all sorts of deprivations and self-punishment as he sought forgiveness for sin: "If anyone could have earned heaven by the life of a monk, it was I." But as Luther discovered, "good works" didn't satisfy. He was constantly uneasy about his eternal security, worrying he would fall short.

Moving to Wittenberg University, where he obtained a doctorate in the Bible and became a professor, Luther in 1513 and 1514 began to lecture on the Psalms and studied the epistle to the Romans. During these studies, Luther found the answer his anxious soul had sought.

"At last meditating day and night, by the mercy of God, I ... began to understand that the righteousness of God is that through which the righteous live by a gift of God, namely by faith. ... Here I felt as if I were entirely born again and had entered paradise itself through the gates that had been flung open," he wrote.

Such a revelation was not without consequence. Instead of accepting the works employed by many of his co-religionists to try and earn God's favor, and spurning the fundraising tactic of selling "indulgences" for the departed, Luther tenaciously clung to righteousness by faith and preached it. In 1517, his "95 Theses" were tacked to the door of Wittenberg Cathedral, sparking what is now known as the Protestant Reformation.

His break with the church of his youth was not without peril or cost. But he stood his ground and Luther's followers developed a theology that swept the world. Today, Protestant faith has touched every corner of the globe and reached the lives of millions.

At the end of his life, Luther's harsh utterances toward his theological opponents tarnished his reputation. Yet today, Luther is best remembered, not for his failings, but for his faith. He found that the key to a right relationship with God was in believing and receiving Christ, a legacy which lives on today.

Reflect: How long would you be willing to pray for something you desired from God? Jesus told us to "pray and not lose heart" (Luke 18:1). Remember the story of the persistent widow (Luke 18:1–8)?

Dig Deeper: Habakkuk 2:4; John 3:36; Hebrews 11:6, 7

Luz

From Facebook to Faith

"Every good gift and every perfect gift is from above, and comes down from the Father of lights, with whom there is no variation or shadow of turning" (James 1:17).

Luz sat down to peruse Facebook—never expecting that her life was about to change.

She didn't have much of a social circle and kept her life simple. She mainly focused on God and her teenage grandson, Christian (who was diagnosed with autism), of whom she had full custody.

Luz was reared in the Catholic faith, but she rarely attended church. When her parents did take her to church as a child, the services were in Latin and she couldn't understand what was being said.

Now, on Facebook, she discovered something intriguing—a promotion for a series of meetings hosted by an evangelist with a ministry called Amazing Facts. She wrote down the date and reminded herself several times to not forget and miss opening night.

Luz and Christian arrived for the first evening, and both immediately found the Bible information fascinating. They returned for the next night—and the next. While Luz felt a little hesitant about the church sponsoring the event, she was pleasantly surprised to discover that she was enjoying the meetings more and more. Her reservations quickly melted away.

Sometimes, it wasn't easy to attend every night. But she noticed that whenever she hesitated about whether to go, Christian would speak up and say, "I want to go." They never missed a night!

Soon the church members and the evangelist began sharing additional Amazing Facts resources, including magazines, Bible lessons, DVDs, and more. Luz devoured them and said, "I enjoyed every message!"

Luz felt her understanding of God growing abundantly, whereas before she'd struggled with all sorts of daunting questions. She became particularly convicted about the beautiful truth of the Sabbath and decided to commit her life to this deeper walk. At the end of the series, Luz and Christian were baptized together into God's remnant church, joyfully testifying to their new journey of truth.

Today, Luz knows that she has purpose and reason in her life—to share with others the blessings she has found, especially about the Sabbath. "I invited my neighbors to the church," she reports, "and soon they will marry and go down together into the baptismal waters."

Luz can now thankfully testify to others about her new walk with God. "I have not stopped talking about all the blessings that God has for everyone who believes in Him."

Reflect: How many blessings has God given to you? See how many you can count up in one minute.

Dig Deeper: Luke 6:38; 2 Corinthians 9:8; Philippians 4:19

Leroy

Doing the Right Thing, Part 1

**"I will instruct you and teach you in the way you should
go; I will guide you with My eye" (Psalm 32:8).**

When Leroy's golfing partners discovered he would not play on Saturdays anymore, they were shocked. One day they spotted Leroy's wife, Ann, on the green, and asked her when she was getting a divorce. "Isn't that what's required when you're married to someone who joins a cult?" She assured them they were not splitting up.

Leroy grew up in a small town in Colorado and faithfully attended church each Sunday. He went to a parochial school for eight years. After getting married and spending time in the military, his church attendance became more sporadic. "I wanted to do what I wanted to do," he recalls.

The couple moved around, started a family, but eventually ended up back home where Leroy worked on construction with his father. He also started attending his Sunday-keeping church more regularly and was even a deacon for about eight years.

One day, Leroy got a card in the mail offering free Bible study lessons. "They were from some place out in California named Amazing Facts," he shares. "I never heard of them and probably would have thrown the card away if I knew it was from a Sabbath-keeping organization." But he filled the card out and left it sitting on his work bench in his locksmith shop.

"I'd come to work," he explained, "and see that card staring me in the face." Finally, he mailed the card and received the first lesson of the *Amazing Facts Bible Study Guides*. He immediately started working on the lesson. After sending in the answer sheet, he received another lesson, and then another.

Eventually, he came to a study on the Bible Sabbath. "After I mailed that one in, I received a call from Amazing Facts asking if I'd be interested in visiting a local Sabbath-keeping church," he remembers. He was, and when he called the small church in town, he got an answering machine. So he temporarily gave up.

Then he remembered working with his dad on building a house for a family member who was a Sabbath-keeper. So he called his cousin Genevieve, who happened to have the pastor's cell phone number. Leroy called the pastor who invited him to church that coming Sabbath. He accepted the invitation.

When Leroy attended the Sabbath-keeping church for the first time, he thought to himself, "What have I gotten myself into?"

Reflect: Have you ever invited someone to church? Remember, God wants to use you as a pathway to truth for another person. Many are waiting to be invited home.

Dig Deeper: Psalm 5:8; John 18:38; Acts 8:30–32

Leroy

Doing the Right Thing, Part 2

"Always be ready to give a defense to everyone who asks you a reason for the hope that is in you, with meekness and fear" (1 Peter 3:15).

After studying the *Amazing Facts Bible Study Guides*, Leroy decided to attend a Sabbath-keeping church for the first time. "It was communion Sabbath," Leroy shares. "When members got up to leave for the foot-washing service, something we never did in my Sunday church, I thought to myself, 'What have I gotten myself into?'" Three times he tried to stand up and walk out, but he stayed. Week after week he kept attending without his wife.

Eventually, a church elder studied with him and answered several of his questions. Leroy decided to be baptized. When he first starting going to this new church, his wife, Ann, told him, "It's okay for you to go to the Sabbath-keeping church, but don't ask me to go along with you." A few days before he was to be baptized, his daughter called and said, "Dad, you need to invite mom to your baptism."

So he invited Ann to his baptism. She came and was treated so kindly by the ladies of the church, she later told her husband, "You know, I think I'm going to start going to church with you." He picked up a packet of *Amazing Facts Bible Study Guides* from a rack at the church and gave them to his wife. Eventually, Ann was also baptized.

Leroy shares, "One of my daughters thought I was joining a cult, and when my son was also concerned, I sent them both a set of Bible study guides." After his son looked them over, he called his sister and said, "Don't worry about dad." He concluded that this Sabbath-keeping church was not a cult after all. He later called his dad and told him, "I think you're doing the right thing."

Leroy and Ann have shared the study guides with several of their children and attended church with some of them when visiting during holidays and vacations. "If someone had sent me a book, I would have probably put it on the shelf or tossed it. But the *Amazing Facts Bible Study Guides* were the best thing for me." He explains, "These packets are the best resource for convicting people of the truth. All they need is a willing heart to do the lessons."

Reflect: If someone asked you about your faith, what would you say? Develop a short testimony that you can share with others on how God changed your life.

Dig Deeper: John 15:16; Colossians 4:5, 6; 2 Timothy 1:8

Abraham

From Idolatry to Patriarch, Part 1

**"So Abram departed as the had spoken to him, and
Lot went with him. And Abram was seventy-five years
old when he departed from Haran" (Genesis 12:4).**

For decades, Jewish young people in synagogues across the United States have been taught the story of Abraham—originally named Abram—from a textbook written by James Isaacs.

The story of Abraham as told in Isaac's *Our People* history is more expansive than what the Bible tells us about the young man from Ur of the Chaldees. One element of Abram's story has endured among those who've read it.

Depending on how it's told, Abram (later Abraham) was either a young boy or a more mature adult when he came to understand that the idols made and sold by Terah, his father, were useless. The real God of the universe took no pleasure in people worshipping carved bits of wood.

One evening, while Terah was asleep, Abram took a small axe and destroyed all the idols save one. Abram placed the axe in that one idol's hands. The next morning, Abram blamed the remaining idol for the "massacre." When Terah remonstrated that the idols were inanimate and unable to do anything, Abram made his point.

Again, that's the legend from a Jewish history book. There's nothing in Scripture to directly support that story. However, one has to wonder why Abram/Abraham found favor in God's sight, and his presumed rebellion against the idolatry of the Chaldeans would have been a great sign to God that here was someone upon whom the Lord could rely.

In Genesis 12:1–4 we read, "Now the had said to Abram: 'Get out of your country, from your family and from your father's house, to a land that I will show you. I will make you a great nation; I will bless you and make your name great; and you shall be a blessing. I will bless those who bless you, and I will curse him who curses you; and in you all the families of the earth shall be blessed.' So Abram departed as the had spoken to him."

Notice Abram's response to God's command: He "departed as the had spoken." One of the hallmarks of those who have been converted is a willingness to do what God says, without hesitation or argument.

God saw something in Abram that indicated faithfulness. May He see the same in each of us!

Reflect: Is your heart sufficiently tender that you can say "yes" without hesitation when God asks? If not, pray for Him to help you change.

Dig Deeper: Nehemiah 9:7; Acts 7:2–6; Hebrews 11:8

Abraham

From Idolatry to Patriarch, Part 2

> **"So he lifted his eyes and looked, and behold, three men were standing by him; and when he saw them, he ran from the tent door to meet them, and bowed himself to the ground" (Genesis 18:2).**

It's fashionable, in some quarters, to imagine that a conversion has to be a dramatic event: Heartfelt weeping, a walk down the "sawdust trail" to the front of a revival tent, or perhaps a deathbed confession. The more drama, spectacle, and publicity that can be attached, the better.

But there are times when conversion—or the evidence thereof—can be quiet, humble, hardly noticed. This incident in Abraham's life is one of these. The patriarch is sitting at "the tent door," the Bible tells us, and sees three visitors in the distance. Abraham jumps up, runs to meet them, and bows low before his guests. Rejecting their demurrals, he insists on offering them due hospitality, and then some.

Abraham told his guests, "My Lord, if I have now found favor in Your sight, do not pass on by Your servant. Please let a little water be brought, and wash your feet, and rest yourselves under the tree. And I will bring a morsel of bread, that you may refresh your hearts. After that you may pass by, inasmuch as you have come to your servant" (Genesis 18:3–5).

Of course, Abraham served more than "a morsel of bread." He had fine cakes of meal prepared, and a roasted calf, hearty fare and not an inconsequential recognition that the guests deserved proper treatment.

It turns out these visitors were more than just coincidental travelers on the road past Abraham's tent, en route to Sodom. They were angels of the Most High, and they made a promise to Abraham: In a year, you and Sarah will have a son.

Abraham's act of hospitality was so important that centuries later the writer of a New Testament epistle invoked it: "Do not forget to entertain strangers, for by so doing some have unwittingly entertained angels" (Hebrews 13:2).

Abraham showed his converted heart by his faithfulness to God in being kind to his visitors. How do we live out our professed belief?

Reflect: If "some have entertained angels unawares," what circumstances can you recall that might fit that description? As we have opportunity, let's be sure to exercise the spiritual gift of hospitality!

Dig Deeper: Leviticus 19:34; Isaiah 58:7; Matthew 25:40

Abraham

From Idolatry to Patriarch, Part 3

> **"Then He said, 'Take now your son, your only son Isaac, whom you love, and go to the land of Moriah, and offer him there as a burnt offering on one of the mountains of which I shall tell you" (Genesis 22:2).**

For reasons known only to God, Abraham was asked to make a sacrifice no parent would want to contemplate: Take "your only son Isaac" and sacrifice him on Mount Moriah.

We've seen Abraham's willingness to obey God when the Lord spoke to this ex-Chaldean. Told to leave Haran, Abraham upped and went. Seeing unknown visitors at his front door, Abraham ran after them, bowed down, and begged to serve them as if they were long-lost relatives.

But now! The child of promise, the one whose birth Sarah doubted, the one who remained after Ishmael was sent away. The heir to everything Abraham had. This child—albeit not an infant—was to be offered not merely as a sacrifice, but as a "burnt offering" to the God who had promised to make of Abraham "a great nation" (Genesis 12:2).

It's beyond comprehension for any parent to imagine this. There's sacrifice, and then there's this, something miles beyond a grain offering, or the dedication of a fatted calf.

Yet Abraham obeyed. He didn't inform Isaac immediately of the plan, but merely took a party that included his son to Mount Moriah, and built an altar away from his servants. Now it was just Isaac and Abraham—and a task too awful to contemplate or explain.

"But the Angel of the called to him from heaven and said, 'Abraham, Abraham!' So he said, 'Here I am.' And He said, 'Do not lay your hand on the lad, or do anything to him; for now I know that you fear God, since you have not withheld your son, your only son, from Me'" (Genesis 22:11, 12).

Abraham passed the test, without spilling a drop of his son's blood. God provided a ram (Genesis 22:13) and the proper sacrifice was made.

This was Abraham's third major test, one that examined the level and depth of Abraham's conversion. That he succeeded says much about Abraham's faith—and about the God who responded to that faith.

Reflect: What sacrifice has God asked you to make—or is asking now—that seeks your "all"? When we understand what the Lord sacrificed to redeem us—sending His "only begotten Son" (John 3:16) to die in our place—is there too much we could give in return?

Dig Deeper: Micah 6:7; John 3:16; Romans 8:32

Elizabeth

God Allows U-Turns

"Walk in the Spirit, and you shall not fulfill the lust of the flesh" (Galatians 5:16).

A few years ago, there was a popular automobile bumper sticker that read: "If you're headed in the wrong direction, God allows U-Turns." Elizabeth knows about this first hand. For four years she was married to a woman. Despite having been raised with Christian influences in her life, Elizabeth and her "wife" were both "into vulgar music, media, and worldly goals," as well as using drugs and alcohol.

One day Elizabeth and her partner discovered Amazing Facts on YouTube and it completely changed their lives. As they listened to Pastor Doug Batchelor, they began to sense a change taking place in their hearts. She recalls, "We became more aware of the truth, and that Jesus is the only hope in this temporary life."

"Both of us realized we were deceived into following the enemy by the lust of our flesh. Amazing Facts taught us about the Bible Sabbath along with other Bible truths." Elizabeth says that while watching Pastor Doug, "the Holy Spirit was at work as we learned more and more truth. Our desires changed."

The two women—now living celibate lives—got in touch with a local Sabbath-keeping church and began Bible studies with the pastor and his wife. This led to their "full conversion and baptism," as Elizabeth explains. "And there's no doubt," she adds, "that Amazing Facts was a key factor in our Christian conversion and growth as believers."

Elizabeth regularly brought home Amazing Facts booklets from church. "I enjoyed reading the different topics. They reference Scripture, which helped me learn many Bible truths. Some booklets helped me unlearn false teachings I had learned before." The ministry has even helped Elizabeth become an evangelist. "I enjoy sharing the printable materials on the Amazing Facts website now. It has been helpful to me in guiding others in their Christian lives."

Her Christian life today "is Spirit-filled," she says. "My life is about serving others out of love and reflecting the Savior." After being baptized, she shares, "My life goal is to lead other people to Christ, helping others know Jesus can help them overcome addictions, sin, vanity, and all of the enemy's deceptions."

Reflect: Have you ever gone down a one-way street in the wrong direction? What could have happened if you kept going? God wants us to quickly turn around if we are following the ways of the world.

Dig Deeper: Romans 13:14; Galatians 5:24; 1 John 2:16

Augustine

Delivered by Truth, Part 1

"For the good that I will to do, I do not do; but the evil I will not to do, that I practice. ... O wretched man that I am! Who will deliver me from this body of death?" (Romans 7:19, 24).

Augustine was born into an upper class home in AD 354, in Roman North Africa in what is known today as Algeria. His mother, Monica, was a strong Christian and a central figure in his life, while his father, who converted to Christianity on his deathbed, was more like a stranger to Augustine.

When just 11 years old, he was sent away to school where he learned Latin literature, along with pagan beliefs and practices. One day, he and some friends stole fruit from a neighborhood garden, not because they were hungry, but because "it was not permitted." He admitted later that his nature "was foul, and I loved it. I loved my own error—not that for which I erred, but the error itself."

At age 17, Augustine went to Carthage to continue his education. His mother labored over the direction of her son's life through prayer and "good warnings." Despite her efforts, he lived a life solely for pleasure and associated with young men who liked to boast about their sexual exploits. He also began an affair with a young woman that lasted for 15 years and resulted in the birth of a son.

Augustine was a brilliant student and an eloquent rhetorician. His interest in philosophy led him to study many different religions. But through personal study, the friendship of Christians, and his mother's prayers, he was led toward Christianity.

While praying in a garden next to a home where he was living in Milan, he poured out his heart to God with "a mighty rain of tears." He prayed for the burden of sin to be lifted from his heart and cried, "How long, how long? Tomorrow and tomorrow? Why not now? Why not this very hour make an end to my uncleanness?"

At that moment, a school child next door was singing a little song that went, "Pick it up, read it; pick it up, read it." He immediately stopped crying and felt convicted to go open the Bible and read wherever his eyes fell on the page. What he read banished his doubts and brought light to his heart.

Reflect: Have you ever wrestled to hear God's voice speak to your heart? You can know messages from heaven by simply opening your Bible and reading the inspired words contained within.

Dig Deeper: 1 Samuel 3:10; 2 Samuel 22:7; Psalm 30:5

Augustine

Delivered by Truth, Part 2

**"Now to Him who is able to do exceedingly abundantly
above all that we ask or think, according to the
power that works in us ..." (Ephesians 3:20).**

After crying with great tears to God for deliverance from sin, Augustine was impressed to open his Bible and read whatever passage came to him. He had been in a garden next to the home where he was living. His friend Alypius was sitting on a bench nearby where Augustine had left a copy of Paul's letter to the Romans. "I snatched it up," he writes, "opened it, and in silence read the paragraph on which my eyes first fell ..."

"Let us walk properly, as in the day, not in revelry and drunkenness, not in lewdness and lust, not in strife and envy. But put on the Lord Jesus Christ, and make no provision for the flesh, to fulfill its lusts" (Romans 13:13, 14).

After reading the passage, Augustine recalls, "There was infused in my heart something like the light of full certainty and all the gloom of doubt vanished away." He closed the book and shared his experience with Alypius who, in turn, read the verse that followed, "Receive one who is weak in the faith ..." (Romans 14:1). Together, the two men made a "full commitment without any restless hesitation."

Augustine then went into the house to tell his mother, who was living with them at the time, about what happened. He wrote that "she leaped for joy triumphant" and blessed her son. She repeated the Bible promise that God "is able to do exceedingly abundantly above all that we ask or think, according to the power that works in us" (Ephesians 3:20). God had turned "her grief into gladness more plentiful than she had ventured to desire."

The Christian writer Ellen White makes this note: "The mother of Augustine prayed for her son's conversion. She saw no evidence that the Spirit of God was impressing his heart, but she was not discouraged. She laid her finger upon the texts, presenting before God his own words, and pleaded as only a mother can. Her deep humiliation, her earnest importunities, her unwavering faith, prevailed, and the Lord gave her the desire of her heart. Today he is just as ready to listen to the petitions of his people" (*Christian Education*, p. 236).

Reflect: Have you prayed earnestly and for a long time for a loved one to turn to God? Never give up. Persevere in prayer with unwavering faith and watch God work in mighty ways.

Dig Deeper: Luke 18:1–8; Romans 12:12; Galatians 6:9

Carol

Centered in Christ

"Resist the devil and he will flee from you" (James 4:7).

Carol's mother wanted to provide her daughter with a nice Christian background, so she took her to a local Catholic church. But when Carol's mother went through a divorce, she was marginalized from that Christian community. Even so, Carol recalls, "I started reading the Bible when I was in grade school, but God was in the background of my life." Without Christ as her focus, her life grew full of oppressive routines and worldly comfort.

As an adult, Carol worked hard to succeed, but admits, "My life was centered around me." Bills would often take all of her earnings and if anything was left over it went to buying drugs. After Carol became pregnant, she began to struggle with extreme feelings of emptiness.

One day, two co-workers were talking about a Bible study. It reminded Carol of the comfort she used to find in God's Word. So she decided to give church another try. Carol picked a Sunday to attend a local church. She took extra care in getting nicely dressed, but on her way out she tripped on the stairs and got her clothes dirty. So she went back to change, but then realized she would already be late. The idea of walking in at an awkward moment on her first time back in church was too much to bear. She said, "I felt that this was a sign that God did not want me, but when I told my friend, she said, 'The devil will do anything to keep you from hearing God's Word.' That sentence changed my life." Carol began attending a Lutheran church full time for the next 25 years.

One day an Amazing Facts seminar advertisement caught her eye, so she attended and didn't regret a single moment. Waves of new information poured over her as her Christian worldview finally began making sense. Carol recalled, "I felt the conviction of the Holy Spirit and started worshiping on Saturdays."

Amazing Facts evangelist Darrin Bartell provided a world of resources for exploring rich Bible concepts. "I learned more at the seminar than I had in 25 years at the Lutheran church," she said. Today, Carol's life is centered in Christ and she thirsts for Bible study and prayer. Nothing keeps her from the Word or from finding ways to share God's love with others.

Reflect: Can you think of a time the devil tried to stop you from attending church or from quiet time with God? Don't let him have the upper hand.

Dig Deeper: Luke 8:15; Romans 10:17; Ephesians 6:11

Twelve Ephesian Men

From John's Baptism to the Holy Spirit's

"All authority has been given to Me in heaven and on earth. Go therefore and make disciples of all the nations, baptizing them in the name of the Father and of the Son and of the Holy Spirit" (Matthew 28:18, 19).

There were 12 men from Ephesus who were followers of John the Baptist. We don't know their names, their occupations, or their marital status. All we know is that they were believers in God, like Paul. But when the missionary-apostle first met these 12 seekers, he discerned that something was missing in their experience—something that these men may not have noticed.

"Did you receive the Holy Spirit when you believed?" Paul asked. "We have not so much as heard whether there is a Holy Spirit," they replied (Acts 19:2).

This presented a dilemma. The men were believers, but they didn't know about Jesus, about His death and resurrection, or about the Comforter He promised, the Holy Spirit. (See John 14:16.) They knew about the message of John the Baptist, but they did not know the One about whom John had prophesied.

So Paul presented to them the great truths that are the basis of the Christian's hope and explained what they had yet to experience of the Holy Spirit. The twelve men were deeply interested and thankful as they listened to Paul's words. Through faith they took hold of the wonderful truth of Christ's atoning sacrifice and received Him as their Savior.

After expressing their belief in Jesus, miracles took place. "When Paul had laid hands on them, the Holy Spirit came upon them, and they spoke with tongues and prophesied" (Acts 19:6). When the apostle prayed over these godly converts, they received, as promised, the gift of the Holy Spirit. And, because of the setting in which they were located, they were able to speak in the languages of other nations, and prophesy.

We don't know the names of these twelve men, but we know their hearts. They were open to inquiry, open to instruction and exhortation, and open to change when they saw a need. May God give each of us the same attitude day by day!

Reflect: Do you know anyone who needs help on their spiritual journey? What lessons from this story stand out for you?

Dig Deeper: Mark 16:17; Acts 2:4; 2 Timothy 1:6

Nick

A Gold and Silver Witness, Part 1

"Here is the mind which has wisdom: The seven heads are seven mountains on which the woman sits" (Revelation 17:9).

Raised in a Catholic home, Nick had a strong sense of loyalty to his faith. However, while stationed with the U.S. Air Force in Germany, he happened upon a television program that shook his world. The speaker led him through the history of the world and its relationship to Bible prophecy, ending with a clear identification of the antichrist.

Nick wondered if his church had lied to him. Convinced that the evangelist was wrong in his interpretations, Nick started studying the Bible in earnest. "I even flew to Rome," he says, "to see if the city really did have seven hills, just as the evangelist stated."

Nick later discovered an advertisement on the web for the *Amazing Facts Bible Study Guides* and signed up. Every day after work, he rushed home to study more about what the Bible has to say about the future and the antichrist. The truths he learned changed his life, and soon he was contacted by an Amazing Facts representative offering to connect him with a local church.

Since Nick knew he would be stationed in Washington State, Amazing Facts put him in contact with a church member in Tacoma, who offered to provide transportation to church each week. This marked the beginning of a new chapter in his life, and eventually Nick was baptized. After leaving the military, he entered into full-time ministry.

Fast forward about ten years, and Nick has been actively sharing with his community the truths he has learned. He also has a special ministry to high school students, in which he uses the *Amazing Facts Study Guides*. He has found them to be an effective way of teaching Bible truths. But God had more blessings in store for him.

Recently, while attending a Christian-sponsored extreme sporting event, he met up with a representative from Amazing Facts. As he learned about estate planning gifts and legacy giving, Nick asked the representative if people ever gifted anything out of the ordinary. One thing mentioned was precious metal collections. Nick says this comment made an unconscious impression on his mind.

Reflect: Can you recall a time when your beliefs were challenged? Did you turn to the Bible to clarify the issue?

Dig Deeper: John 5:39; Acts 17:11; 2 Timothy 2:15

A Gold and Silver Witness, Part 2

> **"'The silver is Mine, and the gold is Mine,' says the of hosts" (Haggai 2:8).**

Nick learned from an Amazing Facts representative that people sometimes gift precious metals to advance God's work. The idea left an impression on his mind.

A few weeks later, a series of circumstances inspired Nick to get radical with God. He prayed, "Lord, how can I get radical with You?" Instantly, he says, his gold and silver collection came to mind. Over the past decade, Nick had been collecting precious metals as a kind of insurance in case of a worldwide financial collapse. Now he faced a dilemma.

Immediately, the conversation with the Amazing Facts representative came to mind. So he prayed, "Lord, if you want me to give up my gold and silver, You have to show me beyond a doubt from Your Word." Then he went to bed.

Early the next morning, he woke up with a verse in his mind, but he couldn't remember where to find it in the Bible. Quickly, Nick got up and searched online for the verse and soon found it. "Who can endure the day of His coming? ... For He is like a refiner's fire and ... will purify the sons of Levi, and purge them as gold and silver, that they may offer to the an offering in righteousness" (Malachi 3:2, 3).

Nick was in a quandary. "I put the ball in God's court, and He served it right back! He provided a verse not just with silver or gold but both. But not only that, the chapter included a promise. "'Bring all the tithes into the storehouse, that there may be food in My house, and try Me now in this,' says the of hosts, 'If I will not open for you the windows of heaven and pour out for you such blessing that there will not be room enough to receive it'" (Malachi 3:10).

The verses convicted him to step out in faith and contact Amazing Facts to donate his collection of gold and silver coins. He says, "I figured there probably wasn't a better verse in the Bible that God could give me—and you can't out-give God!"

Nick wants others to get radical with God, to take Him at His Word, to trust completely on His promises and not in the fleeting securities of gold and silver.

Reflect: Have you ever tried to out-give God? What sacrifice has the Lord made for you? What are you willing to do for Him?

Dig Deeper: Deuteronomy 10:14; Psalm 50:10; Haggai 2:8

Pandita Ramabai

A Defender of Widows and Children, Part 1

"A father of the fatherless, a defender of widows, is God in His holy habitation" (Psalm 68:5).

She was born into poverty, suffering, and heartache. Her father was a Brahmin priest in India when Pandita Ramabai came into the world in 1858. He was a dedicated pilgrim and devoted to a life of penury, yet he believed in educating his wife, a practice strongly condemned by Hindus. When Pandita was eight years old, her mother began to teach her to read and write. She quickly advanced and, by the age of 12, had memorized 18,000 Sanskrit verses.

As her family traveled on pilgrimages around India, Pandita witnessed the extreme suffering of child widows (girls given into marriage at a young age and whose husbands die), women, and children in late nineteenth century India. During a severe famine, her parents looked to the gods for help. The sacred books they studied taught them that if they worshiped the gods in a specific way, gave alms to the Brahmans, and repeated certain prayers, the gods or goddesses would appear to them and give them whatever help they needed.

Sadly, during this famine, her father—aged, frail, and blind—died of starvation, followed by her mother and sister. Pandita and her brother continued to travel, searching for spiritual peace. They walked on foot from north to south, then from east to west, visiting sacred places, bathing in sacred rivers, but losing their faith in the gods.

In 1878, they went to Calcutta where Bengali Brahmins recognized her great knowledge and invited her to lecture. As she studied the great books of her religion, she began to see contradictory teachings. As her doubts about her beliefs grew, so did her growing awareness of the oppression of women in India. She was convicted that something must be done to relieve the predicament of women, widows, and children in her country.

When her brother died, Pandita married a Bengali gentleman. After two years of marriage, her husband died of cholera, leaving the 22-year-old mother alone with a baby in her arms. At this time, she decided to travel to England to study and "fit myself for my lifework." It was a journey that would change the direction of her life.

Reflect: Have you ever witnessed extreme poverty? How does God view the plight of poor widows or children without parents?

Dig Deeper: Exodus 22:22–24; Luke 7:11–15; 1 Timothy 5:3–6

Pandita Ramabai

A Defender of Widows and Children, Part 2

"The watches over the strangers; He relieves the fatherless and widow" (Psalm 146:9).

When Pandita Ramabai saw the mistreatment of widows and children in India, it moved her heart to want to see conditions change. After her husband died, she traveled to England to advance her education. One day, the Christians she stayed with invited her to visit a rescue home for downtrodden women. When she spoke with some of the women who had once been in the home receiving help and were now working to help others, she noted that "they had so completely changed and were so filled with the love of Christ and compassion for suffering humanity, that they had given their life for the sick and infirm."

Then she admitted, "Here for the first time in my life, I came to know that something should be done to reclaim the so-called fallen women; and the Christians, whom our country considered outcaste and cruel, were kind to these unfortunate women, degraded in the eyes of society."

When Pandita asked one of the Christian ladies what made these women want to help other women who were struggling so much, she read to her the story of the woman at the well in John 4. The Christian then spoke of the infinite love of Christ for sinners. Pandita had never heard anything like this in the religious books she had read. It began to dawn on her that Jesus Christ truly was a Divine Savior and that "no one but He could transform and uplift the downtrodden" women in this world.

In 1891, Pandita came to a clear understanding of the true nature of Christianity and was led, by the Holy Spirit, to grasp the deeper things of God. "One thing I knew by this time," she later wrote, "was that I needed Christ and not merely His religion. I was desperate. What was to be done? My thoughts could not and did not help me. I had at last come to an end of myself, and unconditionally surrendered myself to the Savior, and asked Him to be merciful to me, and to become my righteousness and redemption, and to take away all my sin."

God was about to use this humble and brilliant woman to become a valiant defender of widows and orphans in India.

Reflect: Can you recall a time in your life when a new religious truth began to dawn in your mind? When you take time each day to study the Bible, the Lord will speak to your heart in a powerful way.

Dig Deeper: John 16:13; Acts 2:37; Romans 8:14

Pandita Ramabai

A Defender of Widows and Children, Part 3

"[Jesus] said to them, 'Go into all the world and preach the gospel to every creature'" (Mark 16:15).

When Pandita Ramabai, a woman who grew up in an impoverished Brahmin family in India, gave her life to Christ, she began to practically work for the betterment of poor widows and orphaned children in her country. She published her most important book, The High-Caste Hindu Woman, which revealed some of the darkest aspects of the life of Hindu women. It exposed the practice of child brides, the challenges of child widows, and the oppression of women.

In 1889, Pandita founded the Mukti Mission for broken women and orphaned children. She created a safe haven to educate women and provide them with hope. At the risk of her own life, she went throughout India to rescue poor women who were being forced into servitude. At Mukti they fed, nurtured, and educated the women. Many went on to become influential women in India and around the world.

During a severe famine, just a few years after the mission opened, Ramabai traveled through villages with a caravan of bullock carts and rescued thousands of outcast children, child widows, orphans, and other impoverished women. She brought them to a shelter constructed at Mukti where they were fed and cared for. The mission is still active to this day and is now called the Pandita Ramabai Mukti Mission.

Pandita knew seven languages and, in the last decade of her life, worked to translate the Bible into her mother tongue—Marathi—from the original Hebrew and Greek. During the completion of her work, Pandita's daughter died. Then Pandita lost her hearing, but she pressed on with her translation.

The women of Mukti helped to set type for the Marathi Bible, and Pandita would carefully go over the proofs. When she became seriously ill, she prayed that God would give her ten more days to finish her editorial work. After completing her work, ten days later, she went to bed and died in her sleep on April 5, 1922.

Because of her Christian faith, Pandita's story was not widely known for years in India, but over time many came to value her valiant work for the oppressed women of their country. In 1989, the government of India issued a commemorative postage stamp to honor her.

Reflect: If you could bring more Bibles to any country in the world, which country would you pick? Did you know one of the signs of Christ's soon return is taking the gospel to all the world?

Dig Deeper: Psalm 19:4; Romans 10:18; Revelation 14:6

Dee

Coming Full Circle

"Remember those who ... have spoken the word of God to you, whose faith follow, considering the outcome of their conduct" (Hebrews 13:7).

Like so many children in our culture, Dee grew up in a home divided. His parents divorced when he was only four and, he recalls, "I was basically unchurched for most of my life."

As a teen, he faced the same self-esteem challenges that most do, but he says he didn't realize that he was living a "horrible life," as he calls it—using foul language and struggling with other problems. He explains, "I had a girlfriend in high school telling me that she had to break up with me because I wasn't a Christian. I thought, 'That's weird. I believe in God. Why would she say that?'"

In 2001, the terrorist attacks of 9/11 were a personal and spiritual wake-up call for Dee's father. A few years later, his dad found Amazing Facts on television and began watching the *Most Amazing Prophecies* presented by Pastor Doug Batchelor. Eventually, his father asked Dee to join him. Says Dee, "When I first watched the series, I thought, 'I've never heard that before about the state of the dead, the Sabbath, the Ten Commandments, or the rapture. But that's what the text really says!' The more I watched, the more helpful it became."

Dee felt called to find ways to share what he was learning. Amazing Facts websites and resources made witnessing easier. As a young believer, Dee grew rapidly in his walk with God, eventually attending an evangelism training school and being baptized.

After working in ministry for about five years, Dee discovered that Doug Batchelor was going to be the main speaker at a youth event where he would also be conducting a seminar. It was "kind of an amazing full-circle experience" for Dee to meet Pastor Doug—the first preacher to share with him the Bible's full message. "To be able to do ministry with him at that time meant the world to me," he shares, "and to be able to tell him my story and say, 'Thank you,' was a blessing."

Today, Dee continues to grow spiritually and share Christ passionately. He is involved in sharing the last-day message as a full-time traveling evangelist and through video ministry.

Reflect: Who were the key people in your life who introduced you to Jesus? Have you ever stopped to thank these people for the impact they made on you?

Dig Deeper: Jeremiah 3:15; Romans 10:14; 1 Timothy 5:17

The Apostle John

The Disciple Jesus Loved

"Now there was leaning on Jesus' bosom one of His disciples, whom Jesus loved" (John 13:23).

It's a scene out of a movie, perhaps: Someone is at work when a teacher walks by and says, "Follow me." The worker responds without questioning, leaving their job for a life that, on the surface, appears uncertain at best.

If such a thing happened to you at work today, would you drop everything to follow a new leader? What if you knew that it was God the Son who was passing by?

John was one of the two sons of Zebedee, a prominent fisherman of Galilee and, it is believed, a man of some affluence. After all, the Zebedee Fishing Co. had hired help, and Salome, Zebedee's wife and the mother of James and John, was able to spend time on the road supporting Jesus' ministry.

But before Salome went along with the disciples, John and James had to be converted. John was first to follow of these two to follow Jesus; we read in Mark 1:19, 20: "When He [Jesus] had gone a little farther from there, He saw James the son of Zebedee, and John his brother, who also were in the boat mending their nets. And immediately He called them, and they left their father Zebedee in the boat with the hired servants, and went after Him."

Jesus called. John and James responded and followed.

It's one of the shortest conversion narratives in the Bible. There's no report of John pondering the invitation, no deliberation, no debate. John didn't perform a Google search to check out Jesus' background, he didn't look in the morning newspaper, or scan the cable news channels. John knew, clearly by special revelation, that Jesus was no capricious charlatan, but was in fact the Christ, the Son of the living God.

Throughout John's life and ministry—which extended from the windswept plains of Palestine to the island of Patmos to the city of Ephesus—his devotion never wavered, and his influence grew. Jesus was especially fond of John, as noted in the references to his being the disciple "whom Jesus loved," not least because John wanted to remain close to Jesus. John wrote one of the gospel accounts and three epistles. His commission to write Revelation capped a lifetime of study and service; its words still guide believers today.

Jesus called, and John answered. May we each be as responsive to God when He calls us!

Reflect: Is there a call from God you need to answer today? The more we respond to Christ's continuing calls to follow Him, the closer we want to be to the Savior.

Dig Deeper: Matthew 4:21, 22; Mark 15:40; Revelation 1:9

Cornelius

No Partiality

> "In truth I perceive that God shows no partiality.
> But in every nation whoever fears Him and works
> righteousness is accepted by Him" (Acts 10:34, 35).

It was considered taboo during the time of Christ and the early church for Jews to eat with Gentiles (non-Jews). The Mishnah states, "The dwelling places of heathens are unclean." So when Peter received a vision from heaven to visit in the home of a Gentile centurion named Cornelius, it really stretched his faith.

Cornelius was a "devout man and one who feared God with all his household, who gave alms generously to the people, and prayed to God always" (Acts 10:2). Shouldn't that be enough to slip him past the gates of heaven? No, none of us are saved by our works no matter how genuine our efforts. This Roman needed more and God took action to provide it.

"About the ninth hour of the day he saw clearly in a vision an angel of God coming in and saying to him, 'Cornelius!' And when he observed him, he was afraid, and said, 'What is it, lord?'" (vv. 3, 4). The angel then told the centurion to send men for Peter in Joppa.

When Peter walked into Cornelius' home—which was an act of courage on his part—he discovered that the Roman centurion had gathered many to come and hear his words. He explained that while it was the custom of Jews to not associate with Gentiles, "God has shown me that I should not call any man common or unclean" (v. 28).

What followed was a gospel presentation by Peter on how Jesus came to bring salvation through His life, death, and resurrection, concluding with the words, "To Him all the prophets witness that, through His name, *whoever* believes in Him will receive remission of sins" (v. 43, emphasis added).

Then, in a tremendous flood of love from heaven, the message of Peter was affirmed by the outpouring of the Holy Spirit. The Jews with Peter "were astonished ... because the gift of the Holy Spirit had been poured out on the Gentiles also" (v. 45). It was a stunning point of change in the mission work of the early church.

God's work is always astonishing, the work of grace on the heart of anyone who believes, including a Roman centurion who wanted to receive salvation.

Reflect: Is there someone you know, or someone in your town, who could benefit from a personal visit to share the good news? God's love knows no walls of separation.

Dig Deeper: Hosea 14:9; John 17:20; Ephesians 2:12

Tanya and Carey

Promise of Truth, Part 1

"Jesus said to him, 'I am the way, the truth, and the life ...'" (John 14:6).

Tanya grew up in an atheist country located at the crossroads of Asia and Europe. In her early twenties, she and her husband, Carey, came to the United States. She is an engineer in petroleum and her husband is a contractor and they have two sons. Growing up atheist, Tanya gave little thought to God until a neighbor invited her to church in 2004.

"I accepted Christ," she says, "and attended mainstream churches. I was a children's Sunday School teacher, which I loved, but I started to feel empty in my heart. I began wondering, *Am I really a Christian?*"

For a year and a half, Tanya stopped going to church. "One night," she remembers, "I got on my knees and prayed, 'God, I need to know the truth. I feel like I'm going nowhere with You. Please show me the truth.' I cried out in desperation. I can still hear the clear thought in my head. God said, 'Tanya, there is a whole lot you don't know. Are you ready? If I reveal the truth to you, you will be accountable. Are you ready for that?' That scared me out of my socks! I asked, 'God, can I think about that and get back to you tomorrow?'"

Tanya couldn't sleep. After much wrestling, she recognized that she needed to know the truth and was ready to hear it. The next day, she returned to her knees. "God," she resumed, "I do want to know the truth, but I'm afraid. Can you show me under one condition? Can you help me to swallow the truth and be obedient, even though it is hard?" Again, Tanya heard a clear thought in her mind assuring her that if she was willing to follow the truth, God would help her. "I am willing," she prayed.

From that encounter, Tanya began a two-month journey of searching for God's truth, seemingly coming to one dead end after another. "I was so disappointed that I finally decided that I must have dreamed the whole thing up." She told herself that she didn't care anymore, but deep inside she was still searching. In desperation, Tanya decided to do a Google search, looking one more time for the truth.

She typed in the search box: "What Is Truth?"

Reflect: Have you ever boldly prayed that God would reveal truth to you? What happened? Sometimes the truth we need to face is about ourselves.

Dig Deeper: Psalm 119:160; John 16:13; Ephesians 6:14

Tanya and Carey

Promise of Truth, Part 2

"Pilate said to [Jesus], 'What is truth?'" (John 18:38).

When Tanya prayed for God to lead her to truth, she decided to do a Google search, and she didn't care who delivered the message. So she typed in the search box: What Is Truth? "I didn't know what else to type. Then a YouTube video popped up that was titled 'USA in Bible Prophecy' by Doug Batchelor. It was from the *Prophecy Code* series."

Tanya had never heard of Doug Batchelor, and she couldn't believe that the USA could actually be in Bible prophecy. So she listened out of curiosity. "Only a few minutes into the topic, I nearly fell off my chair." She paused his talk and ran to get her Bible. "I thought maybe this guy had a secret Bible or something. But he spoke straight from the Bible. Not just giving his own opinions. The Bible."

Just when Tanya wished she could hear more, the program ended by stating that the entire series was available on the Amazing Facts website. So she kept listening with her Bible by her side. "Twenty-four sermons!" she says. "I listened to the whole seminar in two weeks. Lunchtime, weekends, early in the morning. By the end of the seminar, I really couldn't sleep. I was both impressed and shaken," she remembers. So she went back to her knees and said, "God, now I am accountable. You said You would help me. Either I am following You all the way or I denounce You completely."

Tanya was in agony. She felt she had been lied to by the Christian churches she had attended. "I wrote to my pastors in the 'big' church, but they told me I wasn't a theologian and couldn't understand these things." They told her that she was in the minority with her new beliefs, but she shared Matthew 7:13, "Enter by the narrow gate; for wide is the gate and broad is the way that leads to destruction, and there are many who go in by it." "After that," she says, "I decided to accept the truth that I had found."

Tanya wrestled with how she would make the changes in her life. But God did give her strength, and she found a Sabbath-keeping church located just one mile from her house. She was welcomed and found that the people lived the truth they believed. Her struggle was over.

But then the next battle began. How would she tell her husband?

Reflect: Have you ever experienced a spiritual battle that stretched you to the limit? Remember, God promises to give you strength and wisdom.

Dig Deeper: Proverbs 12:22; John 8:32; 2 Timothy 2:15

Tanya and Carey

Promise of Truth, Part 3

**"For you will be His witness to all men of what
you have seen and heard" (Acts 22:15).**

After Tanya accepted new Bible truth, she wrestled with how she would tell her husband about the wonderful teachings she discovered from Amazing Facts. Carey had been brought up in a strong mainstream Christian church. How could she stand for the Sabbath and the other truths that didn't line up with her husband's beliefs? Indeed, her husband was upset.

After four or five months of struggle in the family, Carey lost his job. "You have to understand," Tanya says, "how unusual this was. Carey is in high demand and has even had to turn jobs down. But now, by divine power, not one single person called him."

During the three months of time that Carey was without work, he decided to go to the meetings that were happening at Tanya's new church. The pastor made a very personable impression on Carey. "My husband was the one who urged me to attend the meetings every night. Carey did not miss one meeting. When we went camping once, Carey made sure we rushed home in order to get to the meeting!"

After the series of meetings were over, Tanya asked Carey what he was going to do about the truth that he had learned. "For a while, Carey was in agony as he tried to decide whether to accept or reject it. I shared with him that I wanted to be baptized. And not just into anyone's name or title. I wanted to be baptized into the truth. I had heard the Bible's message to come out of Babylon. I knew that was for me." Carey shared Tanya's commitment, and soon afterward they were both baptized. Miraculously, the very next day, Carey was offered a job!

Tanya tells people who are searching for truth, "If you are hungry for truth but feel stuck, go to the Amazing Facts website and listen to the lesson on Mark of the Beast and 666. If you find logic in those, then you can trust to listen to the whole series. I send people to the Amazing Facts website all the time, and they have the same reaction I did."

In addition, Tanya advises new believers to share their faith. "Don't hold back on the truth! You don't know what you possess in your hands. People are desperately searching for truth. Spread it around!"

Reflect: Has the Holy Spirit ever prompted you to share truth with someone? Jesus doesn't want us to cover the light we have been given. Let it shine so the world can know Christ!

Dig Deeper: Isaiah 43:10; Matthew 5:15; Philippians 2:15

Matthew

From Publican to Proclaimer

> **"As Jesus passed on from there, He saw a man named Matthew sitting at the tax office. And He said to him, 'Follow Me.' So he arose and followed Him" (Matthew 9:9).**

Levi, a Jewish contractor who collected taxes (tariffs) for the Roman government occupying his country, was living large, as today's saying goes.

He wanted for very little, having the ability to demand revenue from all who passed his way in Capernaum (or, in Hebrew, *Kfar Nahum*, the "village of Nahum"). The city was an important way station between Jerusalem and Haifa and the rest of the Roman Empire. And Levi had the authority, enforced by Roman power, to demand taxes at will.

But unlike today's civil servants, who earn a salary while collecting taxes for the government, Levi was on the commission plan. The more he collected, the more he could take off the top as personal profit. If you think that was an incentive to get every last penny from those coming through town, well, you'd be right.

Something, however, must have been missing. Levi, whom we now know as Matthew, was not liked by the Jewish residents of Capernaum. They viewed him as a turncoat, a traitor serving Rome and harming his people. The money was good, but what was the moral injury to Levi's spirit? How did it feel to be hated by your neighbors, to be viewed with malice even when you went to pray?

Jesus, no stranger to Capernaum, didn't see Levi that way. He saw potential in this man, eyeing Matthew (a rough translation of "God's gift" in Hebrew) and simply said, "Follow Me."

As with John the beloved disciple, Matthew-Levi didn't hesitate. The money was good, but his heart was bankrupt. Jesus offered a way out, and the taxman grabbed it the way a drowning person would take a life preserver.

More than just receiving Christ's call, Matthew invited other social outcasts like himself to meet and hear the Master. The party was so noticeable that religious leaders scoffed at a Teacher who ate "with tax collectors and sinners" (Matthew 9:11).

Jesus' response was pitch-perfect: "Those who are well have no need of a physician, but those who are sick" (Matthew 9:12). Matthew-Levi was sick at heart, as were the other tax gatherers. But Christ was there to call them to a new way of life.

Reflect: No life is beyond the reach of Christ's love, compassion, and calling. Is there someone you know who needs to hear the good news? Are you praying for them *and* reaching out to them?

Dig Deeper: Psalm 41:4; Hosea 14:4; Luke 18:11–13

Eileen

Sheltered by God

"He shall cover you with His feathers, and under His wings you shall take refuge; His truth shall be your shield and buckler" (Psalm 91:4).

Eileen was in a desperate situation. As a 27-year-old mother of four children, she had suffered physical abuse from her husband for 12 years. After being placed in a battered women's shelter, her husband tracked her down. So she ran with her children out into a snowstorm to escape his violence.

She eventually ended up in another town where local law enforcement worked with residents to find her a safe refuge. "God place me in the home of Sabbath-keepers," she recalls. "They protected me and sheltered me." For the first time in her life she heard about the seventh-day Sabbath. "I felt so much joy in learning about this truth."

Unfortunately, her abusive husband once more found her, so she left this family and a church she had grown to love. Eileen spent much of her life trying to avoid the cruel husband of her children. But she never forgot what she learned from the Sabbath-keepers and passed this truth on to each of her kids.

Years later, two of her adult sons told Eileen about a Sabbath-keeping pastor named Doug Batchelor. After a bad experience in one church, she had stepped away from church, but decided to go online and watch a few sermons from this new preacher.

"I was blown away by his love for the truth," she admits, "and his ability to clearly explain the Bible." Eileen was especially touched by an *Everlasting Gospel* sermon titled "The Unpardonable Sin." "I wondered if I had committed this sin and at times even felt tortured by it." But the message eased her heart and gave her hope.

Eileen has been fighting cancer for the last couple of years. "My hope was growing dim until I began listening to Pastor Doug. I have courage again." In one of the darkest hours of her life she found safety in the arms of God.

Reflect: What do you do when your hope is growing dim? You can always find light in the Bible, a sure place of refuge during your darkest moments.

Dig Deeper: 2 Samuel 22:3; Psalm 91:1–16; Isaiah 4:6

Evan Roberts

"Send the Holy Spirit Now"

"But you shall receive power when the Holy Spirit has come upon you; and you shall be witnesses to Me in Jerusalem, and in all Judea and Samaria, and to the end of the earth" (Acts 1:8).

In the early 1900s, the nation of Wales, part of the United Kingdom, was a rough-and-tumble place. Coal mining was a major industry, and the miners were coarse, hard people accustomed to foul language, heavy drinking, and even rough treatment of the "pit ponies," the horses that ferried coal from the mine to the surface.

Evan Roberts, born in 1878, was the son of a miner, albeit a Christian one. When his father was injured in a mining accident, young Evan apprenticed with a blacksmith, but the lad's heart was in preaching the gospel.

There's no date on which Evan's conversion can be pinpointed. He'd been raised in a God-fearing home and embraced the Scriptures and Jesus at an early age.

However, as Evan grew into young adulthood, he found himself being more and more challenged to put his faith into action. Eventually, he became a student at the Grammar School in Newcastle Emlyn, Wales, prior to ministerial training at Trefecca College.

On September 29, 1903, Evan attended a prayer meeting at Blaenannerch Chapel. He prayed fervently for God to "bend" him, and Roberts felt God respond. A little more than a month later, Evan Roberts—having abandoned his ministerial studies to go back home and preach—began a series of meetings at Moriah Chapel in Loughor, Wales.

What happened next could only be credited to the moving of God. Revival broke out in Wales, so much so that Evan Roberts would sometimes go from one chapel to another on the same day, preaching while congregations prayed in repentance. Saloons—known as "public houses"—were emptied of their customers. Mothers and fathers took care of their children instead of indulging bad habits. Even the "pit ponies" sensed a change in how the miners, now working more industriously, treated these beasts of burden. At least 100,000 people came to a saving knowledge of God during that period in Wales.

The preaching effort took its toll on Roberts, and his health collapsed in 1906. As he convalesced, Roberts turned his attention to intercession, sometimes praying for as long as 18 hours a day. He eventually returned to Wales and passed to his rest in 1951.

Not only did the story of the Welsh Revival spread around the world, but Wales also sent missionaries into many overseas lands. Evan Roberts's decision to earnestly seek God had great impact on a small nation!

Reflect: The power of prayer is perhaps the greatest untapped resource on this planet. Are you praying for God's direction in your life, and for His touch in your community?

Dig Deeper: Psalm 22:27; Micah 3:8; Colossians 1:23

"I thank God ... when I call to remembrance the genuine faith that is in you, which dwelt first in your grandmother Lois and your mother Eunice, and I am persuaded is in you also" (2 Timothy 1:3, 5).

Jillian was raised in a Sabbath-keeping church in which she was actively involved in her youth. But when she became a nurse, her new career kept her so busy that she found herself straying from God. City life was fast and her work demanded more and more productivity. "The party scene offered temporary relief," she remembers.

During this time, her mother kept writing Jillian "irritating letters" about Jesus coming soon. "The Holy Spirit was using my mother's letters and prayers to prompt me to come back to church," she explains. (Today, Jillian tells Christian parents to never underestimate the power of prayer in helping guide children back to the Lord.)

Jim (Jillian's husband) speaks respectfully of his childhood family, but admits "we were plagued with a broken home." Yet God was able to shine through these obstacles and minister to Jim. One way was through his grandparents. "My maternal grandmother was a Sabbath-keeper," he recalls. "She was a loving lady who really influenced me." His grandfather was another light bearer. "He taught me how to pray."

As an adult Jim found himself drifting from God, but he continued to find evidences of the Lord's care for him. Many times during his 37 years of flying helicopters, God helped him bring his crew back safely "beyond my capabilities," he explains. The Holy Spirit was drawing him to God. He believed the Bible was God's Word and understood the importance of duty, "but I didn't really live for Jesus," he remembers. There were still things in Jim's life that needed changing.

In the early days of Jim and Jillian's relationship, Jillian worked as a traveling nurse. While she was away, Jim would drop by her cabin in the mountains to care for things. He recalls that because of poor reception the number of TV channels was limited to one. On this single channel he discovered Amazing Facts. "Doug Batchelor was always on," he recalls. "Some people believe in coincidences, but ..."

Reflect: Was there a grandmother, a grandfather, or another relative who positively influenced your life? Why don't you write to that person a letter of thanks for encouraging you in the right direction?

Dig Deeper: Proverbs 17:6; 1 Timothy 5:10; Titus 2:3

Jim and Jillian

Only One Channel, Part 2

"For You have delivered my soul from death. Have You not kept my feet from falling, that I may walk before God in the light of the living?" (Psalm 56:13).

Jim could only get one channel on his girlfriend's television. She lived in a remote place in the mountains. "Doug Batchelor was always on," he recalls. "Some people believe in coincidences, but I know it helped bring us into the church."

After they were married, Jim and Jillian continued to grow in their faith. Jillian shared her thoughts with Jim about the Sabbath. They rediscovered true peace in Christ and began attending a Sabbath-keeping church. But they hadn't made a public statement of their faith and longed for a chance. The couple wanted to be baptized.

When Dave Steward, an evangelist with Amazing Facts, came to their town and conducted a prophecy seminar, they were excited. At church they were encouraged to pray that the event would reach people in the neighborhood. Jim attended regularly but Jillian was unable to go since she was taking care of her mother who was ill.

Jim was blessed by the series and discovered he could purchase CDs of all the meetings and bring them home to his wife. She was thrilled. Jim explains how Dave presented the Word of God in the clearest possible way. "I wouldn't want Dave (a former lawyer) as an adversary in the courtroom!" he smiles. "God is using him in a great way."

One evening, Dave shared a quotation from Winston Churchill who at one time described the folly of his political nemesis by stating, "Occasionally he stumbled over the truth, but he always picked himself up and hurried on as if nothing had happened." Jim was impressed by how many people stumble across the Sabbath truth in the Bible, but usually get up and just go on their way.

Soon after the meetings were finished, Jim and Jillian took their stand for truth and were publicly baptized. Looking back, Jillian appreciates how strongly Amazing Facts held up the Bible as the primary source of truth. Jim was not only touched by Dave's preaching, but felt he became a brother in Christ by his personal interest in them.

If the Lord does not return in his lifetime, Jim explains how he wants to be remembered: "Unworthy encourager, redeemed by the blood of Calvary."

Reflect: Can you think of someone who really needs encouragement right now? Give them a call and listen to them, then offer to pray for them.

Dig Deeper: Psalm 55:22; 1 Thessalonians 5:11; Hebrews 10:23–25

Samuel

Dedicated to God, Part 1

"Then she made a vow and said, 'O of hosts, if You will indeed look on the affliction of Your maidservant and remember me, and not forget Your maidservant, but will give Your maidservant a male child, then I will give him to the all the days of his life'" (1 Samuel 1:11).

Dedicated to the Lord even before he was conceived, the prophet Samuel was, as a child, brought to the temple to serve for the rest of his life. He was a miracle for his barren mother, Hannah, who had prayed desperately to God for him. True to her word, Hannah, as soon as she was able, gave Samuel to be trained in the priesthood under the tutelage of Eli, the high priest.

He was an obedient boy, hardworking and respectful. He did his duties willingly, even when those around him did not. In the temple he stood in stark contrast to Eli's own sons, Hophni and Phinehas, who were themselves priests. Hophni and Phinehas abused their office for their own selfish gains; they were corrupt, licentious, and blasphemous (1 Samuel 2:12–16, 22). "Therefore the sin of the young men was very great before the " (v. 17).

It must have been difficult for Hannah and Elkanah, her husband, to let another raise their son. The behavior of Eli's sons was well-known throughout the land; it would not have been unreasonable for Samuel's parents to fear that their own son could likely suffer from the same parenting. Samuel was the youngest. It would have been natural for him to look up to the sons of the high priest, to adopt their ways and character.

And Hannah and Elkanah did not see Samuel but once a year at "the yearly sacrifice" (v. 19). While Hannah took the care to visit her firstborn, no doubt imparting to him all the guidance she could, what was one day compared to years of daily exposure to such wickedness? Would it not eventually take its toll on so young and impressionable a mind?

But there was something different about Samuel. He wanted to know the Lord, to love the Lord; and as the years passed, he was "in favor both with the and men" (v. 26). Samuel, in spite of all that was around him, dedicated himself to serving God.

Reflect: Do you find yourself in places where you are tempted to forsake God and His ways? Think of Samuel, Daniel, or Joseph and how they remained faithful to God in the midst of evil.

Dig Deeper: Joshua 23:6–8; Ephesians 6:11–13; Hebrews 10:23

Samuel

Dedicated to God, Part 2

**"I am the good shepherd; and I know My sheep,
and am known by My own" (John 10:14).**

As a child in the temple, Samuel learned about God and served Him as best as he knew how. But Samuel had yet to truly know God on an intimate, personal level.

Then, one night, that all changed. Lying in his bed, Samuel suddenly heard a Voice calling his name. Assuming that it was Eli, he hurried straightaway to the high priest's side.

"Here I am," he said.

But it was not Eli who had called him. So Samuel returned to his room.

Three times, he heard the Call and three times diligently rose from his bed. But this third time, "Eli perceived that the had called the boy" (1 Samuel 3:8) and instructed Samuel in how to respond.

This time, when Samuel returned to his bed, God actually appeared before the child and, as before, called him by name, "Samuel, Samuel" (v. 10). Obedient as ever, Samuel answered, forgetting, in his awe, to address God by His own name.

The Lord then proceeded to give Samuel his first prophecy, disclosing what was to happen to Eli and his family (vv. 11–14). It was a somber sentence; and when morning came, Samuel was reluctant to disclose what he knew to his mentor. But after a firm prompting from Eli, Samuel obeyed, repeating all he had been told.

The experience was the first of many the famed prophet was to have in his lifetime of faithfully delivering God's messages to His people. While Eli had failed his own sons in many ways, the high priest nevertheless succeeded in instructing Samuel in the way of the Lord, in obeying Him instead of man, in trusting in His Word above all else.

It was on that night that Samuel met God for the first time (v. 7) and in a very literal way was called into service by Him. It was then that he truly began to know God.

As his mother had promised, until his death Samuel served God: "So Samuel grew, and the was with him and let none of his words fall to the ground" (v. 19).

Reflect: Do you know God on an intimate level? Do you regard Him as your personal Savior? God knows each of us by name. He desires to have a one-on-one relationship with you!

Dig Deeper: Jeremiah 31:33, 34; John 17:3; 1 John 2:3, 4

Gina

A Prodigal Mother, Part 1

"O God, You are my God; early will I seek You; my soul thirsts for You; my flesh longs for You in a dry and thirsty land where there is no water" (Psalm 63:1).

Suicidal, promiscuous, criminal. That was Gina as a teenager.

Abused as a child and pregnant as a teen, she became a thief, a user, and deeply depressed. Before she was 20, she had lost her baby in a premature birth, had been to jail, and had tried to end her life. At 25, she had had three children and two marriages.

"It was either sink or swim," she states. So she swam.

Raising her children and married to a man for security rather than love, Gina began to desire to return to church. Her mother had occasionally taken her and her siblings to services when they were very young. Now Gina felt the need to go back to church with her children. However, she was afraid that the members would treat her poorly because of her past.

Yet her desire kept growing. Finally, she went back to church—several, actually. She visited different churches and even went to their different Bible studies. "I remember at one of the first Bible studies I attended, I heard the ladies talking about this man Jesus, our Savior, and all the wonderful things He did," she recalls. "I began to weep. I was crying because it was the first time ever that I realized that Jesus was a real man [who] walked this earth."

She continued going to the different studies and then to various church programs, including a weekly youth program where she could bring her children. Slowly, she was learning about Jesus, but there was something about this Man that she still did not understand. "I always felt empty, and my hungering and thirsting for more only grew," she describes. She wanted to learn more—but how?

One evening at the weekly youth program, a woman introduced herself to Gina. She was a mother too and had been bringing her children. Over the next few weeks, the two became friends. One night, Gina's new friend invited her to study the Bible with her and her husband. But Gina was hesitant. Would this study be like all the others, leaving her wanting more? But week after week, her friend renewed the offer and, finally, Gina accepted.

Reflect: Have you ever been extremely thirsty? The Bible says, "Ho! Everyone who thirsts, come to the waters ..." (Isaiah 55:1). There is only One who can quench your deepest thirst.

Dig Deeper: Psalm 143:6; Proverbs 25:21; Isaiah 44:3

Gina

A Prodigal Mother, Part 2

**"For I know the thoughts that I think toward you, says
the , thoughts of peace and not of evil, to give
you a future and a hope" (Jeremiah 29:11).**

Gina's husband was adamantly against her taking Bible studies. He did not want anything to do with them, and he did not want Bible studies happening in his home. So Gina went to her new friend's house instead. That first night at Bible study, Gina's friend and her friend's husband brought out a pack of studies Gina had never seen before. They were called *Amazing Facts Bible Study Guides*. They would change her life!

"I was in awe of what I was learning for the first time," Gina recalls. They studied everything—the Sabbath, the afterlife, and the sanctuary. They studied the Bible as Gina never had before, and in those precious pages she now understood the character of Jesus. This was the meat for which she had been hungering, a complete picture of God and what He was doing in her life at that very moment.

Suddenly, however, she became angry—angry at all of those years spent not hearing, not learning the Bible's truths. Her new friends continued to counsel her. They took her back to the Bible and together, they studied forgiveness. "The couple I studied with helped me to work through the anger," she says. Her character was slowly being changed.

Gina's husband was furious as she began sharing her newfound knowledge with her three children and putting into practice what she had been studying. When Gina began keeping the Sabbath, their home became a battlefield. After several years of this hardship, her husband divorced her. Many family and friends also cut off contact with her. But through it all, Gina remained true to the teachings of the Bible. "I have never had as much joy and peace as I have had since discovering the truths of God's Word," she proclaims.

Today, Gina is an active member of a Sabbath-keeping church, involved in health and prison ministry. She volunteers at a local juvenile detention center, a place where she spent some time as a teenager, sharing her testimony to the troubled girls within its walls. "I am healthier and stronger than ever before," she states. "For the first time in my life as a single woman, I have hope for my future."

Reflect: Have you ever had to make a difficult choice—a right choice—that was not accepted well by others? Jesus promises He "will never leave you nor forsake you" (Hebrews 13:5).

Dig Deeper: Job 14:7; Psalm 31:24; Proverbs 13:12

Richard Baxter

A Reformed Pastor

**"He who says he abides in Him ought himself also
to walk just as He walked" (1 John 2:6).**

Many know the names of Martin Luther, John Calvin, William Tyndale as some of the most influential reformers of the Protestant Reformation. But perhaps not as acclaimed is Richard Baxter, an Englishman born in 1615, at the latter end of the Reformation.

Given to idleness and thievery and addicted to gambling, Baxter became a changed young man at the age of 15, when he read Edmund Bunny's version of Robert Parson's *A Book of Christian Exercise*. For the first time, he understood what it truly meant to be a sinner in need of a Savior. He purposed to renounce his old self and start devoting himself to God and His Word.

In 1638, he was ordained in the Church of England. Then began a lifelong career of faith, controversy, and persecution. Baxter soon became a Nonconformist, touting the Word of God over that of man.

In 1641, he began a nearly 20-year residence as minister of the church at Kidderminster. A powerful preacher, he put his sermons on reform into daily practice, cultivating personal, door-to-door ministry and diligently encouraging his fellow clergyman not to neglect their own souls.

An avid writer, he penned not only hymns and poems but also hundreds of theological resources, including his most famous works, *The Reformed Pastor* and the devotional *The Saints' Everlasting Rest*.

A bold advocate for religious freedom, in his later years he was persecuted for his beliefs and even imprisoned at nearly 70 years old. But he continued to soldier on, a more prolific writer near the end of his life than in his younger years.

In 1691, he went quietly to his grave, though his literary contributions to this day remain loud and clear. He was a man who fervently knew the Bible to be true and acted upon that knowledge. What he preached, he believed to the very depths of his soul. His conversion was uneventful, to say the least—simply from reading a book—but his heart was pricked and bowed to true repentance. From those quiet moments emerged a life full of ardent and unceasing devotion to God.

Reflect: Are you awaiting some dramatic miracle from God to transform your life? The miracle of God is a daily transforming of a heart surrendered to Him!

Dig Deeper: 1 Kings 19:11, 12; 2 Timothy 2:8–13; James 1:12

Keith

Unlocked Doors, Part 1

"Now do not be stiff-necked, as your fathers were, but yield yourselves to the ; and enter His sanctuary, which He has sanctified forever, and serve the your God" (2 Chronicles 30:8).

Heavy steel doors closed and locked Keith in prison. With three strikes against him, he sat alone in his small cell and pondered his life. "I'm in a seriously bad situation. I've tried so many times to do the right thing but keep failing." Keith was trapped, not just inside four concrete walls behind a locked door, but in his own thoughts from serving the devil for so many years. In desperation he cried to the Lord for help.

God heard Keith's cry and spoke to his heart about another door. "Why don't you enter My sanctuary?" As he tried to understand what this meant, a prison guard opened his cell door and asked Keith a simple question that changed the course of his life. "Would you like a television?"

Keith grew up in a "normal"—translate that "dysfunctional"—home. His mother left him and his father for a life of partying and drugs. His dad taught him to work hard and be self-sufficient. He also instilled in Keith deep prejudices that later led to violence toward others. In high school Keith joined a group of extreme racist "Skinheads," getting involved in drugs and violence. Over the next 20 years he spiraled downward through the doorways of juvenile halls, jails, detention centers, and eventually prison.

"I went from being a happy kid with some pains in my life to being like the demoniac in Mark 5, alone and in bondage. I was in shackles from head to toe and not fit for society. Just as Jesus walked across the waters and rescued the demoniac, Christ came and set me free."

Keith admits he was tied up in his own anger and hatred. He didn't know anything about God and lived by his pagan beliefs. "I had no interest in Christianity." But sitting behind a locked prison door began to open a door in his thinking.

"Would you like a television?" the guard asked.

"Yes!" he replied.

After plugging it in, he turned on the TV and the first thing he saw was a prison advertisement for chapel services.

Reflect: Have you ever been in a jail or prison cell? What does it feel like to have big, steel doors close behind you? Remember, Jesus is powerful enough to open up any door.

Dig Deeper: Psalm 28:2; Ezekiel 44:16; Acts 16:26

Keith

Unlocked Doors, Part 2

"Stand fast therefore in the liberty by which Christ has made us free, and do not be entangled again with a yoke of bondage" (Galatians 5:1).

After a prison guard gave Keith a TV, he plugged it in, turned it on and the first thing he saw was a prison advertisement for chapel services. Keith attended and learned of other services, including one held by Sabbath-keeping Christians.

One day, while trying to get the digital channels on his television set to work properly, he discovered only four channels worked—while others in his cellblock received 8 to 15 channels. Not only that, all four channels broadcast only one Christian station. Keith soon discovered that one of his favorite programs to watch was by Pastor Doug Batchelor. "I could hardly wait each Sabbath morning for the 7:00 a.m. broadcast. Pastor Doug taught with such clarity, conviction, and love. After six months, I knew where to find truth."

Keith dreamed of one day getting out of jail and walking through the doors of the sanctuary of Pastor Doug's church, but he had to parole in the county of his last arrest, which would prevent him from attending that church. After writing to the church, he wrote up a transfer request to parole headquarters and his prison counselor. Nothing happened for eight months.

One day he was called into the parole office. The lady in charge said, "I don't understand what has happened. I've never seen anything like this in all of my years working here. Your file indicates where you were arrested, but your paperwork says you are from Sacramento. You must know somebody!" Keith's transfer request was accepted.

During his time in prison, a volunteer brought Keith the *Amazing Facts Bible Study Guides* which he completed. "They were awesome studies. Other inmates were also doing the studies." Finishing the lessons prepared him for baptism.

The first Sabbath after his release, Keith walked through the doors of the church and into the sanctuary. God's first call to Keith's heart to enter His sanctuary became a reality. Keith is now a baptized member of the church. He is working to complete a college degree in order to enter full-time ministry.

Keith has walked through many doors in life, but when he entered God's sanctuary that first Sabbath, he knew he had finally arrived home.

Reflect: Is there a door that seems to be shut tight in your life? Pray and ask God, if it is His will, to open that door. There might be a different door the Lord wants you to walk through.

Dig Deeper: Psalm 146:7; Isaiah 61:1; Acts 5:19, 20

Timothy

Paul's Protégé, Part 1

"To Timothy, a beloved son: ... I remember you in my prayers night and day, greatly desiring to see you, being mindful of your tears, that I may be filled with joy, when I call to remembrance the genuine faith that is in you" (2 Timothy 1:2–5).

If you saw an evangelist being stoned for preaching the gospel, would you be eager to train under him? Timothy was. He was a young man whose mother was Jewish but whose father was Greek. Nevertheless, he had been brought up to believe in the true God (2 Timothy 1:5; 3:15).

Timothy most likely met Paul during the apostle's first missionary journey, when Paul and Barnabas stopped in Lystra, a city in Lycaonia, a region in modern-day Turkey (Acts 14:6, 7). At that time, a group of Jews who had previously opposed Paul and Barnabas' preaching followed and discovered the two Christians. The Jews succeeded in inciting a mob, who proceeded to stone Paul and leave him for dead (v. 19).

Outside the city, Paul lay bruised and beaten. But he was not alone. Those to whom he had preached in Lystra, those who had come to believe in the gospel, surrounded him. Despairing, disconsolate, perhaps even praying, these faithful disciples peered down at the still, bloodied body of Paul. Suddenly, it moved! He was alive. By a miracle from God, Paul was alive (v. 20).

What an impression that scene must have made on the mind of young Timothy. The next day, Paul and Barnabas traveled onward, but the fire within Timothy's heart did not die out.

Several years later, when Paul returned to Lycaonia on his second missionary journey, the young disciple had grown in his faith and was even "well-spoken of by the brethren" (16:2). On this recommendation, Paul decided for Timothy to accompany him on his travels.

But before they departed, Timothy consented to be circumcised (v. 3). As a Jew on his mother's side, he knew that any Jews aware of his heritage would be more inclined to respect his witness if he respected their customs. Committed to his calling, he desired to reach as many souls as possible for God's kingdom and to take every opportunity for their salvation.

Reflect: Timothy made a major decision to become a missionary. What must you sacrifice in order to fully commit your life to Christ and share His gospel? "The sacrifices of God are a broken spirit, a broken and a contrite heart" (Psalm 51:17).

Dig Deeper: Deuteronomy 30:6; Isaiah 56:6–8; Romans 12:1, 2

Timothy

Paul's Protégé, Part 2

"But you be watchful in all things, endure afflictions, do the work of an evangelist, fulfill your ministry" (2 Timothy 4:5).

With their small size and preference for solitude, honey badgers are surprisingly known as one of the world's most fearless animals—defending themselves against hyenas, pythons, and even whole prides of lions! Likewise, Timothy may not have looked like much, but he proved to be an enduring force for God.

From Paul's two epistles to Timothy in the New Testament, many surmise that Timothy was a mild-mannered, even timid man. Paul spends some of one letter encouraging the younger disciple to boldness and bravery: "For God has not given us a spirit of fear, but of power and of love and of a sound mind" (2 Timothy 1:7). In the other letter, he seeks to strengthen what some may have seen as a weakness: "Let no one despise your youth, but be an example to the believers in word, in conduct, in love, in spirit, in faith, in purity" (1 Timothy 4:12).

What must it have been like for such a gentle soul in the days of hardship that followed the apostle to the Gentiles and his companions?

During his travels with Paul, Timothy visited several early churches as a messenger for the apostle, bringing comfort and encouragement by his preaching of the doctrine (1 Corinthians 4:17; Philippians 2:19–23; 1 Thessalonians 3:2; 1 Timothy 1:3). When Paul was imprisoned in Rome, Timothy became a source of comfort to the apostle himself. During this time Paul wrote several letters—to the Philippians, to the Colossians, to Philemon—addressed from himself and from Timothy.

Paul's second epistle to Timothy is the apostle's last known epistle, written shortly before his death. In it he gives earnest advice to the younger disciple: "Endure hardship as a good soldier of Jesus Christ" (2 Timothy 2:3); "continue in the things which you have learned and been assured of" (3:14), "rightly dividing the word of truth" (2:15); "[p]reach the word" (4:2). Spread the gospel; study the Scriptures; remain faithful to God.

Did Timothy follow Paul's guidance after the death of his beloved mentor? *Foxe's Book of Martyrs* tells us that indeed Timothy became the bishop of Ephesus and held that position during the great persecution of the early Christian church until his martyrdom in AD 97. His time under Paul prepared him to stand firm in his faith to the end.

Reflect: Have you ever been under fire for your faith?
Is being meek the same as being weak?

Dig Deeper: Isaiah 53:7; Matthew 10:18–22; Romans 1:16

Sheila

Deeper Faith, Part 1

"May the Lord of peace Himself give you peace always in every way. The Lord be with you all" (2 Thessalonians 3:16).

She thought about ending her life. Broken and abandoned, Sheila felt that she couldn't go on. All hope had vanished. When financial struggles and pornography ripped her marriage to shreds, and her husband left her, she felt there was no reason to live. But God had not left Sheila. With only a flicker of faith left, she helplessly clung to Bible truths she had learned years before through Amazing Facts.

As a young adult, Sheila's heart had at one time felt empty. Even though she had grown up in a faith community, even though she believed she had been "saved," and even though she had married her high school sweetheart, she never felt like she had a personal relationship with God.

All of that changed when she attended an Amazing Facts seminar. Her husband convinced her to attend the series. Sheila was warmly introduced to Jesus as her personal Savior and friend. She didn't hesitate to make a full surrender to Christ and she was gratefully baptized. But, she admits, "At that time I didn't know the total life change that would take place in my life."

At first things appeared to be fine in their family, but beneath the surface things were not going well at all. Consumed with day to day efforts to make ends meet, their marriage was about to shatter into a million pieces. Financial problems kept stacking up and then one day Sheila discovered her husband's addiction. When he walked away from the marriage, her world collapsed.

Sheila was devastated. She valiantly attempted, as a young single mother, to support her two young boys. But the pain was so deep that she felt it would be better to just go to sleep and never awaken.

Something deep inside her heart kept her moving forward, however, something she had first discovered through Amazing Facts. Sheila turned to the Amazing Facts website for hope. There she found truth-filled articles that pointed her to Christ. She listened to inspiring sermons that grew her faith and strengthened her trust in God.

Reflect: Have you ever felt abandoned by God? The Bible says, "The is near to those who have a broken heart ..." (Psalm 34:18). Pray and believe He is with you.

Dig Deeper: Matthew 19:26; Ephesians 3:20, 21; James 1:12

Deeper Faith, Part 2

"My brethren, count it all joy when you fall into various trials, knowing that the testing of your faith produces patience" (James 1:2, 3).

After her marriage shattered, Sheila was inspired to practice what she was learning from Amazing Facts. She was determined to cling to the Lord through all her difficulties. One day, she faced a new test. "I was working to make ends meet and realized I didn't have enough gas to get home from work," she recalls. "I didn't know what to do."

She prayerfully decided to trust God and drove to work, even though her gas tank registered nearly empty. That very day, friends came to her work with boxes of food. Tears freely fell down her cheeks as they kindly told her, "This is for your family." In one box was a card with just enough money to fill her gas tank. Sheila praised God for faithfully fulfilling His promises to her.

Eventually Sheila met a godly Sabbath-keeper and remarried. She and her new husband attended an Amazing Facts revival series with her two boys. The meetings revitalized her faith in God and even inspired her nine-year-old son to commit his life to Christ through baptism.

During this time, trials tested their faith. Sheila and her husband ran a successful tree business and always set aside money to pay taxes. But one year, they fell short several thousand dollars. Sheila explains, "We had six weeks to come up with this money. From a human perspective, this looked impossible. We prayed about it, knowing that God has always supplied all of our needs."

With time running out and rain in the forecast—which meant no work—the situation looked hopeless. But Sheila had been in hopeless situations before and found strength from the truths she learned through Amazing Facts.

During the next few days, the temperature plunged and the rain turned into an ice storm. Tree limbs began breaking all over the city and, within hours, people began calling their company to come and clear branches and fallen trees from driveways and yards. They were soon booked for months. In just three weeks they had all the funds to pay their taxes.

Sheila confidently points to Amazing Facts as a heaven-sent ministry that bolstered her faith through dark days.

Reflect: Are you going through a trial right now? Is your faith being tested? Persevere! God is faithful and will see you through this difficulty.

Dig Deeper: John 16:33; James 1:12; 1 Peter 5:10

Chuck Colson

From Dirty Tricks to Serving Christ

"I was in prison and you came to Me" (Matthew 25:36).

By the time he was 39 years of age, Charles Wendell Colson had accomplished something few of his peers could even imagine: he was a special counsel to the President of the United States, Richard M. Nixon.

Within five years, however, Colson—who once boasted he'd "run over his grandmother" to secure a Nixon election victory—would be a different man in a much different place. Instead of The White House, Colson was in a federal prison, convicted of "disseminating derogatory information to the press" about Daniel Ellsberg, an analyst who leaked secret government papers about the Vietnam War to the media.

It was what happened on the night of August 12, 1973, that would change Colson's life forever. Sitting with Tom Phillips, then the head of Raytheon Corp., Colson had to face the question of Jesus' claims on his life. Colson, a former U.S. Marine captain and right-hand aide to the President, broke down and accepted Christ as Savior.

That change allowed Colson to plead guilty to the charge in the Ellsberg case. He was sentenced to a year in jail, and served seven months. But those 210 days changed him. On release, Colson founded Prison Fellowship, determined to bring inspiration and reform to inmates, and comfort to their families. His goal was not only to introduce prisoners to Christ, but to relieve the bitterness inmates had, an attitude that often led released convicts back into the system.

When Colson died in 2012, many praised his conversion. "America is the land of second chances—and few men have made more of theirs than Chuck Colson did. For in addition to loving and serving his country, the former Marine captain and 'president's hatchet man' came to love and serve a God of second chances," Heritage Foundation president Edwin J. Feulner said.

Jonathan Aitken, a Colson biographer, put it this way: "Look at the incredible good he has done. He completely changed the face of faith-based caring for prisoners and offenders, not just in America but across the world."

Chuck Colson's reliance on Christ transformed his life. In turn, Colson remade the lives of countless prisoners, while also touching the culture through radio broadcasts, books, and articles. His legacy lives on today, with Prison Fellowship reaching inmates in 110 nations around the world.

Reflect: A conversion can have a powerful effect on a person's life. What have you been doing with the gift of salvation God has given you?

Dig Deeper: Ezekiel 18:7; Hebrews 13:3; James 1:27

Mikael

The Power of Christ, Part 1

"Call to Me, and I will answer you, and show you great and mighty things, which you do not know" (Jeremiah 33:3).

Mikael's long, dark spiral began with sudden devastation when he was only 11 years old. Literally overnight, his loving, joyful childhood in South Africa changed. His father was brutally attacked and nearly killed—and nothing would ever be the same again.

Before the attack, his dad would play with him and attend his soccer games. Now, Mikael struggled to make sense of the severe brain damage that left his father physically and mentally challenged, with the emotions of a child.

"Having no role model or father figure, I started to go off the tracks when I was a teenager. Although I grew up happy, after my dad's accident, my happiness declined over the years. I lost my joy. My life suddenly plummeted into a lifestyle of drugs and partying every weekend."

For sixteen years, Mikael lived in addiction—to drugs, online gaming, and destructive relationships. Sometimes, out of guilt, he'd return to the Charismatic church of his childhood or visit the Catholic church of his girlfriend. But he often wondered if there really was a God. With a thirst for knowledge, he felt particularly drawn to "experts" who claimed to expose hidden stories and secrets. One documentary particularly impacted him because it dismissed Christianity as a fraud and hoax.

Then, Mikael found something different.

"In 2015, I went to rehab. Once my mind was sober and free from drugs, I could hear the gentle knocking of Jesus on my heart. I asked God to show me the truth and, boy, did He show me the truth!"

While researching for a deeper understanding about Daniel and Revelation and the antichrist, Mikael found Amazing Facts TV. "I downloaded *Foundations of Faith* and *The Prophecy Code* and started watching. I love the way Pastor Doug presents truth—he has this gentle way of presenting. I was in a Christian church for most of my life, yet I'd never heard these things that he was preaching. Over a short few weeks, I started believing. I was convinced the message I heard was the truth."

Reflect: When was the last time you heard the voice of God speaking to your heart? Jesus said, "When He, the Spirit of truth, has come, he will guide you into all the truth" (John 16:13).

Dig Deeper: Isaiah 30:21; John 10:27; Romans 10:17

Mikael

The Power of Christ, Part 2

"For I am not ashamed of the gospel of Christ, for it is the power of God to salvation for everyone who believes" (Romans 1:16).

When Mikael went into rehab to recover from drug abuse, he discovered prophetic truth on Amazing Facts TV. "I also learned foundational truths about the Sabbath, death, hell, and the health message." The day Mikael arrived back home for a family dinner and shared that he no longer ate pork, his startled family asked him if he was becoming Jewish. But several months after adopting a healthy lifestyle, Mikael was thrilled to report that the high cholesterol that had plagued him for years was now normal, and the rest of his health had greatly improved.

Mikael felt like a sponge for Bible truth. He particularly enjoyed listening to the Bible question-and-answer periods with Pastor Doug and his wife, Karen. And when he heard the story of *The Richest Caveman*, Mikael identified with Pastor Doug's testimony, especially what he said about drugs. "Pastor Doug mentions how you cannot be happy without self-control. That's what I was lacking in my life."

But even more than his newfound health or his understanding of prophecy, Mikael considers the Sabbath truth to be his most valuable lesson and gift. "What has helped me to connect with God is the truth about the Sabbath. Out of everything I have learned, this is the stand-out fundamental truth that has energized me. My walk with God has never been so close."

Mikael found a Sabbath-keeping church to begin attending and was welcomed with open arms. He also delights to bring his three precious children to church, teaching them the beauty of God's endless love. "I always did what I wanted to do on weekends, but now my Savior and I have a special 24 hours to connect, relate, and love each other," he says.

"It's such a blessing to feel the power of Christ working in your life to change things that you never believed could change—and not by our strength but through His strength," he says.

Soon, Mikael was baptized. "God showed me light and I stepped out in faith and became obedient. My walk with God is more real and closer than it has ever been."

Reflect: If you could have unlimited power to change just one thing in your life, what would it be? Have you considered asking the all-powerful God of the universe to change that one thing for you?

Dig Deeper: 2 Samuel 22:33; 2 Chronicles 20:6; Job 26:7–14

Mary Magdalene

At Jesus' Feet, Part 1

"But one thing is needed, and Mary has chosen that good part, which will not be taken away from her" (Luke 10:42).

Across the United States is an increasing demand for exorcists. While many scoff at demon possession, Scripture tells us that it is indeed very real.

The Bible speaks of several women who were involved in the ministry of Jesus, but none so prominent as Mary Magdalene. We know little of Mary before she met Jesus, but we can presume that her life was most likely one of deep suffering. Mark 16:9 tells us that Jesus "cast seven demons" out of her. In the Bible seven is the number that represents completion. What must it have been like to have been totally, perfectly in the throes of the prince of darkness?

While we have no account of how the seven demons tortured Mary, Scripture does give us other accounts of demon-possessed people. We are told several times of a young boy whose demon repeatedly tried to kill him, "for he often [fell] into the fire and often into the water" (Matthew 17:15) in fits of epilepsy (Mark 9:18). In the case of the demoniac of the Gadarenes, he was known as a terror who ranged among graves, "crying out and cutting himself with stones" (5:5). Self-mutilating, violently disturbed, sickeningly tormented—these were the kinds of characteristics associated with demon-possessed people.

But Jesus was able to heal them. When He had exorcised their demons, these people became as new. In Luke's account of the demoniac of the Gadarenes, it states that after the Messiah had called the demons out of him, the man was "sitting at the feet of Jesus" (Luke 8:35). He was calm, peaceful, and he wanted to be with Jesus.

Similarly, Luke tells us that after being healed, Mary "also sat at Jesus' feet and heard His word" (10:39). This was her response to His saving her from her demons. She loved and revered Him more than anything or anyone else in her life. She became His faithful disciple.

Here, she is depicted in contrast to her sister, Martha, who was irritated at Mary for not helping to host their guests. But Mary had realized what was important in life. She had firmly made the decision to seek Jesus first and the prize of a life lived eternally with Him.

Reflect: Have you been wrestling with your own demons? Have you tried to fight them off by yourself? Remember that Jesus is the answer, the cure, and the way everlasting.

Dig Deeper: Psalm 27:4; James 2:19, 20; 1 John 4:4

Mary Magdalene

At Jesus' Feet, Part 2

"Assuredly, I say to you, wherever this gospel is preached in the whole world, what this woman has done will also be told as a memorial to her" (Matthew 26:13).

Her brother was dead.

Mary and her family were Jesus' intimate friends while He walked this earth. But Mary's brother, Lazarus, had fallen sick and died. Mary was distraught. But four days later, Jesus brought her brother back to life. It was a miracle that set into motion several major events during the Savior's last days.

Just a week before Passover, Jesus visited his friends in Bethany once more. One evening, there was prepared a supper for Him and His disciples at the house of Simon, a Pharisee whom Jesus had cured of leprosy (Mark 14:3; Luke 7:36). Mary had bought an alabaster box, within which was a very expensive, fragrant oil that she intended for the Savior. As the men sat, Mary, weeping in gratitude, broke the box and poured the oil over Jesus' head and feet, wiping them with her own hair. It was an act of extreme love and reverence, one reserved for a future king.

But as the pungent scent filled the room, Judas, one of Jesus' disciples, objected, pretending offense that the money used to buy the gift was not given to the poor instead (John 12:5, 6). The other disciples began to agree; as for Simon, Jesus saw only disdain in his heart (Luke 7:39). Mary must have been mortified. She had meant to honor her Lord, but now her gift was seen as extravagant impropriety.

But before she could flee, Jesus turned to her. He marked her actions as ones that poured out from a heart of overwhelming gratitude: "Her sins, which are many, are forgiven, for she loved much" (v. 47).

What Mary had done was even more significant than she realized, for she had anointed the Savior for His burial (Mark 14:8). This deed bound her heart to Him, strengthening her devotion and faith for the days to come. And Jesus wanted us to remember it (v. 9). The love that compelled Mary to this act is the appropriate response to the love our Savior bears for us sinners, to His act of dying on the cross that we might live in Him.

Reflect: If you had been at the table with Jesus, would you have viewed Mary's act as strange or even inappropriate? What is your response to the Savior when you think on what He has done for you?

Dig Deeper: Romans 5:6–11; Ephesians 5:1, 2; 1 John 4:16–21

Mary Magdalene

At Jesus' Feet, Part 3

**"Go into all the world and preach the gospel
to every creature" (Mark 16:15).**

The day that Jesus was crucified, Mary stood and watched helplessly with several other devoted women, including Jesus' own mother (John 19:25). There were among His disciples one who had betrayed Him, another who had denied Him, and others who had deserted Him. But Mary had followed the Savior in His life, and she now followed Him to the site of His death.

After the Sabbath passed, Mary Magdalene and several other women visited His sepulcher, bringing spices with which to anoint His body (Mark 16:1, 2). What must have been going through her mind as she approached the grave? Did she remember the alabaster box and the fragrant oil?

Upon arriving at the tomb, to Mary's shock, she saw that the stone that had covered the sepulcher had been moved. The grave had been opened! Fearing the worst, she ran to find the other disciples and relayed to Peter and John the horrible news (John 20:2). The body of their Lord had been taken!

As Peter and John ran on ahead, Mary followed, sobbing inconsolably. So blinding, so all-consuming was her grief that even when she saw two angels in His tomb, even when she saw Jesus Christ Himself alive, she did not realize who it was. It was only after the Savior addressed her by name that Mary understood—and her grief turned to instant joy.

She had the privilege of being the first human being to see the Savior risen from the dead (Mark 16:9). She had the privilege once more to "[hold] Him by the feet and [worship] Him" (Matthew 28:9). Because He had risen, her own life was renewed. Because He had risen, she went forward with new purpose.

At His bidding, she shared the wonderful news of His resurrection to His eleven closest disciples. And while they did not believe her (Mark 16:11), they believed at last when Jesus Himself appeared to them, as He had to her (v. 14).

It is not for us to change a person's belief. It is for us, like Mary, to simply shout it from the lowest valley to the highest hilltop—we serve a risen Savior! He lives! He lives! Through Him we are saved!

Reflect: Have you ever been so focused on something that you did not see the bigger picture? In the midst of our troubles and problems, do we forget that God has already given us the answer?

Dig Deeper: Psalm 91:15, 16; Philippians 4:6, 7; 1 Peter 4:12, 13

Mike and Linda

The God Who Pursues

"All things work together for good to those who love God, to those who are the called according to His purpose" (Romans 8:28).

Linda was raised a Catholic but eventually quit attending church as an adult. Mike, her husband, grew up in a Sabbath-keeping church but drifted far away from its teachings during his teen years and stayed away for nearly three decades.

Moved by their children's interest in adopting a vegan diet, Linda began researching the benefits and discovered the well-known documentary *Forks Over Knives*, available through Amazing Facts. As their minds cleared, Mike longed to return to the biblical teachings of his childhood.

As a compromise, they started visiting the popular mega-churches in their city, and then decided to try a church of the denomination from Mike's youth. Sadly, the church barely differed from the non-denominational churches they visited. However, they met a church member who urged them to watch Pastor Doug Batchelor.

Mike's mother was also encouraging Mike and Linda to watch Amazing Facts. "I had long resisted," says Mike, "but my mom just kept urging us to connect with Amazing Facts. She also sent us Doug Batchelor's biographical book, *The Richest Caveman*. This led us to watch Amazing Facts online."

The messages captured Mike and Linda's attention and gave Mike a sense of returning to the faith that he left. "The turning point in our lives," says Mike, "happened during an episode of *The Landmarks of Prophecy* series that covered the topic of baptism and rebaptism. It was there that Linda and I decided to give our lives to Christ."

Mike and Linda had to do a lot of searching and thinking about the things they were learning. "Linda," Mike explains, "found these Bible teachings to be quite different from what she had grown up believing. But Doug Batchelor presented the truth so clearly and backed it up with the Bible so well that there was no question that this was the truth." After making their decision to follow Christ, Mike gave up his job at an auto dealership in order to keep the Sabbath—a decision he has never regretted.

"We are so glad we kept listening!" says Mike. "Our lives have changed dramatically because of it. Before we gave our lives to Christ, we were roaming through life aimlessly, but now we live for God and seek to glorify Him in all that we do."

Reflect: Have you ever drifted away from God? Remember the story Jesus told of the lost sheep in Luke 15? The Shepherd pursues those who wander from the fold.

Dig Deeper: Psalm 139:7, 8; Zephaniah 3:17; Luke 15:1–7

Constantine

The Greatest

"You will know them by their fruits" (Matthew 7:16).

He gazed upward to the sky—and there, emblazoned above the sun, stood a cross and this mighty creed, "In this sign, conquer."

It is a well-known story, Constantine's famous vision before he became the sole ruler of the Roman Empire. Most believe it to be the pinnacle of his dramatic conversion to Christianity—but was it?

At that time the empire's Tetrarchy was quickly dissolving into a series of civil wars, with Constantine at the forefront. After winning a decisive victory at the Milvian Bridge, Constantine, surmising that the vision had been prophetic, went on to defeat his rivals one by one, attributing his conquests to God. But was Constantine's life truly changed after his so-called conversion? Did his life speak of the almighty, merciful God?

As a self-proclaimed defender of the faith, Constantine instituted religious tolerance by the Edict of Milan, quelling the rage of Christian persecution. He also showered the Christian church with buildings, land, and employment. In his reign the church became rich, powerful, and protected. And while that may seem like a good thing, was it the will of God?

At the same time that the church began to succeed, it also began to be heavily influenced by its celebrated patron. Constantine's favors vastly eliminated the separation of church and state, indebting the church to its earthly savior—himself.

While he claimed Christianity as his faith, he also propagated pagan religions. As a result, the religions of Christianity and paganism began to bleed into each other, mixing, melding, uniting. For example, in AD 321, Constantine enforced Sunday as the day of rest over the biblical Sabbath, paying homage to the Roman sun god.

Constantine was, above all, a politician. His conversion to Christianity was marked by a ruthless ascendance to the throne, all in the name of God. He had his firstborn son and second wife killed after rumors of infidelity, one by poisoning, the other in a vat of boiling water. He purposely declined to be baptized until he knew he was about to die, so as to be absolved of all the sins he believed he had to commit in order to sustain his position.

Was this a man whose heart had been touched by the grace of Christ? As he lay dying, did he feel remorse for his deeds? Was his true conversion actually on his deathbed? Only God knows.

Reflect: How do you know if you are truly converted? Do your actions have any part in it or are we saved only by grace through faith?

Dig Deeper: 2 Corinthians 7:10, 11; Philippians 3:17–19; James 2:18–24

David

Finding a Faith that Works

> **"How can a young man cleanse his way? By taking heed according to Your word" (Psalm 119:9).**

In his first 37 years of life, David wrestled with addictions, suicidal thoughts, and ungodly music. But after watching the movie *Hacksaw Ridge*—the story of a World War II hero named Desmond Doss—he was inspired to find a deeper relationship with God. The faith of Doss, a conscientious objector and a Sabbath-keeper, was new to David and led him on a quest that changed his life.

Before he decided to follow Christ, David's life was pretty "normal" from a worldly point of view. "I went to worldly events, listened to heavy metal music, and had ungodly relationships," he recalls. "I also struggled with depression and anxiety and often thought about taking my own life, sometimes several times a day." Speaking with a Christian psychologist didn't help.

Inspired by the faith of Desmond Doss, David began looking for truth and eventually discovered Amazing Facts. "I was browsing on YouTube one day and looking for religious programs when I first saw Pastor Doug," he remembers. "I felt like I had finally found a pastor whose messages clicked with me." What he heard and the way the Bible was presented changed David's views on how he should live his life.

Since David was a young teen he had struggled with lust and always felt the guilt of viewing impurity, although never enough to stop. "But when I started listening to Pastor Doug, began having daily devotions, and faithfully reading the Word, those thoughts became greatly suppressed." He finally gave his addiction over to God, asked for forgiveness, and prayed for the power to avoid situations that would lead to bad thoughts.

David's life has changed. He says, "I've stopped watching programs that I used to view and I've also quit listening to heavy metal music. My eyes have been completely opened to the evil and sin in the world." He admits that it hurts to remember the things he used to do, especially the pain he brought to God when he shunned Him.

Today, David is on a path to better care for his physical health. He is also committed to staying in the Word and helping anyone he encounters as he keeps moving forward on his own Christian journey. David finally found a faith that works.

Reflect: Are there some books, magazines, or movies that God wants you to stop watching? Confess your sin and commit yourself unreservedly to Jesus.

Dig Deeper: Matthew 5:8; Romans 13:14; 1 Timothy 4:12

Stephanie

The Provider, Part 1

"I have loved you with an everlasting love; therefore, with lovingkindness I have drawn you" (Jeremiah 31:3).

Before she was 12 years old, Stephanie was drinking, smoking, and doing drugs. She was born into a Christian home and even went to a Christian school. But she didn't make friends easily and often felt alone. She was still a teenager when she got married, but that did not fill her aching heart. So she started jumping from man to man, desperately seeking a way out of her own loneliness. She gave birth to two children, was unmarried, homeless on the streets, and finally decided to let her children be adopted by another family.

But she still believed in God and prayed for an open adoption, where she would still be able to have a relationship with her children and they with her. She also prayed that the adoptive family would teach them about Jesus ... and her prayers were answered. Even so, she did not immediately turn back to God, but fell back into trying to find love in another man. She did buy a Bible though, her very own, and when her new boyfriend saw it, he sneered.

"That's not going to help," he told her. So she hid it away.

And on she moved, from man to man, each relationship as broken as the last. Depressed and terribly lonely, her health finally gave way, and she got sick—really sick.

For the next year and a half, Stephanie found herself in and out of hospitals. One day, a chaplain visited and prayed with her. At the time she did not think anything of it. A week passed. She had been released from the hospital and was at home watching a movie about the life of Jesus.

Then, something caught her eye. It was a book on the shelf next to the television, a dusty, old book that she had bought four years ago and had not opened since. It was her Bible.

A spark suddenly ignited within her and in a flash she was reading through the Gospels. Still, she wanted to know more, so she called her mom.

Reflect: Do you know someone who is searching for love everywhere except from God? Pray that they may know and see how much the Lord personally pursues them.

Dig Deeper: John 3:16; Romans 5:8; Zephaniah 3:17

Stephanie

The Provider, Part 2

"We have known and believed the love that God has for us. God is love, and he who abides in love abides in God, and God in him" (1 John 4:16).

After searching to find love for years, Stephanie began reading her Bible and felt a hunger to learn more. When she called her mom and asked for Bible studies, her mother began weeping over the phone. She had been praying for 20 long years that her daughter would someday call and ask for just that. So, on her mother's advice, Stephanie began the online Amazing Facts Bible lessons. It took her just two weeks to complete.

Stephanie called her mom a second time and asked, "Where could I get baptized?" Her mother gave her the name of a nearby Sabbath-keeping church. When Stephanie called, she was invited to a special seminar that the church was holding.

The evening that Stephanie walked through the doors of the church, a lady greeted her, and on this greeter's blouse was a name tag along with the words "Amazing Facts."

Stephanie looked up. "Okay, Lord, You got me," she said.

At the end of the seminar, she was baptized.

After her baptism, Stephanie still struggled with her health, with depression, even with suicidal thoughts. Then one day, she found out that she had lost her job. But she fought back those feelings of abandonment and despair. She put her trust in God and prayed.

Three days later, she received a call from Amazing Facts, offering her temporary work. Stephanie could barely believe it. God had answered her prayer. She did not know how or when or even why Amazing Facts had contacted her as a potential hire, but she did know that God had not deserted her. He cared about her.

"I have no idea how they got my name and phone number, but I do know one thing: God does provide," she smiled.

Today, Stephanie is an active soul-winner for Christ and even uses *Amazing Facts Storacles* for her Bible studies. She also has a special burden for those who struggle with depression. She loves *Bible Answers Live* as a resource, as well as *Sabbath School Study Hour* and the extensive online library. "Amazing Facts holds a special place in my heart," she says.

Reflect: Have you ever questioned God's great love for you? Read the story of Jesus' crucifixion in Matthew 26–28 and reflect on how much heaven gave for you.

Dig Deeper: Romans 8:37–39; Galatians 2:20; 1 John 3:1

Blind Man

Out of Sight

"One thing I know: that though I was blind, now I see" (John 9:25).

He was a beggar on the streets of Jerusalem, a Jew born blind, pitied, reviled.

But one Sabbath day, as he sat among the scum and filth, he heard footsteps, quite close. He heard a sharp sound, like someone spitting, and then a strange, wet kind of noise beneath him on the ground. All of a sudden, something thick and smooth, like mud, was being gently rubbed over and around his eyes.

Then, a Man's voice spoke, and it was like the hands that had touched his face, gentle but sure. "Go, wash in the pool of Siloam" (John 9:7), the Voice said.

So he went, because he trusted this Man—Jesus, He had said His name was. When he reached the pool, he washed the mud (for that is what it was) out of his eyes as he had been told—and just like that, light flooded in, and shapes, and colors. He could see!

Overjoyed, he headed for home, taking in the things that he had all his life heard or touched but had never seen. When he told people of the miracle, they hustled him eagerly to the Jewish leaders, a group of Pharisees, who interrogated him and even his parents (vv. 13–24). But these Pharisees were not amazed or happy for him. They were determined only to prove that the Man who had healed him, Jesus, was a fraud. As they continued to prod him angrily, he answered plainly what he knew: This Jesus was no fraud. He was a true miracle worker "from God" (v. 33). For his honesty he was excommunicated (v. 34).

But he could not blame the Man who had made him whole. His heart was longing after Him; his heart, like his eyes, had been opened. Not long after, a Stranger approached him and spoke. And he realized—it was Jesus. Jesus revealed to him what his heart had been searching for, that Jesus Himself was the Messiah, that He was God with us (vv. 35–37). In response he said to Him, "'Lord, I believe!' And he worshiped Him" (v. 38).

On that day, the blind man was given his spiritual as well as his physical sight. On that day, he was restored to God.

Reflect: Can you have your sight but still not see? Are there things in your life that God wants to show you to which you are shutting your eyes, from which you are looking away? Pray for spiritual eyes to see.

Dig Deeper: Exodus 34:29–35; Matthew 7:21–23; 2 Corinthians 3:12–18

> **"He heals the brokenhearted and binds up
> their wounds" (Psalm 147:3).**

Lori is a photographer and loves to take good pictures. But the picture of her life was far from perfect. She grew up as the youngest of four children. Her father was a blue collar worker who traveled a lot. Unfortunately, he was involved with friends who were caught in a robbery and he was sent to prison for a few years. After her dad was released, their family moved to another state where he found a new job.

One day a man came to their home to say that her father and uncle had been in a terrible car accident. Lori's uncle had survived, but her dad hadn't. Broken and without a husband and father, Lori's family moved back to their original hometown. During this time another dark shadow crossed Lori's life. Her brother began to abuse her. She was scared and never said anything about it. Instead, she tried to put it out of her mind. Years later, when she told her mother about it, her mother's response left her deeply hurt and angry. It took some time to forgive her mom, but she finally did.

Eventually, Lori graduated from high school and met a young man at church. While still dating, she became pregnant and determined to have the baby no matter what. The young man said he loved her and so they were married. But the marriage was anything but bliss. Her husband physically abused her, once kicking her in the stomach while she was pregnant. She thought she would lose the baby, but didn't. Eventually, Lori and her husband had three beautiful children, but the abuse continued. She once dodged a punch from her husband that left a hole in the wall. She covered the hole with a calendar to hide it from the landlord, but it didn't cover the hole in her heart.

One day, while her two boys were in school, she and her 4-year-old daughter went to visit her mother. She needed time to think. When she returned home, she discovered that her husband was seeing another woman and had started divorce proceedings. Her hatred for him grew when she learned that he planned to take custody of their children. It was a nightmare she never wants to go through again. But, by God's grace, things changed.

Reflect: Do you know someone whose life has been shattered by tragedy or abuse? What Bible verse might give this person comfort and hope? Read and choose one from below to share with them today.

Dig Deeper: Psalm 34:18; Isaiah 53:5; Jeremiah 30:17

Lori

A Shattered Life Restored, Part 2

**"The name of the is a strong tower; the righteous
run to it and are safe" (Proverbs 18:10).**

God was leading Lori, step-by-step, out of a pit of despair. She was able to see her children on weekends and holidays. She found a job and eventually remarried. When the church she attended in town closed, a friend invited her to another church which she attended for a time. This church had a prison ministry and Lori became involved in doing photography work at the prison. She was growing spiritually.

But something was still missing in her life. She says, "I had been praying to God for wisdom and a deeper understanding of His Word." One night she couldn't sleep. She tossed and turned and eventually got out of bed and turned on the television. A program came on called *Amazing Facts with Doug Batchelor*. She had never heard of the show before and left it on, listening to the entire program. Lori recalls, "It was meant to be for me to hear that program that morning. Ever since then I have been searching the Scriptures and watching Doug Batchelor on the Internet every night."

Eventually, Lori went online to find a Sabbath-keeping church. She finally found one near her home that she liked and was soon baptized as a new member. Lori says, "If I had not tuned in to Doug Batchelor early that morning when I couldn't sleep, I would not have known what I'd been missing all these years. Pastor Doug is reaching a lot of misinformed people."

Lori thanks God for answering her prayers. "I now know the truth and want to tell others! God continues to reveal new things to me every day." When she thinks back on all that she has been through, she shares, "If there are others who have been through the pain and abuse I have gone through, I want them to know that God can get you through anything! Nothing is impossible with God!"

The hole in her heart is now being filled with Bible truth and the love of Jesus.

Reflect: What do you do when you cannot sleep? Turn your heart to heaven and pray for God's peace and protection. Angels are watching over you.

Dig Deeper: Nehemiah 8:10; Psalm 32:7, 8; John 14:27

Martin Luther King, Jr.

Schooled

"All Scripture is given by inspiration of God, and is profitable for doctrine, for reproof, for correction, for instruction in righteousness" (2 Timothy 3:16).

"Darkness cannot drive out darkness; only light can do that. Hate cannot drive out hate, only love can do that," wrote Martin Luther King, Jr. in Strength to Love, a collection of his most beloved sermons. It was a strongly Christ-like sentiment from a man who was prone to depression and—though it may be hard to believe—two suicide attempts.

We know Martin Luther King, Jr. as a national symbol of freedom, a hero of the civil rights movement, and a recipient of the Nobel Peace Prize. But before his days of nonviolent resistance and inspiring rhetoric, King was a pastor's kid in the Baptist Church.

Born in 1929, Martin was an intelligent child. He, along with his two siblings, had a loving upbringing under parents who, despite raising a family during the Great Depression, always provided for them.

But King, who had a proclivity to question nearly everything, began to have serious doubts about the validity of the Bible. It seemed to him like a bunch of myths. Two instances from his childhood in particular greatly affected his faith. One was the death of his grandmother, to whom he was especially close. Upon her passing, he attempted to kill himself at only 12 years of age. The question of a person's immortality haunted him for years afterward. The other was his first encounter with racism, when one of his childhood friends was not allowed to see him anymore. His parents encouraged him toward the selfless love the Bible says a Christian has, but King struggled to return anything but hate.

However, in his senior year at Morehouse College, King found himself called into ministry. In his early years at the university, it seemed as though his theological doubts would become paradigms. There was so much science that refuted Scripture, so much higher learning to which he was exposed. But it was when he took a course on the Bible taught by Dr. George Kelsey, who was both a learned scholar and a minister, that King began to see the undeniable truths of Scripture.

That one class was the springboard to his acceptance of a deeply personal God. Out of that growing faith blossomed a life's work against social injustice.

Reflect: Is there someone who mentored you or witnessed to you about God? Are you guiding someone else to Christ? "'You are My witnesses,' says the " (Isaiah 43:10).

Dig Deeper: Psalm 32:8; 2 Timothy 2:2; Titus 2:6–8

Ms. Zhao

Never Forsaken

"I will never leave you nor forsake you" (Hebrews 13:5).

"I first started attending church out of fear," Ms. Zhao admits. "I was only nine years old when I heard my neighbor say, 'Believe in God, He can save you. If you don't, you will go to hell and suffer forever and ever.'"

Ms. Zhao came to believe that God was a tyrant who loved to torture sinners. She felt that the Lord had forsaken her because of her sinful life. It led her to wonder if there was any purpose in living. "I tried a dozen times to read the Bible, but I could never make sense of it." When she asked her pastor questions about the Scriptures, he couldn't answer them.

Ms. Zhao, who was 22 years old at the time, became extremely distressed and wanted to end her life. That same year her best friend committed suicide. It only made her more distraught. She asked herself, "What do I believe? Where is God's love? If we are all destined for hell, why not just get it over with?" She decided to follow her best friend's example and take her life.

"But God never forsook me," she recalls. "His love was always with me. At this exact time my pastor, who knew what I was going through, brought me a video called *Cosmic Conflict*. I had never heard messages like this before. I knew nothing about God's love and the freedom He gives me to choose what is right."

From that moment on Ms. Zhao searched the Internet for Pastor Doug's videos and discovered the Chinese Amazing Facts website. When she learned about the true Bible Sabbath, she talked with her Sunday-keeping pastor. "Amazing Facts is full of heresy," he told her. "Stop watching those videos." Other church members told her the same thing. Yet no one could point out any errors in the teaching.

Eventually, Ms. Zhao contacted Amazing Facts and found a local Sabbath-keeping church. "I have learned a lot of truth," she shares. "The church members were glad to help me and cared about me."

Ms. Zhao rejoices, "God never forsook me. He has been leading me with His great love through all these distressing experiences. His love is always with me. I give God all the glory for what He has done. Thank you, God!"

Reflect: Do you know someone who tragically ended their own life? Hopelessness is one of Satan's greatest tools to lead people to question whether life is worth living. Pray and seek to help the despondent with God's promises.

Dig Deeper: Deuteronomy 31:8; Joshua 1:9; 2 Corinthians 4:16–18

Nathanael

See for Yourself

> **"Oh, taste and see that the is good; blessed is**
> **the man who trusts in Him" (Psalm 34:8).**

According to *Foxe's Book of Martyrs*, this disciple brought the gospel to the entire country of India before being martyred by crucifixion. Also known as Bartholomew, Nathanael was one of Jesus' 12 apostles.

But before he became an apostle, Nathanael was a Jew who fervently believed in the Scriptures. Like many, he had expectations of the promised Messiah. The Anointed One was to be their Savior and their King—mighty, majestic, magnificent. What pomp and circumstance would herald Him? What glorious victories would trail Him?

When his friend Philip told him that the Messiah was none other than Jesus of Nazareth, Nathanael was skeptical. The promised Messiah—from an insignificant village not more than a few miles from his own hometown of Cana? "Can anything good come out of Nazareth?" (John 1:46) he replied scornfully.

But Philip did not try to convince him with reason or debate. He merely pointed straight to the source by bidding him, "Come and see." At this point Nathanael could have dismissed Philip's news as a waste of time. But he did not. His faith outweighed his prejudice. He followed his friend.

As they arrived, Jesus, knowing full well what Nathanael had said to Philip, called to him, "Behold, an Israelite indeed, in whom is no deceit" (v. 47).

Nathanael was stunned. He did not know this Man; how could this Man know him?

But Jesus knew Nathanael intimately. He knew that Nathanael earnestly desired to follow His Savior. As truly as God counts each hair on our heads, Jesus had seen Nathanael under the fig tree (v. 48).

Instantly, Nathanael believed. He had experienced Jesus personally. Nathanael knew from that moment on that Jesus, though He could not have looked less like a king (Isaiah 53:2), was "the Son of God" (John 1:49).

And Jesus, in turn, affirmed his faith, giving to Nathanael a clear illustration of His purpose on earth: "Hereafter you shall see heaven open, and the angels of God ascending and descending upon the Son of Man" (v. 51). And Nathanael ended up giving his life that others might believe in that truth—in Jesus Christ our mediator, our ladder (Genesis 28:12), our only way between earth and heaven (John 14:6).

Reflect: Do you tell rather than show? Nathanael was converted when he saw for himself who the Messiah was. A firsthand experience is more convicting than the most eloquent argument for God.

Dig Deeper: Luke 7:18–24; John 10:25–27; 1 John 3:18

Ellen White

A Modern Prophet, Part 1

"Therefore we were buried with Him through baptism into death, that just as Christ was raised from the dead by the glory of the Father, even so we also should walk in newness of life" (Romans 6:4).

The rock soared through the air, heading straight for a small trio of children running across the open expanse. There was a sickening sound, and one of the children crumpled to the ground.

When the child came to, she was lying in a nearby store. Her nose ached from where the rock had struck her. All seemed well at first, but soon after and for the next three weeks, the little girl lay comatose with no memory. It was expected that she would die. But she did not. She lived, albeit with a scar that badly disfigured her small face and a constitution so frail that she could no longer attend school.

And so life had already become a hardship for Ellen Harmon in her short nine years. There was an overwhelming sadness that she was just not good enough. Her appearance certainly was not—her playmates had made that painfully apparent; her education was meager at best. She was worthless.

But in 1840, when Ellen was but 12 years old, she attended a series of presentations by William Miller, a preacher who spoke on a very important Bible prophecy. At the crux of his studies was Daniel 8:14, the verse which he believed affirmed the exact year of Christ's second coming—in 1843. And Ellen believed it too.

After Miller's meetings she devoted herself to preparing for this day, attending more meetings, spending hours in prayer. But she could not shake the sense of her own unworthiness. How could she prepare for heaven? She had nothing to offer.

Then, at one of these meetings, she heard the words that changed everything: There was nothing that she could bring to the Lord; she would never be good enough. But that was the very reason she was to go to Him, with her sins and weaknesses, faithfully dependent upon His great mercy and His patient forgiveness to create her anew.

That same year, Ellen Harmon was baptized. As she came up out of the water, she realized she had been given a new life and a new purpose in God.

Reflect: Have you delayed having a relationship with God because you wanted to become a better person first? Come as you are. You will not become better *unless* you have a relationship with Him!

Dig Deeper: Isaiah 49:14–16; 2 Corinthians 3:4, 5; Ephesians 2:4–10

Ellen White

A Modern Prophet, Part 2

> "'Your brethren who hated you, who cast you out for My name's sake, said, 'Let the be glorified, that we may see your joy.' But they shall be ashamed" (Isaiah 66:5).

In the history of the world, not a few, having received censure from their own churches, have gone on to become influential pillars in new religious movements—among these Martin Luther, Thomas Cranmer, and John Huss.

When Ellen Harmon was baptized, she was accepted into the Methodist faith, the faith in which she and her siblings had been raised. But as she and her family continued to attend William Miller's meetings, dubbed the Advent Movement, there began a rift that widened between them and their denomination.

At first Ellen was plagued once more with doubt. Being baptized was one matter; living as a Christian before Christ's soon return was another. Confused, she could not reconcile the two. In her young mind, God was a merciless judge who would punish forever in the fires of hell any who could not attain to holiness in earthly life. She lapsed into thinking she would never be one of those saved, and it tormented her.

But after two significant dreams about Jesus and on sage advice from her mother, she took counsel from an Elder Stockman, who also believed in the advent message. This one meeting significantly impacted Ellen, in particular her understanding of God's undying love for mankind. She left armed with knowledge, assurance, and a renewed dedication.

That same day, Ellen began her public ministry for God. Soon, more opportunities began to arise for sharing prayer and her personal testimony as well as witnessing to friends and strangers. But as she and other members of her family began to proclaim Jesus' soon coming to members of their own church, they were met with open indifference, antagonism, and derision.

Finally, their pastor privately asked them to resign from the Methodist faith. But Ellen's father refused, reciting several Scriptures in support of the Second Coming. As a result, the Harmon family was held on trial at the church and subsequently disfellowshipped.

Ellen's continuing convictions caused her to be seen as a heretic. But this apparent misfortune bound her ever more to her growing faith.

Reflect: Have you been ostracized for your faith? In these times of trial, hold fast to God's Word, which we are always to obey over the dictates of men (Acts 5:29).

Dig Deeper: Micah 4:6, 7; Acts 1:10, 11; Revelation 2:2

Ellen White

A Modern Prophet, Part 3

"We also glory in tribulations, knowing that tribulation produces perseverance; and perseverance, character; and character, hope" (Romans 5:3, 4).

The popular phrase "egg on one's face" has several theories as to its origin, one of which is the result of a person's terrible table manners. However it originated, the phrase has a single, plain meaning: utter embarrassment.

The proposed year of Christ's return, 1843, was quickly approaching. Ellen and the other Adventists spent those last weeks in dedicated preparation.

But 1843 came and went—and Jesus did not return.

Then began a time of bitter disappointment, made all the more burdensome as tongues began to wag and the ridicule began to fly, resulting in many believers abandoning the movement.

But not Ellen. Though she did not have the answers, she believed the Word of God to be true.

Other Adventists began to take another look at Bible prophecy, eventually concluding that William Miller had the date incorrect. Christ's coming, it was concluded, was actually October 22, 1844.

That single year Ellen describes as the happiest of her life. She was certain of the new date, and consequently, her efforts—and those of other believers—redoubled. They dedicated their short time to calling upon people to repent, to claim the salvation of Jesus Christ, and to prepare for His second coming. Though their work was greatly hindered by the evidences of their first failed prediction, they soldiered on, taking every moment as an opportunity.

But 1844, like the year before, came and went—without the Second Coming. And again, Ellen found herself severely tried and in darkness.

But not for long. She, as well as other believers, turned straight to the Bible once more, studying, and praying. It was their error, not God's. In their humility, patience, and persistence, they were blessed. They discovered that it was not the date that was incorrect but the event, for Daniel's prophecy did not refer to the second coming of Christ but to the start of a specific part of His ministry in heaven.

These two trials of her faith ended up strengthening, not diminishing, Ellen's trust in God. As a consequence, before the year was out, Ellen was to receive a very special message from God that would change the rest of her life.

Reflect: Has your dark hour ever turned into a blessing? The Great Disappointment of 1844 not only led Ellen Harmon to her life's calling, but also kindled the spark that eventually brought about the Seventh-day Adventist movement.

Dig Deeper: James 1:2–8; Revelation 10:8–11; 14:1–6

Ellen White

A Modern Prophet, Part 4

"But God has chosen the foolish things of the world to put to shame the wise, and God has chosen the weak things of the world to put to shame the things which are mighty ..., that no flesh should glory in His presence" (1 Corinthians 1:27, 29).

John the Baptist's birth was prophesied unto his father, Zacharias. Zacharias and his wife, Elizabeth, had been unable to have children, so when the birth of their son was foretold to him, Zacharias thought it an impossibility. As a result of his unbelief, God struck him dumb until after John was born (Luke 1:20).

Soon after the Great Disappointment of 1844, Ellen received a message from God in the form of a vision. When she shared it with other Adventists, the vision was as a balm of encouragement, a bold assurance that they were to continue in their faith, their study of the Word, and in proclaiming the advent message.

A mere week later, Ellen received another vision from God, this time instructing her to persist in relaying these messages to others. Her work would be fraught with resistance, but she was to go forth nonetheless.

Ellen was terrified. She was only 17 years old and already weak for her age; she was no great orator, neither had she any charm or charisma. It seemed impossible. But the conviction kept growing until finally she yielded, asking only that God protect her from any self-exaltation. Receiving His promise, she accepted the call to be God's prophetess.

As she began to share God's messages with others, she was indeed met with a multitude of hindrances, including accusations that her visions were what was then termed "mesmerism" or a kind of hypnosis.

All of these claims distressed her greatly until she began to doubt that her visions were from God. One morning, she shut her mind to a vision, thinking to protect herself from hypnosis. Instantly, she became as mute. All at once, she realized that she had been led astray by man's opinion, that she had disobeyed God and had reneged on her calling. She was then told in another vision that she would regain her speech in less than a day.

When the time had passed and she could again speak, never again did Ellen doubt the responsibility that she had been given or refuse another of God's visions. This was another turning point in her faith, solidifying her future work for the Lord.

Reflect: Have you been resisting God's will? Is self-doubt a form of disobedience to God?

Dig Deeper: Exodus 6:11, 12; 15:13, 19; 2 Corinthians 12:7–10

**"Blessed is he who reads and those who hear the words
of this prophecy, and keep those things which are
written in it; for the time is near" (Revelation 1:3).**

Ellen White is the most translated non-fiction author in all of history. In her lifetime she wrote 40 books and over 5,000 articles; her works have been translated into 148 languages.

At the age of 19, she married James White and continued receiving visions from God, encompassing important biblical truths, like the Sabbath; specific guidance for the Seventh-day Adventist Church, such as in matters of health reform and education; and prophetic events, like the San Francisco earthquake of 1906.

One of these visions came in 1848. In it Mrs. White was instructed to urge her husband to publish the advent message. But since the young couple had no money, Elder White began looking for ways to invest and people who would be willing to help. Unsuccessful, he then began to look for work in order to fund the project.

But Mrs. White was then given another vision, stating that her husband was to write—not labor—and that God would provide the means in faith. Elder White immediately obeyed.

In 1849, the first copies of *The Present Truth* were, with much prayer, printed and distributed. From this eight-page paper was born a lifetime of literature ministry for both husband and wife. The paper's name has been changed several times over the years and is currently still in production as the *Adventist Review*.

Mrs. White also began to contribute her own writings; her first book, now included as a section of *Early Writings*, was published in 1851. Amidst the travels, sickness, and debt, the printing continued. First, a printing press was purchased, and then a printing house—built and paid for by generous donors.

After her husband's death, Mrs. White spent the next three decades not only producing printed works but also speaking, traveling and, with God's mighty Hand, guiding the Seventh-day Adventist Church. She wrote until she could no longer and in 1915, passed to her rest. Faithful to the last, her final words were quoted from Scripture: "I know whom I have believed" (2 Timothy 1:12).

Her prolific career as an author as well as a messenger of God existed simply because she responded to the call to testify of Him who saved her.

Reflect: Ellen White spent her entire life in active ministry for the cause of Christ. What can we learn from her testimony that our light may continually burn brighter for God?

Dig Deeper: 1 Thessalonians 5:16–24; Hebrews 10:24, 25; 1 Peter 3:15

Michelle

Radio and the Rapture, Part 1

> **"When He, the Spirit of truth, has come, He will
> guide you into all truth ..." (John 16:13).**

"Am I getting old?" wondered Michelle as she drove her usual route to work one morning. She noticed that she was growing tired of her favorite driving pastime: listening to dance music. She had always loved bopping and singing along to the latest tunes, but it just didn't interest her anymore. Instead, she felt drawn to listening to talk radio—of all things!

Michelle began exploring the AM dial on her morning commute. She browsed the airwaves listening to different perspectives on the news and world events. But after several weeks, she heard something completely different on the radio.

It was a program called *Bible Answers Live* from a place called Amazing Facts. Michelle was intrigued. She grew up attending many different churches on and off, but she didn't have a lasting connection to any of them. And for her, an in-depth understanding of the Bible had always seemed an unattainable goal.

On each week's program, people called in with questions about the Bible, and a pastor named Doug Batchelor answered them using references from Scripture. Michelle tuned in each morning and listened intently.

While every question piqued her interest, one in particular brought a flashback of memories and emotions from a recent vacation.

"My husband and I traveled across the country to visit family, and while we were there, they recommended a health food store since they knew I'm a vegetarian and into healthy living. But when we showed up on Saturday, the place was closed! I couldn't believe it," Michelle said. "I thought, 'Why would a business be closed on a Saturday, when it's most people's day to shop?'"

"Later, my family told me that the owner was a Christian who worshiped on Saturdays. I thought the notion was ridiculous. 'They just *had* to be different,' I thought. 'Who do *those* people think they are?'"

When Michelle heard Pastor Doug tell one caller that Saturday was the Sabbath, she was shocked. "That's when I discovered his ministry was like *those* people." Michelle flipped the station immediately and went back to her dance music.

But within a few days, she felt a nudge to return to *Bible Answers Live*.

Reflect: Has the Holy Spirit ever nudged you to do something that you thought was a little over the edge? Sometimes we need promptings by the Spirit to grow more deeply in the Lord.

Dig Deeper: Isaiah 30:21; John 14:26; 1 John 5:6

Michelle

Radio and the Rapture, Part 2

"Remember the Sabbath day, to keep it holy" (Exodus 20:8).

When Michelle discovered a new radio program on her commute to work, she was drawn to listen to it. After several days of listening to *Bible Answers Live*, a caller asked about the rapture. Michelle did not agree with Pastor Doug's explanation. She had grown up worrying about the "secret rapture" all the time. When on an airplane, she worried that the pilot would be raptured and the plane would fall out of the sky.

It was all she had ever known. So when Pastor Doug said it wasn't true, she was angry. "How can they be saying this? I've heard about the rapture all my life, and now Pastor Doug said it was not going to happen? Really? No way! I was done with *Bible Answers Live*," says Michelle. "Now I really didn't like those people anymore!"

"After a week went by, I felt that nudging again that I should listen to the program. I didn't want to, but I did anyway," she recalls. The topic that day was the Sabbath. This time Pastor Doug explained it a little differently, describing how Jesus' followers hurried to put His body into the tomb before Sabbath started. Then they all rested on Saturday, even Jesus.

Michelle's mouth dropped open. She says, "The bells went off in my head— ding-ding-ding! Saturday really is the Sabbath, the day of rest and worship! It was clear as it could be. I was shocked. I'm sure my mouth was hanging open the rest of the way home. Even more shocking to me was why the world is going to church on Sunday. I thought, 'How could this even be?'"

Michelle's heart and mind were open to learning more. Soon she learned that she didn't have to be afraid of the rapture but that she still needed to be ready for Christ's second coming. "It was a bit of a shock but also some relief," she says. "As I look back now, I know God had His hand in this, directing me to an AM station that presented truth from *Bible Answers Live*. This is the best thing that has ever happened to me. I am now one of those people! And I couldn't be happier!"

Reflect: Have you ever been led down a new pathway that made you feel uneasy? When we trust in God, He promises to make our pathways straight (Proverbs 3:6).

Dig Deeper: Proverbs 16:9; Isaiah 48:17; Matthew 6:33

Nebuchadnezzar

The King of Kings, Part 1

"The king answered Daniel, and said, 'Truly your God is the God of gods, the Lord of kings, and a revealer of secrets, since you could reveal this secret'" (Daniel 2:47).

Would you believe that the mightiest king in the world once paid homage to a lowly foreign prisoner?

King Nebuchadnezzar had recently ascended the throne of Babylon, the empire that then ruled the world. The young monarch was ruthless, privileged, and arrogant, commencing his reign with a slew of fatal victories against the Assyrians.

But one night, the king had a dream. The Babylonians were a polytheistic nation; they believed that dreams were one of the means by which their gods communicated to them. Consequently, the king demanded that his famed contingent of wise men not only explain the dream to him but also divulge exactly what happened in it.

But his wise men could not do it. "[T]here is no other who can tell it to the king," they told him, "except the gods, whose dwelling is not with flesh" (Daniel 2:11). Enraged, King Nebuchadnezzar ordered for the whole lot of them to be killed.

A small handful of Jewish captives who were not present at the meeting, but who had previously found favor with the king for their intellect and understanding, were also numbered among those to be slaughtered. But after pleading for a delay in their sentence and spending time in prayer with his friends, one of them, Daniel, received a vision from God about the king's dream. He was told that the dream was actually a prophecy foretelling the future of this world all the way to the second coming of Christ.

When Daniel relayed what he had been told to the king, disclosing that God Himself had put the dream into the king's mind (v. 28), Nebuchadnezzar was astounded. He "fell on his face, prostrate before Daniel" (v. 46), and acknowledged Daniel's God as superior to even the highest of Babylonian gods (v. 47).

This was the Babylonian king's introduction to the one true God. Through this experience, God was revealed to be omniscient, real, and deeply personal. Thus began a series of direct communications between God and a king who knew next to nothing about Him.

Reflect: Has God ever revealed His character to you in a dramatic way? What was your view of Him after He did so? What was your view of yourself in relation to Him?

Dig Deeper: Exodus 34:5–9; Psalm 14:1–6; Isaiah 55:3, 8, 9, 11

Nebuchadnezzar

The King of Kings, Part 2

"I see four men loose, walking in the midst of the fire; and they are not hurt, and the form of the fourth is like the Son of God" (Daniel 3:25).

In the secluded dictatorship of North Korea, everyone—residents and tourists alike, no matter their age, religion, or nationality—is ordered to bow before the statues of past rulers Kim Il-sung and Kim Jong-il or else pay the consequences.

During the regime of Nebuchadnezzar of Babylon, something very similar occurred. After Daniel interpreted the dream to Nebuchadnezzar, the king defiantly flouted the future that God had foretold to him. In the king's dream, there was a statue made of different types of materials, and the different materials represented the different nations that would rule the world after the Babylonian Empire passed into oblivion. At the end of the dream, a stone smashed the statue to pieces and became a huge mountain, symbolizing God's heavenly kingdom, which would overrule the other nations and reign for all eternity.

In opposition to this prophecy, King Nebuchadnezzar had built a statue of pure gold, the material that, in his dream, represented his own kingdom of Babylon. Then he commanded that his subjects, regardless of nationality or faith, bow to this magnificent statue. Failure to comply would result in immediate death. "[W]ho is the god who will deliver you from my hands?" (Daniel 3:15) he asked insolently.

While Daniel was not present at this event, his friends were. When all the other people bowed to the king's statue, these three young men stood firm, making known that they worshipped the true God of heaven alone (vv. 17, 18). Upon discovering the offense, Nebuchadnezzar had the three Hebrews thrown into a "burning fiery furnace" (v. 21).

But to his shock, in the midst of the flames, he saw a fourth Figure among the three. He saw God protecting His faithful servants from the fire. He called the three men—completely unharmed—to him and not only praised God as being more powerful than the Babylonian gods once again but also admitted that God had proved him, the king, wrong (vv. 26–29).

That day, the Lord demonstrated to Nebuchadnezzar another piece of His character, that He was a God who saved life, not One who exterminated it. Though Nebuchadnezzar had a lot more to learn about our Deliverer, that day the proud king's heart was turned even further towards Him.

Reflect: Have you ever found yourself in direct opposition to God and His will? What did you do when you realized this?

Dig Deeper: Jeremiah 23:3–6; Ezekiel 18:25–32; Romans 12:21

Nebuchadnezzar

The King of Kings, Part 3

"Now I, Nebuchadnezzar, praise and extol and honor the King of heaven, all of whose works are truth, and His ways justice. And those who walk in pride He is able to put down" (Daniel 4:37).

Clinical lycanthropy is a rare disorder in which a human believes that he is turning into an animal. There came a time when the most powerful ruler in the world actually found himself in this very state.

Years into his prosperous reign, Nebuchadnezzar had another dream which was again interpreted by Daniel. In this second dream, God forewarned the king that he would "be given the heart of a beast" (Daniel 4:16) if he continued in his pride and self-conceit.

But Nebuchadnezzar did not heed God's mercy. Swollen in his riches, satisfied in his splendor, he continued down the doomed pathway. "Is not this great Babylon, that I have built for a royal dwelling," he proclaimed an entire year later while sauntering about his palace, "by my mighty power and for the honor of my majesty?" (v. 30).

And in that same hour, just as God had predicted, the mighty Babylonian lost all reason and, for the next seven years, lived like a beast (v. 33). His beastly heart was now revealed for what it truly was.

At the end of seven years, just as God had promised, Nebuchadnezzar regained his senses (v. 34) as well as all his former majesty as king of Babylon (v. 36). But a powerful change had come over him. No more did he prize his own empire, his own works and luxuries; out of his mouth came no more the haughty prestige. Gazing upward to his Deliverer, he proclaimed only this: To God alone be the glory!

He had learned that, though he was king of Babylon, he was just like everyone else—a sinner in need of a Savior, of the God who had revealed the future, who had saved the three Hebrews from the fire, the God who had saved him from himself. It was not he, Nebuchadnezzar, who was the king of kings; it was God the Redeemer. "For His dominion is an everlasting dominion, and His kingdom is from generation to generation. All the inhabitants of the earth are reputed as nothing" (vv. 34, 35).

Reflect: Are you humbled by God? Why do you think being aware of your own sins is such a significant part of having a relationship with God, especially in these last days?

Dig Deeper: Jeremiah 9:23, 24; Matthew 20:25–28; Revelation 3:17–19

Leonard

Surfing for Truth

"Observe the Sabbath day, to keep it holy, as the your God commanded you" (Deuteronomy 5:12).

Leonard Edwards cannot remember a time that he didn't attend church. He grew up going to services each Sunday, attending choir rehearsals, prayer meetings, Bible studies, and church field trips. When he was a teenager who wanted to hang out with his friends, his father would tell him, "You can hoot with the owls on Saturday nights, but you better be ready to soar with us eagles on Sunday morning because you're going to church!" Even while he was in the Marines stationed in Okinawa, Japan, Leonard always went to church.

A few years ago, Leonard committed to read the Bible from cover to cover. "Those Bible readings opened me up to God in a way I can't describe," he explains. It sustained him just a few years later when his mother passed away. "Studying the Word of God helped cultivate my personal relationship with the Lord that carried me through my time of grief."

Reading the Bible every day gave Leonard a thirst to learn more about the Scriptures. "I wanted to understand what I was reading," he recalls, "and step up my game in my quest for a more personal relationship with God." Leonard began to question some of the doctrines and teachings of his Sunday church. He found and completed a couple of Bible correspondence courses and was convicted by the Holy Spirit to become a Sabbath-keeper.

One Sunday morning Leonard was surfing through all the church channels available on his cable TV subscription. Suddenly, a certain preacher caught his eye. "For some reason," Leonard remembers, "I stopped when I saw Pastor Doug Batchelor. His topic was, 'Why We Keep the Sabbath.'" Through his message and the conviction of God's Spirit he was led to join a Sabbath-keeping church.

"No one uses the Bible better than Pastor Doug," Leonard shares. "He creates vivid word pictures that resonate with me. It helps me understand the Bible in ways I never knew."

Leonard now loves the Sabbath. "The rhythm of life is easier, quieter, and less congested," he explains. "My relationship with God is much stronger."

Reflect: Have you discovered the Sabbath as a day to strengthen your relationship with God? Perhaps you need to rediscover this sacred time.

Dig Deeper: Exodus 20:8; Isaiah 56:2; Mark 2:27

Joseph Bates

The Reformed Sea Captain

> "Fear God and give glory to Him, for the hour of His judgment has come; and worship Him who made heaven and earth, the sea and springs of water" (Revelation 14:7).

Have you ever heard of a sailor who did not drink? In the 19th century, it was virtually unheard of—and that made Joseph Bates the odd man out.

Born in 1792, Bates desperately longed for adventure on the high seas. Finally able to convince his parents, he began his career as a teenage cabin boy, enduring his share of peril, including an encounter with a shark and a shipwreck in ice. He was also held captive during the War of 1812. But none of that cured his desire for more excitement and enterprise on the deep blue.

Disinterested in spiritual things, he married in his 20s and continued sailing, oftentimes away from his family for more than a year at a time. But his wife was a Christian, and before he left for one voyage, she snuck a New Testament into his stack of romance novels. And once he discovered it, he actually began reading it. Soon, he lost interest in all other books.

Now a captain, he yearned to become a Christian, but his profession made him hesitant. How would that look to his crew? But then, something happened that drove him to a decision.

One of his crew had gotten sick to the point of death. Bates was deeply moved to pray for him and for his own sinful self, but at the same time he was terrified at the prospect. Finally, weighed down by the grievous realization that he, an ungrateful fool, had been spared from death multiple times by God—the shark, the shipwreck, the war—he fell to his knees, asking for forgiveness.

The sailor died, but Bates had too in a way. The experience brought him to understand his dire need for God. After that tragic day, a marked change came over Bates. He manned his last voyage as a Christian, replete with daily prayer and a weekly worship service as well as prohibition of alcohol and swearing. Convicted to perform his duties as a husband and father, he quit his maritime life and eventually gave his full support to the Advent Movement, particularly in the areas of temperance, anti-slavery, the Sabbath, and the establishment of the Seventh-day Adventist Church.

Reflect: We must all face the reality of our own mortality. How can death, however scary it may be, bring you to a new understanding of God and your eternal life?

Dig Deeper: Psalm 107:23–31; Matthew 5:4; Colossians 2:12, 13

Rica Marie

Cleansed! Part 1

> "'As I live,' says the Lord , 'I have no pleasure in the death of the wicked, but that the wicked turn from his way and live. Turn, turn from your evil ways! For why should you die, O house of Israel?'" (Ezekiel 33:11).

Rica's early childhood was what many would consider perfect. An only child, she was treated as a princess, and her relatives praised her for everything she did. "I was exposed to material things, and I was content to play video games, go to the malls, and take trips."

Even though Rica was allowed to be caught up in worldly activities, her mother read the Bible to her every day and encouraged her to pray every night. But Rica felt that being faithful to God was just a waste of time. "As a kid, I didn't think these things were necessary. I felt that, as a Catholic, I belonged to God's kingdom, so what did it matter if I was naughty or said bad words as long as I had religion? God would never refuse me."

When Rica reached fourth grade, however, her world turned upside down. "My family started to fall apart. My nanny who was with me ever since I was born left me, and I was forbidden to ever talk to her again. My friends deceived me, and mean girls at school bullied me and judged me for my physical appearance."

Because of the pressure in the family, her mother and her new nanny often directed their anger toward her. "They told me to shut up," Rica recalls, "because I was too 'talkative' and they called me immature and dumb. I sank into depression and became suicidal."

The upheaval in Rica's life caused her to turn from God. "I would glare at the altar and throw the Bible away," she says. "Whenever I was invited to churches, I'd sleep the entire time. My extroverted personality became introverted, filled with agony and anger. I became rebellious and developed a tomboy personality from my newfound male friends at school."

She was also introduced to swearing and impurity. "I became addicted to porn, and my mind was filled with lust. Every day I cut my skin and just cried in front of the mirror, asking God why He had forsaken me. I told God to take my life away and banish me from existence."

Reflect: Can you think of a time in your life when you felt God had abandoned you? Read the Bible verses below to discover God's love for you.

Dig Deeper: Joshua 1:9; Isaiah 41:10; Zephaniah 3:17

Rica Marie

Cleansed! Part 2

"If we walk in the light as He is in the light, we have fellowship with one another, and the blood of Jesus Christ His Son cleanses us from all sin" (1 John 1:7).

One day, Rica's rebellious and depressing life was changed. Her father introduced her to Amazing Facts. "I was deeply moved by what Pastor Doug was saying," she remembers. "I watched sermons, and I watched the video *Cosmic Conflict*, and the closing prayer taught me how to repent. I saw that despite being a sinful person, God still loves me, and I should not be ashamed of admitting my sins to Him. He was just waiting for me to confess."

Rica had formerly avoided confession for fear that God would reject her. She also learned the truth about her former church and decided to dedicate her life to Christ and follow the Scriptures.

After reading the book *The Last Night on Earth* by Joe Crews, Rica chose to obey God in every area of her life. "I quit the three things that were still making me a hypocrite: lust, violent video games, and Christian rock music. Mr. Crews was right. Why gamble your life away and waste opportunities to serve God? Why wait until the seven last plagues strike to get down on your knees and repent?"

Today, Rica shares that she is a whole new person. She is using *Amazing Facts Bible Study Guides* and has formed a Bible study group in her school. "Even though I am being judged as an over-reacting Bible Christian by my relatives and friends, I still continue to talk about the Bible for I am not ashamed of the gospel of Christ. When I'm grown up, I'll preach and I'll raise my children as devoted followers of Christ."

Rica says that she has learned a lot from her experiences, and she thanks God for saving her in her struggles. "I'm not sure who said this quote," she says, "but it describes what I've been through: 'God sometimes takes us to troubled waters not to drown us but to cleanse us.' Without the help of Jesus, I might still be drowning in the dark abyss, cold and alone. I thank God for that precious day when my pain and brokenness were replaced by love from God."

Reflect: We must all face the reality of our own mortality. How can death, however scary it may be, bring you to a new understanding of God and your eternal life?

Dig Deeper: Psalm 107:23–31; Matthew 5:4; Colossians 2:12, 13

Nicodemus

The Christian Pharisee

> **"For God so loved the world that He gave His only begotten Son, that whoever believes in Him should not perish but have everlasting life" (John 3:16).**

The symbol commonly associated with medicine is of a snake wrapped around a pole. Many are ignorant that the symbol originally came from the Bible, wherein God instructed Moses to make a bronze serpent on a pole so that all the Israelites who had been bitten by poisonous serpents could look upon it and be healed (Numbers 21:8, 9).

Nicodemus was a Pharisee, proud, rich, respected. As such, he believed that he had already been granted eternal life. In essence, he did not need a Savior. But Nicodemus had also seen Jesus, heard His teachings, witnessed His miracles. Something stirred within his heart to know more.

He met with Jesus in the dead of night so that no one else would know (John 3:1, 2). In that one meeting, Jesus revealed to Nicodemus the plan of salvation and in particular the true meaning of the bronze serpent. It was not the statue—it was Jesus Christ who healed. He was the Great Physician who gave victory over sin and the gift of eternal life.

A deep struggle surged within Nicodemus. Did he need a Savior? And was that Savior this Man called Jesus? Nicodemus left with that conversation buried deep within his heart, like a seed sown in the earth.

He did not immediately claim Jesus as the Messiah, but he set himself apart from the rest of the Pharisees, defending Jesus against their bigotry (John 7:45–50). That seed in his heart continued to grow until over three years later, when Jesus Christ was nailed to a cross.

As the Son of Man hung there, like a serpent on a pole, Nicodemus remembered His words from that night long ago: "[E]ven so must the Son of Man be lifted up, that whoever believes in Him should not perish but have eternal life" (John 3:14, 15). Realization dawned. In that darkest hour, Nicodemus believed. Jesus Christ had come into the world to die for his— for our—sins.

After the Savior's death, there was no more hiding or fear or shame. When Jesus' most faithful disciples had forsaken Him, it was Nicodemus who helped to bury Him (John 19:39–42). That little seed had finally become a fruitful tree of his burgeoning faith.

Reflect: How long has the Holy Spirit been working on your heart? Even if it has been years, you can still accept Jesus' gift of eternal life now. Choose to serve Him and watch what He will do in your life.

Dig Deeper: Ezekiel 37:11–14; 2 Corinthians 6:2; Hebrews 7:25

Rahul and Sahana

Blind Eyes Opened

"You word is a lamp to my feet and a light to my path" (Psalm 119:105).

Rahul was born and raised by a faithful and devout Catholic family in India. He served as an altar boy in his church which was just 300 feet from his home. He later attended a medical college in northern India. He was eventually baptized into a Sunday-keeping church, got married, and moved to a country in Western Asia to pursue a job in the medical field.

Life became busy with the birth of their two daughters. When their girls were older, they came across a Sabbath-keeping TV network with programs that their children enjoyed.

During this time, Sahana, Rahul's wife, had questions about some of the teachings in her Sunday church. She wondered about the state of the dead and other doctrines that didn't seem consistent with the Bible. She began watching other programs on the Christian network, including presentations by Amazing Facts.

Sahana took meticulous notes as she listened to Pastor Doug Batchelor preach. Day by day her thirst for God's Word was increasing. In the evenings their family would sit down and study the notes she penned. They would carefully check what they were learning and even studied what other churches taught on certain subjects. "We didn't want to be led into a hoax," Sahana says. "Our careful study led us to amazing new insights and our blinded eyes slowly started opening."

They soon became motivated to find God's true church. Rahul invited church elders to their home and his questions usually left them stumped. Family and friends thought they were under the influence of a cult. But they were determined to follow God's Word.

Rahul and Sahana had never attended a Sabbath-keeping church. They welcomed the Sabbath each week and worshiped at home. They often watched Amazing Facts services. When they discovered a Sabbath-keeping church, they joined God's family and were baptized.

Rahul loves to tell about his newfound faith by sharing literature from Amazing Facts. He travels around the world doing seminars in hospitals. Last year, while working in China, he shared material from the Chinese Amazing Facts website with some of the doctors. "It's a great help to be able to give out materials in the language of the people," he explains. "I've also been able to share Amazing Facts materials in Arabic with some of my Arab colleagues."

Rahul and Sahana are grateful for how God has led their family, step by step, toward His light and truth.

Reflect: Pray for people who live in countries where the gospel is being suppressed. When the gospel reaches the world, Jesus will come and take us home!

Dig Deeper: Isaiah 60:1; John 8:12; Acts 13:47

J. N. Loughborough

The Last Adventist Pioneer, Part 1

"It is a sign between Me and the children of Israel forever; for in six days the made the heavens and the earth, and on the seventh day He rested and was refreshed" (Exodus 31:17).

In the Bible, dreams are one way that God communicates with people, from Pharaoh's fat and lean cows (Genesis 41:18, 19) to Joseph's orders to flee to Egypt with Mary and the baby Jesus (Matthew 2:13).

Born in 1832, John Norton Loughborough grew up in an era of religious reform. In his youth he struggled with devotion to God over his friends, but was finally convicted to dedicate his life to God and was baptized as a "first-day" Adventist. At the age of 17, he was called into ministry as a preacher, and at 20, he was married. To support his wife, Mary, he began working in retail, selling locks for windows, while preaching during the weekends.

Then, a series of meetings began to take place in nearby towns. They were given by Adventists who believed Saturday, not Sunday, to be God's holy day of worship. There was great friction between the first-day and seventh-day Adventists, as many were being converted to believe in the seventh day.

One night, during the time these meetings were being held, Loughborough had a dream. In his dream he was attending a meeting which had two rooms, one dim, the other lit. In the bright room was a strange chart of the Jewish sanctuary and the two-horned beast of Revelation 13. Next to the chart was a tall man.

Several days later, Loughborough learned that some of his own congregation had been converted to the seventh day. He, as the minister, was urged to attend that night's meeting and put the seventh-day believers in their place. So, armed with his list of proof texts, he marched into the meeting—and beheld not only the very same chart he had seen in his dream, but also the tall man.

The tall man, whose name was J. N. Andrews, began to speak, disclosing that while he had planned to speak on another topic, he had been impressed instead to preach on the Sabbath. He then proceeded to systematically go through each of the proof texts in Loughborough's list, in the very same order, disproving from Scripture the first-day Adventist stance on the seventh day.

Not long afterwards, Loughborough became a "seventh-day" Adventist.

Reflect: What are the different ways that God has communicated His will to you? Three ways He speaks are through the Bible, providential leadings, and impressions from the Holy Spirit.

Dig Deeper: Numbers 12:6; Joel 2:28, 29; Acts 2:17, 18, 41–43

"Go, sell the oil and pay your debt; and you and your sons live on the rest" (2 Kings 4:7).

After Loughborough converted to the seventh-day Sabbath, a strange thing happened. His business of sash locks gradually began to dry up. Meanwhile, he had an increasing urge to witness about his new beliefs. Still, Loughborough continued to put all he had into his sales. But it was like he was pushing against a brick wall. However many locks he sold, the money kept on dwindling until, one day, he found himself with only three cents to his name.

At a loss, he attended the Sabbath meeting and, there, received a direct message from God. Given to fellow Adventist Ellen White in a vision, the message stated what Loughborough in his heart knew he was supposed to do—go into ministry full time, preaching the advent message.

That would have seemed to decide the matter. But Loughborough continued to wrestle with the conviction on his way home. How in the world could he minister to others when he had no money and a family to support? He was the one who needed ministering!

Deep in struggle, he settled on a sensible compromise: He would wait for God to provide the means, and then he would start preaching. But that did not give him peace either. Finally, he knew what he had to do. He would throw himself fully into ministry and leave it to God to provide a way. Immediately upon making that decision, he had a sense of peace.

Two days later, Loughborough gave his wife their last three cents to buy some supplies. Soon after she left, a man came and proceeded to buy from him $80 worth of locks, leaving Loughborough with an ample amount to start his ministry.

At the close of the next Sabbath's meeting, there arrived a believer named Hiram Edson, who announced that he had been continually impressed all day to travel to this meeting. So, here he was, but for what purpose he did not know. God, however, did know.

Days later, Loughborough and his new companion, Hiram Edson, began a six-week tour of advent meetings. Within a little over a week, the Lord's will for John Loughborough was fulfilled.

With this leap of faith, Loughborough began a life dedicated to the ministry for the Seventh-day Adventist Church.

Reflect: How have you stepped out in faith for God? Are there logical fears holding you back from putting your full trust in Him?

Dig Deeper: Proverbs 3:5, 6; Matthew 6:33; Hebrews 11:6

J. N. Loughborough

The Last Adventist Pioneer, Part 3

> "Behold, the word of the came to him, and He said to him, 'What are you doing here, Elijah?'" (1 Kings 19:9).

Why is it that after our greatest successes, we tend to have our worst relapses?

After dedicating his life to full-time ministry, John Loughborough traveled far and wide preaching the advent message. His meetings brought thousands to hear God's present truth. He witnessed conversions and miracles, even his own healing, and was at the forefront of the Seventh-day Adventist movement. Over and over, it was proven that the hand of God was with him.

But life as an evangelist was also filled with difficulties. There was no regulated pay; more often than not, Loughborough was recompensed in goods instead of money, if he received anything at all. The sheer amount of travel was exhausting, especially during the harsh East Coast winters, and during those times he barely saw his family. Loughborough, like Elijah running from Jezebel, became discouraged.

So in 1856, on an invitation from J. N. Andrews, he decided to move his family to Waukon, Iowa. There was land offered on which they could sustain themselves; at the same time, Iowa was a largely untried territory for the advent message. Loughborough could continue to further the ministry while also living more comfortably with his family.

The prospect sounded so promising, but the reality was unexpectedly not. As time passed, a most frightful change occurred—earning money as a carpenter soon became his top priority and, conversely, the cause of Christ was all but forgotten. In his autobiography Loughborough describes it as such: "At times when about my work, solemn convictions would come to me that I must throw all my energies into the cause of God or die. As I struggled against these convictions, they became less and less" (*Miracles in My Life*, p. 46).

Then, in the midst of a cruel winter, Loughborough was visited by the most surprising of guests.

"What doest thou here, Elijah?"

It was Ellen White. She and her husband, accompanied by two other believers, had traveled all the way from Illinois, narrowly escaping death while crossing the Mississippi, to deliver this message from God.

Three times she asked him this question, to Loughborough's ears a burning rebuke. From this simple Scripture, Loughborough was re-converted and spent the rest of his days steadfast in the work of God.

Reflect: Have the cares of this world overcome your zeal for Christ? Spending time in Scripture, prayer, and with fellow believers will guard you against discouragement and distraction.

Dig Deeper: Joshua 1:8, 9; Matthew 13:22, 23; Luke 10:40–42

Andrew

Living on the Edge

"There is but a step between me and death" (1 Samuel 20:3).

Andrew grew up in northern Mexico, and at age 8, he brought home a five-foot-long rattlesnake. "From there, everything went downhill," he jests. Extreme sports, including cliff diving, swimming with sharks, became his way of finding adventure. "I wouldn't call myself an adrenaline junkie, but the closest I've felt to being alive was when I felt so close to death," he says.

He learned English and was a translator when churches would send short-term mission teams into his area. As he shared their testimonies, he became a little jealous: "I didn't have a life-changing experience, that close encounter with God. I knew He was there, but I couldn't understand Him and didn't want to have anything to do with Him. I felt like I was unworthy of God's love."

Coming to the U.S., Andrew decided to sign up to work on a salmon fishing boat in the summer as a way of earning a fair amount of money in a short time. "When I first stepped onto a fishing boat, I knew I would be a fisherman for the rest of my life," he explains.

Andrew still carried with him the memories of those missionary teams and their testimonies, not all of which lined up with what the Bible actually says. While on a trip to help film videos at an orphanage in Honduras, he casually mentioned the "rapture," and was immediately challenged by his companions: "Are you sure that's in the Bible?"

Andrew was sure: "It's all over the Bible!" he exclaimed. His teammates gave him a DVD of Pastor Doug Batchelor preaching on the subject, which "challenged me on this," he says.

After a summer fishing season, Andrew discovered Pastor Doug's "Prophecy Code" series on YouTube. What he thought would be "sweet" turned out to be a shock: "It was torture because everything I knew was getting tossed out the window. He took away everything I thought was normal and had learned about the book of Revelation."

Andrew was glad to learn the truth of what the Bible teaches about the end times, as well as on other subjects. Ever since, there's been a fire rekindled in his heart. "I have this knowledge that I want to share with people," he says. Through the power of the Holy Spirit, Andrew discovered real living. He now shares the peace he has found with others who are living on the edge.

Reflect: Do you live life on the edge? How might you share God's messages with people who live life close to the edge?

Dig Deeper: Psalm 34:7; Proverbs 14:16; Romans 12:2

Simon the Sorcerer

The Magus

**"For a righteous man may fall seven times and rise again,
but the wicked shall fall by calamity" (Proverbs 24:16).**

Some common words in the English language are actually named after people, words like "jacuzzi," "leotard," and "silhouette." One is even derived from Scripture.

Simon lived in the city of Samaria during the early Christian church. His practice of the dark arts had elevated him to the status of a god, if not the Messiah Himself (Acts 8:10).

But when Philip, one of the church deacons, arrived, Simon was no longer the center of attention. Crowds flocked to hear and see Philip (vv. 6, 7). Philip, unlike Simon, did not promote his own greatness and his own prowess. No, Philip instead told the story of the true Messiah, Jesus, of His love and sacrifice for the human race. Many hearts were touched, including Simon's. He and many others were baptized into the faith (vv. 12, 13).

But Simon also had a love for fame and glory. The miracles that Philip performed fascinated him. What could he do with that kind of power?

A short time later, the apostles Peter and John came to Samaria. As the two apostles prayed and laid hands upon the believers, those whom Philip had baptized were now baptized with the power of the Holy Spirit (v. 17)—but not Simon. He merely watched, awestruck. Why, these two men had even more capabilities than Philip!

Eagerly he rushed forward, thrusting money at the apostles. "Give me this power also," (v. 19) he demanded. But you cannot pay for what is freely given; and what could be bought already had been bought by the blood of Jesus Christ.

Thus was Simon's name etched into history with the audacity of his filthy trade. The word "simony," the sale of ecclesiastical or sacred things, bears his sad moniker.

"Repent," was Peter's reply. "For I see that you are poisoned by bitterness and bound by iniquity" (vv. 22, 23).

But Simon did not see what Peter saw. His response spoke volumes: "Pray to the Lord for me, that none of the things which you have spoken may come upon me" (v. 24). He felt no horror of his own black heart, only a horror of the consequences of having one.

Perhaps most tragic were the multiple opportunities Simon had to turn to God. But after his initial profession of faith in baptism, he chose only to continue in sin.

Reflect: How do you know if you are truly repentant for your sins? Carefully study God's law and you will be led to Christ.

Dig Deeper: Joel 2:13; Matthew 3:8; 2 Corinthians 7:10, 11

Justina

Forever Changed, Part 1

"You will seek the your God, and you will find Him if you seek Him with all your heart and with all your soul" (Deuteronomy 4:29).

Justina grew up as part of a flourishing Mennonite community in a beautiful Central American country. Her parents faithfully lived a simple, wholesome lifestyle with a deeply spiritual focus. She rode to school by horse and buggy, studied diligently, and married at a young age as was the custom of her community.

As a child, Justina began listening to a Christian radio station that her parents permitted in their home. Year after year, she listened and soaked up the Scripture truths she was hearing. Justina especially enjoyed her favorite program, which sometimes aired three times a day—*Bible Answers Live*.

Justina loved hearing simple and plain Bible truths about so many questions that had always troubled her. For instance, she'd wondered about what happened when someone died, and how a loving God would burn people forever in hell. But now she heard solid assurance from the Bible that cleared up her confusion and brought peace to her heart.

When she learned about the seventh-day Sabbath, she carefully searched the Bible herself and wondered why she and her family went to church on Sunday. She asked her father. He answered that they went on that day because Jesus was resurrected on Sunday—a standard answer that many first-day Christians are taught.

But Justina couldn't find anywhere in the Bible that said the commandment to keep the Sabbath holy had now been changed to mean Sunday. So she asked her pastor the same question, and he told her he'd get back to her the next week. But he never did.

Justina went on listening to *Bible Answers Live*, growing more and more convicted in her heart.

When she was eighteen, Justina was able to access a computer. She soon found Amazing Facts online and the free gifts that could be downloaded. "This is great!" she rejoiced. Justina immersed herself in study. "I downloaded forty books from the free library!" she recalls. "I read them all."

What she learned began to change her life forever.

Reflect: Is there a particular religious program or book that helped you discover truths that you never knew before? God promises to lead those who earnestly seek Him.

Dig Deeper: 1 Chronicles 16:11; Proverbs 8:17; Matthew 6:33

Justina

Forever Changed, Part 2

> **"[Jesus] said, '[B]lessed are those who hear the
> word of God and keep it!'" (Luke 11:28).**

When Justina discovered Amazing Facts through a local Christian radio station, she was thrilled to learn new Bible truths. "This is great!" she rejoiced. Justina immersed herself in study. "I downloaded forty books from your free library!" she recalls. "I read them all."

Now Justina found herself forever changed. "I could no longer read my Bible the same way." She was living in a Mennonite community still, but in her heart she was a Sabbath-keeper. "I kept trying to labor with everybody, saying, 'Why do we do this? Why do we believe that?'"

When she learned about healthful living principles in the Bible, Justina gave up pork. Even though her husband didn't see these new beliefs in the same way that she did, he agreed that pork no longer needed to be served in their home.

In the meantime, Justina told her brother Peter about what she was learning. She was thrilled to discover that he'd been studying the Bible on his own and was also convicted that Saturday was the Sabbath. Together they began visiting a Sabbath-keeping church and were soon baptized.

Today Justina continues to share with her family and prays for these seeds to bear fruit. Her husband attends church with her, and she rejoices that her sister wants to be baptized soon.

Justina learned deeper truths through years of listening to *Bible Answers Live*. This is the largest Christian radio ministry in that part of Central America, broadcasting to all of Belize, Guatemala, and southern Mexico. Amazing Facts programs have run on this one station for more than 24 years.

Stories like Justina's are happening wherever Bible programs air all over the world. Pray that God will continue to convict listening ears and forever change lives.

Reflect: Do you know someone who listened to Bible truth on a Christian radio or TV station and it changed their life forever? The Lord can change anyone who seeks Him and surrenders all.

Dig Deeper: Proverbs 16:20; Jeremiah 33:3; James 1:22

"There is a way that seems right to a man, but its end is the way of death" (Proverbs 16:25).

It was said of James White that he, in the winter of 1843 alone, brought over 1,000 people to Christ by preaching the advent message.

But as a child, it did not seem that James White would amount to anything. Due to a severe illness, which cost him much of his sight in his youth, he was not able to attend school until the age of 19. However, with his sight now fully restored, White sped through classes in only 29 weeks. In the process of redeeming the time, however, he had made education his most treasured idol. His lust for the knowledge of the world was insatiable.

As a fledgling teacher, White, one day, had a significant conversation with his mother on the topic of religion, specifically the belief that Christ would return in only a few years. He had had no interest in theology while at school, but as his mother spoke of the Second Coming, his heart began to open to the message. There grew a deep struggle within him. On one side was a great desire to believe the advent hope; on the other was the huge investment to his career.

There came upon him a burden to begin praying for his students, a burden to which he yielded. He then received a distinct impression to visit each of his students and offer prayer for each one. The very thought injured his pride—he, the masterful teacher, admitting that he had joined those foolish believers? It was the absolute last thing he wanted to do. But he could not ignore the thought. He could not focus on anything but it, not even his own studies!

Finally, he relented, beginning his journey. Suddenly, as he walked past an unknown home, there came a deep urge to knock on its door. Again, he relented and to his shock learned that it was the home of one of his students who had recently moved. Diligently, he offered prayer. To his amazement some 25 persons—half the neighborhood—were called to join them. None of them were Christians, but they had recently attended some advent meetings. After praying together, White was greatly encouraged. He visited and prayed with every one of his students.

By the following year, he discovered that much of the town had become Christian. Thus began James White's ministry for God.

Reflect: Has your own pride stopped you from responding to conviction from God? Remember, "The lifts up the humble ..." (Psalm 147:6).

Dig Deeper: Job 28:28; Psalm 10:4; James 4:10

**"Pride goes before destruction, and a haughty
spirit before a fall" (Proverbs 16:18).**

Glossophobia, a fear of public speaking, is the number one fear people have.

But it was not so for James White. In his young life he already had quite a good reason to esteem his own efforts, having accomplished more in several months than most youths did in years. While he still struggled over giving up his scholarly pursuits, he decided to respond to the call with which God had been so persistently pressing him: to be a preacher.

Subsequently, he set himself up to preach to a considerably sized congregation. It was something that he was assured he could do. Given his expedited education, he was used to ascending, to achieving, to taking big steps to accomplish big things. And everyone knew that preaching was a lowly profession compared to the conquests of a scholar. It would be easy for him.

It was in this rather arrogant mindset that James White began his career as an evangelist. As a result, his first attempt was a sour one, ending in confusion and embarrassment in front of a large crowd of attendees. His second attempt was even worse: He got lost in his own sermon and broke off after twenty minutes. What a difference from the ambitious, confident young man in the schoolhouse. He, a teacher, could not even get through one lecture.

White was sufficiently humbled. He realized that in his heart of hearts there had grown a pride for his own intellect and a love for worldly wisdom. He had, in essence, tried to teach about God without knowing who God was. He realized that he was much unlearned in matters of Scripture and untried in the work of the Lord.

After attending several meetings on the advent message, he further came to a realization of his own ignorance. He then fully abandoned all notions of a secular education, committed himself to biblical study, and henceforth approached preaching cautiously, reverently, ensuring he was led by the Spirit of God. It was only then, after understanding his own lack, that God was able to raise him up as a most powerful evangelist.

Reflect: Are you doing the work of the Lord in your own strength? God does not call us into service for Him so that we can show off what we can do but that His glory may be revealed in us.

Dig Deeper: Proverbs 11:2; Jeremiah 9:23, 24; Romans 12:3

James White

Mr. Worldly Wiseman, Part 3

"Love never fails. But ... whether there is knowledge, it will vanish away" (1 Corinthians 13:8).

British politician Andrew Bennett once said, "The longest journey you will ever take is the 18 inches from your head to your heart." It is a journey of utmost importance, not least of all to Christians.

As the Advent Movement was progressing and the allotted time of Christ's second coming was drawing near, James White was in the thick of this journey. He had listened to many preach, had studied the Scriptures and prophecies and history associated with the movement, and had even attended two large camp meetings. He thoroughly believed that Christ would return soon. At this last camp meeting, he became impressed, more than ever, to share what he believed with as many as he could.

He lost no time in preparing his presentations and holding meetings in nearby towns. It was then that something clicked for him. He had, up to this point, loved the advent message personally; in his study of the Scriptures, the scholar within him had thrilled at the unfolding of the precise and exquisite prophecies of the Bible.

But it was not until now that his heart truly began to ache and burn for those hopeful, penitent souls who came to receive God's promises. Before this, the message had been powerful to him; it had changed him. Now he saw that the message, God's Word, had the power to do the same for every person sitting in that meeting hall. How much more precious were those Scriptures to him then!

He now understood the immense responsibility he had to these people. Many desired further guidance, but he, new to the faith himself, was incapable of providing for them. He contacted his brother, an able minister who also believed in the advent message, for help. About a month and a half later, his brother had shepherded and baptized those same people and had set up a church for them as well.

How different from the James White who first took up the mantle of preaching. His pride and contempt and surety in his own abilities—all had been laid in the dust. He now saw the world through the eyes of a converted man, a man who saw each person as a soul beloved in Jesus Christ.

Reflect: What is your motivation for ministry? Do you have the same love for others as Christ has for you?

Dig Deeper: Isaiah 58:6–10; John 13:34; 1 John 3:14–18

Fred and Marianne

Blue Skies, Part 1

"The word of God is living and powerful, and sharper than any two-edged sword, piercing even to the division of soul and spirit, and of joints and marrow, and is a discerner of the thoughts and intents of the heart" (Hebrews 4:12).

Marianne discovered Amazing Facts one day while watching a Christian TV network. Confronted with topics that most churches don't dare to teach, she knew she had to share what she was hearing with her husband, Fred. As they listened, the Amazing Facts speaker said, "Don't take my word for it. Look it up for yourself." So Fred and Marianne did just that.

They continued to thirst for knowledge as they poured through their Bibles. Every point that was presented held strong in scriptural context. Fred was also privy to current events: "I knew the end times were here before I ever got involved watching Amazing Facts." The excited couple sought out new topics as God vivified their search. As their journey continued they began to hear life-changing truths.

One day a pamphlet on the Ten Commandments caught Fred's interest. With newfound energy, he researched every relevant text listed and then concluded, "About ninety percent of the churches have been lying to people. Sunday is dead wrong. It's not a holy day." The couple found themselves rather alone in this discovery.

Fred grew discouraged: "Most churches don't know the truth and they don't want to know." But it remained his policy to never argue with fellow Christians. However, as world events continued to unfold with ever increasing speed just as in the times of Noah (Matthew 24:37–39), their brothers and sisters in Christ stuck to their routines without a care for the world's state of affairs. "Many people want to put their faith in the government," Fred exclaimed, "but God is the only government I need."

Marianne continued to study with Fred, encouraging him. They found their solace in the Holy Spirit, and hope in the Word. They also found a wealth of helpful study guides through Amazing Facts. As Fred studied, he concluded, "When you follow the government, you get angry. When you follow God, you find peace."

But the Lord had even more truths to reveal to Fred and Marianne.

Reflect: Was there ever a time in your life when you didn't want to know the truth about something? Jesus is patient and will keep knocking at the door of your heart.

Dig Deeper: John 14:23; Acts 5:29; Revelation 3:20

Fred and Marianne

Blue Skies, Part 2

"Though now you do not see Him, yet believing, you rejoice with joy inexpressible and full of glory" (1 Peter 1:8).

While studying materials from Amazing Facts, Fred and Marianne continued to be faithful participants in their old church. Fred had attended for 28 years, and Marianne for 35. Fred was even known to dutifully set up for Communion every Saturday night. Impressed by the Word, Marianne urged her husband to consider finding a new church group. So they quit attending. None of their friends ever called to ask why.

They wanted to start their own Bible study group. To help, Amazing Facts put them in touch with a local Sabbath-keeping pastor. Pastor Patrick would visit them two to three times a week. Fred immediately noted that he was not only knowledgeable, but spiritual. "His talk was not cheap."

Fred and Marianne started attending the pastor's church, and were eagerly welcomed into the body of believers. They greatly enjoyed discussing the Bible with their new friends. To their surprise, the other churchgoers knew their Bible well and were familiar with the things they had researched. This inspired them to study for baptism. But Marianne's health was wavering, and a second stroke left her partially blind. But it didn't stop them as Fred continued to read to Marianne every day.

When the Sabbath of their baptism finally came, the deacons discovered the water heater for the baptismal tank was broken. The humble church had not had the pleasure of conducting a baptism in six years. So the leaders recommended that they postpone the event, but Fred and Marianne would not budge. "They were excited and joyful to be born again in God's church," said the pastor, "They are very sincere and committed." They braved the 60-degree Fahrenheit water, even with their medical concerns.

God blessed their decision. "The last few months have been worth a lifetime," Fred emphatically stated. Today, the couple is inspired like never before. They used tips from Amazing Facts to comb the Scriptures for new truths they could apply to their lives. They threw out any idols they had around the house. They also improved their health habits. Fred notes the incredible benefits of health when following Christ in word and deed. "This may sound strange, but now when I walk my dog the sky is bluer and the flowers are brighter."

Reflect: Have you discovered the Sabbath as a day to strengthen your relationship with God? Perhaps you need to rediscover this sacred time.

Dig Deeper: Proverbs 10:28; Luke 15:7; Romans 15:13

Thomas

Cancer Saved My Life, Part 1

> "He said to me, 'My grace is sufficient for you, for My strength is made perfect in weakness.' Therefore, most gladly I will rather boast in my infirmities, that the power of Christ may rest upon me" (2 Corinthians 12:9).

Thomas grew up going from foster home to foster home. None of them were Christian and abuse was pretty common in most of them, not to mention alcohol and drugs. The emotional pain he experienced was so intense that suicidal thoughts were normal for as long as he can remember. "My life was a total mess," he shares, "I didn't trust anybody." He felt like "a piece of worthless junk" and wondered if life was worth living. "If I will never amount to anything, why go on?"

As he searched for meaning in his life, he turned to many things he thought would make him happy. He worked on movie sets, but that brought no fulfillment. He turned to worldly music, but it left him feeling empty. He thought that being married would fill a void in his life, but after five years in a marriage, it disintegrated. At one point he moved across country, but ended up going further into drugs and alcohol. "I felt like I was sinking deeper into the pit of hell."

"I began wondering if God would help me find answers, so I began checking out different churches. I tried the Mormon Church, the Catholic Church, and others. It was a dead end," he remembers. He moved back to where he began, but kept sliding lower into despair. "My life was out of control. I tried suicide several times. I didn't want to live. I was angry and put up emotional walls to keep people away."

When Thomas' health took a turn for the worse, he checked himself into a hospital. The doctor that first worked with him said, "If you had continued drinking and doing drugs, I would have given you about one week to live." After doing several tests, they finally discovered he had terminal cancer, an incurable rare form of leukemia.

Would this be the end for Thomas, or the beginning?

Reflect: Can you think of a difficulty in your life that turned out to be a blessing in disguise? God can use trials to polish gems for His kingdom.

Dig Deeper: Psalm 38:10; 2 Corinthians 4:8, 9; James 1:2–4

Thomas

Cancer Saved My Life, Part 2

"Jesus put out His hand and touched him ..." (Matthew 8:3).

Thomas ended up in the hospital. His life was broken and while lying in bed, his thoughts turned to God. He remembered one of the churches he had investigated eight years before. At that time, he was still doing drugs and didn't take any religion very seriously. Now he called for the pastor of a local Sabbath-keeping church.

The pastor came and prayed with Thomas. He assured him the church would be praying as well. "The funny part about the cancer," he relates, "is that this death sentence became the beginning of life for me. During this time, when all sorts of blood tests were being done and my life hung in the balance," Thomas remembers, "I began thinking once more about God. It was on my deathbed that I realized how much I needed Jesus." When things turned for the worse, Thomas was anointed.

"It was a turning point in my life," Thomas explains, "when I called up Pastor Danny and introduced myself. I told him on the phone that I wanted to be baptized, whether I lived or died. Later, when I was out of the hospital, he actually drove to where I worked. I went out and sat in his car where he prayed for me and then gave me some *Amazing Facts Bible Study Guides*. I took the lessons home and studied them like I had never studied anything before in my life. I prayed equally as hard."

Thomas was so committed to complete the lessons that he went through three of them every day and within a week completed them all. About this time, he went to the doctor for a check-up. He was bewildered when the doctor smiled and left the room. Three times the doctor came into the room to perform a specific test and three times he left smiling. Then he finally came back and threw some papers on the table in front of Thomas and said, "I don't understand, but your readings are all normal! Read them for yourself. By God's grace you made it through."

Thomas was baptized and is now a living testimony of God's power. As he looks back, he shares, "Cancer saved my life. If this disease had not stopped me dead in my tracks, I would have continued with my life of alcohol and drugs. Like many of my friends, I would probably be dead right now."

Reflect: When was the last time you were stopped dead in your tracks? Was God trying to get your attention?

Dig Deeper: Matthew 4:23, 24; Romans 8:28; James 5:13–16

John Mark

Second Chances

> **"Through the mercies we are not consumed,**
> **because His compassions fail not. They are new**
> **every morning" (Lamentations 3:22, 23).**

It took Thomas Edison more than 10,000 unsuccessful attempts to produce the electric light bulb. America's greatest inventor certainly was not shy about taking second chances.

During the Apostle Paul's first missionary journey, there was a young man traveling with him who also ended up needing a second chance. John Mark was a relative of Barnabas, Paul's fellow evangelist, and assisted the two apostles on the trip.

While not much is known of him, there is a high probability that John Mark came to the faith due to the efforts of the apostle Peter (1 Peter 5:13). What is known is that he was an early Christian convert and that he witnessed—if not under the guidance of Peter, certainly through Paul and Barnabas—the mighty power of God.

In the first leg of the mission alone, when on the island of Cyprus, he was privy to a resounding victory of the gospel over the snares of deceit and devilry. But after this, John Mark somehow got cold feet. Scripture records that, having successfully voyaged to the southern coast of Asia Minor, he then deserted Paul and Barnabas and sailed back home to Jerusalem (Acts 13:13).

While we are not told the reason, we are told of the damage this did to John Mark's reputation. During preparations for a second missionary journey, Paul and Barnabas argued heatedly over his usefulness (15:37, 38). While Barnabas desired to give him a second chance, Paul vehemently disagreed. John Mark was a vacillating coward, one who had run for the comforts of home over the privilege of laboring in God's vineyard. But in the end, John Mark did get another opportunity, sailing with Barnabas back to Cyprus (v. 39).

This time, despite the dangers and hardships that surely assailed him, John Mark recommitted his life to God. Aided by the patient guidance of Barnabas, he began what would eventually be the life of a faithful missionary. Several years later, in Paul's own epistles, we find that John Mark is now favored by the Apostle to the Gentiles (Colossians 4:10; 2 Timothy 4:11; Philemon 24). Ultimately, sparse though his own name may be in the pages of history, he gave us a timeless gift—Peter's account of the life of Jesus in the Gospel of Mark.

Reflect: Jesus Christ gave us the gift of eternal life. Do you need a second chance? God is ready and willing to use you if you are willing to be used by Him.

Dig Deeper: Job 33:29, 30; Romans 15:1, 2; Colossians 3:12–14

Mr. Cheng

Finding a Spiritual Home, Part 1

"Look to Me, and be saved, all you ends of the earth! For I am God, and there is no other" (Isaiah 45:22).

When Mr. Cheng from China was young he attended church every Sunday with his mom. But he never really learned the truth about God. After graduating from school, he started work. In his job he experienced some accidents which convinced him that God was protecting him. "From that time I began to have more interest in God, but I didn't attend church," he shares.

Mr. Cheng married a woman who didn't believe in God. "She worshiped many different idols and burned incense to them," he explains. "I deeply regretted worshiping idols with her." In his heart he knew Jesus loved him and he felt the Holy Spirit calling to his heart. But he didn't respond and gradually forgot about God.

Later, Mr. Cheng started his own business running a cold noodle restaurant. One day a salesman came by to promote his products. Mr. Cheng noticed the words on his car: "Those who believe in Jesus will go to heaven. Those who don't believe will go to hell." He asked the salesman about his faith. "I was once more reminded that I should follow after God." So he began attending church on Sunday and reading his Bible. "My spiritual life grew when I read the Bible," he remembers. He even started playing hymns in his restaurant as a witness to his customers.

A few years later, Mr. Cheng watched a Christian film on Noah's ark. Afterward he noticed a link to a movie called *Cosmic Conflict*. He watched it and was so impressed that he visited the Chinese Amazing Facts website. "This is an amazing site!" he shares. "I am so thankful that God led me to Amazing Facts. It has completely changed my life!"

But there was another faith step God had in store for Mr. Cheng.

Reflect: Can you think of a time you forgot about God? Have you ever turned away from the promptings of the Holy Spirit? Get on your knees and ask God to forgive you and help you listen to His call.

Dig Deeper: Psalm 22:27; Acts 15:19; 1 Thessalonians 1:9

Mr. Cheng

Finding a Spiritual Home, Part 2

"Whoever drinks of the water that I shall give him will never thirst. But the water that I shall give him will become in him a fountain of water springing up into everlasting life" (John 4:14).

After Mr. Cheng discovered the Amazing Facts Chinese website, he spent his days watching Pastor Doug's sermons. "My thirsty heart finally found the true source of the Water of Life," he explains. "The Words of God that I heard became my food. The more I ate of the truth, the more I grew." He was so excited about this discovery that he shared Pastor Doug's DVDs with all the different churches in his hometown along with books that he acquired from the Amazing Facts website.

Sadly, his efforts to witness to Sunday church leaders were not well-received. One pastor was indifferent about Mr. Cheng's suggestion to share the Amazing Facts resources with members. That's when he decided to contact an Amazing Facts worker and ask where he could find a true, Sabbath-keeping church. He was directed to a nearby town where he attended and was warmly received.

On a beautiful spring day, Mr. Cheng was baptized into the Sabbath-keeping church. The pastor and members of this church were very kind and treated him like an old friend. "I could see Jesus among them," he relates. "I finally found my long-lost spiritual home. I finally came back to God. I am so thankful for what the Lord has done for me."

Mr. Cheng, is now 34 years old owns four restaurants. "Every day I read my Bible, pray, and share the gospel." He also carefully watches the Amazing Facts website for new materials to be uploaded. He plans to make his business a place to share the good news.

"I am surprised at God's grace toward me," he relates. "I am so blessed and truly want, through His wisdom and strength, to do God's will. I'd like to follow the example of Jesus. May God increase my faith and help me to become more like Christ."

Reflect: Have you ever been so thirsty that you felt like you were going to die? Can you imagine being so thirsty for God that without Him you would perish? Turn to Jesus, the Water of Life, and He will quench your deepest longings.

Dig Deeper: Nehemiah 9:19; Isaiah 49:10; Amos 8:11

Wernher von Braun

Rocket Man, Part 1

"Whatever you do, do all to the glory of God" (1 Corinthians 10:31).

The man largely responsible for landing the first man on the moon was actually a former Nazi.

Wernher von Braun, born into German nobility, had a fascination with space exploration. Though his family was Lutheran, von Braun himself cared more for rockets than God. At 25 years of age, he joined the Nazis and several years later the SS. His passion for rocket engineering, in particular his design of the V-2 "vengeance weapon," led him into a crucial position in Hitler's regime.

There still remains much controversy surrounding von Braun's involvement with the Nazis during World War II. He was a man who did not oppose the use of concentration camp prisoners to build his rockets; but he was also a man whose preference for space travel over German victory led to his short arrest by the Gestapo. Was this a man whose ambitious pursuit of outer space drove his actions more than any moral or political belief? Whether von Braun became disillusioned with the Nazis at some point during the war or whether he simply used the fascist platform as an opportunistic stepping stone in his career is up for debate.

But by 1945, it was obvious to many that Germany was fighting a losing battle. Von Braun and his team secretly decided to surrender to the United States and devised a plan to do so. It was difficult; von Braun and his team were highly prized by the Nazis and closely guarded, more so as defeat appeared imminent. It looked like their fate was sealed: The Nazis could not afford to let them live if Germany lost; von Braun's brilliant mind was too valuable. But after moving locations several times and being separated from the majority of his team, von Braun was finally able to surrender himself, some of his staff, and their work to an American soldier in Austria.

Surprisingly, in a public statement issued after his arrest, von Braun attributed his decision to God. "[W]e felt that only by surrendering such a weapon to people who are guided not by the laws of materialism but by Christianity and humanity could such an assurance to the world be best secured," he said. Was there, after all, a twinge of faith in this ambitious man? Had an interest in God perhaps been awakened through the horrors of war?

Reflect: Do you use your abilities for God's glory? Are the fruits of your labor dedicated to Him?

Dig Deeper: Exodus 36:1, 2; Proverbs 16:3; Colossians 3:23, 24

Wernher von Braun

Rocket Man, Part 2

"The heavens declare the glory of God; and the firmament shows His handiwork" (Psalm 19:1).

Operation Paperclip was the top-secret mission that evacuated Wernher von Braun and more than 1,600 other German scientists to the United States. As a result, von Braun and his former team were now employed by the United States Army. They spent the next few years at Fort Bliss, Texas, building weapons and getting used to American life. For von Braun, the move had been difficult. In Germany he had been respected and highly valued; here in America, there was a decisive suspicion towards him and his team and, from some, even outright dislike. And he still was not any closer to achieving his dream of space travel. His work was confined to boosting U.S. military presence.

But something significant occurred during those early days at Fort Bliss, when a neighbor invited von Braun to church. Von Braun accepted the invite, not because of any personal need but out of a pure curiosity to experience religion in America. What he witnessed drastically overturned his expectations. To von Braun, religion had always been an irrelevant set of cultural rituals, steeped in tradition and uselessness. You would do religion just to say you did it, but it made no real difference in your life.

But when von Braun walked up to that humble, homely church in Texas, he found a group of Christians who truly believed in God and acted like it. It made an impression on him, and there began to be marked changes in his life. He began to speak and write boldly on his views as a creationist scientist, even granting an interview to a pastor entitled "The Farther We Probe into Space, the Greater My Faith." He became an Episcopalian and throughout his life continued to proclaim the glory of God as our Creator, our Judge, and our Savior.

After multiple failed proposals and requests, von Braun was finally able to divert his work from tools of destruction to tools of exploration—eventually becoming the director of NASA's Marshall Space Flight Center. Among the achievements of his illustrious career was the development of the Saturn family of rockets, which included the Saturn V, the rocket that launched Apollo 11 (and other Apollo spacecraft) to the moon.

Reflect: Has your faith been manifested in your life? Has someone else's faith demonstrated the character of God to you?

Dig Deeper: Matthew 11:29; John 13:12–16; Ephesians 5:1, 2

Ruth

I Belonged

"How precious also are Your thoughts to me, O God!" (Psalm 139:17).

Ruth grew up with no spiritual or Bible training and didn't learn about the love of God until after going through some very difficult times in her life. She also lived a lesbian lifestyle from which she gratefully thanks the Lord for deliverance.

While mourning the death of a dear friend, Ruth received an invitation to Bible studies through a flyer she received in the mail. She responded and was contacted by a Sabbath-keeper named Diana, who began weekly studies with her, using the *Amazing Facts Bible Study Guides*.

Prior to finding the Bible study card, Ruth had limited knowledge of even the most common Bible stories, but she was eager to learn, and the people at the Sabbath-keeping church in her town were very kind and welcoming to her. "They didn't look at me like I shouldn't be there. They treated me like I belonged," says Ruth.

Due to her lack of experience with studying the Bible, Ruth had difficulty finding Bible references, but she was determined to continue. She got an electronic tablet that allowed her to find the verses quickly, and she then was able to get through the lessons with more ease. "By lesson three," says Diana, "she accepted Jesus as her Savior and requested baptism."

Ruth's journey has not been an easy one. She has had some real challenges. Several times a ghostly figure appeared to her. At first she thought it was her deceased friend coming back from the dead to visit her. "We had studied that death is a sleep and that our dead loved ones cannot come back to talk with us," shares Diana, "and Ruth came to realize that this was not really her friend visiting her, but an evil angel imitating her."

Ruth and Diana continued to study, using an Amazing Facts book on baptism called *In His Steps*. Once she decided to join God's remnant church, her fear of water became a very real factor when it came time for baptism by immersion. But once again, her faith triumphed. With the support of Diana's husband standing with Ruth in the water, she was baptized one warm summer Sabbath morning.

Reflect: Have you ever been in a situation where you felt like an outsider? Put yourself in the shoes of a guest visiting your church and help them to feel warmly welcomed.

Dig Deeper: Leviticus 19:34; Matthew 10:29–31; 1 Peter 4:9

Apollos

Preacher Man

"Give instruction to a wise man, and he will be still wiser; teach a just man, and he will increase in learning" (Proverbs 9:9).

Imagine you are lecturing at a colloquium at one of the Ivy League universities. You are a postdoctoral fellow and are poised to become the next Einstein of your field. After your lecture, a janitor approaches you and firmly but kindly lists several points that were incorrect in your presentation. What would you do?

Apollos was a Jewish contemporary of the apostle Paul. Described as "eloquent" and "mighty in the Scriptures" (Acts 18:24), he was a powerful teacher, studied, astute, and talented, who had traveled many miles to Ephesus. Crowds gathered in the synagogue to hear this gifted preacher. However, after he had finished speaking, a couple of tentmakers approached him. Their names were Aquila and Priscilla, a man and his wife who were faithful Christians in their own right.

In private, they told Apollos that there were some important facts missing from his vast array of knowledge (v. 26). While Apollos was a devout student of the Scriptures, he had been taught only up to the preaching of John the Baptist (v. 25). He, like John, believed that Jesus was the Messiah, but he was ignorant of the full meaning of that statement, how Jesus' death and resurrection meant salvation offered freely to all men, how Jesus had given us the gift of the Holy Spirit, how the gospel was to go to the whole world.

This meeting with Aquila and Priscilla was a massive turning point for Apollos. It was as though he were holding a single candle up to a portrait before Aquila and Priscilla drew back the curtains and flooded the entire room with the noonday sun. This was the answer he had been searching for, the complementary half of the message he had been preaching. Apollos was not too proud nor too stubborn to be a teachable teacher. With joy he accepted the good news and continued on as a true evangelist. Welcomed into the Christian church, he worked in tandem with Paul as a missionary, bringing many others into the faith (vv. 27, 28; 1 Corinthians 16:12; Titus 3:13).

Reflect: Have you reached a point in your faith where you think you know it all? Are you complacent about your knowledge of God? Humbly seek a closer walk with the Lord and ask for a deeper understanding of His will for your life.

Dig Deeper: Ecclesiastes 4:13; Matthew 28:19, 20; Luke 18:17

John

A Wrong Turn to the Right Place

"Jesus said to him, 'I am the way, the truth, and the life. No one comes to the Father except through Me'" (John 14:6).

While driving on a new delivery route, John missed a turn and had to make his way back. As he drove down the "wrong" street, his mouth fell open upon passing a sign that read "Amazing Facts." This was the ministry that helped change his life! After work, he drove back and was given a royal tour.

"Amazing Facts has been a big part of my walk with Christ," he explains. "Seven years ago I was living in a confused world that included marijuana and impurity." Then one day he saw his neighbor trying to move a mattress down from the top floor of her apartment. After helping her, she asked, "Do you know Jesus?" Then she invited John to attend a Bible study at her daughter's home. He went.

"At this time in my life I was surrounded by non-believers. I never read the Bible," he shares. When he went to the Bible study, the first thing they did was pop in a *Final Events* DVD. "Since that moment," John tells, "I have had a hunger for God's Word.

John started thinking about attending church. As he debated whether to attend, Joanne, his neighbor and Jolene, her daughter, invited him to a series of meetings at their church. After the meetings had concluded, the pastor connected John with one of the church elders named Paul to study the Bible. Every week they went over the *Amazing Facts Bible Study Guides*. John was baptized on his birthday.

Since that time, Amazing Facts has helped John begin his life again in his new marriage and also in sharing with others the truths he has learned.

John was a little frustrated the day he missed his turn on his driving route, but all along God was directing his pathway to Amazing Facts. "I was so glad to be able to say thank you to everyone at Amazing Facts," he says. John was once going down the wrong road in his life, but God caused him to turn in the right direction.

Reflect: Have you ever driven down a one-way street in the wrong direction? God can use any circumstance to turn us around toward Him, and in so doing make us a blessing to others.

Dig Deeper: Psalm 32:8; Proverbs 16:9; Isaiah 48:17

Phan Thị Kim Phúc

Napalm Girl, Part 1

"Eye has not seen, nor ear heard, nor have entered into the heart of man the things which God has prepared for those who love Him" (1 Corinthians 2:9).

A waifish Vietnamese girl, stark naked, runs crying down the street amidst a smattering of soldiers and other children; behind her the sky is lit with the hell of war. It is an iconic, Pulitzer Prize-winning photograph, taken in 1972 towards the end of the Vietnam War. Its centerpiece, nine-year-old Phan Thi Kim Phúc, had, moments before, been caught in the explosion of a napalm bomb which had incinerated her clothes and seared her entire back and left arm.

She was not supposed to survive. Third-degree burns covered 30 percent of her small body. Every morning at the hospital, where she remained for over a year, the nurses would draw a bath to peel off her dead skin. There was always a point when the pain became too severe and she would pass out. Seventeen surgeries later, Kim was still alive and released to go home.

Several years later, the war had ended, and she now lived in a unified Communist country. Two of her cousins who were caught in the same blast had died from their injuries. Why was she the one who had survived? Oftentimes, she wished she had not. She contemplated suicide. The pain was constant, unbearable at times, and there was not enough money for medication. The scars were horrible, disfiguring.

But Kim knew one thing from her experience in the hospital: She wanted to be a doctor. At 19, she began medical school but was abruptly pulled out by her own government and subsequently paraded around to foreign reporters. Her new life as a Communist propaganda tool was filled with fabricated scripts and strict supervision. She loathed it. Already trapped in her body, she was now fast secured in a political web, her one dream vanquished in a puff of smoke.

Her one question was: Why? Why had she been spared to become this shell of a person? What was the point of it all? One day, she found the answer in a pile of library books.

Reflect: Does your life at times seem purposeless? Do the trials you go through seem meaningless and cruel? Ask for spiritual eyes to see God's specific calling for you.

Dig Deeper: Psalm 33:10, 11; Ecclesiastes 3:1–8; Jeremiah 29:11–13

Phan Thị Kim Phúc

Napalm Girl, Part 2

"Reach your finger here, and look at My hands; and reach your hand here, and put it into My side. Do not be unbelieving, but believing" (John 20:27).

Cao Đài is a patchwork of different faiths: Buddhism, Islam, Christianity, to name a few. Its adherents believe in multiple gods, and its goal is for people to become gods themselves. That may sound enticing to some, but for Kim—the severely burned "Napalm Girl"—Cao Đài was the religion in which she had been raised, and it was not doing her any good.

Kim was hurting. Kim was angry. Kim was lost. And no matter how many times she pleaded to her gods for a way out of that cage of suffering and exploitation, nothing happened.

In desperation she went to the library, grabbing book after book off the shelf. One of these had to have the answer, the purpose to her life, the solution to her pain. In the stack was a New Testament; after spending an hour reading the Gospels, Kim discarded the other books. There was something about this Man, Jesus.

The accounts of Jesus' life described how He had been beaten and ridiculed and died a most horrific death, and how He had wept and cried aloud in unbearable suffering—that was like her. He was God, but He had gone through what she was going through, except much worse. He had scars too, like she did, except His were for her. She had never known that about Jesus.

It was this Jesus who held the answers to her most precious questions. From that day forth, Kim continued to study the Bible. She began to realize how much she needed what Jesus promised in His Word. She was filled with so much hate. She hated that bomb and the man who dropped it, she hated that pointless failure of a war, she hated those men to whom she smiled and nodded and for whom she lied.

So on Christmas Eve of that same year, Kim gave her life to Jesus. She asked Him to take away her anger and hatred and bitterness and give her that peace His Word promised—and Jesus did. Kim was finally able to forgive. From there, Kim found her purpose: to share her testimony of what God did for her to the world.

Reflect: Are you holding onto grudges? Are you reliving painful memories? Bring your burdens to Jesus, "[t]he Sun of Righteousness [who] shall arise with healing in His wings" (Malachi 4:2). Let God's forgiveness take your pain and bury it in the deepest ocean.

Dig Deeper: Psalm 34:17–22; Matthew 5:43–45; Luke 6:37, 38

Lilian

Seeking Answers

"Before they call, I will answer; and while they are still speaking, I will hear" (Isaiah 65:24).

Lilian was searching for answers. Born into a Roman Catholic family in Puerto Rico, she observed the traditions of that faith, even when the rites and practices failed to offer her the hope and understanding she desired. Despite her rigorous religious training, many questions and suspicions remained.

"All my life I have wanted to follow Christ, but I did not have much knowledge," Lilian says. "I obeyed the rules of the church but with much doubt. When I was 25, I visited Avila, Spain, and saw a Catholic saint in a glass urn and his finger in a glass container." She was told the other parts of this saint had been divided into relics for other churches. "That experience had a very negative impact on me."

Later in life, Lilian decided to take classes on teaching the Bible but was unsettled when she heard the Bible described as nothing more than "a literary genre." While teaching workshops on prayer, she remained uneasy. "I no longer believed in the intercession of Mary or the saints; I did not pray the rosary or prostrate myself to images," she says.

When Amazing Facts evangelist Carlos Muñoz travelled to her town to present the gospel, Lilian's daughter—who was already preparing to join the church—invited her to attend.

"Hearing about the credibility of the Bible at these meetings swept away my doubts," Lilian says. "When Carlos quoted Jesus in Matthew 15:3 asking, 'Why do you break the command of God for the sake of your tradition?' I remembered the priest's answer to my question about the Catholic Church being based on tradition."

Thanks to the presentations, she says, "I saw clearly the path that Jesus left to us in the Bible and the error I was in for many years. Now I know the coming of Christ is near, and I know I have to share this message with others who are also in confusion as I was."

Lilian was joyfully baptized and says, "I keep the Sabbath because God is my Creator. I changed my diet. I now have new friendships. My husband is surprised, but he supports me, and I pray for his conversion. Peace is with me. I thank God every day for clearing up my doubts and for showing me the way."

Reflect: Have you ever struggled with doubts about God? When you sincerely call to the Lord in prayer, confessing your sins, God promises to lead you into the truth.

Dig Deeper: John 15:17; Hebrews 11:6; 1 John 5:14, 15

David

You Are the Man, Part 1

"The has sought for Himself a man after His own heart, and the has commanded him to be commander over His people, because you have not kept what the commanded you" (1 Samuel 13:14).

At 25 years old, Stan Larkin lived for 555 days with a completely artificial heart while awaiting a donor transplant. His artificial device, called a "SynCardia," even allowed Larkin to play basketball. But while an amazing feat of modern medicine, the SynCardia could never replace a real heart—especially the new heart that God desires to give to each one of us.

David was a man who desired a heart like God's. As a youth, he loved the Lord and wanted to do His will. For this he was chosen by God to replace Saul as king of Israel and was anointed by the prophet Samuel when only a boy (1 Samuel 16:13).

But David's ascent to the throne was not an easy road. His victories, starting with his defeat of Goliath, the Philistine giant, always seemed paired with great afflictions. One day esteemed by King Saul—his son-in-law even—and the next day he became a hunted fugitive. Though beloved by the people, he was persecuted by the king and separated from his family, his best friend, and his wife.

But it was because of these hardships that David leaned so much upon the will of God. He had nothing of his own, no home, no money. His only security was in God. While in rare times he showed flashes of impatience and vengeance, like during his encounter with Nabal (1 Samuel 25:12, 13), or fear and distrust, like when he defected to the Philistines (27:1), David primarily put his trust in God, and when he did so, he flourished. Habitually asking the Lord's counsel in battle, David gained multiple victories against Israel's enemies. Yielding to God as the only righteous Judge, he mercifully spared Saul's life twice over (24:4–7; 26:7–12). Faithfully waiting for years, at the age of 30, David was finally given the throne (2 Samuel 5:4).

His enemies nearly vanquished, his people unified, his kingdom prosperous, David finally settled into his long-awaited rule. Now, for the first time ever, he was at peace. He did not have to run; he did not have to fight. He was in need of nothing, so he thought. And in that moment David stepped away from God.

Reflect: Are you a person after God's own heart? Do you want what God wants or what you yourself want? Trust in God's ways for they are better than your own.

Dig Deeper: Psalm 25:9; Matthew 23:10–12; Acts 14:22

David

You Are the Man, Part 2

"For out of the heart proceed evil thoughts, murders, adulteries, fornications, thefts, false witness, blasphemies" (Matthew 15:19).

On March 20, 1927, Ruth Snyder and her lover, Henry Judd Gray, murdered Ruth's husband in a premeditated crime that resulted in a botched insurance policy, sensational publicity, and eventually a major motion picture. King David, at one time a man so entirely devoted to God, also claims a place among these ranks of infamy.

It was at the height of his glory that David, espying Bathsheba from his rooftop, made the fateful decision to send for her, after being made aware that she was the wife of one of his best warriors, Uriah the Hittite (2 Samuel 11:2–4). Upon discovering that Bathsheba had become pregnant from their tryst, David then attempted to cover up the deed.

David's army had at this point laid siege to the Ammonites, preparing to deliver a crushing blow to their rebellion. But David had called Uriah from the battlefront and plied him with gifts in the hopes that the mighty man would return to his own home and particularly to Bathsheba (vv. 6–8). Perhaps then, thought David, the unborn child could be passed off as Uriah's own, instead of the king's bastard son.

Unfortunately for David, Uriah was too loyal and too conscientious to desert his fellow soldiers for the comforts of his wife and bed. Despite David's multiple attempts, the Hittite remained dutiful to his post.

What was David to do? If his affair was discovered, he would be a disgrace. What would the populace think and say, they who thought so highly of him? What would Uriah do to him and Bathsheba? He might even lose his life. In that desperate mindset, thinking only of his own position and his own reputation, David devised a wicked plot. He would kill Uriah but make it look like an accident, and he would enlist the help of his captain, Joab, to do it. The cowardly murder was carried out, and Uriah died valiantly on the battlefield during the siege (v. 17).

In one final complicit act, David and Bathsheba married so that it would seem as though the baby had been conceived legitimately (v. 27).

And David then thought that he had washed his hands of the bloody affair. But how wrong he was.

Reflect: In times of idleness and ease, have you allowed your heart to stray from God? After giving in to one temptation, have you found yourself giving in to others more easily? Lean on the Lord's strength and He will help you be an overcomer.

Dig Deeper: Proverbs 4:14–17; Matthew 26:41; 1 Corinthians 10:12, 13

David

You Are the Man, Part 3

"Create in me a clean heart, O God, and renew a steadfast spirit within me" (Psalm 51:10).

In December 2003, serial killer Gary Ridgway sat expressionless in court as a barrage of victims' family members hurled their pain, disgust, and fury at him. But then 63-year-old Robert Rule began to speak.

"Mr. Ridgway," the white-haired father addressed him, "[y]ou've made it difficult to live up to what I believe, and what God says to do, and that is to forgive. And He doesn't say to forgive certain people; He says to forgive all. So you are forgiven, sir."

At that, the killer's hard veneer cracked, and his eyes welled up with tears.

When Nathan, the prophet of God, visited David after the death of Uriah, he told the king a story of a rich man and a poor man whose only lamb was slain injudiciously by the former (2 Samuel 12:1–4).

Outraged, David pronounced sentence upon the rich man, "As the lives, the man who has done this shall surely die!" (v. 5).

Immediately, Nathan retorted, "You are the man!" (v. 7). He went on to correspond David's own conduct in his adulterous affair with Bathsheba and his murder of Uriah with that of the rich man in the story.

David, shocked, suddenly realized his sin. The mirror had been held up; the hammer had struck. Horrified, he did not run nor did he deny it. Instead, he confessed, "I have sinned against the " (v. 13).

And the Lord forgave him.

What miracles does forgiveness produce upon the human heart? Can it soften even the hardest of criminals?

David could have ranted, raged, rebelled. But he did not. When told that, because of his own actions, his child with Bathsheba would die and his family be torn apart, he appealed for the life of the child (vv. 10, 11, 14–16). How David must have wished that he could take back what he had done.

But when the child died (v. 18), he did not resist. Instead, he rededicated himself to God and accepted the consequences of his transgressions (v. 20).

In Psalm 51, David wrote a prayer of repentance, pleading for a complete transformation of character. His heart had now returned to its humble state, "broken," "contrite" (Psalm 51:17). Once more he became a man after God's own heart.

Reflect: Have you ever been caught red-handed? What has been your reaction to your own guilt? God wants us to learn from our mistakes so we don't repeat them.

Dig Deeper: Psalm 119:67; Isaiah 55:7; 1 John 1:9

"For this reason we also thank God without ceasing, because when you received the word of God which you heard from us, you welcomed it not as the word of men, but as it is in truth, the word of God, which also effectively works in you who believe" (1 Thessalonians 2:13).

How does a Baptist family struggling with issues like grace and commandment-keeping discover liberating truth? Apparently by discovering Amazing Facts television broadcasts. Jeffery, who lives with his wife, Jennie, grew up the oldest of seven children. "We were a very conservative, homeschooling, country-living, garden-growing family," says Jeffery, "and we were always pretty much the odd ones in the bunch."

Jeffery remembers going regularly to church with his family up to about the age of twelve. Having doctrinal questions but not finding Bible answers to those questions in their church, Jeffery's family left the Baptist religion. "This wasn't easy," Jeffery remembers, "because both of my parents' families were strong Baptists."

Nevertheless, Jeffery's family continued their search for Bible answers. For a few years, they went from small church to small church, but finally opted to have church at home. Each Sunday morning, they would listen to a television broadcast that featured various speakers. One morning, Doug Batchelor was speaking from the *Millennium of Prophecy* series.

"We must have gotten in on the beginning of the series because Sunday after Sunday, my family sat spellbound to Doug Batchelor's preaching straight from the Bible. Each week, we would tune in to hear more on topics that we had thought were only important to us. The intricate detail with which these topics were presented was very important to us. He gained our confidence with more basic topics. Then when new topics, which seemed strange to us at first, like hell and the Sabbath were discussed, it was so amazing!"

Jeffery shares that it is difficult to convey in words just how wonderful it was to be enlightened with truth his family had never before heard. "I thank the Lord for being so patient, loving, and merciful."

Since the *Millennium of Prophecy* broadcasts were limited to 30-minute slots on the station Jeffery's family was viewing, he recalls that they decided to.

Reflect: Did you or your family grow up in a denomination that you later left because of the discovery of Bible truth? Was it a difficult change?

Dig Deeper: Isaiah 40:8; John 17:17; Romans 15:4

Jeffery and Jennie

Straight from the Bible, Part 2

> "He humbled you, allowed you to hunger, and fed you with manna which you did not know nor did your fathers know, that He might make you know that man shall not live by bread alone; but man lives by every word that proceeds from the mouth of the " (Deuteronomy 8:3).

In their search for Bible truth, Jeffery's family discovered Amazing Facts on television. Since the *Millennium of Prophecy* broadcasts were limited to 30-minute slots on the station Jeffery's family was viewing, he recalls that they ordered the entire set in the series from Amazing Facts in order to watch the unedited version. Subsequently, they ordered nearly everything Amazing Facts had to offer on DVD and audio. "We truly have a bookcase full of Amazing Facts materials," says Jeffery.

Jeffery's family began keeping the Sabbath immediately. "It was more like a holiday than a holy-day," he remembers, "but it was a step." Followed by many more steps, the family adopted lifestyle changes that were in line with God's Bible teachings. The newfound excitement for the Sabbath truth was dampened from time to time, however, by the lack of enthusiasm of others.

"At one point," recalls Jeffery, "I dated a Baptist girl whose family had expressed an interest in the Sabbath. But after much discussion, we had to part ways. This experience really made me dig into the Bible for myself and not rely on my parents or Pastor Doug. It also brought me to visit the local Sabbath-keeping church. I also attended a Generation of Youth for Christ (GYC) event, and I was extremely blessed."

Knowing that he would like to meet someone who shared his convictions, Jeffery joined an online singles connection where he met his soon-to-be wife, Jennie. "I thank God for technology that allows us to connect with people of our own faith," says Jeffery. "I wasn't in circles to really relate to other young people of my faith."

Today, Jeffery and Jennie share their faith with other young adults. "Jennie and I are so blessed, and we are eagerly anticipating to see how God will share His message of truth through us." They are also very active in their local church where they teach, occasionally preach, and lead a hospitality ministry. "There is much work to be done," says Jeffery, "and we are ready to be used by Him."

Reflect: God wants to use you to be a witness to your friends and neighbors. Pray for the Lord to open a door for you to share your faith.

Dig Deeper: Psalm 19:7–11; Isaiah 55:10, 11; John 6:63

The Reluctant Convert, Part 1

**"Your word is a lamp to my feet and a light
to my path" (Psalm 119:105).**

The snow is falling softly through the trees; the moon is sleeping behind rolling clouds. Far off burns a small but bright light from a lone lamppost in the middle of a dark wood, the only visible light there is. A small boy crunches through the drifts, his woolen socks wet through. Though he sees the light, for some reason he is heading away from it. He is walking in circles, in zigzags, in every possible direction but towards that light. And he is getting nowhere.

This was C. S. Lewis' experience as a young atheist.

Born into a Protestant family, Lewis loved to read at an early age. Due mainly to a birth defect in the joints of his thumbs, he was thrust towards mental rather than physical labor and, as such, developed a vivid imagination and a keen intellect. In turn he viewed the world poorly, full of limitations and rickety faults. How could—why would—God create such a place? As a result, Lewis began to love the fables in his head, what he knew he could never fully have, more than his dismal reality. This made him a budding pessimist.

Lewis perceived God as a genie who gave out wishes through prayer. So when his mother became ill from cancer, Lewis was disillusioned. When he was nine, his mother passed away.

At boarding school religion became, through his nightly prayers, a complex, grandiose experience to which he could never attain. At preparatory school, he was introduced to the occult—a practice that excited his already active imagination. Among his professors, Christianity was an unfortunate phase through which humanity had slogged before arriving at a higher stage of enlightenment.

So it was by this idealistic faith, a distorted lens largely of his own making, that C. S. Lewis, as a teenager, became an atheist. Though he was relieved to break off from his yoke of religion, he was simultaneously "angry with God for not existing[,] ... angry with Him for creating a world" (*Surprised by Joy*, pg. 115). It was in this contrary state that Lewis began to notice some very strange things about himself.

Reflect: A young C. S. Lewis' understanding of God seemed to have come from multiple sources: his teachers, his own assumptions, the world around him. From where does your perception of God come?

Dig Deeper: Mark 12:24; Acts 17:2, 11; 2 Peter 1:19–21

C. S. Lewis

The Reluctant Convert, Part 2

"'Come now, and let us reason together,' says the , 'though your sins are like scarlet, they shall be as white as snow'" (Isaiah 1:18).

The average human brain, while taking up only 2 percent of a person's total weight, actually uses 20 percent of his total oxygen. That is a powerhouse little organ!

And C. S. Lewis was a mental gymnast. He continued his education at Oxford, became a published writer, and eventually earned a teaching position at his alma mater. But all throughout this time were the most interesting occurrences.

Lewis began to notice his propensity for authors who were notably Christian. He staunchly knew the books he was supposed to enjoy reading—books for hardened atheists, of course! But truth be told, those writings failed to hold his interest. On top of that, his choice of colleagues, the ones that he most esteemed and held most dear—quite a handful were Christians too! And if they were not, they were headed in that direction.

Perceiving what was happening, Lewis consequently proceeded to fight tooth and nail, as a petulant child with a toy or candy he does not want to relinquish. A great battle waged in his mind and in his heart: self or God. But as he read more and thought more and discussed into the wee hours of the morning with his friends, he, the consummate academic, was unable to reason out of the fact. After nearly two decades as an atheist, Lewis admitted that there was a God. A couple years later, he acceded that Jesus Christ was God incarnate.

No catastrophic event had taken place in his life, no miracle, no sudden death—except within himself. And that change began immediately. Lewis started praying again and reading the Bible. He started going to bed earlier in order to wake up for chapel the next morning. As he began to know God—the true God of the Bible and not one of his own imagining—he realized that what he had loved about those books and authors and friends was the resemblance to Christ's character, the holiness, and the goodness.

Like the boy in the snow, he had, kicking and screaming, stepped into that pool of light and, wondering from whence it shone, had gazed upward into the lamp.

Reflect: What are your struggles with God that no one else sees? As "we do not wrestle against flesh and blood" (Ephesians 6:12), so do we have an infinitely more powerful Helper, the Holy Spirit.

Dig Deeper: 2 Corinthians 10:5; Colossians 3:2; Hebrews 4:12

Judy

A Knock at the Door, Part 1

"But the Helper, the Holy Spirit, whom the Father will send in My name, He will teach you all things, and bring to your remembrance all things that I said to you" (John 14:26).

When Judy was a girl, she *almost* attended church. Her mother died of cancer when Judy was only six years old. After this, her father gave her a nickel each Sunday and told her to go to the church around the corner from where they lived. She didn't want to attend and so snuck out each week and spent the five cents on candy. Since her dad wasn't really into church, she always wondered, "Was it my mother's wish that I attend church?"

Hard times came when Judy's father remarried. With Judy being very independent, conflicts erupted in the blended home. But after high school, her step-mother encouraged her to enroll in an X-ray Technician program where she excelled. After graduating from a Midwestern university, she moved out west where she met her husband. A dream job in Alaska didn't pan out for him, so he went south looking for work. Judy said, "Wherever you go in California, don't stop in Sacramento. It's too hot there!" He returned and told her, "I found a job in Sacramento." So they moved.

After two children came along, Judy was working at a Sabbath-keeping hospital when she found out about her husband's motorcycle accident and death. She was devastated. Friends and fellow workers at the hospital were very compassionate and helpful. Even the funeral director she worked with was a Sabbath-keeper. But Judy now had to face life and work as a single mother while raising two girls, and her connection with Sabbath-keepers soon slipped into the past.

Over the years, as her daughters grew, Judy tried several different churches. In the last one, when the pastor went off in a bad direction, she tried to talk with the pastor's wife who said, "When in Rome, do as the Romans." Judy couldn't buy this and quit attending.

Now where would she go?

Reflect: Confusion comes from the enemy. God wants to give you a clear path that lines up with His Word. Remember to acknowledge Him in all your ways so He can direct you.

Dig Deeper: Luke 19:10; Galatians 5:25; Philippians 2:13

Judy

A Knock at the Door, Part 2

"Go therefore and make disciples of all the nations, baptizing them in the name of the Father and of the Son and of the Holy Spirit ..." (Matthew 28:19).

Three years ago on a Sunday morning, while looking for a religious program to watch, Judy happened onto Amazing Facts Television. She says, "I loved it. As I listened, I found myself agreeing with what the pastor said, except when he starting saying that Saturday was the Sabbath. At this point I didn't even know Pastor Doug's denomination. But I went to my Bible and discovered he was right."

Soon she signed up for the *Amazing Facts Bible Study Guides* and began completing them and mailing them in. When she finished the introductory lessons, she moved to the advanced lessons, and then the prophecy lessons. She enjoyed them all and found her understanding of Scripture grow tremendously.

One day, two young students who were going through the Amazing Facts Center of Evangelism (AFCOE) program knocked on Judy's door. The young men found Judy to be very receptive to discussing the Bible. They provided her with more helpful booklets and DVDs. She says, "Those young men taught me to pray in a meaningful way. I always prayed for my own needs, but they helped me to realize how important it is to give praise to the Lord in prayer."

A few months later the two Bible workers invited Judy to attend a prophecy seminar being held by Pastor Eric Flickinger. She gladly attended. Sometimes, when she couldn't find transportation, the young men brought her to the meetings.

"I attended almost every session. Each evening as I left I would bump into an usher named Larry who asked, 'How was it?' I always smiled and said, 'God is speaking to me!'"

Judy was eventually baptized and says she loves her new church home.

"Where would I be without Amazing Facts! They basically saved my life," Judy shares. "I have found so many answers to my Bible questions. They have led me to my church family. They continue to provide resources so I can witness to my neighbors. If there is one thing Amazing Facts taught me, it was to share my faith. You can't just sit in front of a television and say, 'Amen.' Amazing Facts has helped me to get out into my community and witness to others."

Reflect: Have you ever knocked on someone's door and offered to share with them Christian literature? Don't be offended by negative responses. Your loving response can be used by God to melt hearts.

Dig Deeper: Isaiah 53:1; Matthew 5:16; 1 Peter 3:15

Solomon

Word to the Wise, Part 1

> **"Therefore give to Your servant an understanding heart to judge Your people, that I may discern between good and evil. For who is able to judge this great people of Yours?" (1 Kings 3:9).**

Albert Einstein said, "Any fool can know. The point is to understand." In other words, there is a difference between knowledge and wisdom. Wisdom has to do with a person's decisions, his discernment, his conduct; it has to do with what he does with that knowledge. Wisdom encompasses knowledge. The Bible gives us more insight: Wisdom, in particular, is the ability to "discern between good and evil" (1 Kings 3:9).

Solomon was off to a good start when he asked God for wisdom above all else. In a dream the Almighty appeared to him, saying, "Ask! What shall I give you?" (v. 5). Solomon, in reply, confessed his insecurities. He was an inexperienced youth; he was not fit to rule (vv. 7, 8). To some, the aspect of sovereignty might have seemed thrilling, but to Solomon it was only daunting. He held a great respect for the position; his principal concern was to exercise his duty with honor, for he held in his young hands not only his own future but the fate of an entire nation. And God, observing his humble spirit, granted his request (vv. 11, 12).

In the early days of Solomon's reign, Israel prospered as a result of God's gift to their king. In the case of the two women who each claimed maternity of a newborn baby, the public saw their king's sense of justice (vv. 16–28). He was a deliverer who rooted out covetousness, reunited family, and cherished life. In the construction of God's temple, they saw his loyalty and dedication (5:5; 8:17–21). He was a servant-leader who kept his promises, who faithfully worshiped God alone, and who guided his subjects to do the same. His kingship and his character were a shining witness to "men of all nations" (4:34) of the mighty and magnanimous power of the living God.

But as his nation increased in wealth, security, and peace, so did Solomon—though not to his own betterment.

Reflect: If God were to appear to you as He did to Solomon and give you your desire, what would be your request?

Dig Deeper: Proverbs 3:13–26; Matthew 7:24, 25; James 1:5

Solomon

Word to the Wise, Part 2

"Let us hear the conclusion of the whole matter: Fear God and keep His commandments, for this is man's all" (Ecclesiastes 12:13).

The thing about gifts is that they depend as much on the receiver as on the giver. They can be refused or forgotten, even gifts from God.

In his life, Solomon married 700 women from all kinds of religious backgrounds. It was something that the Lord had forbidden not only His people (Deuteronomy 7:1–4) but expressly the king of Israel from doing (17:17). But Solomon did it anyway. The Bible tells us that "Solomon clung to [his wives] in love" (1 Kings 11:2), not willing to give them up for anything. As he did so, his gift of wisdom began to gather dust, forgotten in a dark corner.

He began to love not only these women but also the things that they loved, their idols, their religious rites (vv. 4, 5). The man who once famously returned a harlot's babe to its mother now condoned the ritual of child sacrifice to gods of wood and stone. He even built the altars upon which the children were burned (vv. 7, 8). At the end of his reign, his subjects were overworked and overtaxed (12:4). They had witnessed the tragic decline of their once wise and merciful king, and they were no longer the happy nation of the past.

Solomon himself was unhappy as well. Following his own heart had brought nothing but misery, dissatisfaction, and decay to him: "Then I looked on all the works that my hands had done and on the labor in which I had toiled; and indeed all was vanity and grasping for the wind" (Ecclesiastes 2:11).

Worst of all, it had taken him far from the God whom he once cherished. Now an old man, he realized the destruction he had brought upon his descendants and subjects and the devastation inflicted upon his own witness. As a last effort to right his wrongs, he penned the Book of Ecclesiastes, a warning and guide to all who would walk this earth. After all his experiences, with what wisdom did King Solomon leave us? "Fear God and keep His commandments, for this is man's all" (12:13).

Reflect: At the end of his days, Solomon saw the error of his ways and counseled others to devote their lives to obeying the will of God. What mistakes have you made in your faith that you would most caution others against doing?

Dig Deeper: Job 28:28; Ezekiel 3:17–21; James 5:19, 20

Gaining a Firm Faith

**"Faith comes by hearing, and hearing by the
word of God" (Romans 10:17).**

For 27-year-old Torres, life was confusing and uncertain. He had a wife and a job, but no happiness, no purpose, and no solid connection to God.

"I was completely selfish and self-centered," he recalled. "I was addicted to drugs and fornication. I was just at my absolute worst. I was never happy or content with anything happening in my life."

What made Torres' condition even more depressing was that he'd grown up with the trappings of the Christian faith. Baptized at age 8, his family's weekly church attendance was about the extent of his spiritual experience.

"I never read the Bible with my family," he conceded. "We didn't really pray much together, either, outside of church services."

At his lowest point, Torres thought about being re-baptized, and decided to seek God in prayer, "asking for Him to show me a way." The answer came as he and his wife drove through his hometown.

"I saw the Amazing Facts banner on the lawn of a Sabbath-keeping church about a month after I started praying this prayer," Torres explained. "The prophecy seminar not only confirmed my desire and need for rebaptism, but also introduced me to people who can help train me for ministry and Bible work."

And for a teacher, Torres couldn't hope for better than evangelist Carlos Muñoz—someone who Torres now considers a mentor.

"This seminar granted me the rock-solid foundation and true rededication to Christ that I desperately needed to move forward in my Christian walk," Torres said. "I now have direction. I know that the next step in my walk is learning as much as I can about Bible prophecy so that I can help others see."

At the end of the seminar, Torres was re-baptized, and his wife, who hadn't previously understood the need for baptism, followed Christ's example as well. Torres said other positive changes have also happened.

"My mornings are so peaceful and joyful now," he explained. "I used to wake up and dread going into work. But now, when I arise, I read a chapter of the Bible. I then thank the Lord and pray for strength going into the day. I have seen amazing results regarding my general attitude towards life, which is more positive. I'm much more joyful and at ease now than I have ever been."

Reflect: How do you begin your day? Spend quiet time with the Lord. Invite Him into your life. Read your Bible and you will find peace.

Dig Deeper: Luke 1:37; 2 Corinthians 5:7; Hebrews 11:1

Marvin Olasky

From Communist to Christian, Part 1

"For since the creation of the world His invisible attributes are clearly seen, being understood by the things that are made, even His eternal power and Godhead, so that they are without excuse" (Romans 1:20).

In May 1970, students at Yale University were given weeks off in order to participate in the myriad of anti-war protests held around the nation. America had just gone full throttle into Vietnam, sparking a wave of student demonstrations, replete with the National Guard, tear gas guns, and rock-throwing.

Among them was an undergraduate named Marvin Olasky, a Jew-turned-atheist. While Olasky did not throw any stones, he was angry. He resented those rich, stuck-up pigs who flaunted their fancy clothes and color televisions and carpeted homes.

Born into a poor Jewish home to a father with more brains than money and a mother who was never happy, Olasky grew up trained in the ways of class envy. He attended Hebrew school but learned only that the Old Testament was a culturally significant book of fictional stories. At 14, he became an atheist after reading the likes of Sigmund Freud and H. G. Wells, convinced that God was a coping mechanism for those woefully disappointed by their own parents. Intellectually superior and proud of it, he excelled at Yale, celebrated for his emerging socialist ideology. He reveled in the progressive age of the 1970s, an era of hippies and anti-war rallies, of Black Panthers and feminism, of liberation. He seemed groomed for the Communist Party, which he joined in 1972. But it was during his years at the University of Michigan, while earning his doctorate in American Culture, that Olasky got his first dose of true religion.

It all began one afternoon on November 1, 1973, when Olasky settled down in his room for a bit of light reading. A faithful Communist, he opened Lenin's *Socialism and Religion* for the second time, thinking to brush up on the relationship between atheism and Communism. (Lenin advocated atheism as the basis for Communism.) At 3 p.m., he finished the pamphlet, and instead of heading to the library as he had planned, he merely sat stock still in his chair, churning and chomping on, among others, the following question: "How do I know that there isn't a God?"

Reflect: Have you been taught to believe that the Bible is a collection of fables? How can we know that the Bible is 100 percent factual?

Dig Deeper: 1 Thessalonians 5:21; 2 Peter 1:20, 21; Revelation 22:18, 19

Marvin Olasky

From Communist to Christian, Part 2

"And the Word became flesh and dwelt among us, and we beheld His glory, the glory as of the only begotten of the Father, full of grace and truth" (John 1:14).

For the next eight hours, Marvin Olasky did not move. He simply thought about his life, his family, his motives. It was a decidedly supernatural experience. By 11 p.m., he had reached one conclusion: He was no longer an atheist. Another two hours had him walking in the dead of night all over campus, still deep in thought. At 1 a.m., he reached another conclusion: He was not a Communist.

Oddly, after this grand revelation, Olasky did not do much of anything but continue on with his graduate studies. Preoccupied with this work, he all but forgot about God.

Then one night, while engrossed in perfecting his Russian, a skill required for his doctorate, he came across an old souvenir. It was the New Testament—in Russian. At no time did it cross his mind that this book was about the God in which he had recently professed to believe. It was simply a nail in his academic tool belt. He opened to the first page and began to read the Book of Matthew. But only a few chapters in, to the Sermon on the Mount, Olasky had already gleaned that this was no ordinary book. No mortal hand had written this; this was from a divine source.

But it was not smooth sailing from there. It took several years of internal battling before Olasky admitted that he was a Christian. It took God's stripping out his intellectual pride; it took reading more of His Word; it took meeting his future wife and plying her with recommendations of Christian authors; it took earning his doctorate and getting married and moving all the way to the West Coast.

It was the year 1976. Olasky and his wife had begun attending a nearby church regularly. One day, a deacon came for a visit and, without any preamble, asked him one simple question.

"Well, you believe this stuff, don't you?" asked the deacon.

And after thinking about it, Olasky realized that he had actually been believing for quite some time. A week later, both he and his wife were baptized.

Olasky went on to become a prolific Christian author and editor as well as the pioneer of the Republican Party's "compassionate conservatism" philosophy of the 1990s and early 2000s.

Reflect: How does reading the Bible transform us?
Why is the Bible so meaningful to you?

Dig Deeper: Deuteronomy 8:3; John 5:39; 6:63

From Confusion to Confidence, Part 1

**"Observe the Sabbath day, to keep it holy, as the
your God commanded you" (Deuteronomy 5:12).**

Confusion best describes Lily's upbringing. "I was raised a Roman Catholic," she explains. "We went to church every Sunday, but we never read the Bible. We didn't even have a Bible at home. My parents were in constant quarrels."

Those tensions filtered down to the children. One of her brothers bullied and beat Lily so much so that she twice attempted to end her life, thinking this would be better than the ongoing suffering. She suffered low self-esteem, and was, she said, "pretty much hopeless." On top of this, her language was "foul," Lily admits, and she couldn't break the habit.

Despite the turmoil between her parents, Lily believed her father, who died in 2017, was "a good father to me." He encouraged her to go to college. In 1987, both Lily and her younger brother arrived in the United States for their higher education.

But Lily found a great deal more!

At school, Lily was invited to go to church, and she began attending. She also read a New Testament Bible given to her before she came to America. While her classmates went out partying on Friday nights, Lily stayed in her room reading and praying.

The result? Lily accepted Christ at age 18 on a Good Friday. She knew she belonged to Jesus because, she recalls, "The first evidence that I am His was that my foul language was gone. I've never spoken another foul word since. It's a miracle!"

But after years of being a Christian and worshiping on Sundays, Lily faced a challenge of faith. And it wouldn't go away.

Lily had started listening to Pastor Doug Batchelor on a Christian radio station at work. What he said was new to her, but it all lined up with the Bible, including the question of the Sabbath day.

"I made sure to listen to Amazing Facts every day," she says. "I really couldn't get enough! So many of my questions were being answered." She even downloaded the Amazing Facts app so she could listen to Pastor Doug while she was at work.

But Lily's job as a pharmacist required work on Saturdays. And while it's true that her work helps other people, she also felt called to observe the Sabbath day. A conflict rose up in her heart. What should she do?

Reflect: Have you ever had a conflict between obeying God's commands and the rules of people? Be determined to do what is right though the heavens fall.

Dig Deeper: 1 Samuel 15:22; John 14:15; James 1:22

Lily

From Confusion to Confidence, Part 2

"Now this is the confidence that we have in Him, that if we ask anything according to His will, He hears us. And if we know that He hears us, whatever we ask, we know that we have the petitions that we have asked of Him" (1 John 5:14, 15).

"All my 27 years as a pharmacist, I had to work some Saturdays," Lily explains. "For the past few years, I worked every sixth Saturday." But her newfound faith, truths she learned through Amazing Facts, convicted her to honor the Sabbath every Saturday.

Lily prayed to God to help her know how to obey Him. Then she went to her supervisor and volunteered to work every Sunday so that she could have Saturdays off. Her supervisor brought the request to the manager—but he denied it.

Later, a new supervisor was hired, so Lily made the same request and once more it was denied. Had God ignored her prayer? Should she quit her job? She continued to pray.

Not long after this, out of the blue, Lily's manager approached her and said, "No Saturday work." When she heard his words, she fought to hold back tears of happiness. "God made a way for me to obey Him!"

Today, Lily's faith is strong, thanks to the Bible knowledge she gained from Amazing Facts and the truth brought into her life that has helped her meet many work and family challenges. She is now a confident believer and isn't afraid to meet challenges head on.

Amazing Facts has answered many of her Bible questions about the Sabbath, Bible prophecy, and the afterlife. "I learned more about the Bible in one year with Amazing Facts," she tells, "than all the years I had been in other churches." And she's not keeping all these special teachings to herself. "I am sharing the light given to me with most of my Christian friends," she adds.

Lily is now optimistic about the future. "I am hopeful," she affirms, "I know Jesus Christ." She is also at peace about her father's death and is grateful for hope beyond the grave.

God led Lily from confusion to confidence. Though she was once far from heaven, she now longs each day to be closer to God.

Reflect: What has helped you to meet challenges head on? God will give you both wisdom and courage to face difficulties with confidence.

Dig Deeper: Proverbs 3:26; Isaiah 41:10; Hebrews 13:6

Miriam

Green-eyed Monster, Part 1

"But one and the same Spirit works all these things, distributing to each one individually as He wills" (1 Corinthians 12:11).

The phrase "green with envy" is thought to have come from ancient Greece, where it was readily accepted that envious feelings produced excess bile, which in turn gave one's skin a greenish hue. While not very attractive, the concept nonetheless shows how strong jealousy can be and how much it can affect other areas of a person's life.

Moses' older sister Miriam stands as the first female prophet recounted in Scripture. When Miriam was but a child, she already exhibited the boldness and daring that characterized her as an adult. When her mother hid her baby brother Moses by the banks of the Nile River, Miriam stayed by and watched closely as the Pharaoh's daughter and her maidservants found him in the basket in the water. The Pharaoh had decreed that every Hebrew male child should be slain. Would the princess see the deed done?

Instead of harming Moses, the princess "had compassion" (Exodus 2:6) upon the Hebrew babe. Without wasting a moment, Miriam, sharp as a whip, intercepted.

"Shall I go and call a nurse for you from the Hebrew women, that she may nurse the child for you?" (v. 7) she asked.

When she was told yes, Miriam brought her mother to the royal entourage. Her brother's life was spared, and not only that, he was returned to his real family for a few extra, precious years.

It seems natural then that Miriam rose to a high position among her people. As an adult, she was a faithful follower of God, called "the prophetess" (Exodus 15:20). When God broke the bonds of Egyptian slavery for the Israelites, it was she who led the women in a victory celebration (vv. 20, 21).

But oftentimes the qualities which we deem so essential in a leader—wit, strength, nerve—are the very same which prove to be their downfall. Miriam was a leader in her own right, but she was not the only leader. She had two brothers, Moses and Aaron, who were also God's chosen—Moses above all. Moses was set apart by God for a very special work (Exodus 4:15, 16; Deuteronomy 34:10), and it was beginning to bother Miriam.

Reflect: List some of your natural talents. Do these attributes make you a gifted leader, teacher, or business person? Have you committed these gifts to God?

Dig Deeper: Exodus 31:2–6; Romans 12:3–8; 1 Corinthians 12:4–10

Miriam

Green-eyed Monster, Part 2

"A sound heart is life to the body, but envy is rottenness to the bones" (Proverbs 14:30).

In-laws—the very word produces in many a visceral reaction. One report even concluded that over 60 percent of women determined the cause of their deep-seated misery to originate from their in-laws, in particular their female in-laws.

For Miriam, it was her sister-in-law Zipporah, Moses' wife, who unwittingly roused her ire. Zipporah's father Jethro, with whom Moses had spent 40 years as a shepherd, had counseled his son-in-law to divide some of his leadership tasks among a team of godly men (Exodus 18:17–23). Moses willingly executed the plan, appointing seventy elders and apportioning the Israelites among them—all without the approval of Aaron and Miriam.

Miriam's pride was rankled. How dare Moses not consult her and her brother first! Was it not their right and privilege as leaders of Israel? Who did Moses think he was? She began whispering in Aaron's ear. They were being ousted—and it was all the fault of that conniving Zipporah and her meddlesome father. So consuming was her jealousy that she resorted to technicality, character defamation, and shameless self-promotion (Numbers 12:1, 2).

But it was not only Aaron who heard her complaints: "For the eyes of the run to and fro throughout the whole earth" (2 Chronicles 16:9). God instructed the three siblings, Moses, Aaron, and Miriam, to meet in the sanctuary (Numbers 12:4). There, He rebuked Miriam and Aaron for sowing seeds of discontent against their own brother. None of them was mighty or skilled in his or her own right but had been made His prophets, His messengers, His servants by His grace alone. And of the three, Moses stood alone as God's privileged friend (vv. 6–8).

As a result, Miriam, the instigator, was stricken with leprosy (v. 10). The envy that had eaten her up on the inside was now revealed before all. Though Miriam was healed, in accordance with the sanitary laws she was then quarantined for one week. What must those seven days have been like for her? Humiliated, broken, this great leader had time to think long and hard about what she had done. In complete isolation she had no one to blame—not Zipporah, not Jethro, not Moses—no one but herself.

The Bible records no second act of rebellion by the prophetess. In meekness she passed to her grave.

Reflect: What do you covet? Have you ever gossiped about anyone in order to gain what you want?

Dig Deeper: Psalm 15:1–3; Proverbs 16:27, 28; James 3:14–18

Dan

Big Questions, Bigger Answers, Part 1

> **"The people who sat in darkness have seen a great light, and upon those who sat in the region and shadow of death light has dawned"** (Matthew 4:16).

When 33 hospital patients died in just one day, Dan just about cracked. As a registered nurse in the mid-80s caring for people with AIDS, his belief in an eternally burning hell left him asking, "Where is God in all of this?"

Dan, an entrepreneur and medical training expert is not only a registered nurse, but he also has three master's degrees. He didn't just treat patients at the beginning of the global AIDS epidemic, but he helped establish the nation's first hospital devoted to research on immunological disorders.

All that initiative, however, took a toll on his health: Until recently, he weighed in at 252 pounds and took thirteen medications daily. Dan knew that neither his weight nor the number of prescriptions he carried signaled good things for his future.

One night, Dan was looking for some inspiration on his satellite television service. An observant member of the Mormon church for 26 years, he didn't know about churches that observed the Bible Sabbath—and, to be honest, he had no interest in learning about one.

That was soon to change. When Dan "accidentally" tuned in to a Christian satellite network, he didn't half-respond to the spiritual and health messages that were broadcast there. He dived in, and in less than a year he was baptized into a Sabbath-keeping congregation, something he credits largely to Amazing Facts. There were tremendous health benefits, too, as Dan was to find out.

The first thing he saw on television was a presentation on the state of the dead. Dan was stunned to learn that the Bible's teaching about what happens after death was in no way similar to what he'd been taught growing up. The afterlife had long weighed on his mind. In his early years of treating AIDS patients, most of who succumbed shortly after arriving at the hospital, he became disillusioned with his childhood Pentecostal teachings about the dead either going to heaven or hell—the latter for eternal torment. This sent Dan to the Mormon faith, but even after decades of practice, he remained unsettled.

"Something about what was said rang true in my mind," Dan recalled about his reaction to the message. But he admits that he knew nothing about the Sabbath-keeping faith.

Reflect: Do you know someone who believes in an eternally burning hellfire? You can show them truth that will bring them peace straight from the Bible.

Dig Deeper: Ecclesiastes 12:7; Psalm 115:17; Ezekiel 18:20

Dan

Big Questions, Bigger Answers, Part 2

"Call to Me, and I will answer you, and show you great and mighty things, which you do not know" (Jeremiah 33:3).

When Dan first heard about the Sabbath, he went to the Internet to learn more and discovered Amazing Facts. "I ended up spending an hour and a half online and contacted Amazing Facts because I wanted answers."

This led Dan back to his living room, where he found another program on making healthy lifestyle changes. The presenter shared his testimony of losing weight and being taken off a range of medications after completing the program. It led Dan to try the program out for himself.

In the meantime, he received the first in a series of Bible lessons from Amazing Facts, which he studied with relish. "I completed and sent back the first lesson the day I received it," he says. More lessons followed, and he completed the course quickly.

At the same time, Dan sought out and visited a Sabbath-keeping congregation near his home, hoping that no one from his other church would see him as, according to Dan, crossing such lines is frowned upon.

His mail-in Bible studies opened the door for Dan to attend a lifestyle program where he found not only physical help, but also more spiritual enlightenment. Recently, Dan was even baptized. He adds, "I got off eleven of my medicines, and I dropped 59 pounds, and it just felt amazing not to have to take the insulin anymore," he says.

Dan is excited after what he's learned about the Bible. He credits his personal and spiritual transformation to the Amazing Facts ministry, which not only provided the Bible lessons, but also helped him make personal health a priority. "I feel very appreciative to God for bringing me here, and for what I've learned and what Amazing Facts has done to try to teach me the Bible," he says. "I'm so blown away to see how personal God is, and how He intervenes in our lives. It's amazing."

Dan also cherishes a visit to the Amazing Facts headquarters, where he was able not only to meet Pastor Doug, but also to speak with the people there who personally grade each mailed-in Bible lesson. He says this ministry has changed his life in more ways than one, and it's all thanks to "accidentally" tuning in to a TV channel and finding Amazing Facts online.

Reflect: Is there a lifestyle change that you need to make? God will help you beyond your greatest expectations!

Dig Deeper: Romans 12:1, 2; 1 Corinthians 6:19, 20; 3 John 1:2

Charles H. Spurgeon

The Prince of Preachers

"Look to Me, and be saved, all you ends of the earth!" (Isaiah 45:22).

In January 1892, the city of London, England, was plunged into mourning: Charles Haddon Spurgeon, a preacher not yet 60 years old, had died, months after giving his last sermon.

When Spurgeon's body lay in repose at his Metropolitan Tabernacle church—a 5,600-seat edifice that would be called a "megachurch" today—for three days, 60,000 mourners streamed in to pay their respects. As his two-mile-long funeral procession wound its way through the streets, 100,000 stood in solemn respect. Even the pubs were closed that day.

All this for a Christian preacher. Imagine that!

But Spurgeon was no mere sermonizer. Friends and critics alike knew him as the "Prince of Preachers" for his flamboyant style, his exhortations to the lost, and his uncompromising stand for biblical orthodoxy as he knew it.

It all started with a snowstorm. Then 15 years old, Spurgeon was prevented from reaching his usual church by the brutal weather. He ended up in a Primitive Methodist chapel, where a shoemaker or tailor—the young man wasn't sure which—spoke on Isaiah 45:22 in a rough-hewn manner.

"My dear friends, this is a very simple text indeed," the speaker declared. He added, "It says, 'Look.' Now that does not take a deal of effort. It ain't lifting your foot or your finger; it is just 'look.'"

Going on in a similar vein, this layman's words were used by God to reach Spurgeon's heart. The speaker looked straight at the visitor and declared, "Young man, you look very miserable. And you will always be miserable—miserable in life and miserable in death—if you do not obey my text. But if you obey now, this moment, you will be saved."

Spurgeon heeded the man's call to "look to Jesus Christ" and his life was forever changed. Within a year, he was preaching in his part of the country. Not yet 20, he was invited to do six months of preaching at a 232-member congregation in London. He went to the capital, and never left.

A preacher to thousands—newspapers in Britain and America reprinted his sermons—Spurgeon's impact on ministry is still felt today, with wide distribution of his commentaries. Although chronic illness led to his death before the age of 60, Charles Spurgeon's reach extended far beyond his base in London, and beyond his lifetime.

Reflect: Is there a single verse—or sermon—that made a difference in the direction of your life? Share it with someone. It could help them more than you know.

Dig Deeper: Numbers 21:8, 9; Micah 7:7; Hebrews 12:2

John

The Bullet of Truth

> **"I affirm, by the boasting in you which I have in Christ**
> **Jesus our Lord, I die daily" (1 Corinthians 15:31).**

John Ludwig's life began in Germany. During World War II, his Jewish father was forced to help build concentration camps—like Buchenwald. When John was only four years old, his family was forced to leave everything and escaped with other Jews to Shanghai, China.

For 10 harrowing years John lived in the war-torn city, which was eventually overtaken by the Japanese. One day a group was gathered to be executed. John was among them. People were piled on top of one another when shots were fired. Somehow he survived and was helped by a French and Chinese couple. When John was 14, he escaped to America and began a new life.

Years later, while walking to work one morning in Fremont, California, John noticed a group of people gathering near a hotel. He stopped and talked with his friend who was a police officer. The man told him that at any moment President Gerald Ford would emerge. When he did, people began to applaud. Just then a shot rang out. Someone attempted to assassinate the president, but the bullet meant for Ford ricocheted and hit John, causing him a lot of pain, but not seriously injuring him.

John's wife, Beverly, grew up in the Reformed Church and always had an interest in religion. She first heard Pastor Doug on the radio program *Bible Answers Live*. In 1999, while trying to find a TV program to watch, she says, "For some reason the only channel I could get with my little antenna was 3ABN. That's when I began to listen to Pastor Batchelor preach."

A few years ago, while driving in downtown Sacramento, the couple drove past a Sabbath-keeping church where they noticed a Revelation series on prophecy being conducted by Pastor Eric Flickinger. "We should go," Beverly suggested to John, so they did.

After attending the series and completing the *Amazing Facts Bible Study Guides*, the couple was baptized. Beverly shares, "I really appreciate Amazing Facts and Pastor Doug, because so many of the Bible questions I've had for years have been answered. I have now found real truth."

John laughs, "I'm almost 80 years old [in 2013]. At my age you think a lot about the world ending soon." For a man who more than once faced death, his words are appropriate for us all, no matter our age!

Reflect: Have you ever had a close call with death? Did you know that God calls us to die to self every single day so that He can live within our heart?

Dig Deeper: Mark 8:35; Luke 9:23; Galatians 2:20

Apostle Paul

From Persecutor to Preacher, Part 1

"I am indeed a Jew, born in Tarsus of Cilicia, but brought up in this city at the feet of Gamaliel, taught according to the strictness of our fathers' law, and was zealous toward God" (Acts 22:3).

If ever there was a brilliant student with a bright future, it was Saul of Tarsus. He could boast, "If anyone else thinks he may have confidence in the flesh, I more so: circumcised the eighth day, of the stock of Israel, of the tribe of Benjamin, a Hebrew of the Hebrews; concerning the law, a Pharisee; concerning zeal, persecuting the church; concerning the righteousness which is in the law, blameless" (Philippians 3:5).

Saul (his Hebrew name) was born into a university town—Tarsus—known for education, philosophy, science, and culture. Here he intermingled with Jews, Romans, and Greeks, which gave him the opportunity to learn several languages. Like his father, he was also able to gain Roman citizenship and later referred to himself by his Greco-Roman name, Paul, which means "little."

No doubt, Saul attended a synagogue school in Tarsus and was recognized as a promising pupil. He was sent to Jerusalem to learn at the feet of the greatest Pharisee and teacher of that time—Gamaliel—and was "taught according to the strictness" of Jewish law. His loyalty to his teachers led him to be one of the most brilliant scholars, strictest Pharisees, and passionate for Judaism far above his peers. Certainly, the leaders in Jerusalem marked him as a future force for good and eventually put this zealous young adult on the Sanhedrin board.

Sometimes we think we know who will be the greatest defenders of the faith. We consider educational degrees, test scores, and academic excellence, but without a converted heart, such achievements become meaningless. God had another plan for this cream-of-the-crop young man. And it would take a jolting experience to knock him from his high estimation of himself to see truth.

Reflect: Have you ever known a person who was successful in the eyes of the world, but then experienced a difficult time that led them to the Lord? God can use *anyone* for His glory.

Dig Deeper: Acts 22:1–5; Galatians 1:11–14; Philippians 3:1–6

Apostle Paul

From Persecutor to Preacher, Part 2

> **"They cast him [Stephen] out of the city and stoned him. And the witnesses laid down their clothes at the feet of a young man named Saul" (Acts 7:58).**

Never get between a mother bear and her cubs. That sage advice has a twist, according to some biologists—it depends on the species of bear. The two most common bears in North America are the black bear (Ursus americanus) and the brown bear or grizzly bear (Ursus arctos). Researchers have found that when black bear cubs have been captured in front of their mothers, the mother bear will most often run and hide. But not so with the fierce grizzly. According to Bear.org, 70 percent of human deaths caused by grizzly bear attacks are related to a mother protecting her cubs.

Saul of Tarsus was like an aggressive mother grizzly bear, seeking to protect the Jewish teachings and traditions of his nation. His first appearance in Scripture takes place at the stoning of Stephen in Acts 7. While the chapter ends with him apparently being a coat-watcher during the stoning, the first verse of the next chapter clearly states, "Now Saul was consenting to his death" (Acts 8:1). But it doesn't stop there. "As for Saul, he made havoc of the church, entering every house, and dragging off men and women, committing them to prison" (v. 3).

Stephen's stoning prophetically marked a turning point for the Jewish nation and the infant church. This first period of persecution ravaged the new body of believers, and leading the pack of attackers was Saul. This zealous Pharisee didn't just dislike Christians, he hated them with a passion. "I punished them often in every synagogue and compelled them to blaspheme; and *being exceedingly enraged against them*, I persecuted them even to foreign cities" (Acts 26:11, emphasis added).

Saul didn't try to reason with Christians to change their minds. He didn't write editorials in the local newspaper to raise his concern. He viciously attacked the church. He later told the church at Galatia, "You have heard of my former conduct in Judaism, how I persecuted the church of God *beyond measure and tried to destroy it*" (Galatians 1:13).

What happened next makes the miraculous work of God in Saul's life all the more stunning. Something deep inside this angry man led him to a major turning point.

Reflect: Have you ever felt protective of your faith or your church? How do you feel when you observe Christians being attacked? Paul later considered it a privilege to "suffer for His (Christ's) sake" (Philippians 1:29).

Dig Deeper: Acts 26:1–9; Galatians 1:13, 14; 2 Timothy 3:12

Apostle Paul

From Persecutor to Preacher, Part 3

> **"Then Saul, still breathing threats and murder against the disciples of the Lord, went to the high priest and asked letters from him to the synagogues of Damascus, so that if he found any who were of the Way, whether men or women, he might bring them bound to Jerusalem" (Acts 9:1, 2).**

Saul was on the warpath. Persecution scattered Christians out of Jerusalem and when Saul (who later in Acts is referred to by his Roman name, Paul), found out believers were in Damascus, set off to capture them. He was so intent on crushing the new Christian church—"breathing threats and murder against the disciples of the Lord"—that he asked the high priest in Jerusalem to provide him letters of extradition so that he could drag these "criminals" back to Jerusalem to be jailed.

Around noon, as Saul and a group of men helping him, approached Damascus, a blinding light suddenly surrounded the group—a light brighter than the sun. The stunned men fell to the ground and a voice spoke to the leader. "Saul, Saul, why are you persecuting Me?" (Acts 9:4).

Bewildered, he asked, "Who are You, Lord?" and the Lord replied, "I am Jesus, who you are persecuting. It is hard for you to kick against the goads" (v. 5). Trembling, Saul asked, "Lord, what do You want me to do?" The Lord replied, "Arise and go into the city, and you will be told what you must do" (v. 6).

"And the men who journeyed with him stood speechless, hearing a voice but seeing no one. Then Saul arose from the ground, and when his eyes were opened he saw no one. But they led him by the hand and brought him into Damascus. And he was three days without sight, and neither ate nor drank" (vv. 7–9).

The Holy Spirit had been working on the heart of Saul. Like a goad (a rod used to spur an animal forward), he had been resisting impressions that probably came to him while watching Stephen being stoned. How could he, likely sitting in the council that listened to Stephen speak, overlook this man who had the "face of an angel"? (Acts 6:15).

God was calling to the honest but misled heart of Saul. Now, in blind quietness, he sat thinking and listening to heaven's voice.

Reflect: Have you ever had an experience that made you stop in your tracks and think deeply about the direction of your life? God encourages U-turns in life.

Dig Deeper: Acts 9:1–9; Acts 22:6–11; Acts 26:12–15

Apostle Paul

From Persecutor to Preacher, Part 4

"The Lord said to me [Saul], 'Arise and go into Damascus, and there you will be told all things which are appointed for you to do'" (Acts 22:10).

Saul discovered that he was blind. When Jesus revealed Himself to the zealous persecutor of the church (whom Christ identified with His own being), the Lord told the enemy of Christians to stand up and go into Damascus for further instructions. When Saul stood to his feet, he could not see and had to be led by the hand into the city.

For three days, the sightless Pharisee did not eat or drink as he prayerfully contemplated his encounter with Jesus. But God had not forgotten Saul and, in a vision, asked a disciple named Ananias to visit Saul. The follower of Jesus was hesitant and said, "Lord, I have heard from many about this man, how much harm he has done to Your saints in Jerusalem" (Acts 9:13).

But the Lord told Ananias, "Go, for he is a chosen vessel of Mine to bear my name before Gentiles, kings, and the children of Israel. For I will show him how many things he must suffer for My name's sake" (v. 15, 16).

Ananias faithfully obeyed God, went to the very street where Saul was staying, and placed his hands on him, saying, "Brother Saul, the Lord Jesus, who appeared to you on the road as you came, has sent me that you may receive your sight and be filled with the Holy Spirit" (v. 17). In that moment, "There fell from his eyes something like scales, and he received his sight at once; and he arose and was baptized" (v. 18).

Saul was physically blinded when Jesus revealed Himself on the road to Damascus. Perhaps the Lord wanted him to feel his utter helplessness and need of the Holy Spirit. Maybe God wanted Saul to think deeply about his actions, how he was mercilessly persecuting God's church. After those three days of darkness, a resurrection took place. Not only did he receive his sight, but he was filled with the Holy Spirit.

That's often how conversions take place. We must realize just how dark our life has become without Christ. And when we cry for help, the Lord sends the Spirit ... who leads us to making a commitment to Jesus and His body of believers through baptism.

Reflect: When did you last witness someone's baptism? What stood out for you as you watched the ceremony? God wants us to demonstrate our full commitment to Him through baptism.

Dig Deeper: Acts 9:10–19; Acts 22:12–16; Acts 26:16, 17

Jon

Needing Answers, Part 1

"I am persuaded that neither death nor life, nor angels nor principalities nor powers, nor things present nor things to come, nor height nor depth, nor any other created thing, shall be able to separate us from the love of God which is in Christ Jesus our Lord" (Romans 8:38, 39).

Jon grew up in a secular home with no religious background. He had questions about life like other young people. He often wondered what the future held for him and what his purpose was in being alive. His parents had no answers for their searching son.

Because his family moved around a lot, Jon found it difficult to adjust. By the time he entered high school, his grades were terrible and he had a problem with authority. "I started smoking at the age of 14 and drinking by the age of 15," he remembers. He started getting involved in crime—breaking and entering, selling drugs, and stealing cars.

"I would do just about anything to find some sort of excitement," Jon shares, "anything to find happiness in my life." At one point he overdosed on the recreational drug, ecstasy.

Jon didn't want to be alone and began looking for a meaningful relationship. He found himself in Australia where he met a Christian girl. Initially they really hit it off and were together for about seven years. "Neither of us had a true relationship with God. We excluded Him out of our lives and tried to do everything on our own."

When the relationship ended, Jon fell into a deep depression. "When I came home each day, as soon as the door closed behind me, I would drop to my knees and start crying. I couldn't see the light at the end of the tunnel," he recalls. At one point he tried to end his own life by taking a handful of pills. "I didn't want to die," he explains, "I just didn't want to feel this way anymore."

Jon never felt so lonely in all his life. He would stay in his bedroom and pray for hours each day. "That was the sum of my life at that time—alone, unhappy, and really needing answers."

Reflect: Do you know of someone who is alone, unhappy, and really needing answers? Pray for that person. And then ask God how you might reach out to them.

Dig Deeper: Psalm 27:10; Proverbs 18:24; 1 Peter 5:7

"The righteous cry out, and the hears, and delivers them out of all their troubles. The is near to those who have a broken heart, and saves such as have a contrite spirit. Many are the afflictions of the righteous, but the delivers him out of them all. He guards all his bones; not one of them is broken" (Psalm 34:17–20).

A turning point came when Jon began studying the Bible. He soon found Amazing Facts online and began watching hours of sermons each day. "The more time I spent watching Pastor Doug," he shares, "the more I found answers to the questions I was asking." God gave Jon hope and gradually pulled him out of the darkness.

One day, Jon decided to attend a Sabbath-keeping church. For many weeks he drove to a local church and would sit in the parking lot for about 30 minutes and would then drive home. Finally, he found the courage to enter the church. The people were amazed at how Jon found the church through his own study. He began building relationships with the people, and his life really started changing for the better. Eventually, Jon was baptized.

But he couldn't get enough of God's truth. Jon wanted to read and study more about the new things he was learning in the Bible. So he prayed to God for two things: a new job and a new direction for his life. Within one week, God answered both prayers. He landed a new job and could start right away. His other prayer was answered when two ladies approached him at church and offered to send him to the Amazing Facts Center of Evangelism (AFCOE).

"My life has changed so much since I started following God's path for me," Jon shares. "I'm just so much happier. I realize there is so much more in this world that I can do to help others." At one point in his turbulent life, Jon really needed answers. Now he looks forward with joy to a life of service for God.

Reflect: Think of a time that you served someone, even when you didn't feel up to it. What happened in your heart? God can change how we feel when we obey Him.

Dig Deeper: Deuteronomy 31:8; Psalm 23:4; Philippians 4:19

Ethel Waters

His Eye Was on This Sparrow!

"Are not two sparrows sold for a copper coin? And not one of them falls to the ground apart from your Father's will" (Matthew 10:29).

Carrying an extraordinary 380 pounds on her 5-foot-9-inch frame, the 61-year-old African American woman shuffled into Madison Square Garden to hear a young preacher share a gospel message. His brief "crusade" was to encompass six months of preaching in the heart of New York City, hardly a Bible Belt bastion.

As she sat down, thoughts of her troubles in life bubbled up. The three marriages—her first at age 13—and three divorces. Her never having had children. The amazing success on Broadway, in films, even on the very-young medium of television beginning in 1938. And the money, which rolled in during good times, but was so mismanaged that the Internal Revenue Service was now hounding her for back taxes.

Ethel Waters, unrecognized by those seated near her, invisible to the man on the platform, listened to the sermon. The speaker offered a message of hope, forgiveness, a new start, with heaven at the end of life's road.

Though she had previously been involved with church, Waters had drifted in her spiritual life. Maybe it was so many "firsts" for her: the first to integrate a Broadway show and get equal billing; the first African American to have a television show; the first to star in a coast-to-coast radio show, backed by Jimmy Dorsey's orchestra. Yes, the fame was nice, the money was good, but neither fame nor money could fill the void in her heart. Physically, the years of nightclub entertaining and treading the boards on Broadway's stages eventually took their toll.

Responding to the appeal from the pulpit, she found her life had changed: "In 1957, I, Ethel Waters, a 380-pound decrepit old lady, rededicated my life to Jesus Christ, and boy, because He lives, just look at me now. I tell you because He lives ... I can thank God for the chance to tell you His eye is on all of us sparrows."

For the next 20 years, Ethel Waters sang at evangelistic campaigns held by that same preacher. Her presentation of "His Eye Is on the Sparrow" touched hearts around the world.

Oh, and that preacher? You might have heard of him. His name was Billy Graham.

Reflect: When was the last time you really felt God's love for you? When was the first?

Dig Deeper: Psalm 91:1; Isaiah 8:14; Proverbs 29:25

Sister Muthoni

Mighty Weapons, Part 1

"Though we walk in the flesh, we do not war according to the flesh. For the weapons of our warfare are not carnal but mighty in God for pulling down strongholds" (2 Corinthians 10:3, 4).

What would you do if your child was demon possessed? Take the child to a Pentecostal deliverance church? Visit a witch-doctor? Sister Muthoni in Kenya tried both.

Twenty years ago, Muthoni joined a Sabbath-keeping church. Her husband never did follow her in that decision, and when he died ten years later, he left her alone with two daughters, one in high school, the other in junior high. Muthoni's oldest daughter began experiencing demonic attacks shortly after the death of her father.

One day, a young man came for her, stating that she belonged to "their" family. Muthoni's daughter had never seen the man before, so she refused to go with him. Whether the man was a demon in human form, or a human working with demons, will never be known, but from then on their family troubles got worse.

That night, the daughter received a ticket to attend a secret occult meeting. Thoroughly frightened, she told her mother the whole story of what had been happening. Muthoni called for the church elder and pastor to come pray over her daughter, but nothing seemed to help.

When school started again that year, Muthoni's eldest daughter returned to her boarding academy (nearly all high schools in East Africa, both public and private, are boarding schools), but the demons went with her. Every night now, she was terrorized by demons. Unable to concentrate on her studies, she eventually dropped out of school and began doing drugs and alcohol. At the age of sixteen, she ran away from home and became a prostitute, working at a night club.

In spite of Muthoni's efforts to get her daughter to come home, she refused—until she became sick and was diagnosed with HIV. When she did return home, Muthoni's daughter threatened to kill her. She informed her mother that she had been initiated into occultism, and was now serving and worshipping the devil.

Where could Sister Muthoni find help? She was desperate.

Reflect: Have you ever been in a desperate situation? When trials are overwhelming, it is often then that we most earnestly seek help from the Lord.

Dig Deeper: Matthew 12:12; 2 Corinthians 10:3–5; James 4:7

Sister Muthoni

Mighty Weapons, Part 2

"For we do not wrestle against flesh and blood, but against principalities, against powers, against the rulers of the darkness of this age, against spiritual hosts of wickedness in the heavenly places" (Ephesians 6:12).

Sister Muthoni was desperate to find help for her daughter who had turned from God and was worshiping the devil. Her daughter finally came home after contracting AIDS from her work as a prostitute, and now threatened to kill her mother. What could the distraught mother do?

Muthoni took her daughter to Pentecostal pastors for deliverance, but there was no change. Then she took her to the witch doctor. Again, no help. It seemed that death was the only option for her daughter. During this time, Muthoni stopped attending her Sabbath-keeping church.

Finally, her daughter left home and married a notorious gangster-criminal, leaving Muthoni in tears. The situation had gone from bad to worse and looked like it would never change.

It was after this sad saga, that *Prophecies of HOPE* by Amazing Facts evangelist Michael Wambua, began in Muthoni's town in Kenya. The advertisements offering HOPE piqued her interest, and she decided to attend. The gospel of Christ spoke hope to her heart, and Muthoni decided to accept Christ anew and be re-baptized.

The day before her baptism Muthoni came to Michael and told him the sad story of her life, asking him to pray for her oldest daughter. Amazingly the next morning, Muthoni's daughter showed up in church! During the sermon, she made a decision to accept Christ as her Savior too!

Muthoni was re-baptized that Sabbath, and her daughter is now looking forward to baptism in the future. Mother and daughter both experienced revival in their hearts! What a happy day that was for Muthoni. The deepest longing of this mother's heart was finally satisfied by the power of God to free her daughter from the grip of Satan.

Reflect: Do you know someone who seems to be hopelessly enslaved by the devil? Persist in prayer and intercede on their behalf. Seek godly counsel from trustworthy Christians and don't give up.

Dig Deeper: Matthew 8:16, 17; Ephesians 4:27; 1 Peter 5:8

Zacchaeus

He Came Up Short—Until Jesus Visited

> **"Look, Lord, I give half of my goods to the poor;
> and if I have taken anything from anyone by false
> accusation, I restore fourfold" (Luke 19:8).**

Being a tax collector is often a thankless job. Being one in the Holy Land during Jesus' life was an invitation to be cursed. For one, the Jews who collected taxes did so for Rome, the occupier and oppressor. For another, these tax gatherers were notorious for padding the tax bill so they, the collector, would profit, and handsomely.

That's why, we read in Luke 19:2, the "chief tax collector" in Jericho, named Zacchaeus, "was rich." He knew how his bread was buttered, to borrow an old phrase, and he played the game very well.

But even the worst of us has some nugget of a conscience left—at least we can hope—and Zacchaeus's conscience must have been bothering him. Why else would he take a break from his extortion to run out and see Jesus passing through town?

The Bible says that while rich, Zacchaeus was "of short stature" (Luke 19:3), and so he had to climb a tree to see Jesus. "And when Jesus came to the place, He looked up and saw him, and said to him, 'Zacchaeus, make haste and come down, for today I must stay at your house'" (v. 5).

The rabbis—perpetually scolding Jesus' unconventional ministry outreach to those deemed "unclean" by society—scorned the invitation: Jesus was to dine with a sinner! The tax collector rejoiced, perhaps for the first time in a long while.

When visited by Christ, Zacchaeus was convicted—and converted! He declared, "Look, Lord, I give half of my goods to the poor; and if I have taken anything from anyone by false accusation, I restore fourfold" (v. 8). That was good enough to satisfy Jesus, who declared salvation had come to the tax collector who'd come up short in God's ledger.

As one Christian writer states, "Zacchaeus had been overwhelmed, amazed, and silenced at the love and condescension of Christ in stooping to him, so unworthy. Now love and loyalty to his new-found Master unseal his lips. He will make public his confession and his repentance" (*The Desire of Ages*, p. 554).

Reflect: Has God's mercy ever inspired you to take dramatic, generous action? Is there anything too great to give up for Jesus when you think of all He gave for you?

Dig Deeper: Exodus 22:1–7; Numbers 5:7; 1 Timothy 6:17, 18

Brian

Beyond a Shadow of a Doubt, Part 1

"Blessed are those who hunger and thirst for righteousness, for they shall be filled" (Matthew 5:6).

When Brian first gave his heart to the Lord, he earnestly prayed to understand more about the mark of the beast. Before becoming a Christian, he heard and read about Revelation 13 all the time and knew it was very important. His study convinced him that whatever it was, this power would be very subtle and deceptive. He knew it would sway practically the whole world. "I didn't want to receive this mark," he explains, "which was condemned in the strongest language."

Brian searched for explanations for the mark of the beast in all kinds of sources. "None of them," he says, "provided me with a satisfactory answer." When he gave his life to Christ, he felt assured that the Bible truly was the inspired Word of God and would make this point clear, he believed, "beyond a shadow of a doubt."

A couple months after his conversion, Brian felt impressed to visit the Sabbath-keeping church that his aunt attended. At the time he didn't know a thing about this church. It was just another denomination.

On the first Sabbath he attended church, the pastor concluded with an altar call. Brian raised his hand to indicate his interest in being baptized. After the service he spoke with the pastor who gave him a copy of the first lesson in the *Amazing Facts Bible Study Guides* and said, "A Bible worker will be in touch to study the lesson with you."

Brian was so hungry to learn truth that he went home and immediately studied the lesson. "I was totally blessed by the information in this guide," he tells. "It helped me to understand the Bible in a way I had never understood before. And it was so plain!"

When the Bible worker showed up at Brian's house the following week, they reviewed the first lesson and then she gave him the next lesson titled, "Did God Create the Devil?" That title alone got him fired up about studying this topic. "I knew I would finish this lesson in one day, so I asked if she would leave me more." She hesitantly left five or six more lessons. Most people would be overwhelmed with these many lessons, so it's better to leave just a few. But not Brian!

Reflect: Do you have a hunger for the Word of God? If not, perhaps it is because you might be partaking of things of the world that dull your appetite.

Dig Deeper: Psalm 81:10; Isaiah 55:1; 1 Peter 2:2

Beyond a Shadow of a Doubt, Part 2

"If any of you lacks wisdom, let him ask of God, who gives to all liberally and without reproach, and it will be given to him. But let him ask in faith, with no doubting, for he who doubts is like a wave of the sea driven and tossed by the wind" (James 1:5, 6).

Brian wanted to know the truth about the mark of the beast. A Bible worker was leading him through the *Amazing Facts Bible Study Guides*. He was eating them up! Then he discovered the lessons were available online at amazingfacts. org. "In less than a week," he shares, "I completed the entire set of 14 lessons."

The Bible worker continued to study with Brian, and he was always on top of the lesson. Then he learned there was an advanced set of lessons. Bible workers are trained to carefully hand out a few lessons as people are ready. But the enthusiasm and interest in Brian must have changed her mind. "I praise God that she listened to the Holy Spirit because of my great interest in learning about all these wonderful truths in the Bible," he shared.

Finally, the day came when Brian opened up Study Guide #20, "The Mark of the Beast." As he studied this lesson, his heart throbbed with joy to finally learn from the Bible about the mark of the beast and that it revolves around a day of worship.

"I praise God for answering my prayers and leading me to the *Amazing Facts Bible Study Guides* in my search for truth," Brian relates. "And to add icing to the cake, I not only discovered I could also review these lessons online (amazingfacts.org) but was able to hear a sermon on each topic by Pastor Doug Batchelor. As I listened to him teach each lesson and give his testimony, I knew beyond a shadow of a doubt that God is real and that the Bible is the inspired Word of God!"

Brian was baptized and is now active in sharing his faith with others. He explains, "Everything that once confused me in the Bible has now been clearly answered." Brian understands that a public series of meetings helps many people discover Bible truth, "But for me, I needed to study my way into the church through the Bible. What brought me light were these study guides. Now I clearly know what the Bible teaches, beyond a shadow of a doubt."

Reflect: Recall a time when you doubted something you heard. What removed all doubt? God's Word can clear up all confusion.

Dig Deeper: Matthew 21:21; Mark 9:24; Jude 1:22

Sojourner Truth

Lifting Up Freedom

"Who made heaven and earth, the sea, and all that is in them; who keeps truth forever, who executes justice for the oppressed, who gives food to the hungry. The gives freedom to the prisoners" (Psalm 146:6, 7).

Isabella Baumfree was born into slavery in New York in 1797. As she grew up, she was sold several times and eventually married another slave named Thomas with whom she had five children. In 1827, New York freed all slaves, but Isabella had already left her husband and ran away with her youngest child, Sophia.

She later learned that one of her children, Peter, had been sold into slavery in Alabama. Because Peter had been emancipated under New York law, she sued in court and won his return. She was the first black woman to win such a case against a white man.

Isabella eventually lived with Isaac and Maria Van Wagenen where she had a life-changing religious experience and became a devout Christian. The year 1843 was a turning point for Isabella when she became convicted that God was calling her to be a traveling preacher. She told friends, "The Spirit calls me, and I must go." Thus, she changed her name to Sojourner Truth.

Sojourner became an advocate for women's rights, temperance, and the abolition of slavery. She was a speaker and went on lecture tours, delivering messages that demanded equal rights for women and blacks. For 10 years, Truth spoke before hundreds of audiences. She was also privileged to meet Harriet Beecher Stowe and, during the Civil War, President Abraham Lincoln.

For a period of time, she was friendly with the Millerite movement that preached the soon coming of Jesus, but later left the group. In 1857, she moved to Battle Creek, Michigan and, according to some reports, became a Sabbath-keeping Christian. She died in 1883, and was buried in Oak Hill Cemetery in Battle Creek, in the same graveyard as other Sabbath-keeping pioneers, including Ellen G. White.

Though she was once sold at the age of nine for $100, along with a flock of sheep, this brave woman found Christ and became a spokesperson for the belief that all people are created equal. She once said, "Truth is powerful, and it prevails."

Reflect: Have you ever stood up and spoken out against an injustice you observed? God wants us to stand for truth, especially in these last days.

Dig Deeper: Psalm 119:45; 2 Corinthians 3:17; Galatians 5:1

Teresita

From Nun to Prayer Warrior, Part 1

"Therefore, as through one man's offense judgment came to all men, resulting in condemnation, even so through one Man's righteous act the free gift came to all men, resulting in justification of life" (Romans 5:18).

As a young nurse in the Philippines, Teresita had a deep desire to serve God. She felt impressed to enter a convent and become a nun. Her sins weighed on her heart and she believed that by serving in this way she could be purged of her sinful past.

While attending nursing school, Teresita met "sisters" and a priest. She thought that if she could be like them, she would become holy and pure. When she told her mother of her desire, she begged her not to go. She says, "I was stubborn and rebellious and didn't want to listen to her."

On the day she wanted to enter the convent, her uncle, who was serving as a priest in Rome, was visiting in Manila. She begged him to help her get into the nunnery. The next day they caught a taxi and with his help she was accepted. The decision so shocked her mother that she had a heart attack and was paralyzed for several months.

Little did Teresita think that it would be 21 years before she would leave the monastery. Life in this religious community was rigorous and included doing penance, always consulting the mother superior, and even kissing the floor.

Except hearing the Bible at mass, Teresita never studied the Scriptures. She focused on the lives of the saints and the catechism. But none of these things brought peace to her tortured conscience. The guilt of her sins began to crush her spirit. Praying the rosary, making pilgrimages, confessing to the priest, partaking of communion ... nothing eased the weight of her sin.

Teresita continued to seek peace by doing acts of righteousness. "I felt so empty. I was serving idols instead of the true and living God. I depended on my superiors instead of Jesus."

Then, in an unfortunate encounter with another nun, she disobeyed the mother superior and was asked to leave. Teresita thinks of it now as a "mighty deliverance from God." At the time she pleaded with them to allow her to stay. She had 21 years of a blameless record but was now dismissed.

Reflect: Have you ever been tempted to impress God or others by your own acts of righteousness? These will never save you. Seek heaven's wisdom on revealing Christ to others.

Dig Deeper: Matthew 6:1–8; Romans 6:18; Philippians 3:9

From Nun to Prayer Warrior, Part 2

"Therefore, if anyone is in Christ, he is a new creation; old things have passed away; behold, all things have become new" (2 Corinthians 5:17).

After being dismissed from her convent, Teresita was extremely depressed. "I could not stop the tears. I felt so alone." With only a little pocket money she boarded a ship and left, feeling like life was not worth living. She eventually moved to Canada to help her sister and then moved to New York.

While working in the United States as a night nurse in a hospital, she continued to attend church nearby. She participated in holy mass, in the stations of the cross, prayed through the rosary, and made weekly confessions. One day, the head nurse on her floor—who was a Sabbath-keeper—asked her, "Teresita, why don't you worship God on the Sabbath?"

"What is the Sabbath?" she asked him. Then he handed her an invitation to a series of meetings being held by Pastor Doug Batchelor in mid-town Manhattan called *Millennium of Prophecy*.

On the fifth night of the series she began to attend the meetings with her sister. When Pastor Doug spoke on the antichrist, Teresita was shocked, but earnestly prayed for enlightenment.

She completed the series with her sister and decided to be baptized. Her sister told her, "You've been fooled. You've always been a Catholic. You will die a Catholic." With the pressure of her family on one side and the desire to follow the Bible on the other, Teresita began to study more deeply. About one month after the *Millennium of Prophecy* series concluded, she was baptized into the Sabbath-keeping church where her nursing supervisor attended.

Since her new life in Christ, Teresita has become a prayer warrior and has also participated in several mission trips.

Teresita shares, "I will forever be grateful to Amazing Facts for my conversion. God used Pastor Batchelor to remove the scales from my eyes so that I could see the pure gospel. I can still remember being buried in the waters of baptism, after the series, and taking my first breath upon coming up out of the pool. I said to myself, 'I am rising as a new creature in Jesus Christ!'"

Teresita always wanted to serve God. Though she spent 21 years looking for peace through acts of penance, she now walks in freedom that comes only through the blood of Christ.

Reflect: When have you last felt renewed by the Holy Spirit? Is there something hindering you from God's blessing on your life? Daily invite the Spirit to dwell in you.

Dig Deeper: Isaiah 43:19; Romans 6:4; Ephesians 4:22–24

Esther

Rags to Riches, Part 1

"Do all things without complaining and disputing, that you may become blameless and harmless, children of God without fault in the midst of a crooked and perverse generation, among whom you shine as lights in the world" (Philippians 2:14, 15).

Eleanor Roosevelt holds the record as the First Lady of the United States who served for the longest amount of time—a consecutive 12 years alongside her husband, President Franklin D. Roosevelt. She was known for her unconventionally active take on her role and was an outspoken advocate for human and civil rights. Lesser known is the fact that she was orphaned at only 10 years old.

Another orphan who rose through the ranks of an empire, Esther was an exceptionally beautiful girl raised by her cousin Mordecai after the death of her parents (Esther 2:7). She and Mordecai lived during the peak of the ancient Persian kingdom in the capital of Susa, or Shushan. But they were not natives; they were descendants of a Jewish contingent seized by the Babylonian king Nebuchadnezzar over a century before (vv. 5, 6). Esther was nothing more than an obscure refugee.

But one day, a new decree was issued: All the young virgins from every corner of the realm were to be brought before the king so that he could choose from among them a new bride. Esther, along with all the others, was taken to the royal palace to be overseen by an official named Hegai (v. 8).

Now Esther was not only beautiful in form, she also possessed beauty of character. Brought up under Mordecai's care, she had become a God-fearing young woman. Now ensconced in the Persian palace, she immediately caught the eye of Hegai, he no doubt doubly endeared by her comeliness as well as her kindness. And it was not only Hegai who noticed her: "Esther obtained favor in the sight of all who saw her" (v. 15). So it was that when she was presented to King Ahasuerus, also known as Xerxes I, that he likewise saw what everyone else had and chose her as his new queen (v. 17).

While this may seem like a fairy tale, the life of Queen Esther was so much greater. And unlike a fairy tale, she was not yet to have her happily ever after.

Reflect: In what capacities do you interact with those who do not share your same faith? What are you known for among them?

Dig Deeper: Isaiah 43:10, 12; Matthew 5:14–16; Romans 12:1, 2

Esther

Rags to Riches, Part 2

"Yet who knows whether you have come to the kingdom for such a time as this?" (Esther 4:14).

On May 5, 1945, in the midst of a harrowing Japanese attack in World War II, an unarmed medic saved 75 of his injured comrades by lowering them down a 400-foot cliff. But if you would have asked Private First Class Desmond Doss how he completed that feat, he would have told you that it was not he but God who had spared their lives that day.

As for Esther, she had been queen for some time when she discovered that her life and those of all the Jews in Persia were on the line. Through Mordecai, Esther learned that there had been a new decree written announcing the genocide of all Jewish people in Persia (Esther 3:8, 9). The architect behind it was the prime minister, Haman, who had been slighted when Mordecai had refused to bow to him (v. 2).

Mordecai then requested that Esther beg for the lives of her people directly to her husband. But Esther was afraid. If she initiated a visit to the king in his inner court, Persian law stated that she would be put to death unless the king held out his golden scepter to her, signaling mercy (4:11). She did not want to go. But Mordecai responded with a perspective that changed Esther's mind.

He reminded her of her duty, her heritage, and her faith (vv. 13, 14). His words gave her a purpose; they reminded her that she was not alone. It was God who had brought her to her current station, and it was God who would go with her. Esther decided she would go—but not without much prayer and fasting (v. 16).

Three days later, when Esther entered the king's court, the scepter was held out to her (5:2). The next day, in front of King Ahasuerus and Haman himself, she unmasked the latter as a premeditator of murder (7:3–6). In the end, Haman was put to death (v. 10) and a new decree was written in the Jews' defense (8:5–13).

Esther had submitted to God's calling for her life; through her, God brought about the Jews' deliverance. Although He is not mentioned in the entire Book of Esther, God's providence is all over its pages.

Reflect: What divine appointments have you received from God? What would you be willing to give up in order to fulfill them?

Dig Deeper: Matthew 10:39; Romans 8:28–30; 1 Peter 2:9, 10

Zachary

Once Upon a Murder, Part 1

"In my distress I cried to the , and He heard me" (Psalm 120:1).

The sound was sickening, like a slab of meat being punched over and over again. It echoed off the cold, hard walls of the prison. Thud, thud, thud. It was the sound of someone fighting for his life.

Finally, a small form dropped to his knees—his body a swollen, bruised lump.

There had been four men, all bigger than him. He had fought back, and they had finally left him alone. But he knew there would be more to come. He was "fresh fish," new to prison, and this was his welcome to life behind bars.

God saw Zachary and loved him. Through generous and compassionate believers, this broken and bruised inmate found healing and hope.

Zachary grew up in a big Catholic family, the eldest of four boys. When he was young, he liked going to church, but he liked other things more—alcohol, drugs, guns. He loved guns. He stole, he fought, he dealt, and he lived life with a gang.

One day, he shot a man dead. For his crime, he was sentenced to 25 years in prison.

Now, in that dark, lonely place, bruised and beaten, Zachary looked at his life and was afraid.

At night he was tormented by a demon. It held him so tightly that he could not move or speak. He would wake up sobbing.

And those men who had beat him would come back. How could he stand up to them again? How could he endure another 25 years of this?

That harrowing day, he realized that his prison cell was not his only prison. Zachary realized how weak he really was and just how much he did not want to die. That agonizing day he cried out to God. He explains, "I knew my life was wrong and that my situation was a direct result of what I had done. And I also knew nothing could save me but God."

He cried and cried, as though he would never stop. He told God how sorry he was for all the evil he had caused and pleaded for His help. He also had a growing desire to read the Bible. "In my distress I cried to the , and He heard me" (Psalm 120:1).

Reflect: Did you know God hears the cries of our heart and has compassion for us when we are in great distress? Turn to the Lord when life has beaten you down. He truly cares for you.

Dig Deeper: Exodus 2:23; Judges 3:9; 2 Chronicles 14:11

Zachary

Once Upon a Murder, Part 2

"I have come as a light into the world, that whoever believes in Me should not abide in darkness" (John 12:46).

Zachary was in prison, crying out to God with great sobs. All of a sudden, it was as if the cement blocks of his cell had been parted by an unseen hand, and the sun shone down on him, warm and bright and full. He felt something he never had before—joy.

Three days later, Zachary was moved to another prison. Gone were the men who beat him up. And the demon that had been harassing him in the night? It had gone too. God had answered his prayer.

He began to read the Bible. He signed up for as many Bible studies as he could and got his hands on as many Christian books as possible.

But one day, he found a book that changed everything. In the back of a book titled *The Great Controversy* was an offer to send away for a Bible study by a ministry called Amazing Facts. He sent in the offer and received the lessons. Then he sent away for more lessons, magazines, and books.

Zachary was in awe of the truths taught by Amazing Facts; they were taken straight from the Word of God. He also read *Broken Chains*, Pastor Doug's book about Jesus' encounter with the demoniac of Decapolis, and he began to practically apply the biblical knowledge to his own life. He read *Hero of Hacksaw Ridge* and used it to witness to his three brothers, who are all in the military.

Zachary's brothers noticed a change in his life—in fact, his whole family saw that he had become a completely different person. God had given him a new heart and a new mind to love the things of His Word more than anything else.

Today, Zachary, a murderer turned missionary, shares the truths of the Bible with his fellow inmates. He is now a co-laborer with Christ to help set others free. He is freer now in the confines of his prison cell than he had ever been when living out in the world.

God lead Zachary out of darkness and into the marvelous light of truth. "To serve in the kingdom of God is the greatest thing I've ever taken part in," he says.

Reflect: What do you do when you are surrounded by darkness? How can you let the light of heaven into your life? God is ready to send truth into your mind and heart.

Dig Deeper: Psalm 18:28; Luke 1:79; John 1:5

William Booth

"God shall have all there is of William Booth," Part 1

"Jesus said to her, 'Did I not say to you that if you would believe you would see the glory of God?'" (John 11:40).

At 13, a young boy should be in school, spending his free time at play and study. Instead, William Booth was working for a pawnbroker in Victorian-era England.

"My father was a Grab, a Get," Booth would later recall. "He had been born into poverty. He determined to grow rich; and he did. He grew very rich, because he lived without God and simply worked for money; and when he lost it all, his heart broke with it, and he died miserably."

Not only did Samuel Booth's heart break, but William's father lost the money to send the young boy to school. So William was apprenticed to pawnbroker Francis Eames in Nottingham. There, William saw people at their worst, pawning necessary items to have money for necessities—or addictions such as alcohol.

He also saw what a bad employer would be like. Eames treated Booth miserably, even though the boy was his most reliable employee. After Booth's father died when the lad was 14, William was a source of support for his mother, Mary, and siblings, but he toiled under taxing conditions.

During this period, he began attending the Broad Street Wesley (Methodist) Chapel in Nottingham. On one evening in 1844, he responded to the preacher's messages and surrendered his life to Christ while walking home.

"It was in the open street [of Nottingham] that this great change passed over me," he later wrote. In his diary, Booth offered a solemn vow: "God shall have all there is of William Booth."

A visit to Nottingham from American revivalist James Caughey kindled a desire in the young man to go out and win souls. He would implore those going into the saloons and other places of degradation to instead come to church. Booth would stand on a barrel and preach to open-air "congregations" of two or three people, appealing to them to receive Christ.

Booth left the pawnbroker's shop and set out to share the gospel. But another "conversion," if you will, lay ahead, and with it another life-changing experience.

Reflect: What motivates you to go out and seek the lost? Pray that God will give you a love for lost souls.

Dig Deeper: 2 Chronicles 20:20; John 1:14; Romans 14:17–25

William Booth

"God shall have all there is of William Booth," Part 2

"Believe on the Lord Jesus Christ, and you will be saved, you and your household" (Acts 16:31).

William Booth once saw England's poorest as customers in a pawn shop. Now, the converted man saw the poor, the drunken, and the desolate as objects of Christ's love.

Booth had abandoned the pawnbroker's trade, despite a six-year apprenticeship in Francis Eames' Nottingham establishment. Instead, he became a Methodist evangelist, ending up in London and marrying a young woman who was a spiritually kindred soul, Catherine Mumfort. It was Catherine who motivated and guided the young preacher.

Eventually, Booth worked in the slums of East London and was invited to preach in a tent erected at a burial ground. It was about as far from a traditional Methodist chapel as one could go: the air was heavy with the odors of alcohol and naphtha lamps, and the coarse people were curious about what the young man was saying. On the night of July 2, 1865, "a few souls" came forward to the "mercy seat" at the front of the tent to find salvation after Booth had preached.

Arriving home near midnight, Booth found Catherine waiting up for him: "O Kate, I have found my destiny!"

That destiny involved starting The Christian Mission to East London, where Booth would seek the lost as well as improve the lives of those living there. More distinguished Methodist chapels didn't want the unwashed converts Booth brought to their doors, so he started holding a weekly worship of his own.

By 1878, Booth's mission was raising funds and sharing an annual report with donors. In writing one such report, Booth's now-grown son Bramwell, assisting his father, gave the mission the name we know today: The Salvation Army.

William Booth now wrote, "We are a salvation people—this is our specialty—getting saved and keeping saved, and then getting somebody else saved."

Booth's Salvation Army, with its uniforms, brass bands marching through the streets, and "open air" evangelism outside of pubs and in town squares, sent shockwaves through England. Saloonkeepers recruited ruffians to break up Salvation Army meetings. High-church leaders looked suspiciously upon the informal services Booth's disciples held.

But his movement grew, spreading to America and Canada, and now operates in more than 130 countries and territories. The Army has 2,000,000 church members, each of whom proclaims the message of Booth's signature hymn, "O Boundless Salvation," which says God's grace is "now flowing for all men."

Reflect: How long would you be willing to pray for something you desired from God? Be persistent and never give up!

Dig Deeper: Isaiah 45:22; Habakkuk 2:4; John 6:40

Sharon

"Stop at that Channel," Part 1

"Your ears shall hear a word behind you, saying, 'This is the way, walk in it,' whenever you turn to the right hand or whenever you turn to the left" (Isaiah 30:21).

As the youngest of five children growing up in a Catholic household, Sharon learned to stay out of the way. Drinking and arguing between her parents and older siblings was a way of life. When her dad would come home drunk, Sharon would quickly go hide in a corner with her hands over her ears.

But she also learned to keep up appearances on the outside—pretending everything was fine. This habit continued even as she grew older and suffered an abusive relationship herself.

"I put the face on and pretended to be content in front of people all the time. I always felt inside that I needed to just keep people happy—push down what I was feeling and keep everybody happy around me."

At age 21, Sharon married for the first time and had two children. But she still felt lost inside. Now instead of trying to hide in a corner, she'd go into her closet and cry privately. There were so many days when she only felt motivated to get up and try to keep going because she knew that she needed to take care of her children.

After almost 20 difficult years of marriage, Sharon's husband left her and their children. She was forced to find a job—constantly trying to juggle her meager funds to cover bills. Many days she'd arrive home after a hard day at work to discover that one utility or another had been cut off yet again.

And her children, teenagers now, began making choices that brought more pain. Those were her darkest days.

Looking back, she says, "I was so very lonely and sad. I cried a lot. I'd think, 'Ok, do what you have to do to get through the day. Then go to bed. Then get up.' I felt like a robot."

One night, Sharon sat on her couch flipping through television channels looking for something to watch. "It was like God kept knocking. I could just feel the presence of Him saying, 'I'm here and it's ok—stop at that channel.' And I did."

Reflect: Have you ever heard God speak to your heart? Did you respond? Listen to the Holy Spirit and compare what you hear with the Bible, then move forward in faith!

Dig Deeper: Joshua 1:7; John 10:27; Revelation 3:20

**"He heals the brokenhearted and binds up
their wounds" (Psalm 147:3).**

When Sharon sat down to watch TV, praying for direction, she sensed God telling her to stop at a certain channel. "And I did." It was *Amazing Facts Presents* on Channel 44, and she knew a miracle was happening.

The message of grace that Pastor Doug shared touched her hurting heart. She remembers listening as he shared his own story. And she began to understand the truth about who she was in Christ. Sharon felt the tiniest beginnings of hope.

"I always felt so unworthy. I knew I was just a total mess. But watching the program taught me about the loving Father I never knew growing up. Pastor Doug made it so simple when he shared that it's ok not to be ok. That Jesus will meet you where you're at."

Sharon was hungry to learn more. She sent away for a few of the free pamphlets and then the *Amazing Facts Bible Study Guides*. The more she discovered, the more her life changed.

What she learned from Pastor Doug especially helped her to find healing from past hurts created by all of her painful family situations.

"Pastor Doug taught me how to actually live with people that can be coming up against you. He said to learn to trust God because people will disappoint. Now I live by Proverbs 3:5 and I rely on God to give me strength.

"And another huge message that Pastor Doug really implanted in my mind was 'don't blame the people. The devil uses people to get to you because he knows your weaknesses.'"

Sharon spent years trying to feel approval from the people closest to her—and feeling rejected instead. Now she doesn't carry that burden anymore. Instead, she praises God for how He heals and restores even the deepest pain. In her darkest times, she never would have pictured that God would bring her relationships with her father, her grown children, and even her former husband, to the place of peace she experiences today.

Today, Sharon prays to be the hands and feet of Jesus to everyone around her. "I never knew God—never knew Jesus—until Pastor Doug taught me. For years I was so depressed and filled with gloom. But I am so different today. I have peace. I keep my eyes on Jesus and the cross and I fear death no more."

Reflect: Have you ever felt completely broken inside? Jesus was wounded and knows just how you feel. Throw yourself into the arms of a loving Savior.

Dig Deeper: Job 5:11; Psalm 34:18; Isaiah 61:1

Manasseh

The Prodigal King

**"You shall worship the your God, and Him
only you shall serve" (Matthew 4:10).**

History has known no shortage of depravity when it comes to royals—from Russia's Ivan the Terrible, whose violent temper caused his daughter-in-law's miscarriage and the ensuing death of his own son, to Queen Ranavalona I of Madagascar, who dispatched her enemies by a torturous game involving chicken skin and the poisonous tangena nut.

Included in this hall of infamy is Judah's own King Manasseh. A practicing occultist (2 Chronicles 33:6), he not only loved evil, he abhorred anything good and "shed very much innocent blood" (2 Kings 21:16), including that of the prophet Isaiah. He disdained God and instead "worshiped all the host of heaven and served them" (2 Chronicles 33:3). Worst of all, he led his people into this same apostasy.

Not only did he build shrines for these false gods, he built them in God's very temple in Jerusalem (2 Kings 21:5), even insolently placing within it a representation of the Canaanite fertility goddess Asherah (v. 7). He also sacrificed his own sons to these heathen religions, burning them to ashes upon the altars he had built (2 Chronicles 33:6). In turning away from the true God, he had become the worst of the worst, sunken into an evil more dreadful than even the pagan nations themselves (v. 9).

Chance after chance was Manasseh given to return to the God of his ancestors, but time after time he denied it (v. 10). Finally, destruction came upon him in the form of the ruling empire of the day, the Assyrians, "who took Manasseh with hooks, bound him with bronze fetters, and carried him off to Babylon" (v. 11).

Now the tormentor had become the tormented. It was during this time of shame, fear, and suffering that Manasseh gave his heart to God and, in repentant prayer, asked for His mercy (vv. 12, 13). God answered his prayer, and Manasseh was allowed to return to Jerusalem.

The humbled king immediately instituted a slew of reforms, removing all the pagan sites that he had built, including the Asherah, as well as repairing the neglected items in God's temple. For the rest of his days, Manasseh never forgot his captivity; he worshipped God alone and encouraged his people to do the same (v. 16).

Reflect: Are you in a position of prominence, as a boss, a teacher, a head of household? How do you use that position to glorify God?

Dig Deeper: Proverbs 16:10–15; Mark 10:42–45; Titus 1:7–11

"Seek first the kingdom of God and His righteousness, and all these things shall be added to you" (Matthew 6:33).

Bill's life looked great. His success in industrial sales propelled him up the corporate ladder and to a future filled with achievement. His wide circle of friends and business colleagues saw him enjoying the lifestyle of someone who made good money.

"Anybody looking at me from the outside," explains Bill, "saw a successful up-and-coming manager. But they did not see the self-medication, the frustration, the self-loathing, the depression, the complete dependence on self. In fact, I always felt like I was on the outside looking in."

Despite the outward appearances, Bill was miserable. He wandered down many roads looking for peace and joy, but instead he ended up with two failed marriages. He then drifted into drugs. His anger with himself only grew.

Weary of shallow friends and relationships but still wanting something more in life, Bill joined an online dating service. He chose the name "Tall Blue-Eyed Texan." And there he met Carrie, a woman who had been praying for a long time that God would let her meet a tall blue-eyed Texan who loved the Lord.

Bill smiles sharing the story. "I'm 6 feet 4 inches tall, live in Texas, and have blue eyes. Exactly what she was looking for—well, almost. I didn't know the Lord, let alone love Him."

So Carrie helped Bill get to know Jesus for the first time. She had grown up in a Sabbath-keeping home but was attending a non-denominational church when they met. As Bill listened to Carrie share, he came to love and accept Christ as his Savior.

For the first time, Bill began finding the peace he'd longed for—and true love. Carrie became his wife, and they attended church together every Sunday.

But doubts remained. "The one thing, though, that I couldn't shake," Bill says, "was that feeling of being on the outside looking in—of not really belonging."

Bill's job eventually led them to another state, and he and Carrie tried out several Sunday churches. Nothing ever quite fit. Although Carrie shared with him about the Bible Sabbath and sometimes talked about returning to a Sabbath-keeping church, Bill figured it didn't matter on which day you worshiped as long as you worshiped.

But behind the scenes, a friend of theirs was already praying they would become Sabbath-keepers.

Reflect: Do you know of someone who has prayed (or is praying) for you? God wants you to intercede for a friend in need.

Dig Deeper: Romans 8:26; Ephesians 6:18; 1 Timothy 2:1

Bill

A Praying Friend, Part 2

**"As newborn babes, desire the pure milk of the word,
that you may grow thereby, if indeed you have tasted
that the Lord is gracious" (1 Peter 2:2, 3).**

Bill and Carrie were looking for a church, but behind the scenes, a friend of theirs was already praying they would become Sabbath-keepers and felt impressed to send them a set of *Storacles of Prophecy* Bible lessons from Amazing Facts.

Carrie was eager to study them, and Bill agreed. "As we went through them, I was amazed at what I was learning." They also watched Amazing Facts presentations. "Pastor Doug is a great teacher and speaker. And what he was saying were things I had never heard before, but they made perfect sense. What spoke to me most though was the teaching on the Sabbath. That really hit home. I knew it was right."

It took some time, but Bill and Carrie eventually decided to try attending a church that kept the Sabbath. However, Bill was pessimistic. He felt concerned about how Sabbath-keeping would affect his life and doubted that he could adapt to such a huge change in his weekly routine—especially with the demanding requirements of his career.

"I travel frequently for my job, managing a business, and I was always working or thinking about work. But as soon as we started observing the Sabbath, I realized what a blessing it was in my life. The Sabbath taught me to set work aside for one day and focus on God and my family. I discovered that I have been able to do more with the six days than I could ever do with seven."

And Bill realized he'd found the last piece he'd been searching for. "I finally felt at home in a church. The Sabbath became a huge blessing in my life, and that feeling of being on the outside looking in disappeared!"

Next to the Sabbath, Bill considers what Pastor Doug shared about tithing to have the biggest impact on his life. "To me, tithe and Sabbath are tied together. Just as I now accomplish more in six days because I set aside Sabbath to spend with God, I receive more monetary blessings as I tithe faithfully."

Bill and Carrie are active in their church. Bill teaches a Sabbath School class and was recently asked to preach a sermon. "I've gone from an infant on baby food to helping to feed others with solid food," Bill explains.

Reflect: Have you discovered the blessing of returning tithe? It's a way to put God first in your life! You can never out-give the Lord. Watch how He blesses your faith!

Dig Deeper: Philippians 1:9; Hebrews 6:1; 2 Peter 3:18

Arnold Fruchtenbaum

Rescued from Communism,
Converted to Christ

**"For I am not ashamed of the gospel of Christ, for it is the
power of God to salvation for everyone who believes, for
the Jew first and also for the Greek" (Romans 1:16).**

His name may not be a "household word" in many Christian circles, but
Arnold J. Fruchtenbaum, holder of a doctorate from New York University, is a
Jewish believer in Jesus whose influence spans continents and decades. What's
more, it was his family's rescue from communism—twice, in fact—that began
his journey to faith in the Messiah.

Falsely accused of being a Nazi spy, Fruchtenbaum's father, a photographer,
had been imprisoned in Siberia. Arnold was born in the easternmost part of
Russia in 1943; after World War II, the family returned to Poland, which was
not a hospitable place for his family. In 1947, the Fruchtenbaums escaped to
Czechoslovakia, only to have that nation seized by communists the next year.
Posing as Greeks, the family escaped to West Germany and were befriended
by a Lutheran pastor who directed the America-bound family to a Jewish-
Christian mission in Brooklyn. Arnold and his mother were helped there.

In meetings at the mission, Arnold found faith in Jesus. This did not please
his father, a descendant of Orthodox Jewish teachers who was still committed
to Judaism. The young man was ordered not to contact Jewish believers or
read Christian Scriptures while in the family's home. Arnold surreptitiously
maintained contact, however, and never abandoned his faith.

After high school, Arnold was sent packing by his father, who didn't want a
Jewish believer in Jesus in his home. Arnold graduated from Cedarville College,
a Christian school, with a degree in Hebrew and Greek. He continued his
studies at Dallas Theological Seminary and earned his NYU doctorate writing
"Israelology: The Missing Link in Systematic Theology."

Having spoken around the world about Jewish belief in Jesus,
Fruchtenbaum continues his work through Ariel Ministries, which has
outreaches in eight nations, including Israel.

Reflect: Looking at a changed life can change the direction of your
own life. Has someone's personal testimony deeply impacted you?

Dig Deeper: Psalm 119:46; Isaiah 53:1; Hebrews 4:12

Calvin and Bonnie

Complete Answers, Part 1

"Always be ready to give a defense to everyone who asks you a reason for the hope that is in you, with meekness and fear" (1 Peter 3:15).

Bonnie grew up with an atheist father. She only remembers going to church once with her mother on Easter. About three years ago she and Calvin were attending a Baptist church. They were looking for answers to their Bible questions and were just not satisfied with "partial" answers that were not straight from the Scriptures.

One day Bonnie asked her neighbor friend, Evelyn, "Why do you go to church on Saturday?"

Evelyn simply replied, "Because it's the Sabbath."

Bonnie then asked, "Then why do you think I go to church on Sunday?"

"Because it's convenient," Evelyn smiled. That's where the conversation ended ... for the time being.

Lloyd and Evelyn planned to go to California for the winter and Calvin and Bonnie agreed to look after their place while they were gone. Before leaving for California, Evelyn invited Bonnie over so she could show her where everything was located in case something came up.

As they walked past Evelyn's bookcase, Bonnie noticed a whole row of old VHS tapes. Bonnie and Calvin had just quit receiving satellite TV the day before and felt it would be better just to watch videos and DVDs. So they were looking for interesting programs to view. When Bonnie saw the old VHS tapes, she asked Evelyn, "What are all these?"

Evelyn replied, "They are a series of programs about Bible prophecy called *The Prophecy Code* filmed in 2005."

"Would you mind if we watched them while you're gone?" Bonnie asked.

"Help yourself," said Evelyn, and soon after, they left for California.

Calvin and Bonnie just couldn't get enough of these Bible seminars and soon bought their own set (on DVD) from Amazing Facts. They received free booklet offers and later purchased the Prophecy Study Bible.

A couple months after first watching *The Prophecy Code*, Bonnie and Calvin made a decision that changed their lives.

Reflect: Has someone ever asked you about your religious beliefs? The Bible encourages us to be prepared to answer for our faith.

Dig Deeper: Matthew 10:19; Mark 13:11; Luke 12:12

Calvin and Bonnie

Complete Answers, Part 2

"You shall receive power when the Holy Spirit has come upon you; and you shall be witnesses to Me ..." (Acts 1:8).

When Bonnie and Calvin's neighbors asked them to watch their home while they traveled west for the winter, they began watching *The Prophecy Code* series they found in their home. Before leaving, the Sabbath-keeping neighbor said, "Help yourself!"

A couple months after first watching *The Prophecy Code*, Bonnie and Calvin showed up in church one Sabbath with a whole list of questions. They continued to come and study. After watching the series once, they watched it again and became convinced that Saturday was the Bible Sabbath. Eventually, they completed studies and were baptized.

Bonnie says, "I just love the materials I get from Amazing Facts. Pastor Doug speaks in a way that I can understand. His messages are so inspiring and informational. I'm always requesting the free offers for the booklets because I like to share them with my friends and neighbors. When I'm talking with them about the Bible and they ask a question I can go right to these booklets which are so clear."

Calvin and Bonnie like to share Amazing Facts materials with their neighbors. Some will listen to them, some will not. More than once someone has said, "I know Saturday is the Sabbath, but I'm comfortable just sticking with my old church."

Sometimes Bonnie gets asked Bible questions and she doesn't know the answers, so she will go back to her *Amazing Facts Bible Study Guides* and the booklets she has collected to find information. And she still comes to church with questions for her pastor.

When Bonnie took a friend to the doctor, she brought along a few Amazing Facts booklets to read while she sat in the waiting room. Often she will guide the conversation to spiritual things and draw people into a discussion about the Bible. God has opened many doors for her to share her faith.

Bonnie says, "Our beliefs are strong. We used to struggle to go to church each week, but now we look forward to going to bed early on Friday evening and getting off to church before services even begin. We just love our church family and spend lots of time with them, especially on the Sabbath."

Reflect: What makes some people more excited about sharing their faith? Do you have a love relationship with Jesus that prompts you to witness for Christ?

Dig Deeper: Matthew 5:16; John 15:7; Colossians 3:16

The Samaritan Woman

The Gift

"Come, see a Man who told me all things that I ever did. Could this be the Christ?" (John 4:29).

Today, "The Woman at the Well" wouldn't be that much of an oddity, at least not in the U.S., or Britain, or many other places. But in her day, she was part of a minority in Palestine who was looked down upon by the religious and cultural elite in Israel. Although that wasn't the spectacle of her first-century life. It was her "backstory."

This woman, who met Jesus in the middle of the day at a well in Samaria, was notorious. Married far more than once, she was in an illicit relationship. In Jesus' time, it was so much of a scandal that she could only collect water from the community well during the height of the midday sun. To go when the rest of the townsfolk were there would only invite ridicule.

When the woman arrived at the well, Jesus engaged her: "Give Me a drink," He said (John 4:7). In that culture, this was an invitation to a conversation. She'd probably had such invitations before, and some of those had led to her five marriages, maybe even her current unmarried relationship.

Knowing that Jesus was a Jew, she asked Him why she was being asked to fetch a drink. The Jews had long looked down on the Samaritans; the Bible says they "[had] no dealings" with her people (John 4:9).

That's when Jesus revealed Himself, albeit subtly: "If you knew the gift of God, and who it is who says to you, 'Give Me a drink,' you would have asked Him, and He would have given you living water" (v. 10).

When Jesus told the woman what she already knew, that she had been married five times and was now living with a man to whom she wasn't wed, the light began to dawn. "Sir, I perceive that You are a prophet" (v. 19). When she described the Messiah as revealing all truth, Jesus answered, "I who speak to you am He" (v. 26).

This revelation turned the woman into an evangelist; she told the men of the village, "Come, see a Man who told me all things that I ever did. Could this be the Christ?" (v. 29). The men followed her and listened to Jesus.

Divine insight made a disciple of the Samaritan woman—and an outreach worker as well!

Reflect: After she recognized Jesus as the Messiah, this woman evangelized her community. What are you doing to reach your neighbors? Pray and act this week!

Dig Deeper: Psalm 46:4; Isaiah 12:3; Acts 9:11

Nicole

Craving the Truth, Part 1

"Now the works of the flesh are evident, which are: adultery, fornication, uncleanness, lewdness" (Galatians 5:19).

Nicole sat at her computer searching online and praying for something profound. It seemed as though she had spent her entire life searching for one thing or another. Starting with her earliest years, she longed for a way out of the poverty and pain of her childhood. She was tired of stealing quarters just so she could buy something to eat.

After finishing high school, Nicole began searching for a job that would take her far away and offer her a better life. She was thrilled when a friend showed her a newspaper ad seeking dancers for a resort. It seemed to be an answer for so many of her troubles. She had always wanted to be a dancer, and the promised pay was good. Her family even helped her purchase a one-way bus ticket, so Nicole set off with starry visions of dancing in a fun musical show.

Looking back, Nicole says, "What I found when I got there burst my bubble fast. A seedy-looking guy, a rundown building, and girls on stage wearing practically nothing." Young and alone, she felt defeated. "I was hours away from home with no money, scared out of my mind, and with what appeared to be no choice but to take the job."

In desperation, Nicole reasoned that no one would ever find out if she danced just enough to afford a ticket back home. But once she started down that path, things didn't go as she'd hoped. The years began to pass, one after another, with her life growing darker all the time.

Occasionally, during the most difficult times, Nicole would remember how she sometimes visited church as a child. She wondered what it would be like to know more about God. "I was a dancer for a little over twenty years. Once you're in that world, you're worn away and introduced to all kinds of things that lead away from Him."

As much as Nicole longed to be closer to God, she now knows she was looking for Him in all the wrong places. After searching for truth in the Kabballah, tarot cards, spiritualism, and other places, Nicole felt like her life was broken and beyond repair.

But God had not left Nicole.

Reflect: Have you ever walked down a pathway away from God? Did the Lord ever leave you during that time? The Bible says God goes to great lengths to pursue His lost children.

Dig Deeper: Matthew 5:28; Mark 7:20–23; 1 Corinthians 6:18

Craving the Truth, Part 2

"Peace I leave with you, My peace I give to you ..." (John 14:27).

One day, Nicole made a decision that changed everything. "I looked at my life and affirmed that I had nothing to show for it. I decided then to turn away from my former choices. The next day, I met the man who would become my husband."

Nicole recalls, "I prayed and had a feeling of the love of Jesus washing over me. He loves me, and no sin is so great as to make that not so."

That's when a new search began. "I was simply craving the truth," she says. Studying on her own, Nicole discovered that the Sabbath was actually Saturday and not Sunday. But she found herself increasingly disheartened to discover that most Christian churches observed Sunday as their day of worship. Nicole's constant prayers became centered on asking Jesus to lead her to His true church.

She still remembers the moment when the light dawned and she knew her prayers were answered. "I landed on the Amazing Facts website," she shares. "Here I was praying and asking Jesus to lead me to His true church, and what do you know, I was on the website at that very moment. It all clicked."

Nicole saw a treasure house of discovery open to her. "Listening to Pastor Doug talk about the importance of confession and explain how to do it, I started confessing up a storm. I believe this is what kicked off such a remarkable life-changing experience for me."

Today, living in Australia with her husband, Nicole continues to listen to Amazing Facts and grow in God's healing. "I can hardly begin to put into words what it's meant to have the Word opened up to me like this. Thank you so much for this profound ministry. Praise God! I just needed the truth."

She adds, "It's quite an extraordinary feeling to finally be at peace when you've struggled for most of your life and haven't been able to make things work on your own."

Nicole feels overwhelmed with abundance as she continues to witness God's transforming power in her life. Today, her prayers are filled with thankfulness for the blessings of a wonderful marriage and a home of her own. "I'm more at peace than ever before. I am resolved to live a clean life and to follow Jesus in every way because I want my love for Him to be evident."

Reflect: Do you have God's peace in your life? Surrender all to Jesus and let Him pour out His love into your heart right now. Then God's love will shine out of your life and bring light to people around you who are walking in darkness.

Dig Deeper: Isaiah 26:3; John 16:33; 2 Thessalonians 3:16

Stan Telchin

Betrayed

"Did not our heart burn within us while He talked with us on the road, and while He opened the Scriptures to us?" (Luke 24:32).

Stan Telchin was born to a Jewish family in 1924, and grew up during the Great Depression. He learned early on that material security was very important. This background drove him to achieve great success in the insurance business. By the early 1970s, Telchin, his wife, and their daughters lived in a suburban home, had a housekeeper, and four BMW sedans parked in the driveway. His eldest daughter was a student at Boston University.

One Sunday evening, the phone rang. Stan was planning his next week's insurance business when he was stopped short by Judy's disclosure. His daughter "told me with great caution that she had come to believe that Jesus is the Messiah. I was speechless, outraged and I felt betrayed. How could a child of mine join the enemy?"

This upended the entire family. Stan's wife, Ethel, banged cabinet doors and pots and pans in the kitchen. Judy's sister, Ann, was heartbroken. And Stan? He felt rage and anger build up within him yet managed to maintain his composure. "You're coming home for spring break soon," he told Judy. "Let's talk about this then."

Spring break came and went, and Stan was left with more questions than before. Judy told him, "Daddy, you are an educated man. Read the Bible for yourself and make up your own mind. It is either true or it is false and if you read it carefully and ask God to reveal the truth to you, He will."

Taking time from his business, Telchin dove in: "The very next night, I picked up the New Testament for the very first time. I was prepared for a book of hate aimed at the Jewish people, but I found it to be a book written by a Jew, for other Jews, about the God of Abraham, Isaac and Jacob and the Messiah He sent to His people."

Finally, Stan had to decide: What would he do with this Jew named Jesus, a Messiah for the Jewish people, whose gospel accounts are also very Jewish? At 7:15 in the morning on July 3, 1975, Stan Telchin surrendered his life to Jesus.

After writing his story in *Betrayed!*, he spent the next 37 years in pastoral ministry, evangelism, and writing, with an emphasis on reaching his fellow Jews with the good news.

Reflect: Do you know someone whose affluence, pride, or bias is blinding them to the gospel? Have you prayed for an opportunity to reach them?

Dig Deeper: Psalm 39:3; Isaiah 50:4; Hebrews 4:12

"He who walks with wise men will be wise, but the companion of fools will be destroyed" (Proverbs 13:20).

Ashlee had a big dilemma. "I wanted to serve God, but I also wanted to fit in." As a young adult, she became weary of living a double life and needed to make a change. She grew up in a devoted Christian family who loved God and each other. They went to church every Sunday, and Ashlee was active in youth groups and at Bible camps. She accepted Christ into her heart and desired most of all to never let down God or her parents.

When Ashlee was very young, she didn't recognize that her dad was different. He was just a regular dad who loved her and did everything he could to help her succeed. But when she started school, she found out that he was famous. Her father played for two professional football teams, winning two Super Bowls during his career.

That made her different from the other kids—and not always in a good way. Ashlee found herself the target of jealousy and bullying at school. "I wanted to be liked by my peers, but I wasn't. I'd walk around thinking, 'Who's going to accept me? Who will I sit with at lunch today?' Kids can say some really harsh things, and that gave me great insecurity."

By the time she reached high school, Ashlee faced a huge decision. As a gifted athlete herself, she says, "Everything we did at home was based around sports. It created such a bond between me and my father and older brother. Athleticism was my talent and something I loved. I was really good at a lot of sports, but I knew that if I was actually going to make it and get a scholarship, I needed to pick one and focus. I chose soccer."

Ashlee won a full scholarship to a university and became captain of her soccer team. Now peer pressure returned in another form, this time threatening her relationship with God. "It's really difficult to go to a school that is not based on God at all. I did plug into some Christian groups, but I also wanted to fit in with my team. I was living a double life because I wanted to serve God, but I also wanted to fit in."

Reflect: Have you ever been part of a group that did not have the same values you did? Should you stay in that group as a witness or leave it? Remember, God is calling Christians to change the world, not be changed by the world.

Dig Deeper: Proverbs 1:10; 1 Corinthians 10:13; Galatians 1:10

Hitting the Jackpot, Part 2

"I know your works. See, I have set before you an open door, and no one can shut it; for you have a little strength, have kept My word, and have not denied My name" (Revelation 3:8).

Ashlee felt like she was trying to swim upstream and couldn't breathe. "I was so sick of the struggle, of going back and forth. I wanted to do whatever it took to get right with God, but I was dabbling in the world. I didn't want to be lukewarm anymore. Then I heard Him speak one word to my heart: 'Go.'"

Eventually, Ashlee finished her schooling and headed to another school to further her education. There she met Andrew, who was also on fire for the Lord, and together they prayed about God's direction for their lives. "Our motto in life was that we wanted to live in reckless abandon for our Creator, whatever that looked like."

After they were married, Ashlee and Andrew spent the summer living apart. She was coaching soccer in New Jersey while Andrew was in Alaska. During that time, Ashlee learned that the seventh day was the Sabbath of the Bible, not Sunday.

She thought, "If this is really the way of God, I want to go on Saturday." She found a local Sunday-keeping church that also held Saturday evening services and began attending them.

One day, as she and Andrew talked on the phone, he carefully introduced a new topic. "He said, 'I don't want to cause any problems, but I think we should go to church on Saturday.' And I said, 'Oh, that's no problem. I'm already going to church on Saturday!'" Both Ashlee and Andrew knew then that God was working to show them truth at the same time.

When Andrew picked her up to drive home at the end of the summer, he shared that someone had given him a set of audio messages ten years earlier called *The Prophecy Code* by a ministry called Amazing Facts and a speaker named Doug Batchelor. Andrew hadn't listened to them until recently, but now he wanted Ashlee to hear them too. For the entire drive home, they played *The Prophecy Code*.

And God began to perform a miracle in their minds and hearts.

Reflect: Can you recall a time when God showed you a new truth? What did you learn? Why not share that truth with someone else today!

Dig Deeper: Ezekiel 11:19; Romans 12:2; 2 Corinthians 3:18

Ashlee

Hitting the Jackpot, Part 3

> "I will give you the treasures of darkness and hidden riches of secret places, that you may know that I, the , who call you by your name, am the God of Israel" (Isaiah 45:3).

When Andrew picked up Ashlee to drive home at the end of his summer of fishing in Alaska, he shared *The Prophecy Code* series with his wife. For the entire drive home, they listened to the whole series.

"My heart was changing in that car ride," Ashlee says, "because I was learning more about God. Everything I was hearing was Scripture proving Scripture proving Scripture. God became more real to us than He had ever been before."

As soon as they reached home, they looked up Amazing Facts online and were thrilled to discover all the materials available. "We thought we'd hit the jackpot!" Ashlee laughs. "We're kind of Amazing Facts-obsessed!"

Ashlee and Andrew started devouring every sermon. In addition to learning more about the Sabbath, she was thankful to discover that hell wasn't a place of eternal torment. "Thinking about hell would really upset me before. I didn't want to think about a God who would burn someone forever. It seemed sadistic and unloving."

She also felt relieved to learn that the Bible teaches that when people die they go to sleep. "I'd hear how people believed that the spirit of the dead came back as animals or would send messages, and that was creepy to me. I was super glad to know the truth and realize that it was very clear; there is no message from the dead."

Ashlee was especially thrilled with how the prophecies of Daniel and Revelation took her life-long walk with God even deeper. "The most important thing is Christ and His sacrifice and accepting His grace. But I found that knowing about prophecy just strengthened my faith even more. It gave me evidence that God is real because all of His prophecies came to pass."

Looking back through her life, Ashlee says, "There's no way I can doubt God—ever. I didn't know all this information before, but I knew He was real because He showed up for me and transformed my life. He healed me and gave me everlasting life."

Ashlee says, "Scripture is empowering and comforting now. I have a direct line to God through prayer and His Word. I don't need to be a theologian to read Scripture and know Scripture. All my answers are right there."

Reflect: Do you have a question that has troubled you? Turn prayerfully to the Bible and ask the Lord to reveal His treasures to you.

Dig Deeper: Proverbs 2:4, 5; Matthew 6:19; Luke 12:33

"Finally, brethren, whatever things are true, whatever things are noble, whatever things are just, whatever things are pure, whatever things are lovely, whatever things are of good report, if there is any virtue and if there is anything praiseworthy—meditate on these things" (Philippians 4:8).

According to a 2005 article by the National Science Foundation, a person has between 12,000 and 60,000 thoughts a day, and of those thoughts, 80 percent are negative. What happens when those negative thoughts are combined with one's faith?

In John 11, Jesus and His 12 disciples had since departed from Judea due to the hostility of their own people, the Jews. But now, Jesus expressed the need to go back to His friend Lazarus.

"Rabbi," asked the disciples incredulously, "lately the Jews sought to stone You, and are You going there again?" (v. 8).

But Jesus was determined to return. One of the 12, Thomas, resigned to his fate, responded mournfully, "Let us also go, that we may die with Him" (v. 16).

There was no hope in that reply. To Thomas, following Jesus to Judea meant certain death. How blind Thomas was to think that walking with Jesus brought only destruction and defeat. He did not know that he was with the Creator Himself, the One who gave life to him and to all. Even when Jesus resurrected Lazarus from the dead, Thomas did not understand.

When His Master was crucified, Thomas was crushed. And when His Master was Himself resurrected and began to show Himself to His followers, Thomas was skeptical.

"We have seen the Lord" (John 20:25), the other disciples told him.

You would think that this would have been the most wonderful news for Thomas, words he had been most longing to hear. But Thomas did not leap for joy or sing praises or cry happy tears. In his heart he was sorely wounded. They had seen the Master, but he had been left out. What made them more special than he?

"Unless I see in His hands the print of the nails, and put my finger into the print of the nails, and put my hand into His side, I will not believe," he stated obstinately.

It was, in reality, an ultimatum. "You do what I say on my terms! You play by my rules—or else!" That was what Thomas was really saying.

But people ought to be careful about giving ultimatums to God ...

Reflect: Have negative thoughts blinded you from seeing who God truly is and what He is currently doing in your life? Pray for eyes to see and ears to hear the Spirit's call.

Dig Deeper: Psalm 37:7, 8; 94:16–19; Romans 8:5–11

Thomas

Glass Half-Empty, Part 2

"Now faith is the substance of things hoped for, the evidence of things not seen" (Hebrews 11:1).

The days following Christ's death were precarious times for the now 11 disciples. The Jewish leaders had succeeded in murdering their Master; certainly they would be next, His most devoted associates. So they hid themselves and met in secret. It was during one of these times that they had first seen Jesus, without Thomas.

About a week later, they gathered together again. This time, Thomas decided to join them. It was in this sequestered hideout that Jesus appeared to them once more for the express purpose of answering Thomas' ultimatum.

Quite suddenly did their Master appear. As He had done before, He did not use the door or any secret passageway. He simply "stood in the midst" (John 20:26) of them.

"Peace to you!" He declared, as He had the previous time. Jesus' purpose was to bring peace, to clear away the doubts and anxieties.

Thomas was stunned. The door had remained shut; no one else knew they were there. Then did Jesus address him directly, "Reach your finger here, and look at My hands; and reach your hand here, and put it into My side. Do not be unbelieving, but believing" (v. 27).

Jesus knew the explicit details of Thomas' terms and met them one by one. But now that his demand had actually been granted, Thomas saw how his own negativity had made him foolhardy, proud, and insolent.

"My Lord and my God!" (v. 28) was all he cried.

Thomas no longer needed to touch the scars; he believed fully and immediately that Jesus Christ was "flesh and bones" (Luke 24:39), that He truly had risen from the dead, that He was the living God, for "[i]n Him was life" (John 1:4).

Jesus gently rebuked him to a greater faith: "Blessed are those who have not seen and yet have believed" (20:29). The majority of believers nowadays have not had the privilege, as had Thomas, of an eyewitness account of the Messiah. Had all others required one in order to believe, there would be vastly fewer Christians in the world.

The fact that Jesus reached down to draw Thomas out of his doubt, as He has time and again for us all, humbled the disciple and in an instant turned his stubborn heart into a willing one, eager to follow Christ to the end of his days.

Reflect: Are you asking for unnecessary signs from the Lord? In what other ways can your faith grow?

Dig Deeper: Deuteronomy 7:17–19; Isaiah 41:10; James 1:5–8

"Come to Me, all you who labor and are heavy laden, and I will give you rest" (Matthew 11:28).

When Cyril was 10 years old, his mother became a Christian. "My mom ensured we went to church every Sunday and I grew up thinking I knew the truth and felt quite assured," he says. "I attended one of the modern Pentecostal churches in Nigeria." His church was patterned after one of the popular mega-churches in the United States.

Although he was an active part of this church family, Cyril eventually began to feel a deep emptiness. Hungering for answers, Cyril regularly attended prayer meetings and other church programs. But he somehow still felt there was something significant, even essential, missing from his experience. "I wasn't [just] a Sunday to Sunday Christian," he says. "I attended midweek meetings, and all the conferences, etc. Sadly, it all felt so shallow and peripheral after a while. It was clear to me that the truth entailed much more than what I got." The problem was that Cyril had no clue how to nail down that truth.

While Cyril was struggling with this spiritual emptiness and dissatisfaction, a manager in his office gave him an invitation to a particular meeting. "She sold it in a very interesting way—that the meeting would appeal to me as it would be an intellectually stimulating experience. She concealed the fact it was a church meeting."

Up until then, Cyril had made a point not to regularly attend other churches because there were so many choices and he felt they were all basically the same and could offer him nothing more. The one exception was the Roman Catholic Church because it appealed to his sense of sanctity and reverence. So it was only out of very high regard for the manager that he decided to attend the meeting.

"My secret resolve," he says, "was to attend once and be freed from the commitment." But the Lord had other plans!

The meeting Cyril attended was a Daniel and Revelation seminar on videotape, and the speaker was Pastor Doug Batchelor. Here, for the first time, Cyril was exposed to the undiluted gospel of Jesus Christ. At the beginning of the series, the message Cyril heard was very unsettling, as he had never studied the book of Daniel and initially found this new light extremely challenging.

"After the first day, I was genuinely upset," he recalls.

Reflect: Can you think of a time in your life when you were genuinely upset when confronted with the truth? It's often a giant opportunity to grow in Christ!

Dig Deeper: Job 15:31, 32; Proverbs 14:12; John 14:6

Cyril

A Cure for Emptiness, Part 2

"Whoever drinks of the water that I shall give him will never thirst. But the water that I shall give him will become in him a fountain of water springing up into everlasting life" (John 4:14).

When Cyril first attended a church video seminar on the book of Daniel by Pastor Doug Batchelor, he admits, "I was genuinely upset. I grew up as a Christian and had attended church and Sunday school frequently, but the book of Daniel and the insights from the message were completely foreign to me." However, it was clear from that first meeting that he had found the cure to his emptiness. Cyril did not need an invitation for the rest of the series but sat eagerly in the front row each time, absorbing truth after truth.

Pastor Doug's messages helped Cyril understand key doctrinal issues. He was especially grateful for the clear insights he received on the subject of speaking in tongues—something he had previously misunderstood.

"At some point during the meetings," Cyril shares, "I remembered I hadn't been properly baptized, so I approached a friendly brother in the church and asked questions." Cyril was baptized on a Sabbath at the end of the series.

Cyril believes his life has been impacted tremendously by the work of Amazing Facts. He says, "The multitude of messages and interviews I listened to were very important to my stability in the church. I have learned to trust God from day to day. Very important to me is the need to be able to ensure that I can help intellectuals appreciate the veracity of the Bible."

His favorite program on the Amazing Facts website is the Sabbath School Study Hour. "I love Bible study," he remarks, "and it is always a blessing to get fresh perspective that is much deeper and broader than mine."

Today, Cyril feels blessed to be part of a Sabbath-keeping congregation. "I have found people here who have helped my faith a lot," he says. He is currently active in his church and is happy to be part of an army of young professionals engaged in mission work to reach some inaccessible regions of Nigeria. He also serves as an ordained elder.

Reflect: God wants you to be an inspiration in the body of Christ. What can you do to be a blessing to someone at church this week?

Dig Deeper: Acts 20:35; Galatians 5:13; 1 Peter 4:10

Lee Strobel

The Case for Christ

"And if Christ is not risen, your faith is futile; you are still in your sins!" (1 Corinthians 15:17).

There are those who have accused Lee Strobel of fabricating certain facts in his best-selling book *The Case for Christ*. Especially under fire is his purported method of objective investigative journalism. These arguments cannot be ignored and certainly cripple not only the case but the cause for Christ. But underneath all the controversy, there is one undeniable truth: Lee Strobel was an atheist who had a change of heart.

From a young age Strobel, it seemed, was a natural newspaperman. At 13, he single-handedly produced a four-page paper for neighborhood delivery. He worked first as a journalist and then as an assistant managing editor. He got married and eventually had two children with his wife, Leslie.

He was also a cynical atheist and violent alcoholic. During one argument with Leslie, he managed to kick a hole through the living room wall. As a child, his daughter routinely avoided him. When he would come home—usually drunk—she would head for the safety of her bedroom.

When Strobel moved his family to a new home, Leslie became best friends with their new neighbor, Linda. Linda was a Christian. The more time Leslie spent with Linda, the more she would hear about Jesus. Then Linda began asking Leslie to attend church with her, and finally Leslie went—and went and went. One day, she came home and told Strobel that she was a Christian.

Strobel was furious. His first thought was of divorce. He then became determined to prove to Leslie that Christianity was nothing but a cult. The next weekend, he joined her at church and then proceeded to spend almost the next two years trying to disprove the existence of Jesus Christ. At the end of that time, on November 8, 1981, after Strobel weighed all of his research and evidence, he had to admit that he believed Jesus Christ was not only a real person but also the Son of God.

He traded his career in journalism for one as a Christian teaching pastor, author, and speaker. Most of all, he became a different kind of husband and father. He stopped drinking, worked on his anger, and spent more time with his family. Witnessing this transformation, his five-year-old daughter announced that she also wanted God to do in her life what He had done in her father's life.

Ultimately, one fact is certain: God transforms people's hearts.

Reflect: How has God affected your relationships with your family members? If you are unsure, you might ask them.

Dig Deeper: Psalm 127:3–5; Mark 10:6–9; Ephesians 6:4

Vickie

Finding God Again

"Train up a child in the way he should go, and when he is old he will not depart from it" (Proverbs 22:6).

Vickie's mother raised her in a Sabbath-keeping church, read her Bible bedtime stories, and showed her how to pray. Her mother even taught her about Bible prophecies.

But over time, books and movies of mixed morality crept into Vickie's life. And worse, she was unaware of the danger. Influenced by entertainment, secular education's evolution agenda, and excessive schoolwork, she stopped attending church. Though Vickie maintained an intellectual belief in God, her faith dwindled.

God kept calling to Vickie's heart. In her search for peace she began attending a Sunday-keeping church. But this did not satisfy the deepest questions in her mind. Doubts continued to plague her.

When Vickie had reached the depth of her despair, a member from her old Sabbath-keeping congregation asked if she would help out with their church services. "She had always been a really kind lady," Vickie recalls. "I did not have the heart to say no."

After a few weeks of assisting at church, Vickie found herself one Sabbath in the middle of an enthusiastic discussion among some members. The pastor, who was part of the discussion, shared how God did not promise a life on this earth without hardships, but did promise to give strength to His followers. His statement filled Vickie with hope. "It made me want to find God again."

Vickie had earlier stumbled across an online ad for Amazing Facts. Saving the link for future reference, she continued searching for truth elsewhere. "Satan began to strike harder," Vickie recalls. Despite her open-minded, earnest seeking, Vickie faced discrimination for her new beliefs at her Sunday-keeping church. "I hadn't given God complete control," Vickie remembers, "but once I did, I felt relief."

She asked God to help her obey the truth, no matter where it led. Then something miraculous happened. "After I prayed," Vickie shares, "I recalled the Amazing Facts website I had been saving." She immediately got online and watched every video she could find that was relevant to her questions. It was a turning point in her Christian journey.

The result of her online learning through the Amazing Facts website was mind-boggling. Though Vickie experienced setbacks, her persistent search for truth was rewarded and she gave her heart completely to the Lord and was baptized into God's remnant church.

Reflect: Do you know of someone who was raised in the church, and then left, and came back? God cares for all of His sheep!

Dig Deeper: Psalm 13:5; Romans 5:8; 1 John 4:16

Judah

The Engineer, Part 1

"'Woe to the rebellious children,' says the , 'who take counsel, but not of Me, and who devise plans, but not of My Spirit, that they may add sin to sin'" (Isaiah 30:1).

Christian detractor Niccolò Machiavelli, whose most famous treatise *The Prince* details how to acquire and retain political power at any cost, became the father of a philosophy that both fascinated and terrified throughout the ages.

If the term had been defined in his lifetime, Judah, the fourth-eldest son of the Hebrew patriarch Jacob by his first wife Leah, would have been decidedly Machiavellian. While his eldest brother, Reuben, was a flaccid, vacillating man, and his next two eldest, Simeon and Levi, were prone to brute violence, Judah decimated by ruthless schemes, calculated necessity, and sheer opportunism.

Judah married a Canaanite, a rebellious act typically forbidden among his people (Genesis 28:1), and by her had three sons. When his firstborn son, Er, died prematurely, he passed Er's widow, Tamar, onto his next eldest son, Onan, as was customary at that time (38:7, 8). When Onan died soon after, Judah returned Tamar to her family under the false pretense that she would be given to his third and last son, Shelah, once he came of age to marry (v. 11). But it was all a lie. His actual plan was to constrain his daughter-in-law to be a childless widow for the rest of her life, not wanting Shelah to meet the same untimely end as his brothers. Judah did not care about Tamar's fate, particularly harsh in those days.

After the death of his own wife, Judah one day traveled to a nearby town for work and, while there, slept with a prostitute whose face he never saw—leaving as a deposit for his payment the equivalent of today's identification documents, his signet, cord, and staff (v. 18). When he attempted to send her payment, however, the prostitute was nowhere to be found (vv. 20–22).

He then received news that Tamar had become pregnant "by harlotry" (v. 24). Snatching the opportunity to be rid of his previous obligation to his daughter-in-law, he pronounced a death sentence upon her, only to discover—by receipt of his signet, cord, and staff—that she was the very prostitute with whom he had slept (vv. 25, 26). Tamar had had a scheme of her own, and he had been squarely beaten at his own game.

But Judah was not done yet.

Reflect: Have you devised cleverly laid plans for your own life? What say does God have in those plans? Make it a habit to lay all your plans at the feet of Jesus so He can direct you.

Dig Deeper: Proverbs 19:21; Ezekiel 8:12; Hebrews 4:13

Judah

The Engineer, Part 2

"But he who hates his brother is in darkness and walks in darkness, and does not know where he is going, because the darkness has blinded his eyes" (1 John 2:11).

On May 23, 1862, in the Battle of Front Royal during the American Civil War, Captain William Goldsborough captured and imprisoned Charles Goldsborough. They were brothers. The battle marked the only time in U.S. history that regiments from the same state, Maryland, fought against each other.

Judah had a half-brother named Joseph from his father's second wife, Rachel. Judah, along with his nine other brothers, hated Joseph. Joseph was pampered by their father, Joseph was a tattletale, Joseph was a goody two-shoes. When Joseph innocently relayed his strange dreams, which seemed to foretell his rise to power over his own family, the brothers taunted him enviously, "Shall you indeed reign over us? Or shall you indeed have dominion over us?" (Genesis 37:8).

So when Joseph, on instruction from their father, visited his older brothers, the siblings "conspired against him to kill him" (v. 18). Though Reuben succeeded in delaying their scheme, once he had left, Judah came up with what he thought was a marvelous idea.

"What profit is there if we kill our brother and conceal his blood? Come and let us sell him to the Ishmaelites, and let not our hand be upon him, for he is our brother and our flesh" (vv. 26, 27).

Whether Judah's conscience had smitten him is debatable; what is not is his callous knack for capitalizing upon human suffering, and that of his own family member no less. Thus, Joseph was sold, and their father fed a lie about wild animals and Joseph's bloody coat (vv. 31–33).

Over two decades passed, and the brothers' homeland in Canaan was now ravaged with famine. They had no more crops, no more food. They would starve to death slowly but surely. No clever scheming could get them out of this disaster. There was but one hope—Egypt, the one place that still had a supply of grain. On their father's command, the 10 brothers started the long and arduous journey to the foreign land, leaving behind their youngest brother, Benjamin, whom Rachel had died giving birth to and whom their father, now that Joseph was gone, treasured all the more.

What awaited them in Egypt would be the surprise of their lives.

Reflect: Do you dislike someone you know you should love? Should our feelings dictate our treatment of people with whom we do not get along?

Dig Deeper: Leviticus 19:17, 18; Proverbs 10:16, 18; 1 John 3:14, 15

Judah

The Engineer, Part 3

**"We are all one man's sons; we are honest men;
your servants are not spies" (Genesis 42:11).**

Since he and his brothers had sold Joseph into slavery, the years had not been kind to Judah. Guilt weighed heavily upon his conscience. He could see what their deed had done to their father; it had broken him. Instead of ridding themselves of Joseph, the brothers had actually cemented him forever in their memories and in their father's heart.

It was a very different group of men who now arrived in Egypt to buy grain from the governor, a man of renowned intelligence and savvy. But from the start, things seemed to go wrong—very wrong.

"You are spies!" (Genesis 42:9) accused the governor before interrogating the brothers further.

When they answered honestly about their father and youngest brother, Benjamin—even mentioning Joseph—the governor only locked them in jail (vv. 13, 17). Then, after three days, he ordered that they prove their story by fetching their so-called younger brother while he held one of them, Simeon, hostage (vv. 18–20, 24).

The brothers turned to one another; in all of their minds was the same thought: They were finally getting what they deserved. Then said they, "We are truly guilty concerning our brother, for we saw the anguish of his soul when he pleaded with us, and we would not hear; therefore this distress has come upon us" (v. 21). Joseph—his young, innocent, tear-stained face was ever before them, and they the cold-blooded mercenaries. There was no defense, no avoidance; all of them plainly admitted their part in the crime.

But then the governor did a strange thing. He gave the brothers the grain they had purchased—but did not take their money. It was after they had already left Egypt when they realized: Every man had had his money returned to him in his sack of grain (vv. 27, 28, 35). It was a terrible moment for them, for what if the governor thought they had stolen from him—when they were trying to be honest? But Joseph had been honest with them too, and they had repaid him brutally.

And oh how they dreaded telling their father the governor's demand. The patriarch would never let Benjamin return to Egypt with them—especially after what had happened to Joseph.

As expected, Jacob refused (v. 38). What were they to do now?

Reflect: Have you borne a secret guilt too long? Confess your heavy burden to Jesus first; let His healing lead you (Acts 3:19).

Dig Deeper: Psalm 32:1–5; Jeremiah 3:12, 13; Hosea 5:14, 15

The Engineer, Part 4

**"I myself will be surety for him; from my hand
you shall require him" (Genesis 43:9).**

Over a millennium later, Judah became an ancestor of the Messiah, Jesus Christ. It seems fitting, therefore, that Judah represents a type of Christ.

After Jacob's refusal to part with Benjamin, the famine continued to rage. Eventually, the grain ran out (Genesis 43:2). They had to return to Egypt or else starve. Judah reminded his father of the governor's request: This time, they must bring Benjamin (vv. 3–5).

But Jacob only lamented all the more.

Undeterred, Judah made the most important decision of his life: He decided to take full responsibility for Benjamin's safety (v. 9). He was not willing that they all—his children, his brothers' children, his father—should die that slow and painful death as well as leave Simeon to rot in an Egyptian dungeon.

Jacob, faced with Judah's plain common sense, finally gave his consent.

So the brothers set out again for Egypt and its mysterious governor, careful to bring enough money for their previous sacks of grain as well as the new grain they were to buy. How far had they come from the greed and deceit of their youth. Upon their arrival, they solicitously inquired after their returned money and, being assured it was no mistake, were, along with a liberated Simeon, treated to a magnificent feast with the governor himself.

Again, their sacks were filled with grain and, felicitous, they began their journey home. But before long came the governor's steward after them, accusing them of stealing the governor's precious silver cup. Though the brothers protested their innocence, the cup was discovered in none other than Benjamin's sack of grain. Benjamin's punishment was to remain in Egypt—a slave for the rest of his life.

When confronted by the irate governor, it was Judah who answered. He did not make excuses. Even though in truth all the brothers were innocent, he took the blame upon them all (44:16). Humbly did he petition the governor for Benjamin's freedom, eloquently expressing his father's love for his youngest son and his own love for his aging father. Lastly, he willingly offered himself in place of Benjamin (vv. 33, 34), as Jesus offered Himself as our Passover Lamb.

This loving act of sacrifice was all the proof the governor needed. By this he knew that his brothers had truly changed, for the governor was none other than their lost brother Joseph.

Reflect: Have you ever given sacrificially for someone else? What did that act do for your faith?

Dig Deeper: Leviticus 17:11; 1 Samuel 15:22; John 15:12, 13

Lucy

Peace at Last

"These things I have spoken to you, that in Me you may have peace" (John 16:33).

Lucy is no stranger to grief and loss. At the age of 14, she lost her older sister and her sister's three children in a house fire. Later she suffered the death of her mother. Shortly after this her daughter-in-law died suddenly, leaving Lucy's son alone with two children. "My world was being torn apart," Lucy says. "My head was in a constant spin."

Lucy was inconsolable and wanted to see no one. When she decided to reach out to the pastor of her church, she learned that he, too, had passed away two months earlier. It seemed that everywhere Lucy turned, there was more loss. "I had no relief from my pain and I felt I had no one to turn to," she recalls.

Thinking about death and wanting to die, Lucy did an Internet search asking the question, "What happens when we die?" The search took her to an Amazing Facts website where she found the answer to her question. "Pastor Doug's explanation was so soothing and comforting to my troubled and damaged soul," she says. "I was able to live again!"

Even though Lucy's mother was Catholic and her father was Jewish, neither of her parents taught religion in the home. When Lucy found the Amazing Facts website, she found words of comfort which helped her cope with all her losses. "I'm the youngest of eight children," she explains. "We were never raised with the truth, so everyone went their own way. But when I found God's truth, I wanted to share it with my family."

Unfortunately, Lucy's desire to share her joy was met with laughter and scoffing. She recalls the sadness of trying to share the truth about death with her brother. Her sister-in-law squelched her brother's interest by convincing him to believe in reincarnation and ghosts. "When they left my home, I had tears running down my cheeks. Amazing Facts has been the glue that keeps me in the fold of God."

From despair to peace, the Bible truth about death brought comfort to Lucy's heart. As she continues to grow, she shares, "My goal is to live my life in the character of Jesus and teach what I have learned to anyone who is willing to receive it."

Reflect: Have you ever suffered a deep loss and felt overwhelmed by grief? Jesus will put His comforting arms around you. Ask Him to come close and He will.

Dig Deeper: Psalm 56:8; Matthew 5:4; Revelation 21:4

Blaise Pascal

Boy Genius Twice Converted

> "Each one's work will become clear; for the Day will declare it, because it will be revealed by fire; and the fire will test each one's work, of what sort it is" (1 Corinthians 3:13).

Blaise Pascal never saw his 40th birthday, but his relatively brief life left an indelible mark on the world. Born in 1623, in France, his mother died when Pascal was three years old. The remaining family—his father and two sisters and the boy—moved to Paris. By the age of 19, he'd invented a mechanical calculator and sold 50 of them to affluent families.

He made other discoveries in mathematics and science related to fluids and pressure. In 1646, his father's serious injury caused Blaise to contemplate and embrace religion, only to backslide five years later when his father died.

On November 23, 1654, as Pascal was preparing for bed, he had a spiritual experience that lasted nearly two hours. He wrote a brief testimony of this "Night of Fire" and had it sewn into his jacket lining, where it was found only after Blaise Pascal died.

From that night, Blaise Pascal dropped his work in mathematics and instead concentrated on theological writings. He became famous for a book known as "Lettres Provincials," or "Provincial Letters," written under a pen name, which defended Jansenist theology from attacks by the Jesuits. Readers relished not only Pascal's arguments, but also his use of humor and satire to make his points.

In his mid-30s, Pascal began writing "Defense of the Christian Religion," an apologetic treatise. In August of 1662, Blaise Pascal fell ill with convulsions and died without completing the book. "May God never abandon me," were reported to be Pascal's last words.

Friends collected Pascal's notes and drafts for his apologetic book and published them as "Thoughts of M. Pascal." Under the French word for thoughts, "*Pensées*," those words have endured for more than 350 years as a compelling defense of the Christian faith. It remains in print today, read and studied around the world.

His theological writing is not his only living memorial: A computer programming language, Pascal, would be named in his honor centuries later.

Reflect: One night of intense spiritual experience changed Blaise Pascal into a devoted disciple. Can you recall a similar experience? And if not, have you prayed for one?

Dig Deeper: Isaiah 28:17; Jeremiah 23:29; 2 Peter 3:10

Gene

Brought Back to Life, Part 1

"Yea, though I walk through the valley of the shadow of death, I will fear no evil; for You are with me" (Psalm 23:4).

Gene came to a turning point in his life and realized that the way he was living needed to change. As he drove home from work one day, he asked Jesus to come into his life and take over. Slowly, the Lord began to work. Gene and his wife began to occasionally attend a Sunday church again, usually on special occasions like Easter or when there was a guest speaker.

Soon after, while watching TV, a new program caught Gene's eye. It was called Amazing Facts. "I was immediately attracted to the title of the program because I like facts. I base my life and my work as a rancher on solid evidence. When Pastor Doug Batchelor spoke of a free offer on the program I ordered it. The resource I received spoke of the Standard Oil Company president reading Exodus 2:3 and the pitch used on the basket in which Moses was laid as a baby. Since I had been working in and around the oil industry for over 10 years, the article grabbed my attention."

For several months Gene continued receiving materials from Amazing Facts, but eventually this stopped coming. "I saw Pastor Doug preach a few more times on the television, but then I couldn't find his program anymore, even though I tried again on several occasions."

Several years later, Gene went through a life-changing experience while undergoing surgery for cancer on his right kidney. The operation was only supposed to take a couple of hours, followed by two days in the hospital and a couple weeks to recover at home. But during the procedure, things went downhill fast.

During the operation, Gene began bleeding and the surgeon had a difficult time stopping it. At one point, after the surgeon had done his best, Gene was sent into recovery. Then the doctor met with his wife, June, and two daughters, and said, "Gene is bleeding and I don't know why. His blood pressure is dangerously low and I can't do anything about it."

Immediately, Gene's family began to pray. Then the doctor, with the help of other physicians, took Gene back into surgery. His two-hour surgery ended up lasting 14 hours, but God brought him through.

Reflect: Have you ever faced the possibility of imminent death? Where did your thoughts turn? God is just a prayer away. Turn to the Lord for He will hear your every cry for help.

Dig Deeper: Psalm 86:1–7; Jonah 2:1; John 11:25

Gene

Brought Back to Life, Part 2

"I am the resurrection and the life. He who believes in Me, though he may die, he shall live" (John 11:25).

Six months after almost dying on the operating table, Gene was back in surgery. While recovering he found it difficult to sleep. Early one Sunday morning, he came across Amazing Facts. Fifteen years had passed since he had last watched Pastor Batchelor preach. "I was so excited! My wife was still sleeping so I didn't awaken her, but the following Sunday I did wake her up so we could watch it together." As they listened, they knew God was telling them this was Bible truth.

About a month later, Gene woke up at 4 a.m. and prayed, "Lord, what do you want me to do today? Where do you want me to go?" Later he woke up June and told her that God impressed him that they should visit a Sabbath-keeping church about 40 miles from their home. When they arrived, he told his wife he would go in and check it out. She was cautious and skeptical and waited in the car.

Gene was warmly greeted at the door and told the man who shook his hand that he wanted to know about his church. "I asked what they believed about Jesus. He kindly answered my questions. Then he said they were having Sabbath school and invited my wife and me to join them." So Gene got his wife and they attended the class.

Just a few days after this, he spoke with a friend who told Gene about the children's program at his church. Gene had never asked him which church he attends, but on this day he did. He was surprised to discover it was a Sabbath-keeping church. "I knew God was confirming my prompting to attend church that previous Sabbath."

A couple of days after this took place, one of Gene's employees came by the office with her husband. They started talking about spiritual things and she said, "Why don't you and your wife come and visit our church." Once more, he discovered it was also a Sabbath-keeping church! Twice, God affirmed Gene's choice to visit that church.

Gene and his wife soon began taking Bible studies and were eventually baptized. They still enjoy watching Amazing Facts online. Gene believes God saved his life on an operating table so that someday he could discover the way to eternal life.

Reflect: Have you ever asked God to give you a confirmation to a choice you needed to make? The Lord is gracious in hearing our prayers and answering them according to His perfect will.

Dig Deeper: Mark 11:24; John 15:7; Ephesians 6:18

James, Brother of Jesus

The Resurrection Changed Everything

"'Is this not the carpenter, the Son of Mary, and brother of James, Joses, Judas, and Simon? And are not His sisters here with us?' So they were offended at Him" (Mark 6:3).

Blended families are not a new thing, not at all. You can find one of the most prominent in the Gospels: It appears Joseph, Jesus' earthly father, had another family with a spouse who died. When Joseph and Mary were married, those brothers and sisters were part of the package.

Yet while the siblings may have gotten along well enough, when Jesus' ministry began, fissures developed. First the break came with the neighborhood: they knew the family and couldn't believe Jesus was somehow "special" or apart from the others.

Then, those brothers wanted Jesus to announce His ministry at an inopportune time, the Feast of Tabernacles. "Now the Jews' Feast of Tabernacles was at hand. His brothers therefore said to Him, 'Depart from here and go into Judea, that Your disciples also may see the works that You are doing. For no one does anything in secret while he himself seeks to be known openly. If You do these things, show Yourself to the world,'" we read in John 7:2–4. But Jesus replied, "You go up to this feast. I am not yet going up to this feast, for My time has not yet fully come" (v. 8).

James was one of those brothers who (v. 5) "did not believe in Him." Jesus instructed John, a disciple but not a relative, to care for Mary, in words directed from the cross. James is nowhere to be found. Yet James also wrote a New Testament epistle and was a leader of the Jerusalem church.

What happened? The Bible offers no details, but it's believed that when James saw the resurrected Jesus, he believed. And, he put action behind that belief, sharing the good news and serving the church.

Nothing—not growing up with Jesus, not seeing glimpses of His divinity, not following with the disciples—nothing convinced James until he saw Jesus resurrected. The bad news was that it took James that long. The good news, actually, the great news, is that we each can encounter the resurrected Christ and believe!

Reflect: Do you know someone who encountered the resurrected Christ, through preaching or through Scripture? Can you see the change in their life?

Dig Deeper: Isaiah 53:2, 3; Luke 7:23; John 14:22

Teri

Mrs. Nobody, Part 1

"Do not fear therefore; you are of more value than many sparrows" (Matthew 10:31).

"I make people sick to their stomachs," Teri thought.

Her two sisters looked a lot like their mom, but not Teri. She looked like her dad. But her parents were separated now, and her mother had remarried. So living in her mother's home, she felt out of place. Teri's two sisters could play the piano, and they were both really smart and did well in school too. But not Teri.

She had never thought much of herself. She left home at a young age to get married. She was away from her family, but she was still, in her own words, "a sad sort of person living a small life." She and her husband didn't have much. Sometimes it seemed like they were just living to survive, not living to live. They had two children, but their children grew up and left home; then it was just her and her husband. She took to drinking, and she drank a lot.

And life passed on in this way, in this thin strip of survival—drink, sleep, work—until one day God miraculously intervened.

When Teri and her husband discovered that they could afford the Internet for the first time, they promptly signed up. It opened up whole new vistas for them.

Searching online, Teri and her husband learned about the seventh-day Sabbath of the Bible. They believed in what they heard, especially Teri's husband, and so they began to keep the Sabbath in the small ways they knew how. As more time passed and life continued on for them, the truth about God's special day continued to hold fast—like a lone stream trickling in a dry desert.

As Teri's husband continued searching online, he came across the Amazing Facts website. What he discovered and shared with Teri dramatically changed their lives. Not only did the site have a ton of information about the Sabbath, it had so much more—Bible studies, devotionals, and an online store full of books and DVDs!

Reflect: Have you ever felt like a nobody? What does Jesus really think about you? If you are unsure, study the Bible verses below and you will discover just how much you are loved.

Dig Deeper: Genesis 1:27; Psalm 139; John 3:16

"I have loved you with an everlasting love" (Jeremiah 31:3).

Teri and her husband were amazed to find so much information about the Bible in one place! The resources they discovered at amazingfacts.org were heaven sent.

Teri began studying the *Storacles* online and fell in love with them. Whenever she had a question, she wrote directly to Amazing Facts and, to her delight, an Amazing Facts correspondent answered her questions quickly and clearly. And these weren't automated responses either—they were responses from real, live people who cared about her, who wanted her to learn and to understand the God of the Bible for herself. "I liked learning the reasons behind the way I believe," she adds.

As Teri came to understand Bible truths more fully—especially the Sabbath—her own life brightened and her world enlarged. The dry feeling in her heart, that she was a nobody, began to change as messages from heaven helped her to bloom. After completing all of the *Storacles*, she was delighted and astonished to receive two free Amazing Facts books! "Not bad," she thought for someone who dubbed herself "the stupid one in the family."

Teri has since quit drinking. Instead of pouring herself a drink every morning, she spends a quiet hour with God and an Amazing Facts devotional. She and her husband have started attending a Sabbath-keeping church. Instead of her husband spending free time watching movies, they now spend time together watching Amazing Facts on Roku. Teri also adamantly shares the Amazing Facts website with her loved ones—spreading the gospel in what ways she can.

Little by little, with God's power, Teri and her husband have been making changes in their lives. A tiny stream of truth that started with the discovery of the true Sabbath, has become a gushing river, overflowing with the love of God. "God is so good!" writes Teri. "I am like a fountain inside when I think about how great He is." As Jesus said to the woman at the well, "The water that I shall give him will become in him a fountain of water springing up into everlasting life" (John 4:14).

Though Teri once felt like a Mrs. Nobody, she now knows that she is a precious somebody in Jesus.

Reflect: Are you experiencing God's love flowing inside of you like water springing up into everlasting life? If not, Jesus invites you to ask, for He will freely give.

Dig Deeper: Isaiah 41:10; Romans 8:35–39; 1 John 4:19

Paora Te Uita

The Gospel of Peace

**"Now the fruit of righteousness is sown in peace
by those who make peace" (James 3:18).**

Early Christian theologian Tertullian once wrote, "The blood of the martyrs is the seed of the Church." The statement was true in his day, and it remains true today.

In 1835, in the midst of a series of wars among an indigenous Polynesian people group called the Māori, a Christian mission was established in the North Island of New Zealand. Attending the mission's school was a girl named Tārore, the daughter of a Māori tribal chief, Ngākuku. One day, the missionaries gave Tārore a copy of the Gospel of Luke translated into her own language. The small book was treasured by Tārore and kept in a basket around her neck.

But as the violent battles increased, Tārore and the other students were evacuated to Wairere Falls, the tallest waterfall in New Zealand, where they made camp for the night. That night, warriors from another tribe attacked the camp. In the ensuing chaos, 12-year-old Tārore was killed and her precious book stolen.

Ngākuku's tribe was furious; revenge was the only option. But Ngākuku did not agree. He had learned about the God of the Bible and believed that vengeance belonged to God alone (Deuteronomy 32:35). And so, in an unprecedented act of mercy, nothing was done. There was, for once, peace.

Meanwhile, Paora Te Uita returned to his village. His band of warriors had recently raided a camp near Wairere Falls; in his hand was Tārore's Gospel of Luke. But of what use was it? None of them could read anyway.

Then one day, a visitor arrived in Uita's village who could read. So the visitor was given the stolen volume and from it read the beautiful words of inspiration. And Uita began to change. He realized that what he had done—the murders, the thefts, his very way of life—was wrong. He sorrowed deep in his heart; he knew what he must do next. He made his way to the village of his enemy and asked for Ngākuku's forgiveness. And Ngākuku granted that forgiveness. There was even a church built in honor of the deed.

But that was not all for Tārore's little book. Her spilt blood carried it all the way to the South Island, where it eventually helped to spread the gospel of peace to the whole of New Zealand.

Reflect: Have you been zealous that someone gets his or her just reward? Does your opinion change when you remember Christ's death for you?

Dig Deeper: Matthew 5:38, 39; Acts 9:1–6; Revelation 6:9–11

"For the living know that they will die; but the dead know nothing" (Ecclesiastes 9:5).

Clare scrolled through the videos on YouTube—boring, boring, boring.

Her life was not terrible. In fact, it was pretty good in a lot of ways. She lived with her boyfriend in a nice house in China; she had an easy job at the supermarket and was almost finished with pharmacy school. She was doing well in her classes, doing well financially, and doing well in her relationship. All her check boxes were marked, all her ducks in a row. She had no complaints. What more could she really ask for in life?

But the truth was that all her life, Clare had hoped that there would be more, more to this existence than just being "fine," than just being "okay."

She looked wearily at the screen. What was she even looking for?

Something caught her eye. She clicked on the video and watched the entire thing. It was about the reasons behind a celebrity's death. After it ended, Clare sat back, stunned. Something clicked in her mind. Rapidly, she began searching the Internet. Hours turned into days, which turned into months. Six months later, she came to a conclusion—one that would change her life forever: There was a God.

Clare had been raised Buddhist since she was 12 years old. And what was more, she was studying to become a pharmacist—a scientist. How could she believe in a god? But she did.

One night, she found herself on YouTube again. This time, the video that caught her attention was an interview with a man named Roger Morneau. He was telling the story of how he became a Christian, and he talked a lot about how the devil tried to stop him from knowing the true God of the Bible. Clare was floored. In the video Roger Morneau had listed reincarnation, the theory of evolution, and Sunday worship as the three major deceptions of the devil.

Clare explains, "As a Buddhist, I believed in reincarnation. As a science student, I believed in evolution. These things are actually not true. So, it was a big 'Aha!' moment for me. I knew that God was talking to me through that video."

Reflect: Think of a time in your life when you had a big "Aha!" moment, a time when God spoke to your heart. What did you learn? Share it with someone else.

Dig Deeper: Deuteronomy 4:29; John 14:21; Romans 1:20

Clare

The Buddhist Scientist, Part 2

"Choose for yourselves this day whom you will serve" (Joshua 24:15).

God was speaking to Clare, a Buddhist scientist who had listened on the web to Roger Morneau speak about evolution and reincarnation. And what was that "Sunday worship" thing all about? Mr. Morneau professed to be something called a Sabbath-keeper instead. Curious, Clare searched the Internet for the word "Sabbath-keeper"—and up came the Amazing Facts website. It was exactly what she needed. Delighted, she saw a list of Bible studies that she could complete online and entirely for free. She went through all 24 *Storacles* lessons, drinking in the information like one who had spent her entire life in a drought.

Then she watched the entire series of *The Millennium of Prophecy* with Pastor Doug Batchelor. By the end, she realized that she needed to make the biggest decision of her life. "The Holy Spirit kept convicting me sermon after sermon," she says, "that I needed to forsake everything in order to follow Christ. The messages moved my heart and appealed to me to make major decisions in my life." When Pastor Doug shared how no person can follow two masters, it brought conviction.

Clare identified with people who attempt to serve two masters. She was living these two lives that were gradually growing further and further apart. By this point, she had graduated and become a pharmacist. She was still living with her boyfriend in their comfortable home and was now working at a successful job. It seemed as though she were painting this perfect picture of her future. Years of time, effort, and money had been invested into this life. But it was all so empty—her friends, her work, her relationship. It was meaningless because it was Christ-less.

She knew her life had to change, so she made a decision.

Clare searched online and found the nearest Sabbath-keeping church, showing up the very next Saturday. She was warmly greeted by church members and was soon invited to study the Bible with them. That church became Clare's home church and that church family, her family. She eventually left her home, her job, and her boyfriend. She was baptized into that church and now lives as a medical missionary in China, ministering in health and lifestyle programs, giving Bible studies, and leading out in prayer meetings. And her own father and mother are now studying the Bible too.

Reflect: Do you need to make a decision in your life? Is there something the Holy Spirit is convicting you to change? Will you choose to make that change? Right now? God will help you if you trust and obey.

Dig Deeper: Deuteronomy 30:19; John 15:16; Ephesians 1:4

Elijah

The Greatest Show on Earth, Part 1

"As the God of Israel lives, before whom I stand, there shall not be dew nor rain these years, except at my word" (1 Kings 17:1).

Buffalo grass, a hardy vegetation native to North America, lies brown and dormant during a drought and within two hours of rainfall turns green again.

The prophet Elijah famously predicted a drought in the time of King Ahab, who was the most wicked of all the rulers of Israel (1 Kings 16:33). Ahab had married a woman named Jezebel, who was the daughter of a high priest of Baal—the false god of the Canaanites (v. 31). Jezebel also worshipped Baal and was a powerfully seductive influence upon her husband's religious beliefs and policies. Consequently, during Ahab's reign idol worship remained rampant in Israel, and many Israelites turned away from the living God.

Now came God's strong warning against their sin, told directly to Ahab by Elijah the prophet (17:1). The drought persisted for three and a half years, during which time dearth and famine ravaged the nation. But through it all, God protected Elijah, hiding him from the king, who held the prophet responsible for the country's troubles, and from the clutches of Jezebel, who hated all he stood for (v. 3). Instead, God sustained Elijah by ravens, which brought the prophet food, and provided a stream, which gave him water (v. 6).

God then further preserved his prophet in the home of the widow of Zarephath. In that home Elijah, the widow, and her son witnessed God's direct intervention in their lives multiple times; not only did God save his prophet, He also delivered the widow and her son from starvation, miraculously providing enough food for all of them from just a "bin of flour" and a "jar of oil" (v. 14), and even brought the widow's son back from the dead after a devastating illness took the boy's life (vv. 17–22).

Certainly, Elijah knew that God's loving hand was upon him. How his faith must have been strengthened during that time; how the ravens' daily toil must have repeatedly reminded him of God's almighty power and tender concern.

Now the time had finally come when God was to show Himself to the people of Israel. And Elijah, who, like the buffalo grass, had lain dormant for a season, was about to return.

Reflect: How many times has God's Word, instructions, or impressions explicitly spared your life? We can trust that, no matter how improbable, God always does what He says He will do (Ezekiel 12:25).

Dig Deeper: Isaiah 14:24, 27; Lamentations 2:17; Luke 21:33

Elijah

The Greatest Show on Earth, Part 2

> **" God of Abraham, Isaac, and Israel, let it be known this day that You are God in Israel and I am Your servant, and that I have done all these things at Your word" (1 Kings 18:36).**

Imagine the anticipation, the fervor Elijah must have felt the day he returned to Israel. Finally, after three and a half years of patiently enduring, hoping, ruminating on the day that God's wayward people would see the error of their ways, Elijah met with the king.

"Is that you, O troubler of Israel?" (1 Kings 18:17) asked the weakly king upon seeing him.

But Elijah's response was steadfast, as straight as an arrow and as bold as a lion: "I have not troubled Israel, but you and your father's house have, in that you have forsaken the commandments of the and have followed the Baals" (v. 18).

Then Elijah requested that all the Israelites be gathered for a public demonstration of worship that pitted him against 450 false prophets of Baal (v. 19).

The spectacle began. Also present were King Ahab and another 400 false prophets. Elijah and the prophets of Baal were to build altars and prepare sacrifices and then petition their respective deities to accept their sacrifice by fire (vv. 23, 24).

The prophets of Baal assembled first. Though they danced and screamed and desperately flagellated themselves all day, there came no answer from above (vv. 26–29).

Now came Elijah's turn. At his feet was an altar, long since trampled and forgotten, that had once been used to worship the true God (vv. 31, 32). Faithfully, calmly, orderly, the prophet set about rebuilding it, digging a moat around it, and placing his sacrifice. Then, he requested water to be poured, drenching the altar and leaving no room for doubt (v. 33). To the crowd the difference between Elijah's process versus that of the prophets of Baal must have seemed like night and day.

Then Elijah prayed for God to accept his offering. It was a humble prayer of praise and intercession (vv. 36, 37). Instantly, fire struck the altar—and even the water (v. 38). It was an unmistakable, undeniable, undefeatable sign. The people, awestruck, worshipped God (v. 39).

What a victory had been won that day! Elijah's utter reliance on, and his unyielding confidence in the Almighty shone like a diamond in the rough. But could anything shake that trust?

Reflect: Has your faith in God ever led you to do something bold, something brave for His glory? Step out in faith and watch God part the waters.

Dig Deeper: Joshua 1:9–11; Acts 4:29–31; Hebrews 4:16

Elijah

The Greatest Show on Earth, Part 3

> **"[B]ut the was not in the wind; and after the wind an earthquake, but the was not in the earthquake; and after the earthquake a fire, but the was not in the fire" (1 Kings 19:11, 12).**

During World War I, desertion from the army was considered a grave offense. Great Britain alone captured 291 deserters and executed them by firing squad.

After Elijah's triumphant display, God ended the drought (1 Kings 18:44, 45). Elijah had waited years for this. But now that it was over, what was next? Perhaps he expected an apology from the king or Israel's complete reform. All he got was a death threat from the queen (19:2).

And Elijah, who had so recently demonstrated such courageous trust in God, faltered. He did not ask God's guidance; he simply "ran for his life" (v. 3). He was bitterly disappointed. All his high hopes for Israel had been dashed. He wanted to die (v. 4).

Fortunately, God did not want that.

"What are you doing here, Elijah?" (v. 9) asked the Lord.

But Elijah evaded the question, instead unleashing a bout of self-pity (v. 10). All those years spent hiding, finally the long-awaited event, all those people watching, all the work he had done—had it all been for naught?

God then taught Elijah a very important lesson. He brought before His prophet three mighty powers: a wind, an earthquake, and a fire—all forces of nature that would seem to aptly represent the Almighty. But God deliberately did not associate Himself with any of them. Instead, He showed Himself as "a still small voice" (v. 12).

To Elijah, the visuals were clear. Just because something was big or loud did not mean that it was powerful. Just because Elijah had prepared a grand display to showcase God's might did not mean that people's hearts had been converted. It is only the deeply personal, endlessly compassionate leading of the Holy Spirit that can transform a soul. Elijah had assumed that his work had been finished after God had rained down fire from heaven, but what if his work had just been the beginning? What could God have accomplished through him had he not deserted at the first peep from Jezebel?

But God, ever patient, gave Elijah another chance to continue as His messenger. After that quiet rebuke, Elijah had no more complaints. Instead, he obediently did all that the Lord asked of him.

Reflect: What is your understanding of God's process in winning souls? What role do you have in that process?

Dig Deeper: Psalm 19:7; Jeremiah 3:19–22; Acts 2:29–41

. . . .

"How long, O ? Will You forget me forever? How long will You hide Your face from me? How long shall I take counsel in my soul, having sorrow in my heart daily? How long will my enemy be exalted over me?" (Psalm 13:1, 2).

Kim's father fell quickly to cancer and died at age 64. It turned her world upside down.

"He was my everything. We were close. His death horrified me," she explained. "I comforted him through countless eight-hour chemo sessions, but the fear in his eyes ... it still bothers me today." He didn't know where he was going when he died. Kim didn't either.

He called himself a Christian. He was a dedicated police officer who daily put his life on the line. He was "a good person." But deep inside he was scared and confused.

He taught Kim that obedience to biblical principles was unnecessary, even fanatical. "Temperance in all things" seemed to be his motto, but he was clearly living a life of biblical disobedience. He dismissed church attendance by saying, "It's just a club."

All this left Kim confused and wondering *How is living in sin temperate?* Is it possible to sin just a little? Despite her father's shortcomings, she didn't understand why God would make a good man suffer. She genuinely feared for his salvation.

At the same time, Kim says, her life was a mess. She married a non-believer and pursued worldly lusts for more than 20 years. She had a big house, new cars, money ... whatever she wanted; but with babies at home, and a husband who visited a bar every night and ordered her not to call him, she drifted into despondency.

Hip-deep in hypocrisy (Kim's words), without solid biblical knowledge or a good church background, Kim got quite mad at God. She divorced her husband. Shortly thereafter, her father died. She swirled deeper into darkness and further away from God.

Throughout all these trials, Kim felt that Satan was keeping her in a prison of guilt. She cried and drank wine daily. Kim also learned she had cancer. She considered herself "a messed up, heartbroken, out of control, disobedient, worthless, fornicating, bad sinner"; yet somehow she sensed God tapping her on the shoulder telling her He loved her.

Distraught, Kim went looking for answers. And God responded ...

Reflect: Some people have to hit rock bottom before looking up. Have you ever been so low that you felt abandoned by God? Call to Him and He will answer you.

Dig Deeper: Psalm 13:5, 6; 2 Corinthians 12:9; 1 Peter 5:7

"Whoever hears these sayings of Mine, and does them, I will liken him to a wise man who built his house on the rock" (Matthew 7:24).

Kim was in despair over her life and went looking for answers. God responded, using an Amazing Facts presentation on YouTube. She shares how "I began to feel God's compassion as He began to guide me, drawing me step-by-careful-step through a spiritual process resulting in a new and deeper understanding of the Bible."

God sent Daniel, a new Christian, into Kim's life. They eventually married and together began searching for a church. They soon found a Sunday-keeping church and began attending services. All the while they continued watching Amazing Facts videos.

In their new church, the pastor encouraged everyone to read the Scriptures to make sure he was on track. Kim and Daniel did and discovered that he was teaching confusing doctrine contrary to the Bible. So they left this church and kept searching. They eventually attended eight different churches from varying denominations and found all of them were in conflict with what they were learning online from Amazing Facts.

Kim questioned these pastors about ignoring certain Bible teachings. They often gave excuses about why obedience was not necessary for all biblical teachings. She didn't understand how her father, and now these pastors, could pick and choose what they wanted to obey. Surrounded by hypocrisy and inconsistency, she felt the Christians around them used "grace" as a "get-out-of-hell-free card."

"By contrast," she explains, "what we were learning from Amazing Facts was logical, consistent, and most importantly, biblical."

One day Kim and Daniel listened to Pastor Doug preach on the seventh-day Sabbath. It was as if a veil had been lifted from her eyes. "Everything from childhood to the present that I had suspected was false or hypocritical was proving to be so," she explains. This Sabbath message helped them know that they had found God's true church, the remnant people of Revelation.

Kim and Daniel found a local Sabbath-keeping church and are now happily attending a church that teaches and believes according to the Bible. Their previous conflict and confusion over Bible truth is completely gone. Kim believes, "I have no doubt that God divinely guided us to Amazing Facts." She was once hip-deep in hypocrisy, but today she is standing on solid ground.

Reflect: What do you do when you hear a religious speaker say something that doesn't seem to agree with the Bible? Look it up in the Scriptures. Pray for wisdom to speak up if necessary.

Dig Deeper: Matthew 7:21–23; Luke 6:46–49; 1 John 2:4

Corrie ten Boom

The Deepest Ocean, Part 1

> **"For if you forgive men their trespasses, your heavenly Father will also forgive you. But if you do not forgive men their trespasses, neither will your Father forgive your trespasses" (Matthew 6:14, 15).**

"When we confess our sins, God casts them into the deepest ocean."

It was a concept that Corrie ten Boom had advocated again and again to people all over the world, urging them to a life of reconciliation after the horrors of World War II. But did she truly believe it herself?

The ten Booms were a well-respected Christian family of watchmakers in the Netherlands. In the Second World War, the ten Booms became part of the Dutch underground, with Corrie eventually finding herself as one of its local leaders. In all, the ten Booms, through the use of a secret room constructed in their home, helped to save 800 Jewish lives and, additionally, countless other resistance fighters.

Then, on February 28, 1944, the family was betrayed by an informant and arrested by the Nazis. Several family members were soon let go, but Corrie's father died in prison, and Corrie and her oldest sister Betsie were transferred twice, finally settling at Ravensbrück, a concentration camp for women in Germany.

Corrie was filled with hatred for Jan Vogel, the informant who had done this to her family. Without a doubt, she would have taken his life if given the opportunity. But when she brought up his name to Betsie, her sister felt quite differently.

Betsie thought only of Jan's hard heart, the suffering he had inflicted upon himself through his heinous deed. He did not know the love of God; he did not know the merciful Savior. His was a life trapped in the devil's game. He was the one who was really lost. Betsie was not like Corrie. She had no hatred in her heart for this man; instead, Betsie prayed for his soul.

It was one of the mysteries about her sister. On that first night of air raids, when the war had finally reached their country, Betsie had fervently prayed for the Germans as they dropped bombs on their heads. When they had first been imprisoned, Betsie had spoken with such compassion about the female guards and God's ability to change their hearts.

Her sister, it seemed, could love even her most vile persecutor. And Corrie knew that was exactly what the Bible said to do. But how was it possible?

Reflect: Have you ever been betrayed by someone you trusted? What is God asking you to do about it?

Dig Deeper: Psalm 103:10–12; Isaiah 43:25; Mark 11:25

"Now hope does not disappoint, because the love of God has been poured out in our hearts by the Holy Spirit who was given to us" (Romans 5:5).

Corrie and Betsie spent four months at Ravensbrück. In that time, they witnessed God's many miracles, including the nightly Bible readings they shared with hundreds of women.

But Betsy's health was declining. She died on December 16, 1944, two weeks before Corrie's release. To the end, Betsy remained adamant about not only forgiving their enemies but pointing them to Christ.

Now, without her constant companion for the first time in her life, Corrie was eventually guided by God to found two rehabilitation centers, fulfilling prophetic visions that Betsie had had while they had been imprisoned. One of the centers she set up in her old family home for former members of Holland's Nazi Party. She even wrote a letter to Jan Vogel, finally forgiving him for what he had done.

But Corrie still had much to learn. It was 1947, and Corrie had begun to speak publicly about her and Betsy's experiences in the concentration camps. Her mission was really Betsy's mission: to preach about the necessity of forgiveness after the war.

After one of her talks in the heart of Germany, a man approached her. She recognized him immediately. He had been one of the guards at Ravensbrück!

He spoke earnestly to her. He had become a Christian, and how beautiful it was that God had forgiven him of his sins—of all he had done in that camp. But he also wanted to be assured of her personal forgiveness. He held out his hand to her.

Corrie stood like a block of ice. Waves of hatred washed over her; memories of Betsy flooded in. Were everyone else's sins forgiven—including her own—but not this man's? Everything within her screamed, "Yes!"

But she had preached forgiveness. Could she practice it?

She knew she could not—only God could. In that moment, she made the decision to shake the man's hand, the last thing in the world she wanted to do.

"Jesus, help me!" she pleaded. "You supply the feeling."

And He did. As prisoner and guard reached across that forbidden gulf, God destroyed the hatred in Corrie's heart and replaced it with His love.

"I forgive you, brother!" she exclaimed to the man. "With all my heart!"

And she meant it. God had changed her very feelings.

Reflect: Will you ask God to continually supply the forgiveness you do not have?

Dig Deeper: Psalm 34:10; Ephesians 4:31, 32; Philippians 4:19

Grecia

Breaking Away, Part 1

> **"Enter by the narrow gate; for wide is the gate and broad is the way that leads to destruction, and there are many who go in by it. Because narrow is the gate and difficult is the way which leads to life, and there are few who find it" (Matthew 7:13, 14).**

Grecia grew up in Puerto Rico believing in God. Even though her parents believed in the Lord, they never attended church. She occasionally attended services with her paternal grandmother and she prayed to God, but she just didn't go to church much.

"Since I was small I always had a fear of God but didn't really know Him," she remembers. Grecia would wonder if God approved of some of the things she did. She wasn't reading her Bible and didn't have much of a relationship with the Lord. She thought she could just worship God in whatever way she wanted.

As an adult she joined a church and became fond of the pastor and made many friends among the members.

One day a client named Indiana dropped by Grecia's workplace and began talking about Bible teachings she had never heard of. "It caught my attention," she shares, "and I wanted to learn more about God." Indiana, who happened to be the mother of Amazing Facts evangelist Carlos Muñoz, handed her a paper telling her where she could watch her son's online videos on the book of Revelation in Spanish.

"From the very first one, I loved watching these programs!" Grecia recalls. "I knew these were meant for me." The Holy Spirit began working in her life. She watched several talks each day and even brought some to work. "What I heard changed my life and my way of thinking."

Soon Grecia began to feel uncomfortable attending her church because she started seeing that it was not in harmony with the teachings of the Bible. "I felt bad and didn't know what to do," she explains, "so I prayed for God to direct me." She loved her pastor and fellow members, but knew something must change.

Reflect: Have you ever had to end a relationship? Seek God's will and in the end it will all make sense. Doing what is right is better than doing what is popular.

Dig Deeper: 1 Chronicles 16:11; Joel 3:14; Philippians 4:6

Grecia

Breaking Away, Part 2

"Send out Your light and Your truth! Let them lead me; let them bring me to Your holy hill and to Your tabernacle" (Psalm 43:3).

Grecia loved her pastor and fellow members, but was learning new Bible truth that didn't agree with her Sunday-keeping church. She knew something had to change.

Soon after she prayed, Indiana, who introduced her to the online Revelation programs, told her that a special series of meetings would be taking place in their town on the book of Revelation. They would be held by Amazing Facts evangelist Carlos Muñoz. "I was so excited that I attended all the meetings and made the decision to be baptized into God's Sabbath-keeping church!"

Grecia tells how the Amazing Facts meetings clearly explained the plan of salvation through the sanctuary service. They helped her to grow closer to Christ and develop a relationship with Him. "I now understand more about God's Word and, thanks to the Holy Spirit, want to keep studying the Bible," she says. "More than anything else, I want to share these truths with other people."

Besides completing the *Amazing Facts Bible Study Guides* in Spanish, Grecia continues to enjoy watching sermons in her own language on the Amazing Facts website. She also appreciated the way Carlos emphasized the importance of a close relationship with God. One Bible study tip he shared especially stuck with Grecia. "He told us, 'A verse without context is a pretext!'" Grecia also was thankful for the way Carlos encouraged everyone to make it a priority to pray, read the Bible, and share the gospel with others.

Grecia is so thankful for how God answered her prayers. The prophecy seminar helped her break with her old church, walk in the truth, and keep the Sabbath. During this seminar Grecia's sister and a friend from her old church were also baptized.

"The Amazing Facts prophecy seminar totally changed my life," she shares. "I have fallen more in love with my Lord every day and have decided to follow Jesus in Spirit and in truth. Amazing Facts has strengthened my faith and prepared me to share God's love so that others can come out of darkness and into the light."

Reflect: Have you ever shared the light of God's truth with another person and then watched their life change? There is nothing more rewarding than to be a witness for Christ and see hearts touched.

Dig Deeper: John 8:12; 2 Corinthians 6:14; Ephesians 5:8

The Thief on the Cross

"Remember Me"

"Then he said to Jesus, 'Lord, remember me when You come into Your kingdom'" (Luke 23:42).

He was one of the most anonymous people in Scripture. All we know is that the "malefactor" (as the Authorized Version calls him) was one of two thieves who were crucified alongside Jesus on a dark Friday some 2,000 years ago.

We don't know his name. We don't know where in Palestine he came from. We know nothing of his education, his family, or even his career—if he even had one. We just know he was a thief the Romans wanted dead before sundown.

Initially, *both* of the thieves being crucified had mocked Jesus. The chief priests chided, "If He is the King of Israel, let Him now come down from the cross, and we will believe Him. He trusted in God; let Him deliver Him now if He will have Him; for He said, 'I am the Son of God'" (Matthew 27:42, 43). But in the very next verse, we read, "Even the robbers who were crucified with Him reviled Him with the same thing" (verse 44).

Did you catch that? Both robbers mocked, both reviled. Until ... one malefactor, who we know so little about, did a 180-degree turnaround. Hearing his compatriot demand that Jesus prove His divinity by saving them together, the now-penitent thief said: "Do you not even fear God, seeing you are under the same condemnation? And we indeed justly, for we receive the due reward of our deeds; but this Man has done nothing wrong" (Luke 23:40, 41).

Some have suggested that when this thief heard Jesus say, "Father, forgive them; for they know not what they do" (Luke 23:34 KJV), this man was convicted of his own sin—and his personal need for a Savior. The Bible doesn't give us a reason for the thief's repentance, just the word that he did. And for Jesus, that was enough!

As Luke recorded it: "Then he said to Jesus, 'Lord, remember me when You come into Your kingdom.'" And on that very day, Jesus assured him, "You will be with Me in Paradise" (Luke 23:42, 43).

Salvation! In a sentence! What hope that should give us all!

Reflect: Do you know of people who experienced a "180-degree turnaround" in their view of God and Jesus? Were you such a person? The Lord allows U-turns!

Dig Deeper: Psalm 106:4, 5; Isaiah 53:10–12; Acts 16:31

Todd and Shirley

Jaw-Dropping Truth, Part 1

"Beloved, do not believe every spirit, but test the spirits, whether they are of God; because many false prophets have gone out into the world" (1 John 4:1).

Todd and Shirley came from a Catholic background. They were both confirmed in the Catholic Church, and Todd had been an altar boy. The couple met through their work, experienced love at first sight, and have been married for fourteen years [as of 2015]. They have five children whom they cherish.

Although Todd and Shirley were brought up in the Catholic Church, they felt a growing discontent with calling the priest "Father" and also with making confession to a priest. "We also found all the idols in the church unsettling," says Todd. "We just felt something was wrong and slowly stopped going to church."

When Todd and Shirley moved to Arizona, they became concerned with seeing evil symbols and started researching the Illuminati, the new world order, and the mark of the beast. In order to learn about these symbols, they watched YouTube videos, but as they gathered information, they just felt confused. "We had this uncontrollable feeling of doom," says Todd. "We felt really lost with no hope, but we didn't know what to do. I would lock myself in a room and watch videos for hours. I also drank and cursed quite regularly."

One day while Todd was watching videos, trying to figure out the answers, up popped a link to a Doug Batchelor video on the mark of the beast. "I continued to watch other videos, and then another video of Doug Batchelor popped up. I still did not watch his video until it popped up again!" Todd believes, as he looks back, that God was trying to get his attention.

"I finally watched the video," says Todd, "and it was jaw-dropping. I knew something good was happening inside me. So I watched another video by Pastor Doug about the pope and the antichrist. Everything I was learning seemed right and logical. Pastor Doug said to check out what he was saying and not to believe just another man but to look up the Scriptures. And I did."

Reflect: Has God ever tried to get your attention when you were looking in the wrong place for answers? Often the Lord is reaching out to us even though we are not searching for Him.

Dig Deeper: Deuteronomy 7:7, 8; Job 7:17; Matthew 13:44–46

Todd and Shirley

Jaw-Dropping Truth, Part 2

"For you were once darkness, but now you are light in the Lord. Walk as children of light (for the fruit of the Spirit is in all goodness, righteousness, and truth), finding out what is acceptable to the Lord" (Ephesians 5:8–10).

When Todd heard Pastor Doug encourage listeners to check out everything he was saying with the Bible, he did. Todd felt alive inside and knew he had to share this new found truth with Shirley, but he was apprehensive as he felt his wife might cling to her Catholic background and be offended by the studies that had placed the pope in a bad light. To Todd's surprise, though, Shirley accepted the truth of the Bible and from there, the two of them started a joint journey into God's Word.

A study of the Sabbath was a turning point for Todd and Shirley and they stepped out to find a Sabbath-keeping church. They found one in town, and their pastor says the congregation deeply loves their family. "The things they have learned since leaving the Catholic Church seem to have been practically a banquet feast for them," the pastor says.

"We don't feel lost anymore," says Todd. "We now have the best marriage we have ever had, and we're considering renewing our vows in our new church. Our whole house is very happy, peaceful, and loving. There is no more drinking, cursing, yelling, or locking myself in the bedroom. We are learning how to love our neighbors and we are honoring the commandments because we love God and don't want to hurt Him anymore. We can't wait for church each Sabbath. God is always first in our lives, and we love Him above all."

Todd and Shirley completed the *Storacles of Prophecy* studies, and watched a number of faith-building messages. They continue to study the Bible and use several research tools from Amazing Facts, including The Bible Timeline (timeline.biblehistory.com). Shirley shares her faith with co-workers by first directing them to amazingfacts.org and encouraging them to watch the videos. She also hands out booklets.

Todd and Shirley are thankful for the jaw-dropping truths they have learned which have transformed their lives from despair to joy!

Reflect: Are you part of a church family? What is your favorite part about being connected to the body of Christ? Remember, it's important to not only gain a blessing at church, but to be a blessing to others—for love shows we are Christ's disciples.

Dig Deeper: Psalm 119:160; John 17:17; Ephesians 6:14

Mitsuo Fuchida

Living in Infamy, Part 1

**"Therefore be merciful, just as your Father
also is merciful" (Luke 6:36).**

At 7:48 a.m. on December 7, 1941, the sleepy calm on the island of Oahu was suddenly broken by the piercing sound of dive bombers, torpedoes, and gunfire. Japan's naval air arm, in a surprise attack, had ambushed the Pearl Harbor naval base, killing 2,403 Americans and effectively entering the United States into World War II.

The man who led the slaughter, Mitsuo Fuchida, was a zealous aviator who, from childhood, had idolized Japan's war heroes. Fueled by historical Western dominance and the Immigration Act of 1924, which barred all Asian nationals from the United States, Fuchida fervently hated any and all things American. After the attack on Pearl Harbor, Fuchida's dream was realized, and he returned to Japan a celebrated war hero.

But what was not so well known was the flight commander's near-death on that infamous day. Upon landing his aircraft, Fuchida learned that, besides the fact that his plane was hit no less than 21 times, one of the cables for his controls was dangling literally by a thread. If that cable had broken, he would certainly have not survived.

Surprisingly enough, that was not the last time this famed soldier escaped death. Six months later, in the crucial Battle of Midway, his life was uncannily spared by an emergency appendectomy, which kept him grounded on the carrier *Akagi*. With all four Japanese carriers destroyed in the battle, Fuchida, had he been flying, would have had no choice but to crash along with the rest of his pilots. As it was, he did not come away unscathed, breaking both his ankles when the Americans bombed the *Akagi*.

Then, in August 1945, Fuchida, who had been in Hiroshima planning an aerial maneuver, was, for some unforeseen reason, sent some 500 miles away for a meeting. It was only when he awoke the next morning that he heard about the atomic bomb that was dropped on the city he had just left. But it was not only that. Fuchida, part of a small team of officers, was then ordered back to Hiroshima to assess the damage. Weeks later, all of those other officers—except for Fuchida—died from radiation poisoning.

Did this mere mortal have superhuman powers, or was there something or Someone else at work here?

Reflect: Have there been instances in your life where you have been spared from death? What has been your reaction to your new lease on life?

Dig Deeper: Psalm 68:19, 20; Proverbs 24:11; Titus 3:4–7

Mitsuo Fuchida

Living in Infamy, Part 2

"Be kind to one another, tenderhearted, forgiving one another, even as God in Christ forgave you" (Ephesians 4:32).

After Japan's surrender in 1945, Fuchida was called to participate in the Tokyo Trial, one of the war crimes tribunals which took place at the end of the Second World War and that focused partially on the inhumane treatment of prisoners. Disgusted with the ordeal, Fuchida decided to conduct his own research on American treatment of Japanese prisoners of war—determined to prove the victor's hypocrisy.

He decided to meet a boat of returning Japanese prisoners and to his surprise discovered one of his friends who had been thought dead. Even more of a shock, when Fuchida asked about his friend's treatment at the hands of his American captors, his friend told him of a nurse whose missionary parents had been killed by the Japanese during the war but who nevertheless tenderly cared for him and his fellow prisoners as a mother would her own sons. Fuchida was stunned.

The next year, during his second summons to the war tribunal, Fuchida was handed a small pamphlet. It was the true story of an American soldier who had been captured and brutally tortured by the Japanese. While imprisoned though, that soldier was given a Bible and, after reading it, became a Christian missionary in Japan, the country of his enemies. Again, Fuchida was baffled. He could not understand the soldier's actions. Why love? Why not revenge?

He was intrigued by the God of this Bible. So the following year, in Shibuya Station in Tokyo, the very same place he had received the pamphlet on the American soldier, Fuchida bought a Bible. As he read, he became fascinated with the character of this singular God, this Jesus who humbled Himself as a man. But it was when he read of Jesus' death that Fuchida finally understood. Jesus, tortured, ridiculed, *dying*, prayed for all those who hated Him. He asked for their pardon, for their salvation. It was then that Fuchida knelt down and prayed, asking the God of the Bible to forgive his hatred, his vengeance, his sins.

He became a Christian and for the rest of his life testified of what Jesus Christ had done for him. He was scorned, hated, and even held at knifepoint by his own countrymen but, to the very end, he held fast to his faith.

Reflect: Have you found it difficult to forgive—or be forgiven? Begin by forgiving yourself, then forgive others and you will more deeply experience God's forgiveness toward you.

Dig Deeper: Micah 7:18–20; Matthew 5:43–48; 1 Peter 2:19–25

Melissa

Dying of Thirst, Part 1

"Give no regard to mediums and familiar spirits; do not seek after them, to be defiled by them: I am the your God" (Leviticus 19:31).

Melissa grew up in a home filled with fighting, fear, confusion, and even the occult. She found herself becoming more and more introverted. "For me, the world was a scary place. I was like a mouse seeking safety and comfort in hiding."

To make matters more difficult, Melissa's childhood home was visited by evil spirits. Her mother told her of a time she was praying and heard demonic laughter as her large wooden crucifix on the wall suddenly swung upside down. Yet she unwittingly invited this activity in the home by watching television programs with Melissa about ghosts and other paranormal activity.

Melissa's mother was a devout Catholic and said special prayers, sprinkled her home with holy water, repeated countless rosaries, and did special house blessings. But still, she could not completely cleanse her home of the spirits.

Melissa and her sister were taken to church, baptized, and put into Catholic schools for a short time. But despite all of the religious training, Melissa always knew something was missing. "I didn't really understand God," she recalls. "Everything I did in those days was empty." At age nine she rebelled and quit attending church.

While Melissa's mother told her she would end up spending eternity in hell, she remained uninterested in church. She did not, however, give up entirely on the idea of God. As the years passed, Melissa found herself making lifestyle choices that only added to her emptiness. She became involved in an unhealthy, abusive relationship. She had a daughter whom she adored but a husband who ended up leaving the marriage.

Later, Melissa moved to live near her sister who joined a Baptist denomination. Her sister begged her to read the Bible, but Melissa repeatedly resisted. Finally, while doing an online search for answers to questions about Muslims, Melissa stumbled across a link that turned her life upside down.

Reflect: Have you ever watched programs about the occult or evil spirits? Put these things away and never look at them again. When you do, God will empower you to have a new life in Him.

Dig Deeper: Exodus 22:18; Leviticus 20:6; Revelation 21:8

Melissa

Dying of Thirst, Part 2

"They shall neither hunger nor thirst, neither heat nor sun shall strike them; for He who has mercy on them will lead them, even by the springs of water He will guide them" (Isaiah 49:10).

Melissa was searching for truth when she stumbled across a link to a man named Roger Morneau, who had come out of the occult and become a strong Christian.

Wanting to follow his example, Melissa searched online for a series of Bible studies. The first result that got her attention was from Amazing Facts. They offered a set of twenty-seven lessons, complete with videos and quizzes for each study.

"I eagerly watched Pastor Doug Batchelor explain each study," Melissa recalls fondly. "I enjoyed his presentations, his gentle and sometimes comical approach, and his detailed coverage of each topic. I took notes from each lesson. Like a person dying of thirst in a desert, I had found an oasis of knowledge of biblical truth and was eager to quench my thirst."

Melissa began to piece together answers to many Bible questions and eventually became a joyful member of a Sabbath-keeping church. She is no longer withdrawn and is actively sharing her faith. Now she freely shares the *Amazing Facts Bible Study Guides* with others. "They are clear, thorough, logical, and easy to understand," she says.

Melissa is so excited about giving Bible studies with these guides that she is working to set up her own online Bible study group in order to reach more people.

For others seeking light, she suggests, "Ask God to reveal the truth to you. If you struggle with doubt, honestly tell the Lord. Then ask God to be direct with you. It works wonders."

Melissa is forever grateful for how the Lord led her to God's truth. "It brought me great joy to stumble upon this mountain of knowledge. I have finally found answers to my questions."

At one time in her life, Melissa was extremely distrustful, anxious, and reclusive. "I feared going to church, talking to people, and even talking about God. Now I want to help start a huge revival!" God's truth watered Melissa's heart and caused her to spring to life. Now she wants to share the Lord's ever-flowing love and power with others.

Reflect: Do you know someone whose heart is distrustful. What one thing from the Bible could you share with that person to help them peacefully trust in the Lord? Share that one thing with them this week.

Dig Deeper: Nehemiah 9:15; Psalm 143:6; Song of Solomon 8:7

James, Son of Zebedee

Fisherman Is "Hooked" By Messiah

"James the son of Zebedee and John the brother of James, to whom He gave the name Boanerges, that is, 'Sons of Thunder'" (Mark 3:17).

The life of a commercial fisherman is no picnic. It isn't today (just watch an episode of "Deadliest Catch") and it wasn't in the days of Jesus, although fishing on the Sea of Galilee was far less risky than plying that trade along the coast of Alaska.

James and John, the sons of Zebedee, were in partnership with Simon Peter (and Peter's younger brother, Andrew), when they were called by Jesus to be His disciples. Jesus knew these men, and their profession. He knew what a rough trade it could be, and that these were roughhewn types—a stark contrast to the more educated among the twelve.

"When [Jesus] had gone a little farther from there, He saw James the son of Zebedee, and John his brother, who also were in the boat mending their nets. And immediately He called them, and they left their father Zebedee in the boat with the hired servants, and went after Him" (Mark 1:19, 20).

If the firm of Zebedee & Sons, Fishermen, had "hired servants," we can imagine that this was a well-to-do business, especially if the two sons could drop everything and follow Jesus. What specifically was said to James and John, and why they responded, is not known. Yet their obedience is counted positively in this account.

Less positive is Jesus' designation of the two as "Boanerges," or "Sons of Thunder," which followed their response to Jesus being turned away from a Samaritan village: "And when His disciples James and John saw this, they said, 'Lord, do You want us to command fire to come down from heaven and consume them, just as Elijah did?'" (Luke 9:54).

Having their mother ask for each of her sons to sit at Jesus' right and left hands in the kingdom wasn't a winning strategy either.

But something happened to James after the resurrection. Scripture doesn't give the specifics, but he became a bold evangelist, so much so that he was martyred. "Now about that time Herod the king stretched out his hand to harass some from the church. Then he killed James the brother of John with the sword" (Acts 12:1, 2).

James, a faithful fisherman and a devoted disciple, was truly "hooked" on Jesus. Are you?

Reflect: Some converts start out with a fair amount of impulsiveness. Have you known such a one—and have you seen them transformed by exposure to Jesus' love?

Dig Deeper: Isaiah 11:2; John 1:41; Acts 13:32, 33

Diego

"I Will Never Change My Religion"

"Look to Me, and be saved, all you ends of the earth! For I am God, and there is no other" (Isaiah 45:22).

Diego was a devoted Catholic who, though he never studied the Bible, was so convinced about his beliefs that he would tell others, "I will never change my religion." But then he met Jose, a Sabbath-keeper who shared Bible facts with Diego. "I was initially very hard-headed and refused to listen."

One day, Jose gave Diego an Amazing Facts DVD titled *The Final Events of Bible Prophecy*. As he listened, he realized that his beliefs were wrong. "I had been taught that when people died they went straight to heaven. I was also brought up to believe in a place called purgatory, and that we should worship the saints. My understanding of the virgin Mary, communion, worship on Sunday and more were all based on traditions, but not on the Bible."

Still Diego wasn't ready to accept Bible truth. But he began watching Pastor Doug Batchelor online and Jose continued studying the Bible with him. He learned from Scripture that the Sabbath is on Saturday, not Sunday.

"For a while," he admits, "I tried to retain my old beliefs while trying to hold onto my new beliefs. I tried to consider myself a Seventh-day Catholic, but it just wasn't working. I started worshiping the Lord on Saturday by myself, but still hadn't completely let go of my former views."

Though his parents and sisters consider themselves good Catholics, they didn't attend church. So Diego thought to himself, "I don't really need to attend church either. I can just learn about God on my own." After a couple of weeks, he realized that he was wrong. "I finally made the decision to completely renounce my former beliefs. Never was I going to be fooled again." So he became a Sabbath-keeping Christian.

Diego's parents were not happy about his choice. When he tried to share his new beliefs with them, they refused to listen. "My dad said I was not properly interpreting the Bible. My mother said that her church was correct and is the church God created. But in my heart I knew this was all wrong because I had studied the Bible for myself."

Diego continues to pray for his family to turn from man-made traditions to the Bible. He hopes one day they will ask him about his new-found faith.

Reflect: Is there someone in your family who does not know about Bible truth? How can you reach out to them? Pray for wisdom and guidance from heaven.

Dig Deeper: Isaiah 43:11; Acts 4:12; Ephesians 2:8, 9

Francis Collins

Salvation at a Frozen Waterfall

"When I consider Your heavens, the work of Your fingers, the moon and the stars, which You have ordained, what is man that You are mindful of him, and the son of man that You visit him?" (Psalm 8:3, 4).

Francis Collins is one of the world's most respected genetic researchers. He currently directs the National Institutes of Health, the U.S. government's top medical research body. And even though he was an ardent atheist in his youth, he's now a professed Christian.

Although raised in an Episcopalian family, Collins found his beliefs challenged in college. "I concluded that all of this stuff about religion and faith was a carryover from an earlier, irrational time, and now that science had begun to figure out how things really work, we didn't need it anymore," he told PBS in an interview.

But in medical school, Collins worked with patients whose faith sustained them through difficult trials. Unable to reconcile this with what he called his "obnoxious" atheism, he asked a minister for guidance. The pastor gave him a copy of *Mere Christianity*, the apologetic written by C.S. Lewis. Collins later recalled that on reading the book, "within the first three pages, I realized that my arguments against faith were those of a schoolboy."

Collins' real turning point came on a hike and his spotting a frozen waterfall: "I was hiking in the Cascade Mountains on a beautiful fall afternoon. I turned the corner and saw in front of me this frozen waterfall, a couple of hundred feet high. Actually, a waterfall that had three parts to it—also the symbolic three in one. At that moment, I felt my resistance leave me. And it was a great sense of relief. The next morning, in the dewy grass in the shadow of the Cascades, I fell on my knees and accepted this truth—that God is God, that Christ is his son and that I am giving my life to that belief."

His faith has brought him into conflict with some atheists and some believers, since Collins rejects "intelligent design" and embraces an evolutionary approach. Hope remains, however: just as the onetime "obnoxious atheist" discovered that God does exist, it's still possible that Collins will recognize that by His very words, God "spoke, and it was done" when it came to the creation of the earth and all living things (Psalm 33:9).

Reflect: It's sometimes difficult for those with scientific backgrounds to challenge their peers by declaring their faith in God. Do you know anyone who has trouble believing in God? What can you do to help them?

Dig Deeper: Psalm 19:1; Job 25:5; Romans 1:20

Mou Chou

Broken Ropes, Part 1

**"Blessed be the God and Father of our Lord Jesus Christ,
who according to His abundant mercy has begotten
us again to a living hope through the resurrection
of Jesus Christ from the dead" (1 Peter 1:3).**

Mou Chou was literally at the end of her rope.

Because of her despair in living with an abusive husband, she tried to take her own life. Once, when she tried to hang herself, the rope broke.

Then, by God's grace and through your gifts, the lifesaving good news came to Mou Chou and others in her small village in central China through Amazing Facts videos. After hearing the truth about the Bible in her own language, she gave her life to Jesus and is now a vocal witness of the gospel to anyone she meets, thrilled to share her newfound peace and joy in Jesus Christ.

However, because of growing government restrictions, Christianity in the land of the red dragon struggles to move forward today. But compassionate Christians are providing Mandarin-language resources through the Internet, and growing numbers of believers are being raised up all over China.

Pastor Liang, a Sabbath-keeping minister who uses these Amazing Facts resources in his outreach, traveled to visit this group of new believers in central China. After these Christians watched Amazing Facts videos, they were inspired to keep the seventh-day Sabbath and to live by many of the special truths they found in the Scriptures.

When Pastor Liang learned about this small group of new Sabbath-keepers, he decided to visit and encourage them. The believers had grown to over a hundred souls during this past year. Since the government prohibits large gatherings, these new Christians meet in three smaller groups—one in the city and two in the country. The safest place for these brothers and sisters in Christ to gather is in the mountains, in an out-of-the-way place that requires an arduous 40-minute walk off the beaten path and up a mountain trail.

Sometimes we may complain about small inconveniences in our lives, but when we stop to consider the sacrifices some people make to simply hear the Bible read, it humbles us.

Reflect: Have you ever been at the end of your rope? No matter how dark and discouraging your situation, God can break through with the light of hope. Call to Him now.

Dig Deeper: Psalm 39:7; Isaiah 40:31; Romans 15:13

Mou Chou

Broken Ropes, Part 2

"Declare His glory among the nations, His wonders among all peoples" (Psalm 96:3).

Pastor Liang learned about a small group of new Sabbath-keepers in China and decided to visit and encourage them. Over a hundred souls gathered privately to worship because of government restrictions. One group met in the mountains where they could worship undisturbed.

The pastor spent several days with this group in worship and training, teaching them Christ's method of personal evangelism. The believers were so appreciative of his time that they offered to pay for his traveling expenses, but he graciously refused and encouraged them to use their funds in spreading the gospel in their area. Millions in China—people who have no hope—need to hear God's message for these last days.

It was among this group of fellow Christians that Pastor Liang met Mou Chou. He was also introduced to Nian Zhen, a woman who became paralyzed and bedridden after a severe illness. She was unable to walk, and her husband carried her on his back wherever they needed to go. When this couple heard the pastor was in their area, the husband carried his wife to the Sabbath morning service. After the meeting, the pastor was asked to pray for Nian Zhen to be healed. God graciously answered his prayers. The next time Pastor Liang saw her, she was walking around and caring for herself. She is now a faithful Sabbath-keeper. Praise God!

On his way home, Pastor Liang stopped to visit a village where he once lived, in order to share the truth. His brief time with old friends resulted in a new Bible group starting up. These new Sabbath-keepers were thrilled to learn fresh Bible truths that they had never heard. A short time later, nine from their group gave their lives to Christ and were baptized.

Many Christians would complain if they had to sit on a hard pew once a week for an hour, but people in China choose to worship in isolated places where there are no buildings. And through generous Christian gifts, God is breaking ropes of bondage and helping people like Mou Chou find true freedom in Jesus.

Reflect: Do you regularly give offerings for mission work? God calls us to support our friends in distant places, especially where resources are limited. Pray fervently for the mission work and give generously to help others discover life-changing truths from the Bible.

Dig Deeper: Isaiah 52:7; Acts 13:47; Romans 10:13–15

Hezekiah

Missed Opportunities, Part 1

> "Now do not be stiff-necked, as your fathers were, but yield yourselves to the ; and enter His sanctuary, which He has sanctified forever, and serve the your God, that the fierceness of His wrath may turn away from you" (2 Chronicles 30:8).

In a 2015, Pew Research Center survey on parenting, while 51 percent of mothers rated themselves as good parents, only 39 percent of fathers did the same.

How would Hezekiah's father, King Ahaz of Judah, have rated himself? Second Kings 16 tells us that Ahaz was a wicked king who even murdered one of his sons in a ritual sacrifice (v. 3).

Hezekiah, however, was spared. He grew up as an eyewitness to his father's idolatry, apostasy, and reckless sacrilege. And when he became king in his father's stead, Hezekiah resolved that he would be nothing like him, enacting several major religious reforms: "Our fathers have trespassed and done evil in the eyes of the our God; they have forsaken Him, have turned their faces away from the dwelling place of the , and turned their backs on Him" (2 Chronicles 29:6).

Unlike Ahaz, Hezekiah loved God with all his heart; his most precious desire was to glorify Him (v. 10). As such, Hezekiah destroyed all of the pagan altars and idols (2 Kings 18:4) and raised up the abandoned temple of the living God (2 Chronicles 29:3–19). Neither did he do this alone but encouraged his people along the same path, gathering God's priests, those in positions of authority, and the general public to participate in and contribute to this renewed worship of God.

It was a difficult period. Not all his subjects had the king's same zeal; some even openly jeered at his attempts (30:10). But Hezekiah stayed his course, and the Lord blessed his faithfulness (2 Kings 18:7). The king also eventually succeeded in reinstating sanctuary services, even celebrating the Passover.

But it was not only an internal enemy; Hezekiah also stood against a foreign adversary. During his father's reign, the ancient Assyrian Empire had subjugated the kingdom of Judah as one of its vassals. Against this did Hezekiah openly rebel, provoking a fierce onslaught from the Assyrians. At one point Hezekiah faltered, attempting to appease Sennacherib the king of Assyria with tribute (2 Kings 18:14–16). But Sennacherib was not satisfied; he wanted blood. Hezekiah's defeat seemed inevitable.

Reflect: Are you locked into a certain role, job, or future because of your parents or culture? Remember that we are each made new in Christ (2 Corinthians 5:17). Seek God's design for your life! It will be much more adventurous and fulfilling.

Dig Deeper: Ecclesiastes 3:10, 11; Isaiah 43:18, 19; Revelation 21:5

Hezekiah

Missed Opportunities, Part 2

"They have seen all that is in my house; there is nothing among my treasures that I have not shown them" (2 Kings 20:15).

Legend has it that in 1519, Spaniard Hernán Cortés imprisoned the Aztec emperor Montezuma II, raided Tenochtitlán, the Aztec capital, and oppressed the Aztec people—all because of a rapacious greed for the emperor's treasure. What is so powerful about riches that it can seduce even a faithful man like King Hezekiah?

While faced with the Assyrian threat, Hezekiah fell mortally ill. But after pleading with God, he was graciously granted an additional 15 years of life while also being assured of victory over the Assyrian horde (Isaiah 38:5, 6). Upon asking for a sign of these promises, Hezekiah was given the choice between two miracles and decided to ask the Lord to decrease the time of day. The Lord did as Hezekiah asked (2 Kings 20:8–11).

Word that the solar phenomenon was associated with Hezekiah's recovery reached Merodach-Baladan, the Babylonian king, who then sent ambassadors to Judah. But the arrival of the foreign visitors succeeded only in sparking Hezekiah's pride (2 Chronicles 32:25). Thinking only of his own ambitions, he boasted of "all that was found among his treasures" (Isaiah 39:2) in an effort to make an ally against the Assyrians. He failed to think of it as a golden opportunity to witness of God.

The consequence, foretold by the prophet Isaiah, was sobering: All the riches that the king had eagerly showed off would one day belong to Babylon; not only that, but Judah itself would be destroyed by the very nation Hezekiah had hoped might secure its independence. Hezekiah was cowed, meekly accepting the judgment he had brought upon his entire kingdom (2 Kings 20:19). He had not trusted in God at a time when he was most indebted to Him.

When the Assyrian army once more encamped about Jerusalem, the king had learned his lesson. His sole response was to fall down in prayer: "Now therefore, O our God," said he, "save us from [the king of Assyria's] hand, that all the kingdoms of the earth may know that You are the , You alone" (Isaiah 37:20).

His plea was granted in a fearsome miracle that slew 185,000 of the Assyrian army (v. 36). And Judah was once more spared because of the Lord's mercy and the renewed humility of his servant Hezekiah.

Reflect: What opportunities have you missed? Are you focused on what you can do rather than on what God has done for you?

Dig Deeper: Isaiah 64:6; Jeremiah 9:23, 24; Galatians 6:14

Chris

Lost Boy, Part 1

> **"Not many days after, the younger son gathered all together, journeyed to a far country, and there wasted his possessions with prodigal living" (Luke 15:13).**

By the time he was just 27 years old, Chris had escaped death more than three times. Once was at a drug deal gone bad; another was losing control of his car while drugged up and speeding; another was blacking out while in water. But his life was spared all three times. Why?

Like all Hutterites, Chris was raised in an isolated, rural community that strictly enforced study of the Bible. He was required to attend church daily and to memorize Scripture. As a child, he loved the stories of the Bible, but as he grew older, he began to hate his life: the rules, the order, the discipline—and especially his religion. He wanted out.

At seventeen, he got out. He ran away. Within a year he became addicted to sex and drugs. "Nothing mattered," Chris says. "The only emotion I knew was 'whatever.'" His daily life was a see-saw between getting high and coming down. To feed his addiction, he dealt drugs and even became a drug mule. He had become a cold-hearted creature.

He fathered three children and later married their mother. But none of them, neither his wife nor his children, knew of his addiction to drugs. On his wedding day, he got so high he nearly fainted in front of the judge and the guests. Over the next few years, he abandoned his wife and children three times, paranoid that they would find out about his addictions. But he was drastically losing control.

One morning, he woke up screaming and threatening to kill his wife, thinking she had been angry at him—when it had all been a dream. He had no relationship with his children. He cared for nothing but drugs. He did not want to be the person that he was, but he could not stop himself. He was dying, and he was digging his own grave.

It was at this point, broken, barren, and beaten, that Chris knelt down. In the darkness and the cold, outside of the home and away from the family that he was about to lose, he prayed, "If you are real, God, I need your help."

Reflect: Is there one area of your life that is out of control? Jesus can help you gain control. But you must completely surrender your heart to Him. Are you ready?

Dig Deeper: Ezekiel 34:16; Luke 19:10; Jude 1:22, 23

Chris

Lost Boy, Part 2

"For this my son was dead and is alive again; he was lost and is found" (Luke 15:24).

Chris was a desperate drug addict who cried out to God for help. And his prayer was answered. God did help him. First, God gave Chris the courage to finally admit to his wife his many addictions. Second, his wife did not leave him; she stayed and helped him recover. "She quarantined me in our bedroom for a week [until] I came down," Chris recalls. During that week he became suicidal, but yet again God spared his life. And within months, Chris stopped using drugs for good.

Then came the most beautiful gift of all. He was given a Bible. As he turned its pages, rereading the stories he—it seemed so long ago—used to love, he was changed. It was as though for the first time in his life, he was given the gift of life.

He made friends with his neighbors, God-fearing Sabbath-keepers who introduced him to Amazing Facts. While at their home and watching a sermon by Pastor Doug, Chris saw the free offer for the *Hidden Truth* magazine. With the help of his newfound friends, he ordered the magazine. He began to search for other Amazing Facts programs and loved going through the *Amazing Facts Bible Study Guides*.

Chris was inspired to learn and understand more of this God who gives second chances, who restores breaches, who gives us hearts of flesh. Chris now has his very own relationship with God.

"I started feeling emotions I had long forgotten," Chris says—feelings of joy and peace but also guilt and anguish for the hurt he had caused and the family he had ruined. He wanted, for the first time, to have a genuine relationship with them. As he spent more time with God, he also spent more time with his wife and his three children. His growing love for God created in him a desire to be a loving husband and a loving father.

When he thought of Jesus on the cross, he knew the reason that his life had been spared so many times. It was because Jesus, the Messiah, had come to save people like him. No longer was his one desire for himself, for that next high that never satisfies; now Chris' desire is to share Christ with everyone he meets—and most of all with his family.

Reflect: Have you ever observed someone's life being changed by the Bible? Nothing is more thrilling than helping someone discover Jesus. Go share Him with someone today!

Dig Deeper: Isaiah 43:19; Romans 6:4; 2 Corinthians 5:17

Moishe Rosen

A "Jew for Jesus" Is Born, Part 1

"And He said to them, 'What things?' So they said to Him, 'The things concerning Jesus of Nazareth, who was a Prophet mighty in deed and word before God and all the people ...'" (Luke 24:19).

Martin Meyer Rosen, later known as Moishe, was a "secular Jew" who grew up in Denver. A young woman from Boston, Ceilia Starr, moved into the neighborhood and caught his eye: "She was the prettiest girl in the neighborhood," he would later recall.

By the time she was 16, Ceilia Starr had, in hear heart, declared herself an atheist, rebelling against her orthodox Jewish upbringing. Moishe was a self-described agnostic. The non-faith of young Rosen came as little surprise: he was the not-very-Jewish son of not-very-Jewish parents. A family sporting goods business was more important than activity in a local synagogue, he'd later recall.

The two dated and fell in love. By the time they were 18 years old, Martin Rosen and Ceilia Starr were married. A rabbi conducted the ceremony, even though the couple vowed to be "modern American Jews," eschewing Sabbath rules, dietary restrictions, and other trappings.

Marriage changed things: "When Ceil was pregnant with our first child, she began to wonder about God. She knew there had to be more out there," Rosen said.

Ceilia found answers in reading the New Testament, a book of Scripture generally regarded as "unneeded" by or "off limits" to Jewish people. Mrs. Rosen "discovered that the New Testament was also a Jewish book involving Jewish people, but most of all about the Jewish Messiah," her husband said. Needing further help, Ceilia was visited by a woman from the American Board of Missions to the Jews after the young wife prayed for someone to help her understand the Bible.

This change provoked Martin to wrath. He argued against her, ridiculed the content of some tracts she'd given him, and generally resisted—until he could no longer. Reading the Bible, recalling earlier encounters with Christians who linked Jesus with the Messiah's Jewish roots, Rosen became convinced: he, too, had to follow Christ.

This led to ostracism in their families, a difficult time (to say the least) at the sporting goods store where he worked, and finally a conviction: if Martin Meyer Rosen could find faith, how would other Jews discover the very Jewish prophet named Jesus?

That led to the next chapter of Rosen's life, and it was one that would reshape American evangelism for decades.

Reflect: Have you—or someone you know—suffered in your family because of your faith? How did you respond to the hostility or estrangement?

Dig Deeper: Matthew 21:46; John 6:14; Acts 7:37

Moishe Rosen

A "Jew for Jesus" is Born, Part 2

"Jesus answered and said to him, 'Most assuredly, I say to you, unless one is born again, he cannot see the kingdom of God'" (John 3:3).

After his conversion, Moishe Rosen—then known as Martin—began witnessing to everyone in sight, with predictable consequences. His family essentially disowned him. Bosses and co-workers were hostile. And at the Baptist church he and his wife attended in Denver, various elements of the culture were, to say the least, unfamiliar. Jewish practices and 1950s-era Protestantism had few points of intersection.

Rosen felt a need to change things. He studied at a New Jersey Bible college, and then spent close to 20 years with the American Board of Missions to the Jews, the oldest such evangelistic group in the U.S., now known as Chosen People Ministries.

But long-established missionary groups, however laudable, can become hidebound by tradition. So Rosen struck out on his own, determined to bring the message of Jesus to a generation of young adult seekers—called "hippies" by many—who wouldn't warm to a suit-and-tie presentation.

Rosen and his new missionaries struck out in jeans and t-shirts, the latter emblazoned with phrases such as "Jesus Made Me Kosher." Instead of staid tracts bearing platitudes about heaven, Rosen created "broadsides," informal pamphlets with Jewish jargon and a sense of humor. Finding Jesus wasn't betrayal; it was logical and the search for truth could be fun!

Much of the attention Rosen's followers attracted came from these unconventional steps. Even the name Jews for Jesus was meant to startle. When the opposition got rough, Rosen's troops often received lots of media coverage, which in turn generated questions from those who would be called "seekers."

The public nature of Jews for Jesus' evangelism took hold, particularly when the Supreme Court of the United States ruled that a county ordinance prohibiting witnessing at Los Angeles International Airport was unconstitutional. The ruling put Rosen's movement in the history books.

Unlike some whose leadership of religious groups generate notoriety and public attention, Moishe Rosen didn't attain great wealth. Jews for Jesus has been open and accountable about its finances, and when the time came for Rosen to step out of leadership, an orderly process was in place to find a successor.

Moishe Rosen led a career of preaching the message of Jesus that made an impact on his generation and far beyond.

Reflect: What ministries do you know that are reaching the world in a unique manner? What can you do to reach the world around your home?

Dig Deeper: Colossians 2:13; Ephesians 2:5, 6; 1 Peter 1:2–4

Captivated by Truth

"[The Bereans] received the word with all readiness, and searched the Scriptures daily to find out whether these things were so" (Acts 17:11).

Treva grew up a Catholic, but decided to investigate many other denominations in her search for truth. After a friend told Treva about Roku, a device which offers thousands of channels, she immediately bought this product and began adding channels to her television, including Amazing Facts Television. "At the time," she admits, "I had no idea what AFTV was. I thought it was a branch of the Discovery Channel."

Treva began watching AFTV and was intrigued and captivated by all the biblical truths she had never before heard. As she continued to watch and learn, she heard Doug Batchelor preach about the Sabbath. "I was stunned!" she says. "From that point on, I began to read my Bible like never before; I studied the Word of God with so much passion and rigor that I began to watch AFTV night and day with my Bible by my side."

Looking up the Bible references for herself, she discovered what the Bible teaches about subjects like heaven and hell, health, and baptism. The two most compelling topics for her are the three angels' messages and the cleansing of the temple.

Eager to share her passion for Christ with others, Treva took classes from an evangelism training center that prepares individuals in Bible work, health evangelism, and public evangelism.

Treva loves to share Bible truth with others. She and a group of other church members have created an evangelism ministry called "Knock, Knock." Based on Revelation 3:20, the group goes door to door in the community sharing the good news of Jesus and His soon return. They hand out Lesson #1 of the *Amazing Facts Bible Study Guides* called "Is There Anything Left You Can Trust?" She explains how this title is a great conversation starter, considering today's troubled times.

To those who may be searching for truth, Treva shares, "Everyone should read the Bible for themselves and embark on a personal study of God's Word. If someone is searching for truth, they should go to God in prayer first. Jesus explains in Matthew 7:7 that all we have to do is ask."

That's exactly what Treva did when she was led to—and captivated by—pure Bible truth.

Reflect: Do you search the Scriptures daily? Have you diligently studied the Bible for yourself to determine if the messages you hear coincide with the Word of God?

Dig Deeper: Romans 2:19–24; 1 Thessalonians 5:21; 2 Timothy 4:3, 4

Naaman

The Leprous Captain, Part 1

"Many lepers were in Israel in the time of Elisha the prophet, and none of them was cleansed except Naaman the Syrian" (Luke 4:27).

Leprosy, the dreaded disease so prevalent in the Bible, still exists today, though its definition has changed drastically. Now called Hansen's disease, it refers to a specific type of bacterial infection treatable by antibiotics and much less contagious. The leprosy of the Bible was a different kind of monster—it was a death sentence. And like death, it was no respecter of persons.

Naaman was a very prestigious personage in ancient Syria. A war hero renowned for his bravery and honor, he was a captain of the Syrian army, wealthy, well-respected, and highly valued by Benhadad, the king (2 Kings 5:1). One would think that his was the epitome of a charmed life, except for one extremely important detail—Naaman was a leper.

This was not the kind of disease that stayed locked behind closed doors, a family secret, a skeleton in the closet. Everyone saw this; everyone knew what it meant—even the little captive slave girl that Naaman had brought back for his wife during one of his battles against the kingdom of Israel.

One day, the little slave, she of a pure, compassionate heart, told Naaman's wife of a prophet in her homeland, a man used mightily by the true God who would be able to cure her master (v. 3). And Naaman and his wife believed her. What trust they must have had in the little Israelite, and how powerful a testament to her character and to the work God had done in her young heart!

So, with consent and letters of introduction from Benhadad himself, Naaman journeyed to Israel in search of this prophet. After an audience with Joram, king in Israel, who, if not for the prophet's own interception, might have faithlessly spoiled the Syrian's purpose, Naaman was led directly to the door of Elisha, the very man of whom his servant girl had spoken (vv. 6–9). There he arrived with his splendor and his entourage and bearing a mountain of payment in gold, silver, and clothing (v. 5).

Now the moment of truth had come. Who was this great prophet who could perform so great a miracle?

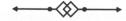

Reflect: How can we find blessings through our physical ailments? Why is it that we seem to seek after God more often and more consistently when we are physically distressed?

Dig Deeper: Exodus 15:26; Psalm 107:19–21; 2 Corinthians 12:7–10

Naaman

The Leprous Captain, Part 2

**"[F]or your servant will no longer offer either burnt offering
or sacrifice to other gods, but to the " (2 Kings 5:17).**

Naaman was about to be tested. In lieu of Elisha, there came a messenger with specific instructions: "Go and wash in the Jordan seven times, and your flesh shall be restored to you, and you shall be clean" (2 Kings 5:10).

Naaman was livid. He had come all this way, and this plebeian could not even spare the time to see him (v. 11)? Then, to add insult to injury, he was expected to *bathe* in that filthy excuse for a river (v. 12)? Was he so degraded that a sewage dump was better than he?

Infuriated, he started for home. But Naaman was generally a reasonable man, and his entourage knew that. It was his pride that had been wounded, nothing more. So they began to talk some sense back into him.

"My father," said his servants, "if the prophet had told you to do something great, would you not have done it? How much more then, when he says to you, 'Wash, and be clean'?" (v. 13).

And Naaman had to admit they were correct. He saw now that it had been his own ego which had gotten in the way of his own well-being.

So he went to the Jordan River and did all that the prophet had commanded—and was healed (v. 14). Amazed, he rushed back to the prophet's home. This time, Elisha came out to meet him.

"Indeed," exclaimed Naaman, "now I know that there is no God in all the earth, except in Israel" (v. 15).

He knew it was not the river itself nor the ritual nor even the prophet who had cured his leprosy. Instantly, Elisha's God became his God (v. 17). A new convert, he still had much to learn, for one, that God's miracles were free gifts, not transactions (v. 16); and he would still have much with which to contend upon his return home to a people and king who worshipped false gods (v. 18). But Naaman had proved in his heart to be a man who sought truth, a man who was willing to admit his faults, a man who would give his all to God.

We know not what happened to Naaman after he returned to Syria, but his genuine conversion was singled out by the Messiah Himself (Luke 4:27).

Reflect: Are you in a position of authority? Are you willing to learn from others, even your subordinates? Remember, "Pride goes before destruction ..." (Proverbs 16:18).

Dig Deeper: Psalm 25:8–10; Proverbs 9:9, 10; 2 Timothy 2:2

Wendy

Finding Faith Again, Part 1

"My eye wastes away because of affliction ..." (Psalm 88:9).

Wendy fondly remembers the little ranch where she and her husband reared their twin daughters. Their close-knit family spent many days enjoying nature while caring for their horses, goats, and chickens. They also attended church together every Sunday.

"Life was very good," Wendy recalls of those early years. But at the time, she had no idea her faith was about to be shattered into a million pieces.

Wendy started every day by setting aside thirty minutes to spend with God, reading her Bible and praying. Her practice was to read through the Bible, chapter by chapter—even the parts that didn't always seem clear.

Death first touched their family when Wendy's mom passed away after a lengthy battle with cancer. Wendy grieved, but she had no idea of the wrenching trials she would face just in a short time.

Just a few years later, her husband went to bed one night as usual, set his alarm to get up for work the next day, and fell asleep. In the middle of the night, he began gasping for air. Wendy woke up and immediately called 9-1-1. The paramedics came, but just 30 minutes later, her husband of 26 years was pronounced dead. "My faith took a huge hit," she recalls, "but this was only the beginning of my trials."

Without her husband's income, and with only a part-time job, Wendy lost her health insurance. A month later, she received notice that her home was in foreclosure.

Within two weeks, her mother-in-law passed away. And just two weeks after that, Wendy received a phone call that her dad had been taken to the hospital. He was placed in hospice care and passed away less than ten days later. Wendy was devastated.

"After each loss, I managed to maintain my faith—until Dad was lying on his death bed." After so many losses, her faith was shattered. "I couldn't see how there could be a God." She began to think that a loving God was a lie. "My whole life had been a lie. My faith died."

Standing by her father after he passed, Wendy began to cry. The hospice worker tried to comfort her with words of faith, but Wendy told her that her faith was gone.

Reflect: Have you ever suffered a devastating loss? Do you know what it feels like to have your world shatter into a million pieces? You can feel the pain of others ... and have empathy like no one else.

Dig Deeper: Psalm 34:18; Ecclesiastes 3:1; John 11:35

Wendy

Finding Faith Again, Part 2

"Weeping may endure for a night, but joy comes in the morning" (Psalm 30:5).

After suffering several devastating losses, Wendy had no idea where to go next. So she turned back to the Bible and the foundation of faith her parents instilled in her so many years ago. Bit by bit, she saw God leading in her life again as He brought her to a new home and a new job.

And after a time, God sent an old friend with a new blessing.

"I first heard about Amazing Facts because a friend of mine had been following Pastor Doug for about 25 years," she explains. He showed Wendy a couple of sermons on YouTube. Not only did she find them informative, but they answered many of her Bible questions. "They were so uplifting and encouraging."

Pastor Doug's sermons transformed Wendy's views of God, Jesus, redemption, forgiveness, lifestyle, and her daily walk with Jesus. "It's as if the truth was just laid out in front of me," she remembers.

Wendy particularly appreciated the teachings that came straight from Scripture and made things so simple. "Amazing Facts lays everything out so clearly," she says. "With my morning devotional time, I would read the Bible over and over and have the same questions each time. Pastor Doug has brought clarity to so many passages that it has changed the way I read my morning devotional each and every day."

Wendy found a new relationship with Jesus. "I always had faith at some level, but Amazing Facts has literally made Jesus come alive to me." He was no longer simply a character in the Bible, but a real and tangible person. "I have a whole new relationship with Jesus, rather than just having a religion."

Her life today is nothing like she'd ever pictured, yet Wendy knows that God prepared a way of help and healing for her—a plan to bring her through the disasters she faced. "I know Satan tried to destroy me and hit me with everything he had. But by the grace of God and the strength of Jesus, he failed. My faith is now even stronger than before."

Reflect: Do you know someone who has suffered deep trials, yet they have become stronger through their sufferings? God is able to turn our sorrows into joy.

Dig Deeper: Isaiah 53:4, 5; Matthew 11:28; 1 Thessalonians 4:15

William J. Murray

The Atheist "Royalty" Member Who Found Jesus, Part 1

"[Y]ou will seek Me and find Me, when you search for Me with all your heart" (Jeremiah 29:13).

During the 1960s and 1970s, a woman named Madalyn Murray O'Hair was something of a celebrity in the United States, appearing on television talk shows and popping up in newspaper articles on a regular basis.

O'Hair wasn't a movie star or a soap-opera actress. Instead, the chain-smoking O'Hair was matriarch of a famous family of atheists, "royalty" among the non-believers, in particular her oldest son, William J. Murray, whose protest of prayer and Bible reading at a Baltimore, Maryland public junior high school led to the banning of such practices by the Supreme Court of the United States.

William J. Murray, about 14 when his mother's lawsuit against the Baltimore schools began—educators had refused to exempt the boy from the schoolroom religious exercises—grew up in a home filled with strife. His father, a wealthy, already-married New Yorker who met Madalyn at the end of the Second World War, only saw the boy once. Madalyn had a second son, Garth, out of wedlock with yet another man. There was no Christian influence in the home to speak of, and Madalyn's mother dabbled in the occult and claimed psychic powers.

The lawsuit brought by Madalyn and William J. Murray was consolidated with another case before the Supreme Court, *Abington School District v. Schempp*. On June 17, 1963, eight of the nine justices ruled in favor of the anti-religion plaintiffs. Only Associate Justice Potter Stewart supported the school boards.

Critics charged the ruling fueled an increased secularization of public education and a rise in unwanted behaviors. Atheists, and some others, cheered at the "eviction" of God from the nation's classrooms.

But young William J. Murray had other things on his mind. He was in a science-oriented high school by the time of the court decision, still an atheist, and looking forward to the future. His mother had turned her anti-school prayer crusade into an organization, American Atheists, and donations poured in from across the land. The group rented an office, printed a magazine, and hired student William J. Murray to operate the printing press at a salary of $50 per week.

In less than 20 years after making history, however, William J. Murray's life would turn in a totally different direction.

Reflect: Standing up for "principles" can have negative effects on a society, as well as positive ones. What principles are you willing to take a stand for—and have you weighed the consequences?

Dig Deeper: Psalm 14:1; Romans 1:18, 19; 1 Corinthians 2:14

William J. Murray

The Atheist "Royalty" Member
Who Found Jesus, Part 2

**"Seek the and His strength; seek His face
evermore!" (1 Chronicles 16:11)**

On one level, William J. Murray had it made: For some time, his income was funded by American Atheists, the organization founded by his mother, Madalyn Murray O'Hair. Then, he got into airline work, rising into management positions where he could be more anonymous than his "atheist royalty" status might have suggested.

William, after all, had been a plaintiff in a Maryland lawsuit that led to the removal of Bible readings and prayers from the nation's public schools. But years in the spotlight, and under the thumb of an abusive, erratic mother, took its toll on William. His first marriage ended in divorce, his daughter from that marriage adopted by Madalyn, who raised the child as an atheist. His second marriage was in trouble. And alcohol, which Murray once saw as a balm, took over his life with devastating consequences.

"I drank a quart of vodka a day and by the time I was thirty I had been married twice," Murray would later recall. "I turned to a twelve-step program to stop the drinking and there found my first awareness of a loving God. Yet that God had no name," he added.

Reading the Bible led him to a saving relationship with Jesus Christ. On Mother's Day in 1980, Murray came out publicly as a Christian, earning this rebuke from the mother he'd not spoken with in years: "I repudiate him entirely and completely for now and all times. He is beyond human forgiveness."

As part of his new evangelism, Murray—who became a Baptist preacher—spoke out about his mother's abuses and excesses, most notably in a memoir, *My Life Without God*, and by speaking across the country. When asked why he opposed her publicly, he said, "I soon found out it was impossible to tell the story without the truth."

Sadly, Madalyn Murray O'Hair's story did not end well: An employee of American Atheists kidnapped her, William's daughter Robin, and his brother, Garth. After obtaining $500,000 in gold coins from the family, the employee and an accomplice killed all three.

Today, William J. Murray lives secure in God's love, and works to guarantee religious freedom for persecuted Christians in other nations. He also lobbies to overturn the Bible-reading-in-school bans that his landmark case created.

Reflect: Finding God and receiving Jesus as Savior changed the course of William Murray's life, and for the better. Do you have (or know of) a similar "radical" conversion story?

Dig Deeper: Lamentations 3:25; Zephaniah 2:3; Acts 17:26, 27

Dan

God's Mirror, Part 1

"He who covers his sins will not prosper, but whoever confesses and forsakes them will have mercy" (Proverbs 28:13).

Years ago, Dan sat in a jail visiting room looking at his mother in disbelief. She'd become a Sabbath-keeper, it seems, and was now urging him to give up pork. She even brought him a pamphlet.

Detained on a marijuana charge, Dan knew how much she loved him and he always listened respectfully when she shared her Christian faith during these visits. But Dan recalls, "I said, 'Mom, pork is all they serve in here—breakfast, lunch, and dinner! I'll starve to death.'" Still, she told him that God would protect him and that he needed to trust Him. That day, Dan stopped eating pork. "I was a huge bacon fan, so that wasn't easy," he says, laughing.

However, once he was out of jail, many of Dan's decisions took him in a starkly opposite direction from his mother's Christian values. For years, he pursued a lifestyle filled with the trappings of the world, including drugs and alcohol.

Then Dan suffered a job accident that resulted in serious injury and pain. When he realized doctors would never be able to fully restore him, he descended into depression. His increased anxiety and daily pain led to even worse substance abuse.

During this dark time, Dan's brother gave him a book about Christ's life, and his sister-in-law suggested he might like listening to a speaker named Doug Batchelor. "I had a lot of time on my hands, so I started watching Amazing Facts," he shares.

Dan went to the Amazing Facts website and began watching "literally hundreds of videos," he estimates. "Pastor Doug has a way of teaching that really captures your attention, and keeps you listening, and makes you think."

But a turning point came when Dan watched an Amazing Facts video on the Ten Commandments. In that message, Pastor Doug used a mirror to illustrate how God's law shows us our sin but that it cannot save us. When the message finished, Dan walked outside. "I started crying," he says. "I was overwhelmed. I realized that I was living in sin, that nearly everything I'd been doing was sin."

In that moment, everything around him seemed to disappear. "I was alone and talking to God." He began to confess all of his sins, asking God to forgive him.

Reflect: Have you ever been so convicted by sin in your life that you actually cried tears of despair? God wants your heart to be broken, so He can make it all new.

Dig Deeper: Psalm 32:5; Matthew 5:4; 1 John 1:9

Dan

God's Mirror, Part 2

> "When [Peter] saw that the wind was boisterous,
> he was afraid; and beginning to sink he cried out,
> saying, 'Lord, save me!'" (Matthew 14:30).

When Dan's heart broke and he acknowledged his sins, the Lord forgave him. He then began attending church with his brother and sister-in-law. And through Bible studies, Dan came to know God in a personal way. It was time to get off the fence and make a decision. "I knew what my sins were. I knew how they had governed my life. God's words were impossible to deny." He made a firm decision to quit drinking alcohol and using drugs and, a few months later, Dan was baptized.

But he didn't know that God had a deeper story still to write in his life.

"The journey of sanctification is not a smooth one," Dan says. "I thought that after I stopped using and got baptized, I was on the road to success and happiness."

But a few years later, while overseas, Dan experienced another serious injury. Once more, he was having to deal with excruciating pain. "I started using again," he shares. "And although I didn't stop going to church, I stopped my home studies and started crowding out the Sabbath." While his wife was shocked by his changes, Dan simply couldn't quit.

Yet once more, God used Amazing Facts to speak to Dan's heart. "I watched Pastor Doug's video about Peter walking on water. But then he turned his face away from Jesus and started to sink. He cried out, 'Save me!'"

Dan realized that he'd turned his eyes away from Jesus after his accident, and that he had started sinking. "Once I realized that I was Peter, I knew I had to turn back to Jesus. I got down on my knees and prayed for the Lord to take Satan's temptations away and give me strength through His Holy Spirit."

Dan has a special message for those who struggle with sin. "When you find yourself growing weak and looking back at the world and you feel yourself sinking, that's when you need to realize that you have the freedom turn away, to look back at Jesus. Your commitment to God is a relationship you need to work on every day. If you come to Him, He'll pick you back up out of the water."

Reflect: When you fall back into sin, are you tempted to make excuses or minimize your situation? Humbly acknowledge your absolute dependence upon God and He will save you.

Dig Deeper: Proverbs 24:16; Matthew 26:41; 1 Corinthians 10:13

"Blessed be the your God ...! Because your God has loved Israel, to establish them forever, therefore He made you king over them, to do justice and righteousness" (2 Chronicles 9:8).

The queen of Sheba is an individual shrouded in mystique, alternately portrayed as a demi-goddess, an oracle, even a kingdom. But the Bible is clear in its depiction: The foreign queen was a real woman who ruled in South Arabia and who had taken note of Israel because of its famous king.

This was during the golden age of Solomon's reign, when he was a faithful servant of God. His deeds had spread far and wide since God had given him the gift of wisdom, and it was because of this that the queen of Sheba had traveled from her distant homeland "to test him with hard questions" (1 Kings 10:1).

It was apparent from the start that the queen did not have any ulterior motive. Her visit was not a political stratagem nor an attempt at a diplomatic alliance; this was a woman who was genuinely seeking, a lady of great influence who sincerely wanted to know more about Solomon's wisdom, his way of life, his nation (2 Chronicles 9:1). What an occasion to witness of the God who gave Solomon this wisdom, who guided his steps, who was the true Ruler of Israel!

So Solomon did exactly that. All the queen's questions were answered (v. 2); and she was able to observe all the king's actions, his daily routine, his interactions with others, his religious practices (vv. 3, 4).

At the end of her visit, the queen came away with one clear picture: It was because of the God Solomon worshiped that Solomon was who he was—wise, gentle, kind. She had seen how he treated his servants, how content his subjects were (vv. 7, 8). She had seen the love of God flowing through this king and his people and that their devotion to God had resulted in an abundant life.

With a heart overflowing with gratitude, she gave to Solomon all she could—gold, gems, spices, wood (vv. 10, 11). In like manner does one when realizing the eternal gifts God has given her, she willingly gives all she is and all she has to God?

Satisfied, the queen of Sheba returned home, forever changed with a newfound knowledge of the living God.

Reflect: The queen of Sheba was touched, not by some extraordinary miracle, but by Solomon's habitual life of faith. Is your life that attractive to others?

Dig Deeper: Psalm 96:1–3; John 15:16; Hebrews 12:1, 2

Sofie
Glued to the TV

"I was hungry and you gave Me food ..." (Matthew 25:35).

Sofie never stepped inside a church during her childhood. Growing up in an abusive family, her young life was filled with turmoil, fear, disappointment, and tragedy. Her alcoholic parents often neglected her. "More times than I can count we went for several days without food," she recalls. Sometimes she went door-to-door asking for money so she and her brothers could eat.

As a young adult, Sofie experimented with smoking pot and drinking. She was filled with anger and explains, "I fought my way through life and didn't let anyone get close to me. I expressed my anger and rage toward anyone in my path." Her heart was full of hate and resentment.

Alcohol and abusive relationships left her a single parent and depressed. Several times she was homeless and had to sleep in her car with her son. People told her that God loved her, but she was angry at God for letting her suffer pain and humiliation.

But eventually Sofie began to turn to God. She was at the end of her rope and cried out, "Jesus, if You want to change me, here is my life. It is Yours to do with whatever You please." Slowly she found that her vocabulary became clean. Then she met a Christian man and together they grew in their faith.

One Sunday morning before heading off to church, Sofie was surfing the TV and came upon Pastor Doug Batchelor. "I found myself glued to every word he was speaking," she remembers. The church she was attending left her hungry for more of the Word of God. "I felt like something was missing in my life." When she heard Pastor Doug preaching, she immediately knew this was the answer.

Sofie signed up for Bible studies and completed the *Storacles of Prophecy* lessons. She loved going through the materials and says, "I wish I could study 24 hours a day!" The lessons opened her eyes to truth and confirmed in her heart that "with God all things are possible" (Mark 10:27). She is now a baptized member of a Sabbath-keeping church.

Today Sofie is actively sharing her faith by holding Bible studies in her home and conducting a motorcycle ministry with her husband. "I'm so in love with the Lord," she shares, "that I could spend all day in His Word!"

Reflect: Do you find yourself glued to the Word of God? Do you hunger to learn more from the Bible each day? Only the Scriptures understood through the Holy Spirit can satisfy your deepest longings.

Dig Deeper: Psalm 34:8; Matthew 5:6; Revelation 7:16

Krishna Pal

The First Indian Convert, Part 1

"How then shall they call on Him in whom they have not believed? And how shall they believe in Him of whom they have not heard? And how shall they hear without a preacher? And how shall they preach unless they are sent?" (Romans 10:14, 15).

In the 1800s, the caste system in India was a powerful mechanism rooted in the belief of reincarnation, where a person would be born into a higher social order (a better caste) depending upon the manner in which he lived his former life.

Krishna Pal was a carpenter living at the turn of the 19th century in Serampore, then a Danish colony in India. He had married within his caste, and his four children were expected to grow up in that same caste.

But one day, while bathing, Pal slipped and broke his arm. So he visited a doctor by the name of John Thomas, a Baptist missionary. After setting his arm, Dr. Thomas began to share, in Pal's own language of Bengali, of something worse than breaking one's arm, worse than any other physical disease out there. Its name was sin, and it had infected every person who had ever lived. But there was good news: God, our Great Physician, had sent a Cure.

Pal was visibly moved. Large tears began rolling down his brown cheeks. He had heard a Christian preach before, earlier that year in the middle of a public market; and he himself, by nature of his trade, had worked previously for the missionaries. Since then, the Holy Spirit had been working on his heart. Pal acknowledged that he had indeed been infected by this disease of sin; he was a cheater, a liar, and much, much worse! But he did not want to be those things anymore.

More missionaries came to visit him, including William Carey, founder of the Baptist Missionary Society, and the good doctor again. Pal was also given something to read. It was the gospel in short form; this too had been translated into his native language. It told of Someone named the Christ, who had saved all people from their sins—even Hindus like him. This Christ, He was the Cure who had been sent!

Pal wanted to learn more.

Reflect: Where and to whom is your mission within your profession? If you are unclear, get down on your knees and ask God to show you.

Dig Deeper: Psalm 96:2, 3; Isaiah 52:7; Acts 13:47–49

> "[T]here is neither Greek nor Jew, circumcised nor uncircumcised, barbarian, Scythian, slave nor free, but Christ is all and in all" (Colossians 3:11).

In Krishna Pal's lifetime, segregation between India's different castes was severe, notable through three different types of public events: marriages, mealtimes, and worship services. For example, it was considered reprehensible for a person of a higher caste to receive food from someone in a lower caste.

After his arm healed, Pal began to study regularly with the Baptist missionaries. Around this time, several books of the Bible, the whole of it having been translated into Bengali by William Carey himself, were now being printed in India. The Indians could now read the gospel for themselves.

Moreover, Pal did not attend his studies alone, also bringing with him his wife and her sister. Eventually, all three believed the Bible to be the express Word of God, that in its precious pages lay universal truths that were to be upheld over the dictates of men, over culture, over tradition.

As such, Pal did the unthinkable: He sat down to a meal with his new missionary friends. It was a public declaration of his faith in the gospel and his belief in a new religion, Christianity. It was, in effect, a deliberate breaking of caste. Pal understood the freedom which the gospel gave, and he now threw off the chains which it had broken. No more separated by a hierarchy of hate, brother ate with brother—each a part of one body, of which Christ is the head (1 Corinthians 12:27; Colossians 1:18). As Christ Himself taught, "One is your Teacher, the Christ, and you are all brethren" (Matthew 23:8).

For this simple act, Pal was condemned by some 2,000 of his neighbors, and he and his family were imprisoned and then released. All this caused his family great fear so that on December 28, 1800, only Pal, along with William Carey's own son, went down into the water to be born anew. He was the first Baptist convert in India.

Using his skill as a carpenter, Pal went on to build a church across the street from his home. Eventually, he became an evangelist as well as a hymnist. He also finally saw the rest of his family baptized in Jesus Christ.

Reflect: What cultural traditions are important to you? How do they hold up against biblical doctrine?

Dig Deeper: Psalm 22:27, 28; Mark 7:7–9; Ephesians 3:6

Vincent and Britny

Healed and Forgiven, Part 1

"Do not rejoice over me, my enemy; when I fall, I will arise; when I sit in darkness, the will be a light to me" (Micah 7:8).

Vincent grew up Catholic and never had a relationship with Christ. Actually, he was never really interested in knowing Jesus at all. When he was 18, he joined the military and was swept away with the world.

He remembers, "I always had on my headphones, listening to satanic music with lyrics that literally blasphemed Christ. One day, while listening to this music, I decided to carve 666 into my knuckles on my left hand, on the index, middle, and ring fingers. I cut deep enough to make sure the scars stayed on my fingers."

Britny, his wife, grew up with a Baptist mother and a Catholic father. She went back and forth between the two, very confused as to which religion would work best for her. "I still remember as a 7-year-old sitting on our front porch singing to God and talking with Jesus. I felt such love for my Heavenly Father at a young age. It filled a void left by my absent father who never had time for me."

Around the age of 14, she started hanging around a crowd that was into drugs, partying, and alcohol. "I got caught up in all of this, including an addiction to prescription pills. It helped me feel numb. That's all I wanted."

Britny fell deeper and deeper into drugs. Her parents lost all control of her. "After one night of heavy partying, I was pulled over and ticketed for thousands of dollars. I was ashamed. I knew my life needed to change. I was 17 and dropped out of high school, got my GED, and started attending college."

Sometime later Vincent met Britny. He recalls, "When we first met, she saw the scars on my knuckles and freaked out. She thought it was very scary." Soon Britny was pregnant and scared. Vincent was only 19 and got an honorable discharge from the Navy. She explains, "We moved in with my parents, eventually got married, and I continued my addictions. After our daughter was born, she became so sick we took her to the hospital."

While they were at the hospital, God spoke to them ...

Reflect: Have you ever gone through a trial that turned out to be a doorway to God's leading? Every difficulty in life can be used by God for good.

Dig Deeper: Psalm 34:14; Romans 12:1, 2; 1 Peter 3:11

Vincent and Britny

Healed and Forgiven, Part 2

**"Heal me, O , and I shall be healed; save me,
and I shall be saved ..." (Jeremiah 17:14).**

While Vincent and Britny were in the hospital with their baby daughter, they shared a room with another patient. One day a chaplain came to visit their neighbor on the other side of the room. Vincent recalls, "While he was there, my wife leaned over and whispered, 'We should talk with him.' I quickly replied, 'No way!' I wanted nothing to do with him or with God." Even though Vincent felt this way, he knew the Lord was longing for him. "Well, my wife ignored my response and stepped over to ask the chaplain to come talk with us."

Britny shares, "I wanted so badly to connect with Jesus. I heard a chaplain come and speak to the people next to us and something told me that this was my chance. My husband, who was my fiancé at the time, told me not to talk to him, but I ignored him and went over and asked him to come over anyway."

She jumped right to the point and asked the chaplain, "Why is my baby sick? Why did God let this happen?" He assured her that God didn't want to see her suffer. Then he shared with the young parents some *Amazing Facts Bible Study Guides* and gave them the *Cosmic Conflict* DVD to watch. "It opened my eyes," she remembers. "It was perfect timing. Vince and I were experiencing so much stress and were on the verge of breaking up every day. I knew that I no longer wanted to live without God."

The chaplain began Bible studies right in the hospital. They completed the series, their daughter recovered, and a few months later both were baptized.

Not long afterwards Vincent had an experience that taught him the depth of God's forgiveness. "My wife noticed that the scars on my fingers were completely gone! The Lord healed my hand from a terrible thing I did against Him. God knew of my struggle to feel forgiven and removed the marks. I felt like the paralytic who was both physically healed and also told, 'Your sins are forgiven!'"

Britny says, "We turned our lives over to Christ and were baptized together and then we were married the following day. Now the only addiction I have is Christ."

Reflect: Do you know someone who is fighting to get away from God, yet this person wants to experience genuine healing from heaven? Pray and reach out to that person today.

Dig Deeper: Psalm 103:2, 4; Jeremiah 33:6; James 5:16

Onesimus

Runaway Slave

> **"For perhaps he departed for a while for this purpose, that you might receive him forever, no longer as a slave but more than a slave—a beloved brother" (Philemon 15, 16).**

In the early Christian church, slavery was prevalent. For every free man, there were three slaves. One historical account records a man by the name of Caecilius as having owned 4,116 slaves. A slave could not marry or own anything. A slave could be tortured in his master's stead during a criminal investigation. And if a slave dared to run away from his master, the punishment, if he were ever caught again, was death.

Onesimus was a slave who belonged to a man named Philemon, a Christian residing in Colossae. For reasons unknown, Onesimus had run away with some of his master's possessions in tow (Philemon 18). All that he was, all that he had, all that he acquired and earned was for his master's gain alone. Why shouldn't he have a better life that he could call his own?

Somehow, Onesimus ended up in Rome. Perhaps he thought that the big city was the best chance he had of starting a new life, some 1,400 miles away from Philemon. But his master's goods went only so far. One thing led to another, and Onesimus finally found himself in the company of the apostle Paul, who at the time was imprisoned in Rome (v. 1). It turned out to be a divine intervention.

The apostle taught him of the gospel, of Jesus Christ, his Savior and Redeemer. Onesimus' heart was moved. He saw now that he had been wrong to rob his master and leave as he did. He gave his heart to Christ, asking for forgiveness (v. 10).

As a result, he began to change. No longer were his actions focused on bettering his own situation, but he became an especial comfort to Paul, tending to the older apostle's needs during his confinement (v. 13).

When Paul requested that the escaped slave return home to Philemon, Onesimus obliged (v. 12). He would willingly return to slavery in order to right his wrongs. If his master, though a Christian, decided to put him to death for running away, so be it. He was a changed man, and he would live his life like one, as a laborer for Christ (Colossians 4:9).

Reflect: Knowing the institution of slavery to be altogether reprehensible, would you have done the same as Onesimus if you were in his position? As Christians, how are we to act in unjust situations?

Dig Deeper: Isaiah 1:16, 17; Titus 2:9, 10; 1 Peter 2:18–24

Daniel

Super Hero for Christ, Part 1

"God did not send His Son into the world to condemn the world, but that the world through Him might be saved" (John 3:17).

Like thousands of boys, Daniel grew up fascinated by Superman. He spent virtually every minute of his free time either watching Superman's exciting adventures on TV, or pretending to be the hero himself.

As he ran around his house playing the starring role, Daniel enjoyed a significant advantage that most people didn't have—his grandmother was a fantastic seamstress. Wearing her realistic custom-made costumes, and armed with his vivid imagination, Daniel leaped and flew triumphantly from one crisis to another.

"I loved doing all the actions!" he says, smiling. "I carried this epic picture of myself fighting the forces of darkness—conquering the bad guy, and saving the world. I wanted to be good and stand for what was right."

When Daniel started high school, he asked a pretty girl named Leanna to be his girlfriend. He was thrilled when she said yes. As they grew closer, Leanna gave Daniel a simple gift that changed his life: A book titled *The Richest Caveman*.

"I wasn't much of a reader but I actually read this book from cover to cover. It awakened a new reality for me. Growing up, we didn't go to church, or pray, or anything. My parents acknowledged God but they were so busy working that religion wasn't a part of our lives.

"But now I found out that there really is a battle going on between good and evil. And there really is a Super Hero—and His name is Jesus. I decided that I wanted to join forces with God and fight the battle against darkness."

As he read the book, Daniel felt especially drawn to the story of Pastor Doug going to church for the first time in his overalls. Even though he wasn't dressed like the other people, Pastor Doug still knew the Bible truths already from the hours he'd spent reading God's Word in the cave.

"I wanted to know these truths that he was seeing."

Reflect: Did you grow up looking to some person on earth as your hero? Have you found Jesus Christ to be the greatest hero of all? Study His life and you will be truly amazed.

Dig Deeper: Matthew 5:43–45; John 15:13; Romans 15:1, 2

Daniel

Super Hero for Christ, Part 2

"You shall receive power when the Holy Spirit has come upon you; and you shall be witnesses ..." (Acts 1:8).

Daniel's girlfriend gave him a book called *The Richest Caveman*. It sparked in him a desire to know the truths that Pastor Doug discovered in the Bible.

When Daniel was a senior in high school, an Amazing Facts evangelist came to town to hold a series of meetings. Daniel and Leanna went to every presentation.

"As I sat night after night, hearing these special truths from the Bible, I thought, 'I would love to do what that man is doing. I'd love to share these truths from the Bible with every one that I come in contact with.'"

At the end of the series, Daniel was baptized. And he also discovered that the Caveman he read about wasn't just the author of a single random book—he actually headed up an international ministry! Daniel eagerly began working his way through all of the Amazing Facts resources available online.

"I became an Amazing Facts addict," he tells people. He read as much material as he could and constantly checked the website for new articles and new videos. "I couldn't wait to see what was coming next."

Time continued to pass and Daniel became more and more active in his church—leading prophecy seminars himself, and even preaching sometimes. Now he was doing what he had first longed to do when he heard the Good News—sharing it with others and seeing their lives changed just like his own life had been transformed.

Although Daniel's mom had passed away while he was in high school, he'd invite his dad to come hear him when he spoke at church. And his dad often accepted the invitation.

Meanwhile, Daniel and Leanna married and began their family. Their involvement in church continued to grow. Any time Amazing Facts would do a worldwide satellite broadcast, their home church would be a host site. Daniel continued to invite his dad for those special events. His dad came because he enjoyed Pastor Doug's style of preaching and he eventually joined the church and was baptized.

Today, Daniel works full time as a graphic designer and evangelist for Amazing Facts. He shares, "Now I work alongside the Caveman telling everyone about the real Super Man."

Reflect: Did you ever wish to do some great work for the Lord? Pray for the power of the Holy Spirit to lead you. God often has us begin with small steps which lead to big advances.

Dig Deeper: Psalm 32:8; Proverbs 16:9; John 16:13

Louise Little

Black and White

> "There is neither Jew nor Greek, there is neither slave
> nor free, there is neither male nor female; for you
> are all one in Christ Jesus" (Galatians 3:28).

Millions know the name of controversial activist Malcolm X, who was assassinated in 1965. But do we ever think of the woman who raised him?

Louise Little was born out of tragedy, conceived when her mother was raped by a white man at 11 years old.

In her youth, she married Earl Little and had seven children with him (the fourth being the future Malcolm X) before his untimely murder at the hands of the Black Legion, an offshoot of the Ku Klux Klan.

Now in her early thirties, Louise was a widow with seven mouths to feed—and America was in the throes of the Great Depression.

She and her children lived in Lansing, Michigan, the only black family in the neighborhood. Around this time, a new family moved onto their street. They were white, but there was something different about them.

They began to visit Louise and the children. They were kind, friendly—like real neighbors. It was a shock to someone like Louise, well-acquainted with injustice and racism. Color did not seem to matter to these new neighbors though. To them, they were all in the same boat, sinners in need of a Savior.

They would talk with Louise for hours, often about the second coming of Christ. They would leave her gifts too, literature about the Bible, and Louise would read them.

After a while, Louise began to take her children to what her new friends called camp meetings, where a large group of people would study the Bible together. Louise and her children especially liked the food, which followed God's dietary laws directly from the Bible.

Eventually, Louise began to see these people as her people. Their faith was now her faith; their identity was her identity. This same God-fearing group of Christians, decades later, became known for keeping the Bible Sabbath.

Unfortunately, Louise's life took a turn for the worse. Her children were taken from her, and she spent the next 25 years in a psychiatric ward—some say unjustly so.

While history does not disclose the state of Louise's faith in her later life, what is clear is that at a time when segregation was the norm, Louise's life was once changed by the love of God, demonstrated through a special Bible-based group of Christians as extending to every creature, no matter the race.

Reflect: How do you view those to whom you witness? God sees every child of His with the same tender regard.

Dig Deeper: Psalm 96:3; Philippians 3:20; James 1:27

Casey

Man Fails, But God Delivers

"My God shall supply all your need according to His riches in glory by Christ Jesus" (Philippians 4:19).

Jesus never fails in saving those who call upon Him, but sometimes people later turn their back on God. It happened with Judas, a disciple of Christ. Casey, a single mother of three, knows what it's like to watch a spouse turn to God and then fall back into substance abuse. Yet the Lord has sustained her through the ministry of Amazing Facts. Even when those we love and trust fail us, God delivers.

Casey had known disappointment before. "My parents divorced when I was 15. We did not have good role models growing up; I have more bad memories than good," she says. In turn, that led to a life of religious confusion. "I did not understand the concept of true faith," Casey explains. "I learned to live off of my emotions rather than Bible principles. My life was a mess."

A change took place when her husband went through a Bible training program. The couple had been separated for a year when he began attending the program in another city. It inspired Casey to begin taking Bible studies with friends and members in a local Sabbath-keeping church. "I learned so many new truths about the Bible," she recalls.

Casey was also introduced to Amazing Facts and she says it really grounded her faith. "When I first started doing Bible studies, I watched Pastor Doug on satellite all the time," she explains. Casey was so excited about what she was learning that she naturally began sharing these newfound truths with others. She now gives Bible studies and gets excited when she can open and present truth with people searching for answers.

Sadly, her husband relapsed and fell back into substance abuse which led to the break-up of their marriage. Such trauma would probably sour other people, but Casey says God has lightened her burden. She still feels compassion for her ex-husband. "I'm not mad at him and I've forgiven him." She is grateful that God has kept her through this difficult time.

In the midst of this emotional storm, Casey has learned that God is faithful. She is a living testimony to the sustaining power that comes from the Lord, even when we are let down by others.

Reflect: Has someone close to you ever let you down? How did you cope? God wants you to depend upon Him as your ultimate source of love and strength.

Dig Deeper: Psalm 62:7; Isaiah 58:11; Jeremiah 17:5

Sergius Paulus

Devil on Your Shoulder

> **"For we do not wrestle against flesh and blood, but against principalities, against powers, against the rulers of the darkness of this age, against spiritual hosts of wickedness in the heavenly places" (Ephesians 6:12).**

Throughout the pages of Earth's history, government and occultism have often walked hand in hand. Even the famous Protestant queen Elizabeth I had as one of her advisors a known occultist by the name of John Dee.

So it should come as no surprise that the Bible also has accounts about dark political influences. During the apostle Paul's first missionary journey, Paul and his company traveled to Paphos, a city on the coast of Cypress. The governor of that region was a man by the name of Sergius Paulus, who Scripture tells us was a perceptive seeker of gospel truth (Acts 13:7). Upon learning of the arrival of Paul's party, Sergius Paulus arranged a meeting with them. It was a wonderful opportunity for the missionaries to share Jesus with one of the officials of the Roman Empire.

But Sergius Paulus was not alone. With him was a man of insidious bearing, a "sorcerer" and "a false prophet" (v. 6). His name was Bar-Jesus, and he was a Jew who had the governor's ear. This was no ordinary lobbyer; this was a man who worked on an emotional, personal, and spiritual level: through the belief system. He had been deliberately spreading lies about the Messiah, about the living God, in an effort "to turn the proconsul away from the faith" (v. 8).

But God, who sees all things, saw through Bar-Jesus' façade of half-truths and calumny and moved Paul, by the Holy Spirit, to pronounce a powerful judgment upon him.

"O full of all deceit and all fraud, you son of the devil, you enemy of all righteousness, will you not cease perverting the straight ways of the Lord?" (v. 10) declared the apostle.

And Bar-Jesus was struck blind, "not seeing the sun for a time" (v. 11).

Sergius Paulus had seen the deportment of the missionaries and had heard "the teaching of the Lord" (v. 12). He had discerned what a vast contrast the gospel was to the whisperings of the false prophet. Bar-Jesus' supernatural punishment was just proof of what the governor had already been told. In that moment Sergius Paulus became a believer.

Reflect: How is the spiritual war between Christ and the devil at play in your life? Invite Jesus to give you full victory over self, sin, and Satan.

Dig Deeper: Genesis 3:15; Zechariah 3:1, 2; 1 Peter 5:8, 9

Jerry

A New Beginning

"If anyone is in Christ, he is a new creation; old things have passed away; behold, all things have become new" (2 Corinthians 5:17).

Jerry was a third-generation member of a Sabbath-keeping church, but fell away from the faith in his teenage years after seeing the personal failings of some youth leaders. As many who run away from the Lord discover, life was not kind to Jerry.

"I became an alcoholic and started smoking," he recalls. Later in life, he quit both of these habits. Though overcoming those addictions was admirable, Jerry was still addicted to his work. "I was a workaholic, working sometimes three jobs at a time," he says. A neck injury resulted in surgery and eventually Jerry had to stop working due to his disability. "I became extremely depressed and at times blamed God for what happened in my life." He compared himself to Job, the Bible figure whose family and fortune were upended by an attack of Satan.

Jerry says, "I hit rock bottom." He attempted to harm his wife and older son, then later tried to end his own life. After eight days in a mental health facility, he asked for a pastor to visit. A Sabbath-keeping pastor answered his call. "God entered my life again at that point," Jerry says. "With the pastor's help I started studying the Bible again. I decided I wanted to live and get better."

A key turning point was studying the *Amazing Facts Bible Study Guides* and watching the *Landmarks of Prophecy* series by Pastor Doug Batchelor. "*Landmarks* really opened my eyes and helped me to remember why we need to turn our eyes to God," he explains. Jerry made a commitment to be re-baptized, dedicating his life to God and spreading His Word.

"Pastor Doug's straightforward presentations also made an impression on me," Jerry says. "He was honest, he didn't preach brimstone and fire, and he read all the facts from the Bible. There were no opinions given, just facts."

Jerry was re-baptized and reconnected to God's family with a new life and lifestyle. "I am now eating healthier. I have a very loving wife, and she has been right by my side through this whole ordeal."

A man who once had problems at home and attempted to take his own life now has a higher calling. "I have dedicated my life to God, I spread God's Word every chance I get," Jerry says.

Reflect: Do you know someone who has turned from God? Don't give up on them; there is hope for every person. Pray earnestly for them to return to the Lord.

Dig Deeper: Isaiah 43:18, 19; Romans 6:4; Ephesians 4:22–24

A Jewish Mother with a Secret

"Let us hold fast the confession of our hope without wavering, for He who promised is faithful" (Hebrews 10:23).

Born in Germany in 1922, Ruth Lieber was a Jewish girl who grew up to become a nurse. She would eventually marry, emigrate to the United States, and have children.

That placid description of her life omits two significant facts. One was that much of her nursing career was spent in Nazi concentration camps, where she had been placed during the Second World War. The other fact: At age 12, she found faith in Jesus, something she would keep very quiet, secret even, for most of her life.

Ruth's encounter with Christians, and the gospel, came when the Nazis came to power in Germany in 1933. Her mother, already gravely ill and hospitalized, was unable to care for the child. Ruth's father fled to Poland to avoid the Nazis.

Ruth ended up in an orphanage run by the Evangelical Lutheran Church. Here, apparently, she found faith, and a German-language Bible she would keep with her throughout her life.

The Liebers ended up in Poland, reunited, just in time for the 1939 invasion by Nazi forces. Her mother was sent to Auschwitz. Ruth never saw her father again.

The young woman was pressed into service as a nurse. Her Christian faith made no difference to the Nazis: She was of Jewish extraction, and so a prisoner she would be. But as a nurse she had some slight privileges, including a way to secure her most precious belongings. She'd hide them in the typhoid-ridden bedding of the other prisoners for whom she cared.

Ruth and her cherished Bible survived the war unscathed. She went to a Jewish hospital to care for Holocaust survivors. After she had seen a premature infant she wished to adopt, the baby's father, widowed when his then-wife died in childbirth, said, "I come with the baby." They were married four weeks later.

Meyer (Yitzchak) Rydelnik knew of his wife's faith, but believed she would outgrow it. He forbade her from expressing it publicly. When she did, in the United States in 1971, he divorced her, leaving their younger children in her care.

Their son, Michael Rydelnik, was embarrassed that his nice Jewish mother was a believer in the Christian messiah. Michael became determined to prove his mother wrong and redeem her for the Jewish faith. Things did not work out the way the teenage boy intended, however.

Reflect: Ruth Lieber Rydelnik clung to her faith during the most trying times the world had seen until that point. Remain faithful, for your testimony can encourage others in their time of need.

Dig Deeper: 1 Corinthians 1:9; 2 Thessalonians 3:3; Revelation 3:11

Michael Rydelnik

Betrayed

"I am not ashamed of the gospel of Christ, for it is the power of God to salvation for everyone who believes, for the Jew first ..." (Romans 1:16).

Michael Rydelnik, the son of two orthodox Jewish Holocaust survivors, was determined to be a "good Jew." And all good Jews knew one thing: They did not believe in Jesus.

When Michael's mother, Ruth Lieber Rydelnik, confided in her son that she, a Jew, did believe that Jesus—*Yeshua* in Hebrew—was in fact the Messiah of all, including the Jewish people, he was unreceptive. When his mother went public, Michael's father moved out and divorced her.

"When my Mom began to talk to me about Yeshua being the Messiah, I was angry," Michael would later recall. "I thought she had betrayed ... me. And then I began to think, 'How could I convince her not to believe this?'"

His plan: Study the Scriptures to prove his mother wrong and win her back. Michael began regular sessions with missionary Hilda Kosner to discuss prophecies about the Messiah.

At one point in their studies, Mrs. Kosner said Michael needed to pray and ask God to guide him. His response was dramatic: "No, no, I don't need to do that. I know Jesus isn't the Messiah." She repeated, "You need to pray about it."

Something happened: "That night, as I was lying in bed ... I got up the nerve and I prayed, 'God, I know that Jesus can't be the Messiah. It's impossible that we've missed him all these years. But if this Yeshua of Nazareth is the Messiah, show me!'"

His opportunity to decide came when his mother invited Michael to view a film about Israel that showed how the Jews' return to Israel fulfilled Bible prophecies, something he could agree with. Then it argued that those same Hebrew prophets predicted Jesus' arrival at precisely the time He was born to Mary. That he rejected.

"I realized I was being a hypocrite. If the Hebrew prophets foretold the coming of Yeshua as the Messiah, if I were going to be a 'good Jew,' I would have to believe in Him. Even if I were the only Jew ever to put my trust in Him, I would still be a good Jew because I put my trust in the Jewish Messiah. That day I decided to put my trust in Him."

Today, Michael is a professor at a leading Bible college, Christian radio talk show host, and the author of numerous Bible commentaries.

Reflect: Michael Rydelnik heard from God when he asked if Jesus was the Messiah. Have you (or someone you know) had a similar experience? If so, share it with others.

Dig Deeper: Psalm 40:9, 10; Isaiah 53:1; Romans 10:17

Claudia

Finding True Love, Part 1

"Beloved, let us love one another, for love is of God; and everyone who loves is born of God and knows God" (1 John 4:7).

Claudia desperately wanted to be loved, but the more she tried to find someone to love her, the more elusive that dream became. She chose to be physically intimate with many men in her search, but she came to realize that she did not have a genuine relationship with any of them.

Claudia was born in Peru to a Catholic family, through which she learned the sacraments and other religious rituals. She believed that there was a God and that He loved her, but she did not know the reasons for her faith. "None of us had a real relationship with Him," she recalls. To her, God was just a hazy figure covered in unfamiliarity. What had He done to improve her life? She felt that God's love was impersonal, an untouchable concept floating somewhere out there.

In her early 20s, Claudia immigrated to America, the land where she thought her dreams would come true. She believed that in the United States, with its many freedoms, she would find someone who would truly love her. She soon began living out her desires and found herself in a new relationship.

Soon, Claudia was pregnant. Thinking that this would be her "happily ever after," she married her boyfriend and gave birth to a baby girl soon after. But her dream of finding someone to make her happy crashed and burned. The marriage disintegrated, and Claudia's identity, so intricately wrapped up in someone else, did too.

Soon after, she began leading a double life—a single woman outside of the home and a protective mother inside. Outside of the home, she was free to be with whomever she wanted. But this newfound freedom did not liberate her; it only made her more confused, more forlorn, and more trapped in sin.

After a particularly difficult breakup, Claudia hit rock bottom. Why couldn't someone just love her? "I couldn't understand why people just hurt and use others," she remembers. She was confused about who she was, about people, and about the purpose of her life. She pored over videos on the Internet, searching for something deeper, something meaningful.

One day, while searching YouTube, she found a seminar by Amazing Facts ...

Reflect: What do you tell a young person who is dreamily in love, but has not put God in the equation? Pray earnestly for wisdom to help discover the right relationship.

Dig Deeper: Romans 5:8; Ephesians 5:28; 1 John 4:9

"We love Him because He first loved us" (1 John 4:19).

One day, while searching YouTube, Claudia—a broken and wounded young woman—found a seminar by Amazing Facts called *The Prophecy Code*. She watched every episode. After that, "I understood what life was all about," she says. Then she watched more from Amazing Facts: *Cosmic Conflict*; *The Final Events of Bible Prophecy*; *Revelation: The Bride, the Beast and Babylon*. She drank in the information and began reading the Bible for the first time in her life.

Claudia then took another step in her search for truth. She went through all of the *Amazing Facts Bible Study Guides* and *Storacles* lessons and discovered God—not the distant, impersonal God of her childhood, but the true and personal God of the Bible. She was introduced to a God who loved her deeply and wanted to save her.

Her worldly dream relationship she always desired began to fade away. Claudia started to understand that healthy relationships are based on mutual love and respect. Furthermore, she learned of Christ's sacrificial love for her, and it made her love Him in return.

"People do the things they do," she reflects, "because they have this emptiness in their hearts that they cannot fill, and it's because we don't know God." The desperation for someone to love her disappeared and was replaced by the knowledge that the God of the universe loved her. It changed her focus from seeking for love from others to thinking of ways that she could love and serve others just like Jesus served her. Now one of her greatest desires is to teach her daughter about what Jesus is doing to save her.

Today, Claudia belongs to a Sabbath-keeping church and regularly studies God's Word. She finally found the relationship that will never come to an end—one that brings true, everlasting joy. "I'm definitely a much happier person," she shares. "God gave me freedom over my sin, and I live in peace with Him because of that."

Claudia desperately wanted to be loved and was eventually introduced to One who told her, "I have loved you with an everlasting love; therefore with lovingkindness I have drawn you" (Jeremiah 31:3).

Reflect: Wounded people often find themselves falling back into bad relationships. What can help a person avoid unhealthy friendships? The Bible is the first place to begin.

Dig Deeper: Psalm 109:22; Isaiah 53:5; Jeremiah 31:3

Job

The Problem of Pain, Part 1

"In the day of my trouble I sought the Lord; my hand was stretched out in the night without ceasing; my soul refused to be comforted" (Psalm 77:2).

A Northwestern University study showed that people suffering from chronic back pain can have a decrease in brain size of up to 11 percent. People commonly regulate pain to a primarily physical realm, but science shows that it affects so much more—and so does the Bible.

Job was one of those people for whom it seemed everything always went right. He was exceptionally wealthy, he had a beautiful family, he was in good health. In fact, he was not one of the greatest but "*the* greatest of all the people of the East" (Job 1:3, emphasis added). He was of an exemplary character as well. He was a father who faithfully interceded for his children (v. 5) and a man whose conduct, personally and professionally, was continually "blameless and upright" (v. 1). All these things were attributed to his wholehearted love for God.

If not for the devil, Job's life would probably have continued on in this manner. But Satan, in his insatiable desire to malign the character of God, set his crosshairs on Job, besmirching him as a petty, opportunistic parasite whose attachment to God went only so far as his love of material gain (vv. 9–11).

So Job's character was put to the test and Satan was given free reign over all of his material possessions (v. 12). As a result, in a single day Job lost everything—his wealth, his assets, his living. Next, the devil massacred his servants and every one of his children (vv. 14–19). But while in mourning for his great losses, Job nevertheless continued to praise God (v. 21).

So the devil returned to God with another accusation: Job was a selfish coward who paid homage only insofar as his personal comforts were concerned (2:5). Thus Job yet again was tested.

Wasting no time, Satan inflicted upon him "painful boils from the sole of his foot to the crown of his head" (v. 7). And though his wife ill-advised him to forsake God, Job still remained faithful (vv. 9, 10).

He still loved God, but he was severely, inconsolably sad and deeply, dangerously depressed. He wanted to die. His world became small, dark, and lonely, like a coffin. He could see nothing but the hopelessness in front of him.

Reflect: Has your pain been so great that it is difficult to focus on anything else? Pray to God for light and strength.

Dig Deeper: Psalm 30:5; Proverbs 12:25; John 16:33

Job

The Problem of Pain, Part 2

> **"I have heard of You by the hearing of the ear,
> but now my eye sees You" (Job 42:5).**

Poet John Keats once said, "Nothing ever becomes real till experienced." How true this was for Job.

What plagued him day and night was that he had not done anything to deserve what had befallen him. Grieved over the loss of his former life, he blamed God, mistakenly believing that He, not Satan, was responsible for his tragic circumstances: "For the arrows of the Almighty are within me; my spirit drinks in their poison; the terrors of God are arrayed against me" (Job 6:4). Throughout his laments his view of God was of a Creator who was ruthless, tyrannical, and unjust. Job was the victim; Job had been wronged, and now Job wanted to be heard! He demanded an answer out of God: "Why have You set me as Your target ...?" (7:20).

Job's friends all had their own answers, espousing their ideas in lengthy soliloquies. But finally, after the men had had their say, God responded. Now it was Job's turn to be questioned (38:3): Did Job create this world and all that was in it? Did he put together the laws of nature?

All of Job's arguments, patched together by vague traditions and a rash deluge of complaints, died on his lips. God was no tyrant, no unjust judge, no impersonal king. Could a tyrant put such beauty in the earth? Could he provide so tenderly, from the chick in the nest (v. 41) to the pride of lions (v. 39)? Could he be so great as to hold the stars in the palm of his hand (v. 31), to shape the mighty behemoth (40:15–19), but to still condescend to an ungrateful servant like himself?

"I am vile" (v. 4) was his reply. "Therefore I have uttered what I did not understand, things too wonderful for me, which I did not know" (42:3).

He realized how foolish and rash he had been. It now seemed no longer so important that his voice be heard. No longer did he see himself as a victim, but as he truly was: "I abhor myself, and repent" (v. 6).

And God, true to His character, did not leave Job in the dust but blessed him with "twice as much as he had before" (v. 10).

Reflect: When Job experienced God personally, his view of God changed, and consequently his view of himself. How does your understanding of the character of God shape you?

Dig Deeper: Psalm 8:3–5; Isaiah 55:8, 9; Ezekiel 18:29

Kip

Rollercoaster Faith, Part 1

"Take heed that you do not do your charitable deeds before men, to be seen by them" (Matthew 6:1).

Kip Johnston was a gambler—with cards, his life, and his faith.

He believed he was a basically moral person. After all, his mother had read him Bible stories and took him to a Sabbath-keeping church. He knew right from wrong. His parents also sent him to Christian schools, but the more he looked at teachers and classmates, the more hypocrites he saw. In his own words, he "was not impressed or converted."

At age 24, a friend confronted his deeply biblical beliefs and led him astray one night. The next day he asked his mother for a Bible and read it for hours. After reading Romans, Kip cried out, "If anybody is out there, I need to know You."

He believed he had a "born again experience," and became a Bible student and street preacher. But it didn't take long for Kip to climb back onto his rollercoaster of rebellion. He went back to motorcycle riding, drugs, and alcohol, and became an accomplished poker player.

At age 30, Kip had $50,000 stuffed in shoeboxes. He read the Bible and prayed by day, but led a corrupt lifestyle by night. Eventually, he lost all his money, but a casino owner hired him to play professionally as a casino insider.

One Saturday morning, Kip was driving home from a shift at a casino still dressed in his suit. When he passed a Sabbath-keeping church, he felt prompted to go inside. By the time he left the service, he had re-embraced Sabbath-keeping. To obey God's law, he decided he would not buy or sell, or work at the casinos, on the Sabbath. His rollercoaster ride was not yet over.

By his own admission, he was "still not fully converted," but had started regularly attending a Sabbath-keeping church, teaching Sabbath school, and occasionally preaching to the small congregation. In an effort to earn a legitimate living, he gave up gambling and learned to drive a long-haul semi-truck.

While on one of his long trips, he watched an Amazing Facts broadcast with Pastor Doug for the first time at a truck stop. He recognized the truths from his youth and knew they were right. He sensed the Lord was reaching out to him, although he didn't fully reach back.

But God was not done reaching out to him.

Reflect: Have you ever practiced religious disciplines like prayer or witnessing to cover up sin in your life? Jesus can see it all and wants to make you entirely clean.

Dig Deeper: Matthew 6:1–7; Mark 7:6; Luke 6:42

Kip

Rollercoaster Faith, Part 2

**"Rejoice with me, for I have found my sheep
which was lost!" (Luke 15:6).**

Kip loved to gamble, but kept moving back and forth toward God and away from Him. One day, while gambling online, a video advertisement by Pastor Doug popped up. Kip remembered him from the truck stop TV, so he clicked the link and began watching Amazing Facts videos one after another while still playing online poker and using marijuana and tobacco.

Eventually, he surrendered the marijuana, then the tobacco, and through the Amazing Facts videos and studies, he became a vegetarian ... and feasted on the Word of God too. Yet he hadn't quit gambling.

Pastor Doug's sermons encouraged him to attend church again and "not go it alone with God." He visited various churches in town, but kept running into "bad theology." In a misguided attempt at self-redemption, Kip handed out Christian literature in the casinos and to street people.

Eventually, he found a Sabbath-keeping church, got involved, and even did hospital visitations; but he still worked six weeks a year on the professional World Series of Poker tour. His pastor saw through him and refused to baptize him.

Eventually, Kip moved to California where he met a pastor who continued to study with him, challenge him, and who eventually baptized him after Kip gave up gambling.

Kip, who was nourished and growing by the spiritual food he was consuming from Amazing Facts, finally prayed, "Lord, I'm tired of this rollercoaster." God's still, small voice replied: "Get into My work."

Kip got his life onto a new track. He has fully turned his back on drugs, tobacco, alcohol, and gambling. He was baptized and, in answer to prayer, later married "a fantastic Christian woman" who wanted to join him in missionary work. Together they spent a year in India building houses, preaching, teaching, and sharing Amazing Facts Bible study materials and copies of Pastor Doug's sermons. The experience humbled him and he says he finally knows what the Lord wants from him.

Today, Kip's wife works as a nurse and Kip again has a gospel literature ministry that takes him door-to-door, to flea markets, and big-box storefronts. His favorite materials to distribute are from Amazing Facts. Kip and his wife are planning more overseas evangelism, but also see the need for mission work right in their own community.

Reflect: Do you know someone who quit attending church because it was full of hypocrites? How do you reach a person like this? Start praying for guidance from the Lord.

Dig Deeper: Hosea 14:1; Joel 2:13; Luke 15:1–7

Jacob DeShazer

Prisoner of War, Part 1

> "Likewise the Spirit also helps in our weaknesses. For
> we do not know what we should pray for as we ought,
> but the Spirit Himself makes intercession for us with
> groanings which cannot be uttered" (Romans 8:26).

After the infamous attack on Pearl Harbor on December 7, 1941, horror quickly translated to patriotism as Americans rallied around the war effort. On April 18, 1942, a small contingency of just over 200 army personnel launched the United States' first significant attack against the Japanese in World War II. The Doolittle Raid, as it was commonly known, was an air strike on Tokyo and its surrounding regions; and its victory, while slim in physical damage, made all the difference for the soul and spirit of the Allied powers.

Among its bombardiers was 30-year-old Jacob DeShazer, a corporal hailing from Oregon. DeShazer had grown up in a devout Free Methodist family but had never truly pursued a personal relationship with God. During high school, his faith waned drastically. In 1940, he enlisted in the army. After Pearl Harbor, an infuriated DeShazer signed up for the Doolittle Raid. He wanted revenge.

In the early morning of April 18, DeShazer's B-25, named "Bat Out of Hell," was the last to launch from the USS Hornet. But as the sixteen bombers careened down upon the East Asia island, a Japanese boat radioed their arrival and the element of surprise was lost. As a consequence, the aircraft were forced to attack earlier than planned.

DeShazer's bombs hit their intended target, Nagoya, a largely populous city in Japan, but the "Bat," along with the majority of the other B-25s, ended up crashing after running out of fuel. As DeShazer and his four other crew members parachuted into enemy territory in China, a woman on the other side of the world jolted awake from her sleep.

She was Jacob DeShazer's mother; and she was experiencing the uncanniest sensation—as though she were falling from a tall, tall height. Deeply agitated, she began to pray. She did not know that at that very moment she was experiencing the very same thing her son was; she did not know that it was he for whom she was praying. But God knew.

Throughout the next three years and four months, the time that her son spent in captivity, she, prompted by the Holy Spirit, continued to intercede for him.

Reflect: For whom do you prayerfully intercede? Do you know of anyone whose prayer for you was answered?

Dig Deeper: Numbers 14:13–19; Daniel 9:3–19; Acts 7:57–60

Jacob DeShazer

Prisoner of War, Part 2

"And God will wipe away every tear from their eyes; there shall be no more death, nor sorrow, nor crying. There shall be no more pain, for the former things have passed away" (Revelation 21:4).

After DeShazer and the rest of his crew parachuted into China, they were soon captured by the Japanese and transported to Tokyo—but not before being subjected to a harsh examination, replete with a brutal beating. In Tokyo, they were reunited with several other Doolittle raiders from another bomber.

For more than three years, these eight men were repeatedly beaten, tortured, and interrogated. They were transferred to several different sites in both Japan and China, held in solitary confinement, and slowly starved.

Three of the raiders, two of them from DeShazer's own crew, were eventually executed by firing squad—and Jacob was supposed to have died with them. The death sentence for the four prisoners had been passed; their names had been given out and even announced in America. But unbeknownst to Jacob, his mother, upon hearing the news, again prayed to God to spare her son's life from the awful penalty. And God answered her prayer. Jacob, for reasons unknown, was spared.

Jacob may not have died that day with his three friends, but he was dying on the inside, filled with a most intense hatred of his captors. So vehement was his hatred that it nearly drove him mad.

But one day, fellow prisoner Lieutenant Robert J. Meder, co-pilot of the other B-25, began talking to Jacob about Jesus. It was the first time in a long time that anyone had done that.

"Jesus Christ is the key to all of this," the lieutenant said.

Jacob was bemused. He knew who Jesus was, of course. But what He had to do with any of this—with the torture, the humiliation, the dark loneliness—Jacob had no idea.

Soon after, Meder died. The Japanese had starved him to death. And Jacob's hatred wormed its way even deeper into his heart, like a canker.

But his friend's words stuck with him; and as the days passed, he continued to ponder them. And in that black and filthy hole, buried deep in enemy country, a seed began to grow ...

Reflect: Have you experienced extreme and prolonged suffering? Have you understood the meaning of your suffering? What happens to your pain once you understand?

Dig Deeper: Isaiah 53:3–5; 2 Corinthians 4:8–10; 1 Peter 4:1

Jacob DeShazer

Prisoner of War, Part 3

> "But I say to you, love your enemies, bless those who curse you, do good to those who hate you, and pray for those who spitefully use you and persecute you" (Matthew 5:44).

After Meder's death, there began to grow in Jacob a longing to understand the hatred that was eating him alive. He remembered his family's faith—it had been said that it had the ability to transform hate into love. How desperately he wished for a Bible to learn how that was so!

Then came a thread of mercy from the most unlikely of sources—Emperor Hirohito. Japan's monarch was not in favor of the inhumane treatment the American prisoners had been receiving. This meant that DeShazer and his companions were now given one Bible to share.

When he was finally able to hold the precious tome in his gaunt hands, Jacob drank in the heavenly words, reading and rereading. He was given the Bible for only three weeks, but during that time, he memorized as many passages as he could, including the Sermon on the Mount and even the entirety of John's first epistle.

But it was when he read this verse that he finally understood: "Father, forgive them, for they do not know what they do" (Luke 23:34). This was it—Meder's key. It was not the faith itself that transformed hearts; it was who the faith was in—Jesus Christ. Jacob's captors did not know Christ, and if they did not know Christ, then how could they know how to love?

Jacob decided to take his newfound faith to a practical level. One day, a guard began to hit and kick him repeatedly, screaming at him to move faster. His first thought was one of hate, but then he thought of Jesus and His instructions in the Sermon on the Mount.

The next morning, when the guard walked by, Jacob smiled at him and greeted him in Japanese. The next day he did it again, and the day after and the day after. A week later, the guard gave him a gift: one beautifully boiled sweet potato.

God continued to change Jacob's heart in prison. On August 20, 1945, at the end of the war, Jacob was released. He went on to become a missionary and serve his former enemies, the Japanese, for the next 30 years. Among those he helped bring to Christ was Mitsuo Fuchida, the captain who had led the attack on Pearl Harbor.

Reflect: Have you seen an act of love change someone's attitude toward you? Remember, love will awaken love in the heart of another.

Dig Deeper: Proverbs 24:17; Jeremiah 29:7; 1 Peter 2:20

Dakota

The Shining Light of a New Day, Part 1

> "I know the thoughts that I think toward you, says
> the , thoughts of peace and not of evil, to give
> you a future and a hope" (Jeremiah 29:11).

Dakota was raised in a Christian home in Arkansas. His parents did their best to raise three millennial children in church, teaching them to respect and obey the Bible.

As a family, they visited many different churches in search of the one that taught all the Bible. He recalls, "This journey to discover truth was difficult at times; however, one day, without us recognizing it at first, the undiluted truth flashed through our home." His parents had discovered the Amazing Facts *Millennium of Prophecy* series with Pastor Doug Batchelor.

At the time, Dakota was just a child beginning kindergarten and was not interested in spiritual things; the truths that his parents had been learning were unknown to him. Fast forward ten years later, and he entered into those spiritual war zones called "public schools." He had soon become so jaded by the world and entrapped in entertainment that the last thing on his mind was God.

Dakota spent most of his time searching aimlessly for any thrill he could get. "All the while, I had no idea that my pursuit of happiness would never be filled by what this world has to offer." At the time, his dad felt a conviction to start a church plant in his hometown. Shortly after, his brother began to share with him the Amazing Facts *Storacles of Prophecy* series. "It was through these insightful Bible lessons that I began to see and recognize for the first time the imperative truths for our time." It opened his eyes to a new purpose.

Inspired by these great truths, Dakota decided to memorize all the Scriptures that he had learned in the Bible lessons and begin sharing them with everyone he possibly could. "I would go to school and spend my lunch time giving Bible studies. Sometimes, I had over fifteen teens attend. Although it was always a struggle attending public school, God continued to convict me of the truth I had learned and reminded me of His matchless power to give me the strength to stay faithful and to graduate."

But before graduating high school, Dakota had another big test to pass. The test was figuring out what he should do with his life.

Reflect: What's the biggest test you've ever faced in your life? Did you pass? God tests us to determine, not our knowledge, but our characters.

Dig Deeper: Proverbs 4:25–27; Jeremiah 10:23; Matthew 6:33

The Shining Light of a New Day, Part 2

"Philip found Nathanael and said to him, 'We have found Him of whom Moses in the law, and also the prophets, wrote— Jesus of Nazareth, the son of Joseph'" (John 1:45).

"When you go to high school these days," Dakota recalls, "they drill into you that you will be a nobody unless you go to college, get a degree, and make lots of money. A big house, fancy sports cars, and other luxuries are all referred to as the 'American Dream.'"

Yet after Dakota saw a lot of celebrities with miserable lives, some to the point of suicide, he knew that the dream wasn't something he wanted. Jesus' words in Mark 8:36 rang through his mind: "What will it profit a man if he gains the whole world, and loses his own soul?" He knew that he must turn his life over to Him in every way. "At that time, I was dating Anna, who would become my wife. I decided to begin Bible studies with her, and I reached out to my friends to share the truths that changed my life."

Dakota's wife and friends were all driving about two hours, three times a week, to study the Bible. The Lord was sending them an avalanche of conviction during every study. He recalls, "It was through these small group studies that I realized I knew the Word of God, but I did not know the God of the Word. It was evident that I knew the doctrines but was still in need of the Great Physician—Jesus Christ. After studying together for three months, five members of the group decided that we were tired of being slaves to a cruel master. Instead, we wanted to be servants of Christ."

The group learned about the Amazing Facts Center of Evangelism and decided to attend their fall program. "I am so glad to say that ever since, my life has changed. Today, I am an Amazing Facts evangelist. My wife and I travel the globe preaching the everlasting gospel to anyone who will come to hear the words of life."

Dakota Day shares, "It wasn't until Philip invited Nathanael to come and see Christ for himself that he believed that Jesus was the Messiah. My prayer is to be the Nathanael for thousands around the world as an Amazing Facts evangelist."

Reflect: Has God ever put it on your heart to begin a small group Bible study? Pray about it. Talk with a couple other people and let God open the door.

Dig Deeper: Mark 16:15, 16; John 1:43–51; 2 Timothy 4:2

Barnabas

The Encouraging Priest

> "And Joses, who was also named Barnabas by the apostles (which is translated Son of Encouragement), a Levite of the country of Cyprus, having land, sold it, and brought the money and laid it at the apostles' feet" (Acts 4:36, 37).

The world is a pretty tough place, so it's nice to have someone in your corner as an encourager. For the early apostles, that uplifting person was a Jewish priest from the island of Cyprus.

From the Exodus until today, those who are identified as members of the tribe of Levi are regarded as *kohen* (priests), exempt from the usual duties of Israelites, including military service (in ancient times, that is). So, Barnabas, whose original name was Joseph (or, Joses), was an unusual person by any standard.

We don't know the details of how Barnabas was converted to following Jesus, but the evidence is clear that he was converted, and soundly so. Unlike the "rich young ruler" (Mark 10) who was unwilling to give up his possessions, Barnabas knew where to place his treasure, specifically in heaven's storehouse.

The Bible's first mention of Barnabas is in Acts chapter 4, where we read that he sold the land he owned and gave the proceeds to the work of the young church. There was no hesitation reported, and no fibbing as we found with Ananias and Sapphira in chapter 5. His first recorded act was to encourage the work financially.

But that wasn't all. He testified in support of Paul, that dreaded former enemy of "the way," when the onetime Saul of Tarsus reported to Jerusalem as a convert. He encouraged the early church. And, as far as we know, he remained faithful until the end of his days.

Arriving in Antioch after being deputized by the leadership, Barnabas not only approved of what he found, but worked to strengthen the fledgling church there: "When he came and had seen the grace of God, he was glad, and encouraged them all that with purpose of heart they should continue with the Lord. For he was a good man, full of the Holy Spirit and of faith. And a great many people were added to the Lord" (Acts 11:23, 24).

This "son of encouragement" won high praise for his work. Male or female, may that be said for each of us, and may we follow Barnabas' example of sacrificial giving and lifelong encouragement of others.

Reflect: Who are you able to encourage today to live a faithful Christian life? Think of one thing you could do to uplift someone toward God.

Dig Deeper: Psalm 112:5; Proverbs 12:2; Matthew 12:35

Dillon

Prophecy Persuades

"I have told you before it comes, that when it does come to pass, you may believe" (John 14:29).

Dillon's early spiritual life was haphazard. "I remember my family going to different churches from time to time but never to any one of them regularly. Sometimes, many years passed before we went to a church again, but we never attended for long."

In high school, Dillon learned to relish being the center of attention, and he became a popular disc jockey at parties. Unfortunately, that led to an involvement with drugs and bad relationships. He says, "Without God, my happiness was found in vanity."

But his intense search for recognition, coupled with a breakup that left him heartbroken, eventually led Dillon into depression. He sought a spiritual solution by going to a meditation class led by a priest. "At first, I found it to be helpful, but then I realized that it was just a superficial relaxation technique."

Meanwhile, his mother and grandmother had joined a Sabbath-keeping church, and his mother came in contact with Amazing Facts. Still suffering the disappointment of an empty spiritual life, Dillon remembered a set of Amazing Facts DVDs his mother had given him. "It was a series of sermons about prophecy," he says. "I had never watched or thought about them until then. But I enthusiastically studied those messages and made notes of all the prophecy events. I was baptized that summer after a likeminded pastor gave me Bible studies."

Dillon says that Amazing Facts' presentations were critical in proving that this newfound faith was worth his attention: "I had a lot of skepticism about Christianity because of my religious education," he admits. "I needed to see just how supernatural the Bible is, and prophecy was one way for me to see that."

What Dillon found changed his life. He's abandoned drugs, alcohol, and being a music DJ at parties. Reading about the benefits of a plant-based diet convinced him to abandon unclean foods. And he's dating a young woman who shares his faith, and they're even contemplating a life of ministry together.

Dillon explains, "I would like to do something significant for the Lord. I feel like everything I know I learned since becoming a Christian. ... I have even become a better student and I'm giving Bible studies to a classmate about the same prophecy that convinced me."

After years of aimlessness and despair, Dillon has found purpose and direction.

Reflect: Does fulfilled Bible prophecy persuade you that Scripture is true? Think about one Bible prediction that has convicted you of the reliability of the Word of God and share it with a friend.

Dig Deeper: Micah 5:2; 1 Corinthians 14:3; 2 Peter 1:21

Count Nikolaus Ludwig von Zinzendorf

Another "Rich Young Ruler"

"A good man deals graciously and lends; he will guide his affairs with discretion" (Psalm 112:5).

Nikolaus Ludwig von Zinzendorf grew up in a Christian home, and thus it's difficult to pinpoint the moment when this young nobleman—a far different "rich young ruler" than the one found in Scripture—received Christ as his Savior.

But there's no difficulty at all in pinpointing when that acceptance made a huge difference in his life.

The world into which von Zinzendorf was born is almost impossible to imagine today: highly agrarian, a peasant class that could hardly dream of rising above their lot in life, and a Protestantism that had lost its way, with dogma and institutional thinking crowding out the spiritual message of the Reformation. And, yes, the Catholic Church was still fiercely opposed to those dissidents who left its precincts. It was a difficult time in which to live.

In October 1721, despite his inclination towards theology and religious work, von Zinzendorf followed family tradition, becoming a judicial counselor to the king at Dresden, Germany. But his heart remained with the minority of Protestants trying to deepen their faith. Within a year, he'd purchased his grandmother's estate, Berthelsdorf, hoping to establish a refuge for those believers driven from their homes in Moravia and Bohemia (today's Czech Republic).

Eventually, discord arose among various factions of the settlers, whose number had reached 300. Von Zinzendorf moved his family to Berthelsdorf and worked tirelessly to calm the troubled spirits and foster unity. He then discovered a charter called Unitas Fratrum (or, Unity of the Brethren), which was used by the followers of Jan Hus (John Huss) years before Luther and the posting of the "95 Theses."

Sharing the message of brotherly agreement and unity, von Zinzendorf's colony of 300 became what is today known as the Moravian Church, a group emphasizing piety and a "religion of the heart." These pietistic people were the first to send missionaries to the "new world" across the Atlantic, and their influence grew. Though relatively small in number, Moravian Christians have remained faithful to the message von Zinzendorf preached, and the God they earnestly desired to serve.

Reflect: Though wealthy, Nicholas von Zinzendorf let his love for God motivate his actions, such as starting a colony for the poor, persecuted believers from Moravia and Bohemia. What is motivating you today?

Dig Deeper: Deuteronomy 15:7–10; Job 31:16–20; Ephesians 5:15

Doug Batchelor

The Richest Caveman, Part 1

"Happy are the people who are in such a state; happy are the people whose God is the !" (Psalm 144:15).

What kind of a childhood do you think the son of an aviation magnate and a "show biz" maven had? If you think it was a happy one, you couldn't be more wrong.

Doug Batchelor grew up with a millionaire for a father and a film critic for a mother. As a child, he quickly learned one thing: Money and fame did not equal happiness. He and his older brother, Falcon, who were both named after airplanes, barely saw their parents. Their father was chasing business deals and drinking himself to sleep every night; their mother, who had begun her career as a songwriter before venturing to Broadway, yearned after celebrity. They were two people who could not be more different: Republican versus Democrat, businessman versus artist, Baptist versus Jewish—though eventually they both became atheists. But neither of them was happy.

And Doug was not happy either. He always felt that he was in the way.

When Doug was only three years old, his parents divorced, and the children were sent to boarding schools and summer camps. In all, Doug went to 14 different schools. You name it, he went to it—public school, Catholic school, Jewish school, even a free school with coeducational dorms. At age five, he was put in his first military school.

At age seven, he began thinking of committing suicide. While in New York, where his mom now lived, he would often find himself on the rooftops of skyscrapers, sticking his toes as far off the edge as possible. Later on, he also began to regularly smoke pot with his mom, who thought it would be safer for her children to use drugs in a controlled environment.

So it was not long before Doug began his first career—in troublemaking. By the time he was 13, he and his friends were robbing homes on one of the Sunset Islands, the exclusive neighborhood off of Miami Beach where his father now resided. He had been to jail and had even stolen from his friends. He did it because he was bored, because he wanted attention, and because he thought no one cared about him.

But all these things that might seem so exciting only made Doug unhappier, so much so that he ran away to Boston when he was only 15 years old.

Reflect: Are you looking for happiness in the things of this world, in other people, in your own achievements?

Dig Deeper: Proverbs 16:20; Philippians 4:4; James 4:1–3

The Richest Caveman, Part 2

"For with the same measure that you use, it will be measured back to you" (Luke 6:38).

Despite the stereotype, many burglaries actually occur during broad daylight. Just ask Doug Batchelor, who spent his time in Boston, ironically, as a thief during the day and a security guard at night.

He had a fake driver's license; he had rented an apartment all for himself; and he had left his family behind.

He knew his dad was disappointed. His dad had expected to pass the aviation business on to him instead of Falcon, who had been born with cystic fibrosis. But at this point Doug did not care. He had had enough of that life.

So he lived life his own way, abiding by one rule of thumb: He never stole from the people whose homes he guarded. Everything else was fair game.

But one day, a fellow security guard and friend had a few words of warning for him. His friend, who knew about his other favorite pastime, believed heavily in karma. Doug was a thief; he would get what was coming to him, his friend predicted.

Doug brushed it off as nonsense, but he could not help but notice strange things beginning to happen. When he woke up one morning, he found his entire apartment had been ransacked. When he plugged in a stereo he had stolen earlier that day, he discovered it was broken. He would stash away money around his room and then, after getting high and drunk, could not remember where he had hidden it. Gradually, he began to get the sneaking suspicion that his friend had been right. There had to be some supernatural being somewhere orchestrating all this!

But it was when he stole a box of Krusteaz whole wheat pancake mix that he was convinced. Later that day, some friends visited unannounced and proceeded to down his brand-new jug of Tang, that nostalgic form of instant breakfast. Doug, looking forlornly at the empty jug, spied the white lid next to it; on it, stamped in blue was the price, $1.19. Amazed, he looked at the Krusteaz box; stamped on it was the exact price, $1.19.

And he thought to himself, "There has to be a God!"

Reflect: Doug's friend called it "karma," but that concept was actually stolen and distorted from the Bible. Scriptures instead tell of a universal principle, commonly labeled the Golden Rule. Have there been instances in your life that you thought were too odd to be coincidences? They very well could have been divine providence instead.

Dig Deeper: Job 11:7–9; Proverbs 16:9; Romans 8:28

Doug Batchelor

The Richest Caveman, Part 3

"There is no fear in love; but perfect love casts out fear, because fear involves torment. But he who fears has not been made perfect in love" (1 John 4:18).

There may be as many as 4,200 different religions in the world—and Doug went through quite a few of them.

After his supernatural comeuppance, Doug, convinced that God existed, was terrified. He had heard of heaven and hell and, with the way things were going in his life, he could predict which of those places he would be going to. So he decided he had better at least try to learn about how this "God" thing worked.

He watched Christian televangelists, but his mom had always assured him that the Bible was just "fairy tales." Plus, all the Christians he knew about were hypocrites. He was quick to move on.

He visited a Hare Krishna temple, but they overpromised and underdelivered: Their "free meal" turned out to be yogurt and raisins. He partook in transcendental meditation; he tried the Jewish faith, the Catholic faith, and he even attempted the Silva Method of mind control. It was like going to a store and trying on a bunch of clothes. The ones he did not like, he tossed aside. In the end he took a little bit from each and made his own religion.

Doug was now 16 years old and still on his own in Boston. But when his dad actually visited, pleading with him to return to school, he relented and allowed himself to be enrolled in a program of his father's choosing. Unbeknownst to Doug though, the Flint School specialized in reforming "bad eggs" like himself. Classes were held on board a ship where, bereft of their passports, the rotten children of rich tycoons were corralled into doing menial chores, like washing dishes, in order to build character.

Well, Doug was having none of it. He caused such a ruckus that finally the captain, also the school's director, made a deal with him just to get him to leave. But before it could reach home, the ship was trapped in a vicious storm. With the main sail in shambles and frigid winter waves and nausea galore, everyone—even the atheists—began to pray for deliverance.

And it was then that Doug learned a very important lesson: God could not be served out of fear. But it was some time before he learned that God needed to be served out of love.

Reflect: Why should we not serve God out of fear? Remember that "perfect love casts out fear" (1 John 4:18).

Dig Deeper: Jeremiah 31:3; Lamentations 3:22, 23; Romans 5:6–8

"Therefore the will wait, that He may be gracious to you; and therefore He will be exalted, that He may have mercy on you" (Isaiah 30:18).

Hitchhiking, a once-popular form of transportation, is actually banned in several states. But fortunately for Doug, it was not banned in Oklahoma.

After surviving the Flint School storm, Doug returned to his father's home for the holiday break. He knew (and so did the captain) that he was not going back aboard that ship. But his father thought otherwise. So when it came time for school to start up again, Doug sold whatever belongings he had to his brother and took off for Palm Springs, California.

He had a plan. He was going to find God in nature. And what better way to do that than in the beautiful desert mountains of the West Coast?

First though, he made a stop in Virginia to visit some friends and promptly lost all of his newly acquired cash to pool and alcohol. Old habits die hard. He made it as far as Oklahoma, but there he remained, broke and stuck—two things that were definitely not in his original plan.

He was a pitiful sight on the side of Interstate 40, dressed for hot Miami in the dead of a "Sooner State" winter. After eight solid hours and no ride, Doug was frozen, sick, and defeated. Finally, even though he knew it would probably not do any good, even though he had been so awful to so many people and did not deserve any mercy, he decided to pray.

He had four very specific petitions: a ride, food, money, and lastly, for that ride to be with a relatively harmless, mentally sound person. His prayer was answered.

The man who picked him up was a born-again Christian who drove him all the way to his destination, all 2,000 miles of it. Doug, the perfect captive audience, was forced to listen to the man's preaching day after day. Along the way, the man paid for every one of Doug's meals, and when they finally arrived in Palm Springs, he gave Doug $40. Doug was floored. All four of his requests had been met. God had taken care of it all—God had taken care of him—and had given him even more than he had been expecting!

But Doug was only just beginning to experience God's abundant mercy.

Reflect: Has the Lord been waiting patiently for you to notice Him? His persistent love is beyond anything you'll find in this world.

Dig Deeper: Isaiah 42:14, 16; Hosea 5:15; Micah 7:18–20

> **"Therefore He is also able to save to the uttermost those who come to God through Him, since He always lives to make intercession for them" (Hebrews 7:25).**

Looking for a rustic getaway? Try The Rockhouse Retreat in Worcestershire, England, a fancy rental property hewn by hand from a 700-year-old sandstone escarpment that costs upwards of $240 per night to book.

A young Doug Batchelor found a much more affordable alternative. Nestled in the heart of Mount San Jacinto at the end of a grueling 4,000-foot climb was Doug's new home, a cave that he lived in for about a year and a half.

He discarded all his clothes and let his hair grow long. Once or twice a week, he would traipse back down the mountain to panhandle or dumpster dive behind the market in town. Over time, he made his cave into a tidy, humble abode, with a sleeping bag for a bed and buckets for his food and even an oven. But it was what had been left in the cave that turned out to be the real treasure.

His cave had, before he moved in, apparently been occupied by someone else. He knew because that someone had left something behind—a Bible.

At the time, he did not think much of it. But as time passed, he dusted it off and began to read. Every morning, he would wake up and munch on some banana bread, warm out of the oven, and read.

When he arrived at the gospels, he began to feel a strange burning in his heart. In his mind was a singular thought that he could not quite avoid, that all he was reading was absolute Truth. Some of the concepts and words were difficult to understand, but when he finished, he knew two things for certain: He was a great sinner and Jesus Christ was the great Savior.

It was then that he fell to his knees and prayed, truly understanding how wretched he was and truly asking God for forgiveness. He knew to whom he was praying now—to Someone who would forgive him and make him as new. Afterward, what peace he felt, what humility, what love.

That hermit of a hippie went on to become a Christian, a pastor, a husband, and a father—and president of Amazing Facts International.

Reflect: It was when Pastor Doug realized his own filthiness that God was able to change him through His Word. The Lord can remake anyone for His glory.

Dig Deeper: Mark 2:17; Romans 5:10; Galatians 2:20

The Rich Young Ruler

Almost

"With men it is impossible, but not with God; for with God all things are possible" (Mark 10:27).

Twice in the gospels, Jesus encounters leaders of the Jewish religion who seek Him out one-on-one. Nicodemus, a leading Pharisee, came to Jesus secretly and—as his later actions attest—became a believer.

The person described in Mark 10:17–22 (as well as in Matthew's and Luke's accounts) as a "rich young ruler" was more than just that. He was a leader in his worship community, a position of honor and privilege earned, in part, by virtue of his wealth. Among the people of that time, having wealth was viewed as a sign of God's favor.

We don't know about this young man's various talents, but we do know that he understood at least the basics of the faith, because when Jesus challenged him about commandment-keeping, the wealthy man replied, "Teacher, all these things I have kept from my youth" (Mark 10:20). Like so many people today, the rich young ruler sincerely believed his own good works were enough to earn a spot in heaven.

Though sincere, the young ruler was sincerely wrong!

Jesus knew his heart, just as He knows the heart of each of us. The rich young ruler may have outwardly observed the commandments, but inwardly he was guilty of a great sin: idolatry. He idolized his wealth and its trappings. When told to forsake those and to follow Jesus as a disciple, the young ruler "was sad at this word, and went away sorrowful, for he had great possessions" (v. 22).

Seeing this, Jesus' disciples heard the Master say it was hard for those who have wealth to enter the kingdom. He declared, "It is easier for a camel to go through the eye of a needle than for a rich man to enter the kingdom of God" (v. 25).

This inflexion point—where wealth and self-regard confront God's calling—is where the Holy Spirit must step in. It's why Jesus said such a conversion was impossible for man, but not for God, with Whom "all things are possible."

The rich young ruler could have found eternal life if he was willing to take himself off the throne of his heart and allow Christ to reign. Perhaps he later did, but we won't know this side of heaven.

Reflect: Wealth and self-love blocked this rich young ruler from following Jesus. Is there something holding you back from following Him today?

Dig Deeper: Job 42:2; Jeremiah 32:27; Hebrews 7:25

Sam

A Troublemaker Finds God

"For you were once darkness, but now you are light in the Lord. Walk as children of light" (Ephesians 5:8).

From a very young age, Sam was always getting into trouble. The cops were called when 4-year-old Sam picked a neighbor's flowers (for his mother). He later set the neighbor's garage on fire. It didn't matter where he was—school, home, down the street—Sam made trouble.

By the time he was an adult, Sam's activities had graduated from mischief to the truly dangerous: He fell in with members of a criminal motorcycle gang at age 18, and started selling drugs, guns, and explosives.

Having a wife and kids didn't change his activities much. At one time, after co-signing on a loan, the first party disappeared. So the gang member who wanted his money back went looking for Sam and threatened to murder him. It sobered him up and he decided he needed to change his life.

One day, when he went out to get his mail, he found a card lying on the ground. He picked it up and noticed that it advertised a free DVD called *Final Events*. After mailing it in, a couple of Amazing Facts Center of Evangelism (AFCOE) students dropped off the DVD. "My wife and I watched it for a week!" he recalls.

Sam later met a Bible worker who gave him Bible studies and invited him to church. "It was a divine appointment," he believes. Studying the Bible changed his marriage and helped him to find peace through forgiveness. After 54 years of smoking, God helped him to stop cigarettes, alcohol, and drugs. He was eventually baptized in God's remnant church.

Today, Sam is a passionate witness for Christ, sharing literature with anyone and everyone. He sets up a table once a month at a homeless shelter and fills it with Amazing Facts resources to hand out. He eventually attended AFCOE and learned even more ways to share his faith.

"I have such a deep desire to share with those who are hungry for truth," he explains. "I was once hungry, and I still am!" Sam used to always get into trouble; now he loves getting into the Word and sharing truth with others.

Reflect: Do you know someone who is nothing but a troublemaker? Never forget how much God loves everyone, even those who seem like hopeless candidates for the kingdom.

Dig Deeper: Romans 8:7; 1 Corinthians 6:9–11; 1 John 3:4–9

Jacob

From Empty to Full

"He sent His word and healed them, and delivered them from their destructions" (Psalm 107:20).

Jacob was at the end of the road.

From the time he was thirteen, drugs became Jacob's life focus. After high school, with police strongly interested in his group of friends, he decided to leave his home town for the life of a vagabond. Hitch-hiking across the country, eating out of dumpsters, sleeping in the streets and in the woods; his heart's desire was to find someplace where the grass was greener.

Years of searching left him empty. Years of drinking weren't enough to chase away the hollowness inside of his heart. One day, Jacob stood at a literal crossroads, not knowing where to go or where to turn. He had given up on life and was hardly able to eat food anymore, with depression overwhelming his soul. It was at this time that a still small voice led him back to his home town where he was introduced to evidence for a worldwide flood.

His search for truth took him to the Bible, where he found the voice of God speaking to his soul. Having been taught that we had evolved and that life was meaningless, the revelation of the love of God and His existence led Jacob to surrender his life and plead to God for help in overcoming his deep depression. The Lord answered his prayers, and Jacob's heart went from sorrow to a yearning to reach others with the joyful truth he had found.

Jacob began to share materials from Amazing Facts and other Christian resources. He began to keep the Sabbath and attend church. The Lord delivered him from depression, addiction, and led him to a life of ministry: giving Bible studies and distributing literature. As of the time of this publication, Jacob has the privilege of serving the publishing department at Amazing Facts.

Jacob says, "If it wasn't for the material published by ministries like Amazing Facts, I would not be where I am today. My life has been completely changed by the Word of God, and I am happy in Jesus. I praise the Lord for the wonderful privilege to have brothers and sisters in Christ, and for the opportunity to work in His vineyard and reach others wandering in darkness like I was."

Reflect: Have you ever felt like you had nowhere to turn? Do you long for a better world? Jesus has a new heaven and a new earth prepared for them that love Him.

Dig Deeper: Psalm 107:17–22; Hebrews 11:13–16; Ezekiel 36:26, 27

Roger Morneau

Former Demon Worshipper

"God is our refuge and strength, a very present help in trouble. Therefore we will not fear" (Psalm 46:1, 2).

It's not every day a satanic cult threatens someone with death for becoming a Christian. Roger Morneau knew that all too well.

Raised in a pious Catholic family, Morneau nevertheless struggled with his faith from an early age, questioning Catholic tenets like burning the wicked for all eternity. By the time he left the Canadian Merchant Navy after World War II, he had cultivated a hatred for God.

Soon after, he ran into an old friend named Roland, who had become interested in spiritualism. Morneau's first séance quickly turned into demon worship as the two were promptly introduced to a satanic cult smack dab in the middle of Montreal's high society.

Morneau sank headlong into a world full of demon ventriloquists, self-typing typewriters, and divination. He participated in worship services to the devil himself and encountered firsthand the alluring deception of selling one's soul for wealth and power. He even won $420 at the racetrack with the help of a demonic dream. The counterfeit existed, the hatred of Christ palpable, and the devil's lust for adoration pervasive.

Now the time had come to officially join this secret society. Morneau hesitated, asking for one week to decide. That night, hardly knowing what he was saying, he cried out, "If there is a God in heaven who cares for me, help me!"

But wasn't it too late? He had already given up on God and was in so deep with the Satanists.

Then, his prayer was answered. At work, God arranged for him to cross paths with a new employee named Cyril Grosse. At break, their conversation led to God. Cyril easily had answers from the Bible for those same questions that had led Morneau to renounce his faith.

That same evening, Morneau sat in the Grosses' home, absorbed in a Bible study with Cyril and his wife. A week later, Morneau had completed all 28 studies and had even attended the Grosses' Sabbathkeeping church. He was convinced that God loved even him.

But his week was up, and Roland arrived to give him an ultimatum: Choose Christ and take a fatal bullet someday, somewhere.

Morneau chose Christ. At 21, he was baptized into Cyril's same Sabbath-keeping church—and died at 73 years old, a husband, a father and grandfather, and God's steadfast witness. Not once did he take a bullet, fatal or otherwise.

Reflect: Do you believe that Jesus Christ can deliver you from all the powers of darkness?

Dig Deeper: John 1:12; Ephesians 6:10–12; Hebrews 4:15, 16

May

The Sabbath-keeping Restauranteur, Part 1

"If anyone serves Me, him My Father will honor" (John 12:26).

It was noontime on Saturday. It was not a particularly special day to most people, not a holiday or a birthday. But to May, it was an incredibly important day. Today was the first Saturday that her restaurants were closed. She had made the decision to close all three of her restaurants for the entire day.

The clock ticked on, well into the noon hour. The front doors would have been jingling open by now. The pans would have been sizzling on the stovetop, the glasses clinking with tea, the crackling chatter of cooks in the back and the wafting laughter of customers in the front. But May knew that if she were to drive by, each restaurant would now be dark and silent.

People had laughed at her. "You'll go bankrupt for sure," they scoffed. Several months ago, she would have thought the same. But she had something now that they did not; she knew Someone now who had changed her whole perspective, not only on the restaurant business but on her life. She knew God, and she had faith in Him.

May had been in the restaurant business for nearly a decade in America. A Chinese immigrant, she spoke no English and knew nothing about God's seventh-day Sabbath. But she discovered a truth-packed program that impacted not only her, but also her sphere of influence.

It all began on that fateful day when she watched a message given by Pastor Doug Batchelor. The Amazing Facts program had been translated from English so that she could understand it. It was a message about the meaning of the Sabbath. For May, it was all she needed. Pastor Doug had pointed her to the Word of God, and she believed. The Lord had given His Ten Commandments on Mount Sinai and they still held true today, and that included His seventh-day Sabbath.

She searched for a local Sabbath-keeping church that spoke her native tongue and found one not far from one of her restaurants. She attended the service, and after it ended, she knew she had a decision to make. There was something tugging at her, not something tangible or something she could see; it was more like the wind through a tree, tap-tap-tapping a branch against the window of her heart. "Will you let me in?" it was asking.

Reflect: Is God tapping on the window of your heart? Will you let Him come in? There is no greater joy than in fully surrendering to Jesus.

Dig Deeper: Exodus 20:8–11; Isaiah 58:13, 14; Revelation 3:20

May

The Sabbath-keeping Restauranteur, Part 2

Day 346
Source:
Amazing Facts

"If you turn away your foot from the Sabbath, from doing your pleasure on My holy day, and call the Sabbath a delight ... Then you shall delight yourself in the " (Isaiah 58:13, 14).

If May truly believed that the fourth commandment still existed today, then that would mean that neither she nor anyone who worked for her ought to be laboring on the seventh day—including those in her three restaurants, her business partner, their entire staff. But she earned her living from those three restaurants. Closing them down on the busiest day of the week would mean reconfiguring employee wages, schedules, food preparation—and, after all that, would it even be feasible to survive the inevitable loss of profit? All of those people were depending upon her, not least of all her business partner, a personal friend.

So May did the only sensible thing she could. She invited her business partner to the Sabbath-keeping church.

Some time passed as May and her partner both began to attend the Sabbath-keeping church. Toward the end of the year, May finally decided to approach her about the biblical Sabbath. She, just like May, was convicted to keep the seventh day holy. They began praying for God's guidance and ultimately decided to close all three restaurants on Saturdays. As for their employees, May and her business partner resolved to keep their wages the same—paying them as though they had worked the seventh day.

Not surprisingly, the restaurants began to lose money. No one could understand why May had made the decision she had—and all for what? For religion? For an old, obsolete law? But May and her partner continued to keep the Sabbath, believing that obeying God was above all else. And slowly but surely, the blessings began to come. Eventually, May's three restaurants began to bring in more and more business and are currently bringing in even more profit than when they were open on Saturdays!

May has since shared Amazing Facts with her friends and family. Now, more than 100 of them spend Sabbath evenings watching Amazing Facts online and gathering together for regular discussion of what they have learned.

Praise God for the seed of faith that a single message had planted in May's heart. From it grew a soul eager to follow the Word of God and lead others to it.

Reflect: Have you ever been in a difficult situation where you were tempted to break God's Sabbath day? God promises to honor those who honor Him.

Dig Deeper: Exodus 16:4; Deuteronomy 5:14; Mark 2:27

Jonah

Anger Management, Part 1

> **"Pick me up and throw me into the sea; then the sea will become calm for you. For I know that this great tempest is because of me" (Jonah 1:12).**

Nineveh was the capital of Assyria, the ruling empire of the day, home to not only the king but also "more than one hundred and twenty thousand persons" (Jonah 4:11). At one point it was the largest city in the world—and, as most cities go, incredibly corrupt. Jonah had been given the task of warning its people of their impending doom (1:2).

But he quailed at the daunting divine request. So he ran away, even going so far as to pay out of his own pocket for a voyage to Tarshish, a faraway city on the southern coast of modern-day Spain, some 2,500 miles in the opposite direction from Nineveh (v. 3).

But one can only avoid God for so long. In the midst of the journey, God caused Jonah's ship to be caught in a powerful storm (v. 4). This storm must have been like no other; so relentless was it that these seamen, weathered though they were, feared for their lives. They did as most do in times of peril: They prayed for deliverance. But they were a motley crew of different ethnicities and faiths, and though they lifted up their voices to all kinds of gods, it was in vain. Meanwhile, Jonah, the only one who worshipped the true God, lay oblivious below deck in a deep sleep (v. 5).

It was only when the captain woke him, desperately pleading with him to pray also, that Jonah realized: This was his doing (v. 6).

When the crew cast lots to find out who brought this trouble upon them, it fell on Jonah, and he was outed (v. 7). He had to admit before them all that he was a coward and that their troubles were his fault. But how wonderful is our Lord that even in the midst of Jonah's disobedience, he was given an opportunity to witness, for when the men persisted in interrogating him, he answered: "I fear the , the God of heaven, who made the sea and the dry land" (v. 9).

Then, to save their own lives, the sailors, though reluctantly and upon Jonah's own request, threw him overboard (v. 15). Immediately, just as the prophet had predicted, the storm ceased. That day, the formerly heathen crew all believed in the Lord God (v. 16).

Reflect: Has God ever used you in spite of yourself? The Lord is gracious and sees what we can become even though He sees what we are.

Dig Deeper: Genesis 50:19, 20; Psalm 76:10; Ephesians 2:8–10

Jonah

Anger Management, Part 2

"I cried out to the because of my affliction, and He answered me. 'Out of the belly of Sheol I cried, and You heard my voice'" (Jonah 2:2).

As the largest fish in the world, the whale shark is in the Guinness World Records at 41 feet, 6 inches long and weighing 47,000 pounds. But while its esophagus would not allow it to swallow a man whole, presumably that of the sperm whale could (and seafarers have attested to it). The Bible does not tell us what kind of gargantuan fish swallowed up Jonah, but it is certain that one did for "the had prepared" it (Jonah 1:17).

After the ship's crew had tossed Jonah to the waves, the prophet spent the next three days trapped "in the belly of the fish" that God had prepared, still very much alive. There, in that dark, maritime grave, he had nothing to do but think about what he had done.

For all his pigheadedness, he had brought not only suffering upon himself but had furthermore embroiled an entire crew of men along with him. He had wanted to get away from God so badly. Now, when he had nothing left, when he was literally at the bottom of the barrel, Jonah wanted no one else but God.

"When my soul fainted within me, I remembered the " (2:7), he prayed.

Jonah knew, just as all those men on board the ship now knew, that God alone could deliver him: "Salvation is of the " (v. 9). Not only could God save him, God *desired* to save him—even after he had foolishly rushed headlong towards death: "The waters surrounded me, even to my soul; .... yet You have brought up my life from the pit, O , my God" (vv. 5, 6), said he.

It was then, when Jonah was in full surrender to God, that God delivered him from the belly of the fish. By the simple power of His Word, God instructed the fish to spit Jonah out onto dry land, and in obedience to its Creator, the fish did (v. 10).

Once more, God made the same request of his prophet (3:1, 2). This time, Jonah went without complaint to the terrible city of Nineveh (v. 3).

Reflect: When we know something is wrong, dangerous, or destructive, why do we keep persevering in that way?

Dig Deeper: Proverbs 7:24–27; 19:27; Romans 1:21–25

Jonah

Anger Management, Part 3

"Then the said, 'Is it right for you to be angry?'" (Jonah 4:4).

Imagine if every person living in New York City suddenly became Christian in a single day. Unfortunately, it seems highly unlikely, right?

Well, when Jonah journeyed to Nineveh on God's command to proclaim its imminent destruction, his prophecy was met with utter, genuine repentance, from the king all the way to the poorest slave (Jonah 3:5–9).

And God forgave the Ninevites, sparing them from destruction (v. 10).

But Jonah was furious. Those people did not deserve mercy! They had lived their lives in selfishness, ignominy, depravity.

Of course, he knew that this would happen. He knew God's character. God was "gracious and merciful" (4:2). Of course He would save them.

And now he, Jonah, would look like an idiot and a liar. All that effort he made, crying up and down the streets of Nineveh—now none of it was going to happen. He was so angry, he could die (4:3)!

But how blind Jonah was. Had he not just received God's same mercy from his own disobedience? Had he not recently repented in the belly of the fish and been delivered? In his pride and self-conceit, he was unable to realize his own hypocrisy.

In a fit he left Nineveh and planted himself just outside it (v. 5). He would not move until that wretched city met its punishment. But as it was very warm, God in His mercy provided a tall gourd to shade the prophet (v. 6). And Jonah sat, satisfied. But the next morning, God caused a worm to destroy the gourd, and Jonah, baking like a bun in the oven, grew furious again (vv. 7, 8).

"It is right for me to be angry," he answered, spiteful, stubborn, and past listening to reason, when questioned by God, "even to death!" (v. 9).

Why did the gourd have to die? He was just the most unfortunate being on earth! Nothing worked for him, nothing went his way—nothing!

But in return God simply asked: Why should all of those people have to die too (v. 11)?

The Bible does not tell us Jonah's reply, but traditionally the prophet is thought to have penned his own book. If he did, perhaps this honest account in itself provides us with a hopeful outcome.

Reflect: Jonah, in his rash anger, would have saved the plant over the people, simply because the plant had been useful to him. What do we prioritize over precious souls for God's kingdom?

Dig Deeper: Luke 10:38–42; 18:9–14; 1 Corinthians 9:11–18

Bernard

From Suicide to Service, Part 1

"[Elijah] prayed that he might die ..." (1 Kings 19:4).

He held the knife, his mind racing. He brought it up to his neck.

Pictures raced through his mind: the drug deal gone bad, the hundreds of thousands of dollars owed, the contracts out on people's lives—but most of all, his family. What would they do to his wife and kids? If it ended with him right here, right now, maybe his family would be safe.

Then he heard a voice, still and small. "It is not your time yet." He struggled to listen.

But there was another voice too, a different and more persuasive voice. It would be so easy to just go through with it. The knife was so close.

Now he was on his knees, the conflict raging within. Finally, he pushed in the knife.

Suddenly the door burst open, and everything went black.

When Bernard came to, he was in the ICU, staring up at a nurse. If the knife had gone in one more centimeter, he was told, he would have lost his voice box.

Later, he learned that his wife had called the police after she had talked to him earlier that day. She had realized that he was going to do something horrible. It was the police who had found him bleeding on the floor and had raced him to the hospital. After all that, the voice had been right. It was not his time. He had been given a second chance.

Bernard had grown up on the streets of New York City, in gangs, with drugs and alcohol, and in the music scene. His dad was Catholic, his mother a Sabbath-keeper. His parents had divorced and, after her own conversion, his mother began to live out her faith.

After getting out of the ICU, Bernard started attending a non-denominational church. But it seemed like something was stopping him at every turn, including a terrible divorce and six months in jail. Finally, he found himself back in his mother's home and driving trucks for a living.

His mom would talk to him regularly about the Sabbath, but all he could remember was how she had sneaked them to church on Saturdays whenever his dad was not around. He hated it. Besides, every good Christian knew that keeping the seventh-day Sabbath was just legalism—right?

Reflect: In truth, God has given all of us a second chance ... and perhaps more. Now is the time to use your lease on life to be a blessing to others.

Dig Deeper: Psalm 143:4; Proverbs 12:25; Philippians 4:10–13

Bernard

From Suicide to Service, Part 2

"Bless the , O my soul, and forget not all His benefits" (Psalm 103:2).

Bernard struggled to accept the Sabbath truth. One day, the strangest thing happened. He heard that voice again, that same still, small voice: "My Sabbath is the true day."

Still, he struggled. He had so many questions about the Sabbath and about God. He began to fast and pray.

Then, one day, he made a delivery at a warehouse and spotted a small book. Then he heard the same voice again: "Read the book." He hesitated, then shook it off.

An hour passed, and someone came to tell him there was a delay with his load. Instantly, there came the voice: "Read the book." Still, Bernard refused, something raging within him.

The minutes crawled by. Three times the man came to apologize for the delay. Three times Bernard heard that same voice. Finally, exasperated, he picked up the book and read it from cover to cover. And he began to weep. Every question he had about the Sabbath, about who God was, was answered in that little book.

After completing Bible studies, Bernard was baptized into a Sabbath-keeping church. His mother also introduced him to Amazing Facts. Most of all, he wanted to become a trained evangelist at the Amazing Facts Center of Evangelism (AFCOE). But he could not afford a cross-country trip and school fees. He was, however, able to go on a funded mission trip to the Philippines. One thing led to another, and years later he was finally able to fulfill his dream—graduating from the Philippines Amazing Facts Center of Evangelism (PAFCOE) ... along with his new wife!

For their first evangelistic series, Bernard and his wife brought 34 souls to baptism. Since then, they have been instrumental in building the only Sabbath-keeping church in that area of the Philippines, on a plot of land given by a Sunday-keeping pastor who had attended their seminars. Oh, and that pastor—he and his entire family were eventually baptized as well.

Bernard has decided to dedicate his life to full-time ministry, which includes a sponsorship program for others to attend AFCOE. This changed man, once ready to take his own life, now thanks God for his life. "I would not give this life up for anything."

Reflect: Do you struggle to hear God speaking to your heart? Open the Bible and then get involved in service for others. Helping others will make God real to you.

Dig Deeper: Mark 10:27; John 14:26; Hebrews 13:15

Peter Hitchens

The "Anti-Theist's" Brother Found Faith

"Against You, You only, have I sinned, and done this evil in Your sight" (Psalm 51:4).

Millions of people knew the name of Christopher Hitchens before they knew the name of his younger brother, Peter. Ironically, both started out very much as "two peas in a pod."

Both were writers, and both plied their trade in journalism and by writing books. Christopher had several best-selling titles and was most noted for *God Is Not Great*, an anti-theist tract that won wide appeal during the "new atheist" movement of the early 2000s.

Peter also wrote best-sellers, most notably his 1998 volume, *The Abolition of Britain*, which began with a bleak contrast between the public mourning in Britain for both Sir Winston Churchill and Diana, Princess of Wales. His concerns were more cultural and political, the latter being poles apart from Christopher's avowed socialist viewpoint.

It wasn't only politics where the brothers diverged, however. As noted, Christopher, who died in 2011, was a committed anti-theist who campaigned against religious belief, saying there was "no evidence" for even the possibility of belief in God. Christopher won wide acclaim for his views from other atheists, but Peter dissented, at one point becoming estranged from his brother for several years.

Why the rift? Peter—who once said he and his brother "had grown out of the nursery myths of God, angels and Heaven. We had modern medicine, penicillin, jet engines, the Welfare State, the United Nations and 'science,' which explained everything that needed to be explained"—and who'd burned a Bible given him by his family in protest—found faith.

It came as the younger Hitchens drifted back to church attendance, first out of respect for tradition, then for something more. Contemplating Rogier van der Weyden's painting "Last Judgment," he saw himself in the images of naked sinners fleeing wrath: Peter saw his sins as worthy of judgment and punishment. If anyone needed saving, he'd later recall, it was Peter Hitchens.

Peter's return to faith marked a shift in his journalism: He began to use Christian arguments to support and explain his political and social views. He wrote *The Rage Against God: How Atheism Led Me to Faith*, a book detailing his journey. And he speaks all over the world about his faith.

Christopher Hitchens won fame for opposing God. Peter Hitchens has found life in Christ and shares his experience with millions.

Reflect: Peter Hitchens found faith when he saw himself as a sinner deserving of judgment. Was that your experience? If so, recall how you made that realization.

Dig Deeper: Psalm 50:4; Romans 3:4; Revelation 19:11

Sauya

A Dream from God, Part 1

"How long will these people reject Me? And how long will they not believe Me ...?" (Numbers 14:11).

"You should believe the message that My servants are presenting."

She woke with a start. It had been no ordinary dream. She had heard that voice—that beautiful, mysterious voice had spoken to her again.

There was to be a group baptism tomorrow, she knew. Her husband and those two young evangelists wanted her to be part of that group.

Well, they were going to be disappointed. But that voice had given her specific details about the baptisms, and her curiosity was piqued ...

Two young men sat together. It was the first month of the new year—and what a way to begin the year! Francis and Eugene had only just completed their training at the Amazing Facts Center of Evangelism in Africa; now they would spend the next month outside the city of Kampala, Uganda, putting to practice all they had learned. Their meetings were going to be held in a few simple tents staked outdoors. They would take turns preaching for the entire month.

But how would people receive them?

They both looked so young, especially Eugene. In the sea of attendees were many who were older. How would they take to two inexperienced boys telling them, guiding them, exhorting them? But God's Word encourages, "Let no one despise your youth, but be an example to the believers in word, in conduct, in love, in spirit, in faith, in purity" (1 Timothy 4:12).

As their meetings went on, Francis and Eugene noticed quite a few Muslims in attendance. The Islamic faith was indeed popular in Uganda, but some had come to hear the truth from the Bible. And then there were those who came because of their husbands, like Sauya.

Sauya's husband was a Sabbath-keeper, and he wanted his wife to give the Bible a fair chance. So Sauya came night after night. But she did not like it.

At one meeting, the subject of baptism was broached. When Sauya's husband asked her about it, she already knew the answer. "No!" was her firm reply. She would not leave Islam, and nothing anyone could say would change her mind.

But Sauya's husband did not give up.

Reflect: How quickly do you turn away from a person who resists hearing the gospel? There is a time to retreat, but sometimes the Spirit urges us to press forward. Pray for that wisdom.

Dig Deeper: Proverbs 15:1; Ecclesiastes 3:7; Acts 2:17

Sauya

A Dream from God, Part 2

"He who believes and is baptized will be saved; but he who does not believe will be condemned" (Mark 16:16).

Francis and Eugene were AFCOE Africa graduates who held a series of meetings in Uganda. When Sauya's husband, who was a Sabbath-keeper, urged his wife to accept Bible truth she heard, she refused. But he did not give up. He asked Francis and Eugene to visit him at home and spend some more time with his wife. "No!" came Sauya's answer again.

The two evangelists did not force the issue. They knew that nothing they could say or do of themselves could move Sauya. It was God—His Word, His Spirit—to which Sauya would respond. What they needed to do instead was to lift Sauya up in prayer to God. And pray they did.

The meetings continued through rain and storm and much prayer. Finally came Francis and Eugene's last message. It touched Sauya so much that she had to admit she had heard the truth. But still, she clung to her religion.

But the two evangelists continued to pray. That night, they knelt down together and offered supplication to God. Those who had chosen to give their lives to Christ would be baptized tomorrow, after the morning's divine service, by one of the Sabbath-keeping pastors in the area. Francis and Eugene prayed that Sauya would be among them.

That same night, Sauya had a dream. That beautiful voice told her the location of the baptisms and the name of the pastor who was to perform them—and even showed her what the pastor looked like. She was told, "You are among the people that I have chosen in this end-time."

When she awoke, Sauya had to see if what the voice had said was true. She went to the service, listening intently. Finally, the baptisms were announced: the location, the pastor, his name—the voice in her dream had accurately predicted them all.

She shot up from her seat. "It is all true," she said in a rush, explaining what God, the Voice, had told her.

"How did you speak with God? And where?" asked Francis.

As Sauya shared the details of her dream, Francis and Eugene realized that God had answered their prayer. That day, Sauya, the former Muslim, was baptized, along with 18 others.

Reflect: There are many ways God can speak to us, but none of them will ever be in conflict with the Bible. Test everything you believe against the Word of God and you'll never be led astray.

Dig Deeper: Romans 15:4; 2 Timothy 3:16; 1 Peter 1:25

The Prodigal Son

Lost and Found

**"[F]or this my son was dead and is alive again;
he was lost and is found" (Luke 15:24).**

Perhaps the most well-known of all Jesus' parables, the Prodigal Son is the last of a set of three teachings about something or someone who is lost.

In this story, a wise and wealthy man had two sons. The younger of the two was the titular prodigal, spoiled, entitled, and self-involved. Fed up with living under his father's roof and authority, he demanded his inheritance straightaway and was given it (Luke 15:12). It was sheer insolence, but the young man did not care; he thought only of himself and what he wanted.

Now in possession of his father's wealth, he got as far away from him as fast as he could. And there, in "a far country" (v. 13), he began to live "the good life"—feasting, partying, spending. Ultimately, he squandered his entire inheritance.

From there, matters went from bad to worse, for "there arose a severe famine" (v. 14), and he could find no other job than "to feed swine" (v. 15), a most horrible fate for a Jew. The pig was an unclean animal, harmful to eat and vile to touch. But the starved prodigal, gazing at the well-fed swine, realized that he would beg to have the scraps from their trough (v. 16). He was worse off than a beast.

It was then that he realized what a fool he had been. He saw himself for what he truly was, ungrateful, indolent, greedy. Immediately, he started for home to plead for his father's forgiveness and for a job as one of his "hired servants" (v. 19).

But he was in for a big surprise. The prodigal, self-absorbed as he was, had never taken the time to get to know his father. He saw the world and the people in it in terms of transactions, consumer goods, and material worth. But his father was nothing like him.

When he returned home, his father had been waiting for him (v. 20). Sorrowfully, the prodigal apologized (v. 21). But there was no talk of servitude, of earning his own worth back. Instead, his father threw a celebration for him, kissed him, dressed him, fed him (vv. 20–23)—not because his son deserved it, but because he loved his son.

Reflect: God loves us the same way the father in the parable loved the prodigal. With such love, why do we so eagerly trade being in the Father's presence for the world's pleasures?

Dig Deeper: Genesis 13:9–13; Numbers 11:4–6; Romans 7:21–25

Wyatt

The Kid Who Became a Satanist, Part 1

"Everyone proud in heart is an abomination to the ; though they join forces, none will go unpunished" (Proverbs 16:5).

It could be argued the deck was stacked against Wyatt virtually from the day he was born: two parents who'd soon split up, no discipline at either of the subsequent homes, practically no spiritual foundation.

Instead of seeking a way to surmount his circumstances, the young boy from Missouri channeled his insecurities into negative action: petty theft, small-scale vandalism, "acting out" whenever the opportunity presented itself, such as an early addiction to cigarette smoking, as well as adopting a "Goth" lifestyle of black clothing, face paint, black eyeshadow, and nail polish.

That soon escalated to drug use and more rebellion. Because he'd be up all night partying, he'd fall asleep in school, earning horrible grades. His dress, lifestyle, and demeanor further alienated young Wyatt from many of his peers, except for other "Goths" and the Satanists he eventually encountered and aligned with.

"I always felt judged by Christians and I never liked them. Even though my mom would send me to church occasionally, as a kid I never felt I belonged there," Wyatt would later recall. "But among the Satanists and when I was involved in Wicca and witchcraft and the Goth group, I felt welcomed, I felt accepted. They didn't judge me for my curly hair or my weirdness that I had or my music I listened to," he added.

Eventually, Wyatt's petty crimes and drug infractions escalated to a point where the legal system could no longer ignore him. He was sentenced to a drug rehabilitation program. Along with exercise, hikes, classes, and groups, one activity was designed to "scare straight" those in the program: a visit to a state prison. But it didn't turn him around. Instead, Wyatt rebelled, stabbing a counselor seriously enough for him to be charged with first degree assault and armed criminal action. The sentence was 20 years in jail.

Once "in the system," Wyatt continued to rebel, spurning his mother's pleas to read the Bible and turn his life around. Wyatt had the "Satanic Bible," he reasoned, and the Christian stuff wasn't true, anyway.

But one day Wyatt picked up an actual Christian Bible and began to read. What happened next stunned Wyatt—and those around him.

Reflect: Wyatt's rebellion landed him in serious trouble. Do you know someone in a similar situation, or have you experienced it yourself? The best next step is to pick up a Bible and start reading it.

Dig Deeper: Ecclesiastes 8:11; Proverbs 14:12; John 17:17

Wyatt

The Kid Who Became a Satanist, Part 2

"For the wages of sin is death, but the gift of God is eternal life in Christ Jesus our Lord" (Romans 6:23).

"Do they have any Bibles there?" Wyatt's mother asked her son during one of their brief phone conversations. He was in juvenile detention, charged with first degree assault and armed criminal action, facing the prospect of decades behind bars.

"And, son, would you read it?" she added.

Convinced by his Satanist colleagues—and the Satanist "Bible" he read—that the Christian Bible was a book of lies, fables, and contradictions, Wyatt didn't have the heart to tell his mother he wouldn't comply. Instead, he uttered a non-committal, "We'll see," and left it at that.

Wyatt walked past the detention center's bookshelf daily to and from the showers. He saw a Bible on the shelf and it irritated him. Finally, Wyatt grabbed a copy and took it back to his cell. He was determined to confirm his prejudices and prove these Scriptures a fraud, once and for all.

Something happened, however, that stunned Wyatt. As he read the real Bible, he found people to whom he could relate, stories that spoke to his heart. Of special interest was the story of David, anointed to be Israel's next king, but still dealing with King Saul, who in madness sought to kill David. In 1 Samuel 24, Wyatt read how David spared Saul's life, and that gesture touched him. In fact, Wyatt knelt and gave his heart to God that moment.

With a Bible and a small radio, Wyatt continued to search for truth. One day he "stumbled" across a program called *Bible Answers Live* while listening to his radio. It was hard to get good reception at first—the station was 500 miles away—so he would stand on his metal bunk and hold his portable radio over his head against the three-inch-thick window merely to hear the broadcast.

Since he could not call in to the program himself, Wyatt prayed his questions would be answered during the weekly broadcasts. Many times they were, but sometimes he learned new things that he had never heard before.

Released from prison six years ahead of schedule, Wyatt Allen attended the Amazing Facts Center of Evangelism (AFCOE) program, became an evangelist, and now shares God's truth with others. God is good, all the time!

Reflect: Wyatt went from a self-hating, face-painting teenager to a man with a transformed life. He and his wife Jenni are now parents and travel across the country, and it's thanks to the power of God's Word!

Dig Deeper: Genesis 2:17; Ezekiel 18:20; John 5:24

> **"And it shall come to pass afterward that I will pour out My Spirit on all flesh; your sons and your daughters shall prophesy, your old men shall dream dreams, your young men shall see visions"** (Joel 2:28).

Annie Smith was early in her life committed to the cause of Christ. At age 10, in 1838, she joined the Baptist Church. Six years later, Annie and her mother, Rebekah, cast their lot with the Millerite movement, which expected the return of Jesus in 1844.

Following the Great Disappointment of that year, Annie turned her efforts to the arts, studying for several years and developing skills in poetry and visual arts.

This concentration on artistic endeavors and secular success worried her mother. Rebekah Smith shared her worries with Joseph Bates, the former sea captain who would help found the Seventh-day Adventist Church. Bates told Annie's mother to write a letter urging the young woman to attend meetings the preacher would have at the home of Elizabeth Temple in Boston, where Annie was pursuing her goals.

The night before the meeting, both Bates and Annie Smith had the same dream: The meeting had begun, the first hymn had been sung, and only one seat, near the door, remained. The door opened and in came a young woman, taking that final chair.

That dream unfolded in real life: Annie had left to attend the meeting on time, but got lost, and only arrived for that last available seat.

"I believe this is Sister Smith's daughter, of West Wilton [New Hampshire]," Bates said. "I never saw you before, but your countenance looks familiar. I dreamed of seeing you last night."

Annie confessed she'd had the same dream. Quickly, she aligned with the fledgling Adventist cause.

Now, Annie turned her talents towards advancing the message and not her worldly success. Within a month, her poem, "Fear Not, Little Flock," arrived at the offices of the *Advent Review and Sabbath Herald* and appeared in print. James White, then the editor, asked Annie—summoned her, actually—to Saratoga Springs, New York, to copy-edit the paper. At first the young woman demurred, citing the damage eyestrain had caused her vision. White persisted, and shortly after Annie's arrival, prayer and anointing with oil resulted in a healing.

Annie's eyes were opened, and what she saw next would change her life—and create a legacy for the nascent movement.

Reflect: Have you had your eyes opened to a situation to which you were blind? God promises to open the eyes of our heart to see Him.

Dig Deeper: Acts 2:39; Isaiah 44:3; Numbers 12:6

"Looking for the blessed hope and glorious appearing of our great God and Savior Jesus Christ" (Titus 2:13).

Annie Smith worked feverishly for James White at the *Advent Review and Sabbath Herald* office. When the Whites traveled to encourage believers, she became, in effect, the editor of the weekly paper.

Poverty and straitened circumstances were not uncommon in the early days of the Adventist Church. The Whites moved from Saratoga Springs to Rochester, New York, and as many as 18 people lived with the Whites at one time.

Annie's writing flourished, however, despite the adverse circumstances. She wrote a total of 45 hymns and poems which appeared in the *Review* as well as the *Youth's Instructor*, aimed at the young people of the growing movement.

The young woman's personal life was far less settled than her professional career, however. Annie came to know, respect, and, apparently, deeply admire John Nevins Andrews, a rising preacher in Adventism. Whether or not her affections were in any way returned, her hopes were dashed when Andrews instead showed interest in another girl.

Crushed, Annie soldiered on, working on her editing and poetry, living with the Whites and others. Tuberculosis invaded the circle of workers there in 1852, but it would be two more years before Annie would come down with the illness. It would take about nine months before the young pioneering church member would succumb to the illness.

During those 270 days, however, Annie remained faithful to her God, and anxious to complete the book of poetry she wished published after her passing. These were poems of faith and dedication to a God and a future Annie could see only in Heaven, knowing that her earthly time was drawing to a close.

On July 24, 1855, Annie Smith summoned up what strength she had and wrote her last poem:

Oh! Shed not a tear o'er the spot where I sleep;
For the living and not for the dead ye may weep;
Why mourn for the weary who sweetly repose,
Free in the grave from life's burdens and woes?

Two days later, at 4 a.m. on July 26, Annie closed her eyes in death, only to await the resurrection. Her younger brother Uriah Smith, himself converted to the Adventist cause in 1852, would for years afterwards sign letters "Yours, in the blessed hope," a tribute to his sister's fixed vision on life eternal.

Reflect: Despite personal disappointment, and even with the prospect of death before her, Annie Smith remained faithful. How do you maintain faith in the face of distressing circumstances?

Dig Deeper: Job 19:25–27; Isaiah 25:9; Colossians 1:25

Nina

As Good as Dead, Part 1

"What then shall we say to these things? If God is for us, who can be against us?" (Romans 8:31).

Nina clutched the Bible close to her chest. Tears poured out of her like a pot boiling over. Her little body shook. "Oh, God!" The words seemed to burst out of the deepest, darkest part of her.

Why didn't He want her? Why? The wail was the loneliest, saddest note—she felt like an orphaned child all alone on a cold city street.

Nina was raised in China's remote countryside.

But something about Nina made her different from all the other people in her village—she was divorced, and instead of a husband, she had a two-month-old daughter. She had no money and no job. People would avoid her; her father would drink and then ridicule her; and everyone was embarrassed by her. To them, she was worse than the filth on the sidewalk.

Nina's mother believed in the God of the Bible and took Nina to a church where members assembled on Sundays. After several visits, Nina also came to believe that there was a God. She desperately wanted to be baptized into her mother's church. She asked three times, but each time she was denied. The members had learned that she was a divorced woman; she was, as they said, a sinner who would be a noxious stain upon their congregation. They would not baptize her; neither was she welcome there anymore.

Nina went home and pressed her Bible close to her and cried as though her heart would break. Even God did not want her. For days she did this. But a strange thing would happen every time. As she sat there sobbing, she would see Someone—a face she did not know—smiling down at her, and somehow she knew what the smile meant. It meant that that Someone was there for her. It made no sense, but she hugged the memory close.

Time passed, and one day, as her father was screaming at her yet again, something in her broke. "You are as good as dead," he ranted. And she felt like she wanted to die.

But something stopped her. Something compelled her to go to the computer instead and get on the Internet. In the search bar she typed the words "preaching by pastors" and there, at the top of the list, was a video by an American pastor.

Reflect: Have you ever felt unwanted? You can be assured that Jesus wants you very much. In fact, Christ died in order to have you.

Dig Deeper: Jeremiah 31:3; John 3:16; Romans 5:6

"So we have the prophetic word confirmed, which you do well to heed as a light that shines in a dark place, until the day dawns and the morning star rises in your hearts" (2 Peter 1:19).

Rejected by her abusive alcoholic father and pushed out of her mother's Sunday church because she was divorced, Nina searched online for hope. She discovered a video by an American pastor translated into her own language entitled, "The Big Statue in Dreams." Intrigued, she clicked on the link.

What she heard and saw gave her goosebumps. She grabbed her Bible and followed along. Though Nina did not know it, she was having her first Bible study on the prophecy of Daniel 2 by Pastor Doug Batchelor.

Nina was a simple girl. She had never learned about the history of the world. But she understood what this American pastor was saying. She understood that the end of the world was close at hand and that her life did matter to God.

Immediately, she ran to tell her mother. But her mother asked only how she could suddenly claim to know so much about the Bible. A day ago, this would have stopped her. But Nina was different now. She went on to tell an aunt of hers and secretly continued to watch Pastor Doug's sermons online.

As she learned more, she yearned for a church that believed as she did—a Sabbath-keeping church like the one Pastor Doug went to. But she knew of none. Suddenly, like sunlight shooting through the clouds, the answer came to her. "There was a voice ringing in my mind," Nina recalls, "that the wonderful truths I've been listening to should have a customer service number."

So she searched for the Amazing Facts phone number online and called. She was given the address of the nearest Sabbath-keeping church. Just like that, Nina's prayer was answered, with a church family and, sometime later, a pastor who gladly baptized her. And because of the aunt whom she first told about Daniel 2, a Sabbath-keeping church was eventually founded in her home village and filled with new members—nearly every member of her mother's Sunday church.

Reflect: When you search for answers from God, and doors seem to close all around you, persist in prayer. Be patient and wait on the Lord. You will not be abandoned.

Dig Deeper: Isaiah 40:31; Amos 5:4; Matthew 7:7

Roman Centurion

Killing Jesus

"For with the heart one believes unto righteousness, and with the mouth confession is made unto salvation" (Romans 10:10).

It was a Friday, a day like any other. But that was all about to change.

There were three to be crucified that day. A Roman centurion was to oversee the ordeal. There was one criminal who had arrested his attention. According to the Jews, this Man had claimed to be the Son of God.

There began preparations for the Man's death. The centurion ordered the Man scourged. Then the Man was dressed as a harlequin king, and all bowed in ridicule before Him. And the centurion, though he was one of them, gazed upon the Man and could not understand how He seemed so noble.

Now back in His own clothes, the Man, stumbling, could not carry His own instrument of death. So another was plucked from the crowd to do so. The centurion strode along, looking down upon the Man's shaking form.

Finally, they arrived outside Jerusalem at the site of the crucifixion. There the Man was stripped naked and nailed to His cross. The centurion and his soldiers split the Man's articles by lot and offered the Man the customary drink to numb the pain—but He refused.

The centurion was mystified. Who would go through all that suffering with his wits about him?

Then came the Jewish leaders, their insults soaked in sarcasm. One of the criminals hanging next to the Man joined in, but the other strangely rebuked his fellow offender, addressing the Man as God. The Man replied, His voice full of love and promise, so different from His abusers. All this fell upon the ears of the centurion.

At noon the sky suddenly turned dark. For the next three hours, the centurion, his soldiers, the crowd waited in inky blackness; and something within the centurion burned vividly, fervently as he thought on the Man dying above him.

In a burst of pity, someone gave the Man some vinegar for His thirst. After that, the Man lifted up His voice in a cry like no other and—it happened so quickly—died.

Immediately the earth began to shake violently. When it was over, the centurion looked up at the Man's lifeless body. He could utter nothing else but: "Truly this was the Son of God!" (Matthew 27:54).

Reflect: During His worst moments on earth, the Savior changed hearts. What must the centurion have experienced when he realized he had just killed God? Do we crucify the Savior in other ways?

Dig Deeper: Psalm 118:22; Acts 3:13–21; Hebrews 6:4–6

Brian

A Voice on the Radio, Part 1

"No one can come to Me unless the Father who sent Me draws him ..." (John 6:44).

The little boy sat in the pew, his feet dangling off the floor. His tousled little head could barely see the priest on the platform in front of him. He stared curiously and shifted toward his mother. He wanted to know so many things about what the priest was doing and saying, and the questions tumbled eagerly from his lips. But in one swift motion, his mother pulled him from his seat and took him out of the church. His mother's grip was hard, like iron. As the blows fell on him, he was reminded repeatedly that he was to be absolutely silent during mass.

Brian was born into a Catholic family—to a father whom he rarely saw and a mother who regularly beat him and his siblings. And when the children reached the age of 15 or 16, they were considered adults and were expected to leave home.

Brian also knew about alcohol and parties. His parents would drink and turn their home into a dancehall for themselves and their friends. "People were happy when they drank," says Brian. So at 10 years old, Brian had his first drink. As a teenager, he smoked his first joint. Before he was 15, he had tried every drug he could find and was regularly smoking, drinking, and partying.

At 15, just like his other siblings had, he left home. He eventually married and had two children of his own. He began to verbally abuse his wife and continued in his addictions. And life went on this way, year after year, until Brian had become a middle-aged man. And life would have continued to go on this way had it not been for one long and lonely night—and a voice on the radio.

Brian was driving home from work one evening. There was nothing interesting on the radio at that time of night, just one bad song after another. He punched a button on his dashboard, automatically scanning through the stations. Bad song. Next station. Bad song. Next station. Then—"Do you want to hear an amazing fact?" called out a clear voice.

"Yeah!" Brian said to his radio.

And as he listened to the voice, it told a story he had never heard.

Reflect: Do you know someone who has a distorted picture of God? You might be a voice to share a true understanding of a loving heavenly Father who longs to redeem that person.

Dig Deeper: Exodus 4:10–12; John 15:16; Romans 8:28

Brian

A Voice on the Radio, Part 2

"Call to Me, and I will answer you, and show you great and mighty things, which you do not know" (Jeremiah 33:3).

While driving home from work one evening, Brian stumbled onto a Christian radio program. As he listened to the voice, it told a story he had never heard. His hand stayed over the button on his dashboard.

"You know there was another man who sacrificed everything for you?" the voice continued.

Well, Brian had heard this story. This story meant terror and punishment and all things evil in the world. No thanks. "Jesus freak," he thought to himself, and his finger reached for the button.

But then another voice came on. It had a cheery, lilting sort of accent. Brian hesitated. He realized the two voices were hosting some kind of call-in program about the Bible. The second voice gave out a phone number for people to ask their questions. People were calling about all kinds of questions—Bible verses, biblical concepts, God's character, God's actions, and passages they did not understand. Brian was stunned.

"Asking a question about God is a sin," he thought. He once had the marks from his mother to prove it.

But after every question, the first voice would answer the caller calmly, patiently, and always with more verses from the Bible. Sometimes the second voice would join in too. Brian listened, enrapt, to the full hour of *Bible Answers Live*—a program heard every week on radio stations all around the world.

"I learned more about God in that hour than I did in all the 12 years of Catholic school," he shares. "I heard about a loving and caring God, even though I had turned my back on Him, He was ready to forgive me and help me redeem myself. I started to want not only to know Him, but I wanted a relationship with Him."

From there, Brian began listening to more Amazing Facts programs. He downloaded the Amazing Facts app and read through all the Bible studies. He began studying the Bible for himself. He came to know those two voices—Pastor Doug Batchelor and Pastor Jëan Ross—very well. He has since dedicated his life to Jesus and has begun a journey with God that will last a lifetime and beyond, to eternity.

Reflect: Have you ever hesitated to ask a question about God? The Lord is open to any inquiry you may have, including your doubts or anger. Turn your heart heavenward and ask God anything. He will hear you.

Dig Deeper: Proverbs 8:17; Isaiah 55:8, 9; 1 Corinthians 13:12

Kristi

God Was Waiting for Me

**"See, I have set before you an open door, and
no one can shut it ..." (Revelation 3:8).**

One Saturday morning, Kristi went for a walk with her six-year-old son through her town in the Republic of Estonia. She soon noticed that they were passing a Sabbath-keeping church. Months before, she'd learned from a former co-worker that they worshiped on Saturday. It seemed to Kristi as though God was calling her to come inside.

Kristi had grown up knowing almost nothing about Christianity. Sometimes she glanced through a small children's Bible she'd received as a gift, but as she grew older, her interest turned to the occult and New Age.

She smoked heavily, drank, and partied—even after giving birth to a son when she was twenty years old. But no matter how much she partied, her sense of hopelessness grew.

Now as Kristi stood outside the church, she felt afraid to go in. But she couldn't ignore the faint stirring of hope inside—the thought that she might be able to find something real and meaningful beyond the front door, if she just had the courage to take a step forward.

"I felt like God was waiting to meet me there," she says today. Kristi decided to answer the gentle invitation and went inside and sat down in a pew.

The message she heard was like cool refreshing water to her thirsty spirit. She felt like she'd come home. But she still had so many unanswered questions. Eager to learn more, she began searching online and was thrilled to discover some video sermons by a pastor named Doug Batchelor.

"Every time I had a question, I would find an Amazing Facts sermon about it," she shares. "I was so happy knowing that a powerful God loves me, and wants a sinner like me. Pastor Doug has helped me a lot with his video sermons. I love listening to Amazing Facts on YouTube and on the app."

God revealed His love to Kristi and she made the life-changing decision to join the family of God. "I was baptized in the summer of 2017," she reveals, "and began to let go of all that displeases God. I know God is cleansing my whole life. So much has happened since I began walking with God."

Reflect: Has the Holy Spirit ever prompted you to walk through a door? Maybe you need to go back to church or maybe witness to a friend. Listen to God and walk forward in faith!

Dig Deeper: Psalm 56:13; Isaiah 9:2; 1 John 1:5–7